Truth and Democracy

DEMOCRACY, CITIZENSHIP, AND CONSTITUTIONALISM

Rogers M. Smith and Mary L. Dudziak, Series Editors

Truth and Democracy

Edited by

Jeremy Elkins and Andrew Norris

PENN

UNIVERSITY OF PENNSYLVANIA PRESS

PHILADELPHIA

Copyright © 2012 University of Pennsylvania Press

Published by
University of Pennsylvania Press
Philadelphia, Pennsylvania 19104-4112
www.upenn.edu/pennpress

Printed in the United States of America on acid-free paper

10 9 8 7 6 5 4 3 2 1

Library of Congress Cataloging-in-Publication Data
Truth and democracy / edited by Jeremy Elkins and Andrew Norris. — 1st ed.
        p.   cm. — (Democracy, citizenship, and constitutionalism)
    Includes bibliographical references and index.
    ISBN 978-0-8122-4379-6 (hardcover : alk. paper)
    1. Democracy—Philosophy.   2. Truth—Political aspects.   3. Political ethics.   I. Elkins, Jeremy.   II. Norris, Andrew, 1960–   III. Series: Democracy, citizenship, and constitutionalism.
JC423.T725   2012
321.8—dc23
                                                            2011025503

For our daughters

It is not foolish to believe that any social and political order which effectively uses power, and which sustains a culture that means something to the people who live in it, must involve opacity, mystification, and large-scale deception. Reasonable people can believe . . . that human beings cannot live together effectively, at least on any culturally ambitious scale, if they understood fully what they are doing. It is not necessarily foolish to believe these things, but they may not be true, and we can still live in the hope . . . that they are not.
—Bernard Williams, *Truth and Truthfulness*

Contents

Introduction: Politics, Political Theory, and the Question of Truth

Jeremy Elkins and Andrew Norris

WE LIVE IN a political culture that is deeply ambivalent about truth. On the one hand, it is said that there are basic truths on which our politics must be grounded. We are told, for example, by the right (mostly) that a certain version of liberal democratic capitalism is the end to which all of human history has been directed, and that the abandonment of the belief in a Judeo-Christian god and adherence to his universal moral commandments leads to radical relativism; while on the left (mostly) we have witnessed the growth of a universal human rights discourse that holds certain truths to be self-evident, as well as a renewed reverence for the natural sciences as a paradigm of rational inquiry and a bastion of truth against superstition and faith. Yet at the same time, we hear from various quarters that the very idea of "political truth" is necessarily tyrannical or hegemonic. And so, for example, from the right comes the insistence that any public valuation of goods,[1] even if concluded through a democratic process, is inherently authoritarian, while from the left we are told that "truth-talk" stands as a threat to the very possibility of cultural and epistemic pluralism.

There are, no doubt, many reasons for this ambivalence. Surely the skepticism about or dismissal of truth is in part a response to some of the claims that have sometimes been made for and about truth—about its nature, about access to it, about what it can do for us—and about what has sometimes been done in its name. And yet in the actual lives that we lead we cannot consistently avoid claims of truth; much of what we do and say is in fact unintelligible except as resting on an implicit commitment to truth and other virtues that themselves depend on some notion of truth. And so like many of those exaggerated claims with which we live, the dismissal of truth is reserved for particular occasions, paraded about to great effect, and then stored in the back room while the regular business goes on. Even Richard Rorty, despite his sometimes much more extravagant dismissals of the idea of truth, at times acknowledged that most people are quite right to be concerned about having adequate information available and not being lied to by public officials, and he argued that while we need not focus on truth, truth is one of the valuable consequences—"a bonus"—of political freedom.[2] It is hard to maintain that it makes no difference how attentive we are to the specific conditions of the world that we seek to affect, or that the quality of the decisions that we make is wholly unrelated to the strength of the evidence behind them and the care of the analysis underlying them. And though there will obviously always be differences of judgment—about the evidence itself, about what to do about it, and so on—even with respect to the political-philosophical differences that come into play, most will believe that at least their own views are based on truthful (if contested) propositions about the world.

Yet the anxiety about talk of truth remains great: that once any such talk is allowed through the door, it must bring with it a history of metaphysical baggage and a future of political domination. In the academy, this anxiety has perhaps been greatest in the humanities and in political theory, where many have responded to it by either rejecting or avoiding the whole topic. John Rawls and many of those who have followed in his path have, by and large, taken the latter tack and explicitly put aside questions of truth on the grounds that not doing so will undermine the possibility of consensus on fundamental political principles and encourage the imposition of "comprehensive doctrines," while many of those influenced by poststructuralism have treated the concern with truth as a threat to plurality and as bound to the dangerous utopian fantasy of overcoming political agonism. Appeals to truth are thus said, on the one side, to threaten consensus and, on the other, to undermine a healthy dissensus. More fundamentally, many worry that concern with questions of truth suggests a return to the idea of a "true world attainable [only] for a man who is wise, pious, virtuous,"[3] threatening that part of the Nietzschean (and following that, the Heideggerian and Arendtian) project of recovering the world of "appearance" from its Platonic denigration.

Against this tendency to reject or neglect questions concerning truth, a number of voices have been raised in recent years. Prominent among them was that of Bernard Williams, who in his final book, *Truth and Truthfulness*, noted the ironically simultaneous commitment within the humanities to truthfulness on the one hand and to the "rejection of truth" on the other, and who asked, sensibly enough, "If you do not believe in the existence of truth, what is the passion for truthfulness a passion for? Or—as we might also put it—in pursuing truthfulness, what are you supposedly being true to?"[4] But for Williams, as for other critics of (what he dubbed) the truth "deniers," the problem was not merely conceptual and the question by no means idle. The neglect of truth, as Williams put it, had significant consequences both for "real politics" and for the humanities. We share that view. The volume we have assembled is concerned with "real politics"—that term taken broadly to include already within it ordinary reflections on political life. It is also concerned with the discipline of political theory, particularly insofar as the kinds of questions that it asks might fairly be thought of as continuous with the kinds of questions and reflections that members of a polity might, at least in principle, engage in with respect to it.

The broadest question that motivates this volume is whether our politics and political reflections should be concerned with truth at all. But there is also a second, more complex question: the question not of whether but of *how* truth should matter. And while the volume itself (in contrast to a few of the essays within it) rests on an affirmative answer to the first of these questions, it does not present a single answer to the second. Nonetheless it rests on the assumptions that a concern with the latter question itself matters for our politics; that the character of our politics depends in part on what kinds of truthful inquiries it promotes and how it deals with various kinds of disputes about truth; and that the question of how truth ought to come into play in our politics is an important political and not merely theoretical question. The volume as a whole, apart from any of the particular reflections on these questions offered in the essays it collects, is intended to reopen the question of truth and its place in political life to more sustained attention than it has in general received within the discipline of political theory. It grew out of the belief that, whatever may be said about particular claims that have been made about or in the name of truth, a serious engagement with the problems of social life cannot do without questions of truth; that questions about truth are inevitable in any society that takes politics seriously; and that questions of truth are not adequately resolved by dispensing with them.

*   *   *

Like various claims that have been made about truth, the contemporary dismissal of "truth-talk" too has a history. While in its academic versions, it has often been represented as an "anti-essentializing" response to (those woefully overessentialized terms) the "Enlightenment" and "Liberalism," the skepticism toward claims of authority based on the possession of "the Truth" is, no less than skepticism toward claims of authority based on revelation and tradition, itself part of Enlightenment and liberal thought. Indeed these traditions of thought are characterized in part precisely by *both* a commitment to truth—and the associated notion of objectivity—*and* a recognition that among the truths to be recognized are the plurality and subjectivity of human life, and the limitation, for that reason and others, of human understanding. Neither of these two strands of thought—which include, on the one hand, the objective facts of plurality, subjectivity, and finitude and, on the other, the necessarily perspectival aspect of objective judgments—is limited to these traditions, and wherever they have together appeared, so too have attempts to deny one or the other. It is not, then, surprising that today we should find once again the inclination to deny one or the other of these: the most arrogant claims to the possession of truth and the dismissal of truth in the name of subjectivity.

There are a variety of forms of this, some of which we already noted. In the field of political theory itself, the subjectivist strand appears, for example, in the tendency to slide from the important recognition that plurality is an irreducible fact of political life that must be respected to the absurd thought that any particular differences are simply irreducible facts that must be respected as such; and from the worthy recognition that the appeal to truth has sometimes been invoked in an attempt to eliminate political difference to the unwarranted thought that any concern with truth in politics—or in any case one that goes beyond such elementary virtues as not lying—must have this as its aim or implication. Similarly, and aided in part by a vulgarization of certain strands of poststructuralism, the thought that all we have of the world is how it appears to us too often slides quickly into the thought that all we have is immediate appearance. Confronted with the existence of a plurality of opinions and recognizing that there will always be differences of judgment, the unarticulated thought seems to run that nothing more can be said about *these* differences except how to respect them, and that because truth cannot set us free of our differences, questions of truth have no role to play. Yet at the same time, these ideas themselves are often held with a kind of dogmatic contentment. And like many ideas that are held in that way, these have largely, and ironically, resisted their own historicization. Thus while history is appealed to for evidence that all is flux, that every notion, no matter how solid it may appear, is transient, and that the world therefore is a world of appearance, that idea itself is too often held as though our grasping of it were the end of history—as though only now, finally from the privileged position of the present, can we see the foibles of those who did not understand the contingency and historicality of their own ideas.

In one respect, it not surprising that in these movements of thought Nietzsche has become such a central figure, for Nietzsche himself often wrote as though mankind were at the end of its history—that is, that we had come to the end of a history of a certain kind of creature—and that the end of this history and this creature was bound up with the end of a certain idea of truth. But for Nietzsche such dichotomies as that between truth and appearance, and truth and perspective, were themselves *part* of that history; and in this way Nietzsche's understanding of the demise of truth in the contemporary world was itself much more deeply historical than that of many of those critics of truth who take themselves to be writing, in part, under his name. The specific form of nihilism to which modern man has been led is, Nietzsche thought, the consequence of a particular understanding of truth, namely, as something otherworldly, and of a particular, correlative understanding of this world as a mere show. And it was because of this that that form of nihilism must ultimately be self-negating.[5] The beginning of a different history thus requires, in part, rethinking the question "What is truth?"—a question that had been "turned on its head" so long as "someone who champions nothingness and negation passes for the representative of 'truth.'"[6] Nietzsche's assertion in his late works that the will to truth is will to power was indeed an attempt to unmask a particular conception of truth. But it is only on a vulgarization of the idea of "will to power," and of other Nietzschean ideas (such as that truth is "a kind of belief which has become a condition of life") and the dismissal of other of his thoughts on truth (such as that the "*measure* of a man is how much of the *truth* he can endure without *degenerating*") that this can be read as a rejection of the idea of truth in general.[7] For Nietzsche, the history of mankind was inseparable from the history of its understanding of truth, and the question of mankind's future was similarly bound up with the *problem* of truth. But the thought that the solution to that problem is simply to abandon the idea of truth, or talk about truth, in favor of appearance is a symptom of the disease, not its cure.[8]

It is, for us today, also perhaps a symptom of a broader cultural trend in liberal societies toward the glorification of subjectivity. Liberal societies depend on the bracketing, in political life, of certain kind questions of truth—such as, paradigmatically, the truth of religious beliefs—and there is a sense in which such matters might thus be regarded as "subjective" from the perspective of public reason. But this has at times led, unfortunately and mistakenly, to the idea that questions of truth *in general* must be bracketed in our politics, and to the associated idea that beliefs concerning any such questions can be correct or valid only within the larger "value system" of the individual or discrete community. Such relativism can limit itself to a simple subjectivism in which each belief is true insofar as it is held by (and true for) the individual or community, or it can go further and declare truth irrelevant to such beliefs, which are justified instead by their emotional or ritual significance to those who hold them. In one respect, then, it is only an apparent paradox that the beliefs thus held all too often take on a dogmatic tone, for in the absence of any confidence that one's beliefs might be justified by the appeal to how things really are, the virtue in most request is stridency.

The intense and increasing focus on subjectivity in late modern life and the commercialization of its signs and vehicles have greatly contributed to these tendencies. The apotheosis of the market as the means for distributing social goods in a pluralistic society easily leads to an individualism in which preference—or more specifically, preference as revealed in market decisions—is treated as the sole ground of value. Yet at the same time, capitalism itself tends to promote not only concentrations of political and economic power, but with them various forms of authoritarianism, including ideological. And if in one sense there is a tension between the subjectivism that appears within the market and the dogmatisms that surround it, the common casualty is the orientation to *questions* of truth. For that orientation is threatened on the one side by the denial that there is such a thing as truth that matters and, on the other, by the smug assurance that it is already ours.

The end result of this is a society in which truth is either passed over in favor of "tolerance" or missed though a strident refusal to entertain alternative points of views and possible criticisms. In his recent book *Truth: A Guide*, Simon Blackburn assails the shared intellectual laziness of that culture, seconding William Clifford's demand in "The Ethics of Belief" that one has a right to a belief only when one has "honestly earned it by patient examination, not by stifling [one's] doubts."[9] Blackburn argues that one reason that this demand is so easily skirted is the common assumption that the expression of belief is an attempt at manipulation and not a contribution to a cooperative endeavor. Blackburn recalls, "It is sometimes said that one of the casualties of the general suspicion and mistrust that permeated the old Soviet Union was that the distinction between truth and other motivations to believe tended to break down. Upon hearing a purported piece of information, the reaction was not, 'Is it true?' but 'Why is this person saying this?—What machinations or manipulations are going on here?' The question of truth did not, as it were, have the social space in which it could breathe."[10] While totalitarian regimes are characterized in part precisely by their much greater capacity to suffocate the "social space" of truth, it is not hard to recognize parallels to what Blackburn describes in our own political culture. Thus we find the widespread tendency, in both the popular press and what passes for much sophisticated commentary, to focus on the rhetorical, strategic significance of political claims (and the acts that rely on them), while leaving aside sustained attention to the question of their plausibility as an account of the world. Here too, albeit in a different form, the question of truth is deprived of the social space in which it can "breathe."

A volume such as this can hardly do much to restore that social space. Perhaps the most that it can do is to point to the significance of it for political life, to suggest why it still matters, and to indicate some of the kinds of questions and problems that must arise if such a space is to be restored and sustained. In line with this, we have sought to produce a volume of essays that will initiate a conversation, not close it. Our aim here is neither to offer a unified argument nor to attempt a comprehensive canvassing of contemporary positions. We have structured the volume in four sections, each of which includes two or three primary essays and two or three secondary essays written in response to the questions raised by those. These essays approach the question of truth and politics from a variety of perspectives, in diverse vocabularies, and within the context of a variety of specific concerns. Our aim has been to foster a dialogue, and we hope that the cumulative force of the primary and secondary essays is to suggest the importance of attending to truth in democratic political life, while at the same time remaining very aware of what such attention *cannot* do. There is—one hopes needless to say—no suggestion here that questions of truth are *all* that matter to politics or, absurdly, that focusing on such questions will resolve all of our political disputes; nor do we read any of the particular essays as suggesting either such thing. Just as it is important to ask how questions of truth ought to matter for our politics, it is necessary as well to ask about their limitations, and of what we have no right to expect from an engagement with them. There is no simple answer to either of these, and the exchanges presented here suggest, we hope, some of the complexity of both.

From Nobel Lecture: Art, Truth, and Politics

Harold Pinter

IN 1958 I wrote the following:

> There are no hard distinctions between what is real and what is unreal,
> nor between what is true and what is false. A thing is not necessarily
> either true or false; it can be both true and false.

I believe that these assertions still make sense and do still apply to the exploration of reality through art. So as a writer I stand by them but as a citizen I
cannot. As a citizen I must ask: What is true? What is false?

Truth in drama is forever elusive. You never quite find it but the search for
it is compulsive. The search is clearly what drives the endeavour. The search is
your task. More often than not you stumble upon the truth in the dark, collid-
ing with it or just glimpsing an image or a shape which seems to correspond
to the truth, often without realising that you have done so. But the real truth
is that there never is any such thing as one truth to be found in dramatic art.
There are many. These truths challenge each other, recoil from each other,
reflect each other, ignore each other, tease each other, are blind to each other.
Sometimes you feel you have the truth of a moment in your hand, then it slips
through your fingers and is lost. . . .

So language in art remains a highly ambiguous transaction, a quicksand,
a trampoline, a frozen pool which might give way under you, the author, at
any time.

But as I have said, the search for the truth can never stop. It cannot be adjourned, it cannot be postponed. It has to be faced, right there, on the spot. . . .

Political language, as used by politicians, does not venture into any of this territory since the majority of politicians, on the evidence available to us, are interested not in truth but in power and in the maintenance of that power. To maintain that power it is essential that people remain in ignorance, that they live in ignorance of the truth, even the truth of their own lives. What surrounds us therefore is a vast tapestry of lies, upon which we feed.

As every single person here knows, the justification for the invasion of Iraq was that Saddam Hussein possessed a highly dangerous body of weapons of mass destruction, some of which could be fired in 45 minutes, bringing about appalling devastation. We were assured that was true. It was not true. We were told that Iraq had a relationship with Al Qaeda and shared responsibility for the atrocity in New York of September 11th 2001. We were assured that this was true. It was not true. We were told that Iraq threatened the security of the world. We were assured it was true. It was not true. . . .

Everyone knows what happened in the Soviet Union and throughout Eastern Europe during the post-war period: the systematic brutality, the widespread atrocities, the ruthless suppression of independent thought. All this has been fully documented and verified.

But my contention here is that the US crimes in the same period have only been superficially recorded, let alone documented, let alone acknowledged, let alone recognised as crimes at all. I believe this must be addressed and that the truth has considerable bearing on where the world stands now. Although constrained, to a certain extent, by the existence of the Soviet Union, the United States' actions throughout the world made it clear that it had concluded it had carte blanche to do what it liked. . . .

I was present at a meeting at the US embassy in London in the late 1980s.

The United States Congress was about to decide whether to give more money to the Contras in their campaign against the state of Nicaragua. I was a member of a delegation speaking on behalf of Nicaragua but the most important member of this delegation was a Father John Metcalf. The leader of the US body was Raymond Seitz (then number two to the ambassador, later ambassador himself). Father Metcalf said: 'Sir, I am in charge of a parish in the north of Nicaragua. My parishioners built a school, a health centre, a cultural centre. We have lived in peace. A few months ago a Contra force attacked the parish. They destroyed everything: the school, the health centre, the cultural centre. They raped nurses and teachers, slaughtered doctors, in the most brutal manner. They behaved like savages. Please demand that the US government withdraw its support from this shocking terrorist activity.'

Raymond Seitz had a very good reputation as a rational, responsible and highly sophisticated man. He was greatly respected in diplomatic circles. He listened, paused and then spoke with some gravity. 'Father,' he said, 'let me tell you something. In war, innocent people always suffer.' There was a frozen silence. We stared at him. He did not flinch.

Innocent people, indeed, always suffer.

Finally somebody said: 'But in this case "innocent people" were the victims of a gruesome atrocity subsidised by your government, one among many. If Congress allows the Contras more money further atrocities of this kind will take place. Is this not the case? Is your government not therefore guilty of supporting acts of murder and destruction upon the citizens of a sovereign state?'

Seitz was imperturbable. 'I don't agree that the facts as presented support your assertions,' he said.

As we were leaving the Embassy a US aide told me that he enjoyed my plays. I did not reply.

I should remind you that at the time President Reagan made the following statement: 'The Contras are the moral equivalent of our Founding Fathers.'

The United States supported the brutal Somoza dictatorship in Nicaragua for over 40 years. The Nicaraguan people, led by the Sandinistas, overthrew this regime in 1979, a breathtaking popular revolution.

The Sandinistas weren't perfect. They possessed their fair share of arrogance and their political philosophy contained a number of contradictory elements. But they were intelligent, rational and civilised. They set out to establish a stable, decent, pluralistic society. The death penalty was abolished. Hundreds of thousands of poverty-stricken peasants were brought back from the dead. Over 100,000 families were given title to land. Two thousand schools were built. A quite remarkable literacy campaign reduced illiteracy in the country to less than one seventh. Free education was established and a free health service. Infant mortality was reduced by a third. Polio was eradicated.

The United States denounced these achievements as Marxist/Leninist subversion. In the view of the US government, a dangerous example was being set. If Nicaragua was allowed to establish basic norms of social and economic justice, if it was allowed to raise the standards of health care and education and achieve social unity and national self respect, neighbouring countries would ask the same questions and do the same things. There was of course at the time fierce resistance to the status quo in El Salvador.

I spoke earlier about 'a tapestry of lies' which surrounds us. President Reagan commonly described Nicaragua as a 'totalitarian dungeon'. This was taken generally by the media, and certainly by the British government, as accurate and fair comment. But there was in fact no record of death squads under the Sandinista government. There was no record of torture. There was no record of systematic or official military brutality. No priests were ever murdered in Nicaragua. There were in fact three priests in the government, two Jesuits and a Maryknoll missionary. The totalitarian dungeons were actually next door, in El Salvador and Guatemala. The United States had brought down the democratically elected government of Guatemala in 1954 and it is estimated that over 200,000 people had been victims of successive military dictatorships.

Six of the most distinguished Jesuits in the world were viciously murdered at the Central American University in San Salvador in 1989 by a battalion of the Alcatl regiment trained at Fort Benning, Georgia, USA. That extremely brave man Archbishop Romero was assassinated while saying mass. It is estimated that 75,000 people died. Why were they killed? They were killed because they believed a better life was possible and should be achieved. That belief immediately qualified them as communists. They died because they dared to question the status quo, the endless plateau of poverty, disease, degradation and oppression, which had been their birthright.

The United States finally brought down the Sandinista government. It took some years and considerable resistance but relentless economic persecution and 30,000 dead finally undermined the spirit of the Nicaraguan people. They were exhausted and poverty stricken once again. The casinos moved back into the country. Free health and free education were over. Big business returned with a vengeance. 'Democracy' had prevailed.

But this 'policy' was by no means restricted to Central America. It was conducted throughout the world. It was never-ending. And it is as if it never happened.

The United States supported and in many cases engendered every right wing military dictatorship in the world after the end of the Second World War. I refer to Indonesia, Greece, Uruguay, Brazil, Paraguay, Haiti, Turkey, the Philippines, Guatemala, El Salvador, and, of course, Chile. The horror the United States inflicted upon Chile in 1973 can never be purged and can never be forgiven.

Hundreds of thousands of deaths took place throughout these countries.

Did they take place? And are they in all cases attributable to US foreign policy? The answer is yes they did take place and they are attributable to American foreign policy. But you wouldn't know it.

It never happened. Nothing ever happened. Even while it was happening it wasn't happening. It didn't matter. It was of no interest. . . .

Listen to all American presidents on television say the words, 'the American people', as in the sentence, 'I say to the American people it is time to pray and to defend the rights of the American people and I ask the American people to trust their president in the action he is about to take on behalf of the American people.'

It's a scintillating stratagem. Language is actually employed to keep thought at bay. The words 'the American people' provide a truly voluptuous cushion of reassurance. You don't need to think. Just lie back on the cushion. The cushion may be suffocating your intelligence and your critical faculties but it's very comfortable. This does not apply of course to the 40 million people living below the poverty line and the 2 million men and women imprisoned in the vast gulag of prisons, which extends across the US.

The United States no longer bothers about low intensity conflict. It no longer sees any point in being reticent or even devious. It puts its cards on the table without fear or favour. It quite simply doesn't give a damn about the United Nations, international law or critical dissent, which it regards as impotent and irrelevant. It also has its own bleating little lamb tagging behind it on a lead, the pathetic and supine Great Britain.

What has happened to our moral sensibility? Did we ever have any? What do these words mean? Do they refer to a term very rarely employed these days—conscience? A conscience to do not only with our own acts but to do with our shared responsibility in the acts of others? Is all this dead? Look at Guantanamo Bay. Hundreds of people detained without charge for over three years, with no legal representation or due process, technically detained forever. This totally illegitimate structure is maintained in defiance of the Geneva Convention. It is not only tolerated but hardly thought about by what's called the 'international community'. This criminal outrage is being committed by a country, which declares itself to be 'the leader of the free world'. Do we think about the inhabitants of Guantanamo Bay? What does the media say about them? They pop up occasionally—a small item on page six. They have been consigned to a no man's land from which indeed they may never return. At present many are on hunger strike, being force-fed, including British residents. No niceties in these force-feeding procedures. No sedative or anaesthetic. Just a tube stuck up your nose and into your throat. You vomit blood. This is torture. What has the British Foreign Secretary said about this? Nothing. What has the British Prime Minister said about this? Nothing. Why not? Because the United States has said: to criticise our conduct in Guantanamo Bay constitutes an unfriendly act. You're either with us or against us. So Blair shuts up.

The invasion of Iraq was a bandit act, an act of blatant state terrorism, demonstrating absolute contempt for the concept of international law. The invasion was an arbitrary military action inspired by a series of lies upon lies and gross manipulation of the media and therefore of the public; an act intended to consolidate American military and economic control of the Middle East masquerading—as a last resort—all other justifications having failed to justify themselves—as liberation. A formidable assertion of military force responsible for the death and mutilation of thousands and thousands of innocent people.

We have brought torture, cluster bombs, depleted uranium, innumerable acts of random murder, misery, degradation and death to the Iraqi people and call it 'bringing freedom and democracy to the Middle East'. . . .

Death in this context is irrelevant. Both Bush and Blair place death well away on the back burner. At least 100,000 Iraqis were killed by American bombs and missiles before the Iraq insurgency began. These people are of no moment. Their deaths don't exist. They are blank. They are not even recorded as being dead. 'We don't do body counts,' said the American general Tommy Franks.

Early in the invasion there was a photograph published on the front page of British newspapers of Tony Blair kissing the cheek of a little Iraqi boy. 'A grateful child,' said the caption. A few days later there was a story and photograph, on an inside page, of another four-year-old boy with no arms. His family had been blown up by a missile. He was the only survivor. 'When do I get my arms back?' he asked. The story was dropped. Well, Tony Blair wasn't holding him in his arms, nor the body of any other mutilated child, nor the body of any bloody corpse. Blood is dirty. It dirties your shirt and tie when you're making a sincere speech on television.

The 2,000 American dead are an embarrassment. They are transported to their graves in the dark. Funerals are unobtrusive, out of harm's way. The mutilated rot in their beds, some for the rest of their lives. So the dead and the mutilated both rot, in different kinds of graves. . . .

I know that President Bush has many extremely competent speech writers but I would like to volunteer for the job myself. I propose the following short address which he can make on television to the nation. I see him grave, hair carefully combed, serious, winning, sincere, often beguiling, sometimes employing a wry smile, curiously attractive, a man's man.

'God is good. God is great. God is good. My God is good. Bin Laden's God is bad. His is a bad God. Saddam's God was bad, except he didn't have one. He was a barbarian. We are not barbarians. We don't chop people's heads off. We believe in freedom. So does God. I am not a barbarian. I am the democratically elected leader of a freedom-loving democracy. We are a compassionate society. We give compassionate electrocution and compassionate lethal injection. We are a great nation. I am not a dictator. He is. I am not a barbarian. He is. And he is. They all are. I possess moral authority. You see this fist? This is my moral authority. And don't you forget it.'

A writer's life is a highly vulnerable, almost naked activity. We don't have to weep about that. The writer makes his choice and is stuck with it. But it is true to say that you are open to all the winds, some of them icy indeed. You are out on your own, out on a limb. You find no shelter, no protection—unless you lie—in which case of course you have constructed your own protection and, it could be argued, become a politician. . . .

When we look into a mirror we think the image that confronts us is accurate. But move a millimetre and the image changes. We are actually looking at a never-ending range of reflections. But sometimes a writer has to smash the mirror—for it is on the other side of that mirror that the truth stares at us.

I believe that despite the enormous odds which exist, unflinching, unswerving, fierce intellectual determination, as citizens, to define the *real* truth of our lives and our societies is a crucial obligation which devolves upon us all. It is in fact mandatory.

If such a determination is not embodied in our political vision we have no hope of restoring what is so nearly lost to us—the dignity of man.

PART I

Opinion and Agreement

Chapter 1

Concerning Practices of Truth

Jeremy Elkins

> Nothing is more inconsistent than a political regime that is indifferent to truth; but
> nothing is more dangerous than a political system that claims to lay down the truth.
> The function of "telling the truth" must not take the form of law, . . . [but] it would
> [also] be pointless to believe that it resides by right in the spontaneous interplay of
> communication. . . . The task of telling the truth is an endless labor.
> —Michel Foucault, "The Concern for Truth"

IN POLITICS, TRUTH has taken a beating in recent years, and from two directions. From one side, the very idea of truth has been attacked as, at best, an
unnecessary, grandiose, and distracting superfluity and, at worst, a remnant
of metaphysical foundationalism, an enemy of democracy, and a tool of political domination. From the other side, we have seen truth, never very secure to
begin with on the battlefield of ordinary politics, suffer a series of especially
cruel beatings: at the hands of a previous presidential administration—perhaps the most contemptuous of truth of any in American history, for whom
"reality," as one of its senior members famously boasted, was not a constraint
on but only an artifact of the exercise of political power;[1] in the increasing
success—and hubris—of partisan propagandists in and out of government in
being able to create public narratives ranging from the marginally plausible

to the outright absurd; and in the frequent refusal of the "responsible press" to assess these narratives rather than merely report on them—to name just a few of the most significant of these recent assaults.

Neither the philosophical nor the partisan attacker of truth is likely to want to identify very closely with the other, and this only partly because in recent years (this has not always been the case) the first sort of attack has come primarily from the left and the second primarily from the right. More important, the partisan attackers will need to deny, at least publicly, that truth is a target, while the theoretical attackers of truth-talk will insist that the politics of deception—and especially of that special variety of deception with which Harry Frankfurt's now famous essay was concerned[2]—are not what they had in mind: that the critique of truth-talk was never meant to deny the simple and politically important virtue of not lying, of "truthfulness" (as it is sometimes put) in contrast to "truth."

Yet for political theorists who have an interest in taking the world seriously, the *problem* of truth can no longer be dismissed as though it were merely a vestige of vulgar philosophical realism and the obsession of political naïfs. To the extent that our thinking about political life is meant to have a serious relationship with our political life, it can no longer be sufficient merely to reiterate, over and again, the kinds of sins that have been committed in the name of truth. We have heard—and rightly so—much about the harms that certain claims of truth have caused to politics. But in light of what our politics have become, now is as good an occasion as any to revisit the question of whether the theoretical deprecation of truth-talk may not have stated its case too strongly; whether the only important political virtue in relation to truth is that of not lying, or whether there is more to it than that; and whether the *question* itself of truth is not one that is necessary for our political life.

Truth and Knowledge

Hanging over much of the theoretical discussion of truth in politics is, as I have just said, a concern with the uses to which the language of truth has sometimes been put, and it is important to begin by recognizing the general and legitimate grounds of that concern. What *is* the danger that a focus on truth might pose for democratic politics and from which the abandonment of truth-talk is meant to deliver us?

One kind of answer to that question would take us straightaway to the metaphysical or ontological: that such a focus must necessarily take us in the wrong direction because there can be no such thing as truth in political life. Few people, however, hold such a view in just that form, among the reasons for which is that it is self-defeating: one would need to have the same access to truth—or to the realm that truth would occupy—to know that it is, as it were, not there. But that difficulty itself suggests a better version of the answer, which is also the more common one. This answer focuses not on the possibility of truth, but on the conceit of knowing it—or, more precisely, knowing, with respect to the matter at issue, all that there is to know. That conceit is indeed an ancient one, at least as old as there are records of humans speaking about such matters as truth and knowledge. And as far as we know just as old is the recognition of it *as* a conceit, the wariness about it, and the sense of its danger, both to the individual soul and to the city. The sense of that danger and the felt need to restrain it are at the very basis of most religions: in the Western biblical tradition, for example, history begins precisely with this conceit, and the Messianic age characterized in part by its overcoming. The concern with this conceit is equally at the origin of the Western philosophical tradition: in the figure of Socrates, who sought to undermine the certainty of those who claimed true knowledge and who sought to show why it is that in "political practice [*politikē praxei*]" "knowledge cannot be our guide."[3] Yet so powerful is the tendency toward that conceit that both religion and philosophy have themselves often succumbed to it, and in the many examples that could easily be cited of the harms that truth has inflicted on politics, the dogmas of various religious and philosophical systems would figure prominently.

The nature of this conceit concerning truth, and the basis for recognizing it as a conceit, depend centrally on the disjunction *between* truth and knowledge: between the impersonality inherent in the idea of truth (as that term is usually understood) and the necessary particularity of any individual person who would claim knowledge of it. The attempt to deflate claims to truth-knowledge thus commonly involves pressing, in one form or another, on this disjunction. And it is not surprising that deflationary projects should thus so often direct our attention back from the impersonal object that is claimed to be known to the agent who claims to know, and to her particular relationship to the knowledge that she claims—her perspective, her motives, her desires, and so on. Nietzsche's version is only one of many, but it is among the most naked.

The will to truth which will still tempt us to many a venture, that famous truthfulness of which all philosophers so far have spoken with respect . . . Is it any wonder that we should finally become suspicious, lose patience, and turn away impatiently? . . . *What* in us really wants "truth"?[4]

Nietzsche himself suggests a number of specific answers: for some, the "prefer[ence for] even a handful of 'certainty' [over] . . . a whole cartload of beautiful possibilities"; for others, the desire to re-create the world in the image of one's own personal "memoir," and to impose one's own "moral[ity] (or immoral[ity]) over the whole of being."[5] But common to all such desires is the urge to objectify one's particularity:

> Anyone who considers the basic drives of man . . . will find that . . . every single one of them would like only too well to represent just *itself* as the ultimate purpose of existence and the legitimate *master* of all the other drives. For every drive wants to be master—and it attempts to philosophize in *that spirit*.

The will to knowledge is thus not

> the father of philosophy; but rather . . . another drive has, here as elsewhere, employed knowledge [*Erkenntniss*] (and mis-knowledge [*Verkenntniss*]) as a mere instrument.[6]

It is easy enough to be reminded here of Paul:

> For sin, taking occasion by the commandment, deceived me . . . [7]

And for good reason. For the Christian narrative is also a deflationary story, an attempt to unmask the will to truth-knowledge. Sin (*hamartía*: "missing the mark") is brought into the world by a willfulness, born of, in Milton's telling of the tale,

> Vain hopes, vain aimes, inordinate desires
> Blown up with high conceits ingendring pride . . .
> to know of things above this world . . .
> . . . to make Gods of Men.[8]

It is the conceit of being able to know the truth that in the Christian narrative continues to corrupt mankind's relationship with what is divine—including, ironically, its relation to the "truth in the [divine] law."[9]

Politics and Truth

The concern with the conceit of truth-knowledge is indeed ancient and perennial. Our focus here, however, is the political. And if we ask in that context what precisely is thought to be the harm caused by this will and this conceit, we can identify two common answers. The first is what we might call the traditionalist or conservative account, which refers here not to a particular partisan identification, but to a strand of thought that in various forms is widely shared, and that was given perhaps its most famous expression in modern Western thought by Edmund Burke. For Burke, the claim of individual reason to possess the truth of society was, indeed, one of the great political conceits, and some of his most virulent criticism was directed at the "self-sufficiency and arrogance" of those who, "never experienc[ing] a wisdom greater than their own," imagine that they can craft a political order on the basis of their own reason. Such attempts, Burke insisted, are, in fact, "wanton caprice" and "arbitrary will" masquerading as truth. The alternative for Burke was not blind, mechanistic adherence to social convention (which would simply be a preference for a different form of conceit to possess the truth—namely, that our existing social arrangements are necessarily the best they can be for us), but rather an attitude of diffidence toward social institutions and practices, one characterized by the rejection of abstract reason as the basis for political decisions in favor of *understanding*. While those who approach society from the perspective of abstract reason "act as if they were [its] entire masters . . . changing the state as often and as much and in as many ways as there are floating fancies or fashions," "destroying at their pleasure the whole original fabric of their society," and breaking the "link" of "one generation . . . with the other," those whose judgments and deliberation are guided by a desire to understand the "commonwealth and the laws" approach them rather with the deferential respect of "temporary possessors and life-renters," guardians of an "inheritance" and of "a partnership . . . not only between those who are living, but between those who are living, those who are dead, and those who are to be born." This stance toward society does not "at all," Burke emphasized, "exclud[e] a principle of improvement," for institutions of the state clearly may need reform, and the law may need to grow. The disposition to understand means rather that "no man should approach to look into" the state's "defects or corruptions but with due caution, that he should never dream of beginning its reformation by its subversion, that he should approach to the faults of the state as to the wounds of a father, with pious awe and trembling solicitude." And it means that one ought not to treat the law as though it were "a heap of old exploded errors," to be "subject to" nothing more than "will" and one's own reason as if starting fresh, but ought rather to recognize that "with all its defects, redundancies, and errors," it is the repository of "the collected reason of ages, combining the principles of original justice with the infinite variety of human concerns." "By adhering in this manner and on those principles to our forefathers, we are guided not by the superstition of antiquarians, but by the spirit of philosophic analogy," through which we "fortify the fallible and feeble contrivances of our reason" and "[temper] with an awful gravity" "the spirit of freedom" that would "[lead] in itself to misrule and excess."[10]

If in this view, then, the great harm of the truth-knowledge conceit is that it fails to appreciate the wisdom embedded in inherited institutions and practices, a second answer to the question of the harm of that conceit—these are by no means exclusive of one another—also involves a failure of understanding, but of a different sort. We can refer to this as the pluralist answer, and we have already touched on one version of it in Nietzsche's reference to the "whole cartload of beautiful possibilities" that the "will to 'truth'" may preclude.[11] A somewhat different version—and one that has influenced many of the political theorists who have argued recently for setting aside questions of truth in politics—is given by Hannah Arendt in essays such as "Philosophy and Politics." Arendt's focus in that essay is on Plato and Socrates, but in this, as in all of her political writings, her eye is ultimately on the present; and her portrait of a Socrates who "had made new demands on philosophy precisely because he did not claim to be wise" is meant to suggest what political discourse—*dialegesthai,* or "talking through"—might look like when it is freed from the "tyranny of truth." For Socrates, the aim of (what we would call) philosophical inquiry was not, as Arendt puts it, to discover "truth as the very opposite of opinion." Rather,

> to Socrates, as to his fellow citizens, *doxa* [opinion] was the formulation in speech of what *dokei moi,* that is, of what appears to me. This *doxa* had as its topic . . . the world as it opens itself to me. The assumption was

that the world opens up differently to every man, according to his position in it. . . .

[Socrates'] method had its significance in a twofold conviction: every man has his own *doxa*, his own opening to the world, and Socrates therefore must always begin with questions; he cannot know beforehand what kind of *dokei moi*, of it-appears-to-me, the other possesses. He must make sure of the other's position in the common world. Yet, just as nobody can know beforehand the other's *doxa*, so nobody can know by himself and without further effort the inherent truth of his own opinion. Socrates wanted to bring out this truth that everyone potentially possesses. If we remain true to his own metaphor of *maieutic* [midwifery], we may say: Socrates wanted to make the city more truthful by delivering each of the citizens of their truths.[12]

Pluralism comes in many varieties, not all of them as fundamentally perspectival with respect to the idea of truth itself as the Nietzschean or Arendtian. But at least for those forms of pluralism for which plurality is both part of the human condition and itself an affirmative good, the worry has been that a politics that rests on the belief that one can know the truth and that is focused on discerning absolute standards will result in a failure to understand the complexity of the world and the situation of human beings within it. It will too easily lead into the temptation to mandate for others a particular way of life and too often end up restraining political dialogue by privileging those who are thought to have special access to truth while circumscribing the kinds of voices that are recognized as legitimate: privileging the "rational" over the "affective," the articulate, formally crafted argument over the sometimes clumsy attempts to articulate novel and incipient ideas, the voices of the well-educated over the less well-educated, of those accustomed to the space of the public and the rhetoric of power over those who have been excluded from it, and so forth. More generally, the fear is that an emphasis on truth will too often promote insularity in our thought and an unwillingness to take seriously the perspective of others, for if we believe that we know the truth or what reason demands, the point of our speech will be to bring others over or to coerce them into compliance; we will be, as it were, evangelicals not ecumenists. Our task, as one common version of the pluralist argument goes, ought rather be to promote a society in which various kinds of diversity are not only tolerated, but understood as ways of being human and living a human life, and to cultivate a more open and "multivocal" politics in which competing perspectives and discursive modes are joined in an ongoing conversation and productive confrontation about who we want to be and how we should proceed.

There is much to be said for all of this. That appeals to truth and reason have at times, in intention or effect, unduly narrowed the range of voices, ideas, and perspectives—that claims to truth-knowledge have, in short, had their victims—is undeniable. Yet as with any political vision born of victimhood, there is the danger of imagining liberation as merely the mirror image of victimization, as domination stood on its head, and in so doing, of reinscribing the very divisions through which domination was constructed: in this case, the oppositions of truth and contingency, truth and plurality, truth and opinion, reason and emotion, and such. After we have recognized, as we ought to, the inflated claims that have sometimes been made concerning truth-knowledge, the question of truth, de-inflated and now with its scare quotes removed, still remains. Is there something in us that might *still*, and justifiably, want truth? Is there still something in our political life that needs it?

*   *   *

As it so happens, we can get a start on an answer by returning to those two accounts—Burke's and Arendt's—that I have taken as representative of, respectively, the traditionalist and the pluralist critiques of truth-knowledge, although I shall return to them now in reverse order.

I have already quoted Arendt's felicitous statement of that key pluralist idea: that "every man has his own *doxa*, his own opening to the world," because "the world opens up differently to every man, according to his position in it." But this implies an important thought: that we can only understand the plurality of *doxai* as perspectives ("opinions" or "judgments" or "appears-to-me"s) *on a world*. That is, it is the world that opens up to perspectives, and not those perspectives that constitute the world. Arendt, in the same passage from which I have quoted, herself says something very much like this.

> The assumption was that [while] the world opens up differently to every man . . . the "sameness" of the world, its commonness . . . or "objectivity" (as we would say from the subjective viewpoint of modern philosophy) resides in the fact that the same world opens up to everyone.[13]

We no longer live in a society in which public discourse about matters of common importance could consist so centrally of individual conversations of the Socratic sort, nor need we adopt as the primary aim of truthful inquiry about public matters the very Socratic goal (which he, or Plato, rightly regarded as bound to the idea of friendship) of improving those whose views are mistaken. But although the Socratic answer is not sufficient for us, the basic question of how to "make the city more truthful" is no less ours. And as Arendt's language can remind us, a politics of truth need not depend on a claim to possess absolute knowledge of the world or universal laws, but follows simply and directly from the idea that beyond our opinions there lies a world.[14]

What is meant here by "world" is just that which is, or that which can be had, in common, and which must stand in contrast, therefore, to the distinct and particular perspectives that we have on it. The critic of truth-talk who suggests that appeals to truth must be references to something "out there" is in one important sense right: namely, that claims of truth must refer to something—a world, *our* world—that is outside of one's own statements about it or beliefs about it. That "I could be wrong" (or that I don't know, am unsure, etc.) or that "things are (or could be) different from how I want them to be" (or how they were, how they will be, etc.) are sufficient to ground a concept of truth. It follows, in other words, from the fact of belonging to a world that one's views about what it is and about how things in it *are* can be subject to evaluations of veracity—not whether they correspond to the world in some naked, noumenal essence, but whether we have good enough reason for accepting them in light of everything we know as well as what we reasonably, under the circumstances, might come to know. And when those views become the basis for claims *on* the political community—claims of how we should understand ourselves, how the coercive force of the state should be employed, how collective resources should be employed, and so forth—a politics that takes seriously that the "world opens up differently to every man" must be concerned with questions about how such views ought to be evaluated.

This, then, takes us back to Burke, for whom the ability to evaluate such views was among the basic requirements of politics. I have referred to Burke's famous contempt for claims of political truth derived from "speculative" or "abstract" reason, and of his characterization of political movements that seek to restructure the "fabric of . . . society" in accordance with such reason as a kind of arbitrary will. Yet for Burke, this was only one variety of arbitrary will. By "arbitrary will"—or "will" *simpliciter*, as he commonly used the term—Burke meant, more generally, will unbridled by genuine understanding. And if behind one form of dangerous political will lay the arrogance of abstract reason, behind another lay the untutored "passions."[15] (This form of will amounted roughly to what Aristotle called *propeteia*, the "rashness" of those who are too "hasty" or too "vehement" to "wait for reason" [*ouk anamenousi ton logon*] and who are thus prone to be guided by *phantasia*.)[16] Thus while Burke, when confronted with claims of political will grounded in abstract reason, tended to emphasize the immanent wisdom of existing institutions, and, when confronted with the demand for transparency issued by that "empire of light and reason," emphasized the importance of those "pleasing illusions . . . necessary to cover the defects of our naked, shivering nature," when confronted instead with the demands of untutored passion, stressed the guiding and taming force of reason. "If government were a matter of will," Burke argued to those who had just elected him, "yours, without question, ought to be superiour. But government and legislation are matters of reason and judgment, and not of inclination," and (he wrote elsewhere) the "dominion" of "will" is "dangerous" when it is "set above reason and justice." If political reason ought not to be confused with the discovery of eternal truths, so too must it not be confused with mere "opinion," "will," "pleasure," "inclination," "desire," and "passion."[17] This is not because the latter are irrelevant to politics, but because they are not enough: among the great threats to politics, Burke rightly thought, is that opinion, will, and inclination would take themselves as such to be a sufficient basis for public policy and that "reason and judgment" would be "subservient" to the naked "will" and "inclination" of electors whose "determination precedes the discussion."[18]

The ultimate object of political reason was, for Burke, the "general good."[19] By this he did not, of course, mean a "brooding omnipresence in the sky" or "a way things really are independent of us." The "good of the commonwealth"—that "rule which rides over the rest"[20]—was, for Burke, rather what we might call a paramount regulative ideal in terms of which all political deliberation must proceed. But as such, it implies that what it is good or right to do politically may be different from what any particular person might want, or what even a majority of persons might in its "hasty opinion," think is right.[21] Determining the general good, though it is not about discovering an object that exists independent of us, is nonetheless in it own way a *pursuit* or an inquiry, and like other undertakings, can be done better or worse. The idea that politics aims at the general good was meant for Burke, in part, to emphasize the *demands* of political judgment. To engage responsibly in that judgment is "no easy task," for it requires the "unit[ing of] circumspection with vigour": the ability and the disposition to gather information and to weigh evidence, to understand the character of existing institutions and the possibilities for their reform, to learn from history and to anticipate events, to attend to the opinions, passions, and sentiments of the people without "running into the perilous extremes of servile compliance or wild popularity," to understand the various kinds of "interests" that make up the society, and to imagine the effect of alternative courses of action on the future well-being of each and all.[22] It is true that Burke was not "a Hegelian proponent of a 'real will' as distinct from what men apparently want"; nor did he have any illusion that all well-considered political judgments would reach the same conclusion. Nonetheless, he insisted that "men have no right to what is not reasonable and to what is not for their benefit," and that it is only "when great multitudes act together" through institutional arrangements designed to replace mere will with reasoned judgment that we "recognize the people" at all.[23]

None of this was, for Burke, simply a matter of ascertaining the truth. Yet if he did not regard the concern for truth as a sufficient basis of political reason, neither did he ever doubt that it was necessary. Of certain kinds of truth claims, such as those asserting absolute natural rights as a basis for political programs, Burke was indeed wary, for these, he lamented, tend to be "all extremes," whereas political judgment often requires "balances between differences of good, in compromises sometimes between good and evil, and sometimes between evil and evil." Because of this, "in proportion as" "the pretended [abstract] rights of . . . theorists" "are metaphysically true," they "are morally and politically false."[24] But just as Burke's dismissal of "speculative" reason as a ground for political judgments in no way implied a rejection of reason per se, so his criticism of reliance on abstract, metaphysical truths in politics was with their character as abstract and metaphysical, rather than their character as truth claims. The point of politics for Burke was not to tally opinions, but to test them, not simply to empower political will, but in large part to evaluate it, and in this, a respect for truth was crucial. "Such is the power of truth," he remarked, that sometimes even from the mere statement of it we must "draw irresistible conclusions." But more generally, and even when considerations of truth did not issue in such compelling conclusions, a respect for truth was for Burke part of what distinguished a politics that sought to comprehend the world from a politics of mere will. It was for that reason that, he warned, "great kings and mighty nations have been undone" by "rejecting truth and listening to flattery."[25]

Underlying a good deal of the contemporary criticism of talk of truth in politics there runs, it seems, a very particular idea of what role truth would have to play in our political life if it is to play a role at all. That idea, and the fear that it motivates, is that if considerations of truth are allowed into our politics, they must be in the form of a claim of absolute knowledge of the world, of telling us what we ought to (or actually do) want, and/or in charting our course for us; that if truth matters it must be, as Michael Oakeshott put it, *apodeictic*: capable of "proving or disproving the 'correctness' of political proposals."[26] Yet surely this is not the only role for truth. It was certainly not at the basis of the Socratic project of making the city and its citizens more truthful. Nor was it what Burke had in mind. He did not think that truth could very often, of itself, tell us what to do, yet he insisted that reasonable judgments could not do without it. For both Plato's Socrates and for Burke, each in his own way, the commitment to truth was bound to the recognition that the world is not simply reducible to our understanding of it. Yet for both, the concern for truth in politics was not how to eliminate that gap, but how to act in light of our recognizing it.

Truth and Certainty

If the point of attending to truth in political life were to "prov[e] or disprov[e] the 'correctness' of political proposals," the relevant ideas about truth would have to have at least two characteristics: they would have to be *known* with *certainty*, and they would have to provide an *absolute* standard of conduct. So great has been the influence of the apodeictic conception of truth that Arendt, despite her veneration of the Socratic project of making the city and the opinions of its citizens more truthful, nonetheless insisted elsewhere that the "tyrannical" character of truth made it unsuitable to the doxastic nature of politics, and that the "pursuit of truth" could thus only be "performed from outside" the "political realm."[27] In "Truth and Politics," Arendt did not reject the idea of truth or deny its importance. On the contrary, part of her concern in that essay was precisely to protect factual truth from political deception and manipulation. "Facts inform opinion, and opinions, inspired by different interests and passions, can differ widely and still be legitimate [only] as long as they respect factual truth," for truth (as she puts it in her Heideggerian closing remark), is nothing less than the "ground on which we stand and the sky that stretches above us." If we understand by truth, she writes, that "which men cannot change at will," it is truth that determines the very "borders" and the "whole sphere" of the "political realm" itself, and the respect for truth and the protection of truth-tellers are necessary to protect politics against the pursuit of "profit, partisanship, and the lust for domination" that seeks to transcend the proper bounds of the political realm.[28]

It is just because of this forthright acknowledgment of the importance of truth to politics that Arendt's insistence that the pursuit of it must remain outside of politics is so striking, and that we have good reason to think that it rests on something like an *apodeictic* conception of the role that truth would have to play if it were part of that "realm." While Arendt recognizes in passing a variety of "modes of truthtelling," there are indeed only two to which she devotes any attention: those "rational," "absolute," philosophical truths concerning "man in the singular" (which when asserted in the "sphere of human affairs . . . strikes at the very roots of all politics and all governments"), and "factual truths," which she tends to identify with "brutally elementary data" about which there can be no genuine disagreement and which provide a limit on political opinion. Taking these as the paradigms of truth, she argues that "all . . . truth . . . peremptorily claims to be acknowledged and precludes debate . . . [whereas] debate constitutes the very essence of political life. In matters of opinion, but not in matters of truth, our thinking is truly discursive."[29]

The categorical distinction between "matters of opinion" and "matters of truth" is, however, a legacy of the apodeictic conception. To see how limited a conception that is, we need only consider a few examples of common political truth-claims:

1. Democracies do not (or are less likely, as compared to . . . , etc.) go to war with each other.
2. The long-term goal(s) of the U.S. administration (or of XYZ in that administration) with respect to the U.S. presence in Iraq (as of the year . . . , etc.) was. . . .
3. "The predominant model of liberal democratic institutions, in which the same representative body lays down the rules of just con-duct and directs government, necessarily leads to a gradual trans-formation of the spontaneous order of a free society into a totalitar-ian system conducted in the service of some coalition of organized interests."[30]
4. "To separate [Negro children] . . . from others of similar age and

qualifications solely because of their race generates a feeling of inferiority as to their status in the community that may affect their hearts and minds in a way unlikely ever to be undone."[31]

While these are all claims about (in Arendt's language, describing truth-claims) "things as they are,"[32] they are neither claims of "factual" truth in the sense of "brutally elementary data" nor claims of the kind of "absolute," "rational" philosophical truth that Arendt associates with the legacy of Plato. And while any of these views could, of course, be held with the assurance that one has come into full possession of the truth, none of them need be. Alternatively, one can, with respect to any of these propositions, *suspect, tend toward, think, believe, opine, be fairly certain of, hypothesize, accept provisionally, have faith in*, or stand toward it in dozens of other epistemic modalities. The stance that one has toward the proposition does not, however, alter its character as a proposition about things as they are. There is no contradiction between holding an opinion as such and having it aim at the truth. (This is, indeed, why the Socratic project of delivering the citizens of the truth of their opinions is a wholly intelligible one, and why for Plato's Socrates the alternative to knowledge was not mere opinion, but "true opinion [*doxa alēthēs*].")[33] But if these are, or can be, opinions, they are not opinions of the sort that Arendt in "Truth and Politics" sharply distinguished from "truth," and for which the essential criterion of "validity" is its "representativeness," and therefore the number of "viewpoints" it takes into account. ("The more people's standpoints I have present in my mind while I am pondering a given issue, and the better I can imagine how I would feel and think if I were in their place, the stronger will be my capacity for representative thinking and the more valid my final conclusions, my opinion.")[34] For opinions concerning the sorts of ordinary propositions that I have listed, the primary criterion of validity is not representativeness, but accuracy, and the stance that one has toward the claim is properly a function of the strength of the evidence that is, or can be reasonably made, available.

If these kinds of ordinary political truth-claims need not be held as a matter of certainty, neither need they be taken to "prove" the "correctness" of political proposals. The first two propositions are quite abstract and, even if believed to be true, would be consistent with very different political programs. The last two examples may be thought more determinate in their political implications. But not even Hayek believed that elected bodies ought *never* to lay down rules of just conduct. And the final claim could in principle be equally well accepted by someone who thought that it was a good reason for eliminating segregation and someone who thought that it was a good reason for keeping it. So far from precluding debate, these sorts of propositions may invite it, both with respect to their validity and, to the extent that they are thought to be valid, with respect to the question of what the implications should be for political programs.

None of this would matter much if it were simply a terminological question of whether to refer to the "pursuit of truth" as occurring "inside" or "outside" of the "political realm." But how we understand the relation of truth to politics itself has political significance; it matters to how we structure various political institutions and to what we ask of them. I have referred to Arendt's concern with preserving the integrity of both truth and politics; it would be a sad irony if the denigration of both was assisted by just that separation between them that Arendt thought was necessary to protect them. There is, however, good reason to think that this has happened. The clearest case of this is perhaps the press, one of those institutions that Arendt singled out as necessary for protecting politics, but that, because its responsibility is to report on factual truths so plain that (she argued) "no action and no decision are, or should be, involved," could do so, she insisted, only "from outside the political realm."[35] Yet the more the press's responsibility with respect to the truth is conceived as limited to reporting on facts that are sufficiently "brutally elementary" and certain that no action and no decision need be involved (although strictly speaking, that is not true even with respect to such facts), the less we will ask of the press. And on this conception of the proper relation of truth to politics, the more it is apparent just how many decisions the press must make about what to cover and how to cover it, the more suspect the press will be held. Similarly, for official political institutions, the notion that their responsibility toward truth is *limited* to respecting brutally elementary truths certainly held opens up an enormous space in which "things as they are" plays little or no role. (I shall discuss both kinds of institutions in more detail shortly.) The notion (of which Arendt's account is just one version) that truth and politics belong to separate realms can easily have the effect of discouraging us from taking up just those very crucial political questions of *how* political institutions ought to confront competing claims about how things are. And it is the neglect of those questions that, I want to suggest, may be the greatest casualty of the attempt to eliminate "truth-talk" from our political life.

All of this brings us back yet again to Burke. For Burke, one of the primary and defining responsibilities of political institutions was to elevate public opinion and to restrain the imperiousness of political will—including that form of political will that is characterized by, in Arendt's phrase, "profit, partisanship, and the lust for domination." Burke himself thought that such a task was best entrusted to that natural aristocracy that, "bred in a place of estimation . . . [with the] leisure to read, to reflect, to converse," and capable of "draw[ing] the court and attention of the wise and learned, wherever they are to be found," could "stand upon such elevated ground as to be enabled to take a large view of the wide-spread and infinitely diversified combinations of men and affairs in a large society" and provide the greatest degree of vigilance, foresight, and circumspection.[36] This particular vision is no longer widely shared; in the movement toward universal suffrage it became a commonplace that that aristocracy had it own partial interests and was more than prepared to use the power of the state to advance them.[37] But the general *idea* that for Burke lay behind the need for a natural aristocracy supported by a limited electorate has outlived his own conception of what specific institutions that idea required to be realized: it is the idea that a healthy politics requires mediating institutions to resist the tendency of untrammeled and unmediated political will. For us as for Burke, the role of such institutions is not reducible solely to questions about truth; but it cannot be understood without any attention to them.

I began the discussion of truth and politics by considering what I referred to for shorthand as "traditionalism" and "pluralism" as two kinds of answers that could be given to the question of the harm that "truth"—or, more specifically, the conceit of knowing it—poses for politics. But neither traditionalism nor pluralism is itself a political program, and recognizing the virtues of each merely opens the door to further, more concrete, political questions. Thus every society that has self-consciously looked to tradition has (like Burke) regarded it as a condition for preserving particular traditions that they be *just*, and any such society must therefore, with respect to any particular tradition, judge whether it is one worth preserving as it is, or whether it needs to be (in Burke's words) "improved"—or in the form that this more commonly takes, how to interpret a particular tradition so as to be able to regard it as just. Similarly every society that has recognized pluralist virtues has had to decide not *whether* pluralism, but what *kind* of pluralism: for example, *which* differences to respect, and what *kind* of respect they deserve. Although, once again, the responses to these questions need not always involve truth-claims, and will never involve only that, they often will include questions of truth and truth-claims, and insofar as they do, the question of how to treat those claims will have to be addressed. There is no simple answer to that question and none that can be generalized across all cases; while for some kinds of conflicts the best answer may be to set aside or "bracket" conflicts about truth, this is neither always possible nor always desirable. Pursuing these sorts of questions, so far from threatening traditionalist or pluralist values, is part of the process of political judgment that is necessary for giving them effect.

* * *

I have meant to argue that, contrary to the apodeictic conception, according to which the point of truth in relation to politics is, as far as possible, to eliminate it, a concern with truth and questions about truth are ordinary and necessary features of democratic politics. This is so in at least two respects. First, insofar as political opinions are opinions about the world, they commonly involve thoughts about (however modestly understood or tentatively held) "how things are." Second, because it is an essential characteristic of politics that political opinions, including opinions about truth, will involve disagreements, a second-order political question must be how the political community in general and various political institutions in particular ought to act in light of these. Insofar as questions of truth are involved, answers to the second-order question (which, of course, will also involve disagreements) will be *about* truth, but they need not be about trying to *resolve* conflicting truth-claims, at least not in any absolute sense. They are better and more generally understood as debates about what to do in light of our concern with how things actually are, in light of the competing views that members of the society have about that question, and in light of the limitations of our knowledge.

It has been part of my argument that the way in which questions of truth matter in political life is often more complex than is usually recognized in the dismissals of truth-talk. I shall now want to offer several illustrations of these second-order questions, and it should not be surprising that these will not only discuss that complexity, but reflect it, requiring us to go fairly deeply (the first example especially so) into some specific institutional controversies. Because of the length of these, I shall limit myself to two primary examples. But these should be sufficient to show how questions about truth, so far from displacing politics, are necessarily bound up with it, and why these questions deserve more and not less of our attention.

The Origin of Life

As a first example, let us consider the contemporary U.S. debate over the teaching of the origin of complex life forms in public schools. In recent years, those who have criticized the monopoly of evolutionary theory in the public school curriculum have made a number of different arguments, including arguments of both tradition and pluralism.[38] Although there are many variations, the two common arguments, in basic form, run as follows.

1. The establishment clause of the first amendment, as it has been developed by judicial decisions, prohibits the government from taking
   a position on the truth of religious doctrine. The Supreme Court has
   put this idea in various ways, among them that the government may
   not endorse a view that sends "a message to nonadherents that they
   are outsiders, not full members of the political community, and an
   accompanying message to adherents that they are insiders, favored
   members of the political community," and that it "must be neutral
   in matters of religious theory, doctrine, and practice. It may not be
   hostile to any religion or to the advocacy of nonreligion; and it may
   not aid, foster, or promote one religion or religious theory against
   another or even against the militant opposite. The First Amendment
   mandates governmental neutrality between religion and religion, and
   between religion and nonreligion." Yet the teaching of "evolutionism" is a direct denial of a central tenet of religious doctrines held
   by many, and as such is tantamount to establishment of an official
   governmental position on religious truth.[39]
2. Even if the first amendment does not *require* that agencies of the state
   refrain from teaching evolution as the sole account of the origin of
   complex life, the principle of intellectual pluralism (itself an "underlying purpose of the first amendment") demands that students be
   exposed to a variety of scientific theories.[40] Evolutionary accounts are
   one theory; "creation science" and "intelligent design" are others.[41]
   For while the mainstream scientific position is evolutionist, there
   are "highly-qualified scientists who" argue "that . . . there is strong

evidence that life and the universe came about in a different manner, one perhaps less inconsistent with religious doctrine" or with design by a creator.[42] Particularly, then, when what is at issue is a belief deeply held by millions of citizens, students ought to be exposed to the arguments for both positions.

Each of these is, in part, an argument from tradition. And each is an argument for pluralism. The first argument rests on an interpretation of the constitutional tradition of religious pluralism; the second is an argument both about the tradition of intellectual pluralism and about the general virtues of pluralism. Neither is, on its face, implausible. So how should we approach such claims?

There are several immediate possibilities that offer little help. First, there is no dismissing these claims on grounds of sincerity; many of those who espouse "creation science" or "intelligent design" believe it as deeply as others believe in evolution as a comprehensive account of the origin of complex life. Second, we obviously cannot get very far simply by reiterating the Arendtian caveat that political opinions (in this case, concerning what the state should teach) must "respect factual truth," for the dispute here involves competing claims about factual truth. And third, we cannot simply take the opposite tack and ignore questions of truth, wiping our hands of it all with the sanguine assurance that, as Rorty insisted, if we only "take care of freedom"—by, for example, "having information freely available"—"truth will take care of itself."[43] Whether that is enough in other circumstances, it is not enough when what is at issue is how to spend limited resources—including, as in this case, time. We cannot, even if we wanted to, teach everything; and while it would be a poor educational system that taught everything it taught as truth, the question is whether, in deciding what to teach, truth can ever come into play, and if so whether this is such a case.

There is another response with which we may immediately be confronted. The question of the relation of science to truth has had no shortage of attention in contemporary philosophical literature. Against the idea that questions of truth should come into play here, the familiar argument may be heard that the natural sciences cannot, any more than the social sciences or the humanities, give us "the truth," if by that we mean a picture of "How Things Really Are." Instead, it might be said—this is only one possible conclusion of that general argument—that we should simply ask more forthrightly such questions as what ways of thinking about the world are, in a broad sense, most useful to us. And if we follow that route, the scientific account of evolution will have no special status: the debate over what to teach about the scientific origin of complex life will not look any different in kind from (although it may be more complicated in detail than) a debate about whether to use scarce resources to offer art classes.

I do not want to enter directly into the debate over whether or how far science can tell us "how things are" in the natural world.[44] Instead I want to focus on the secondary thought that if science cannot give us that truth, the concept of truth can having nothing to do with scientific evaluation or with the evaluation of science. That conclusion follows naturally from the identification of truth with the knowledge of it—the idea that truth as a concept is applicable only to what can be known with certainty. (Or as Rorty puts this idea, in support of it, truth is not a useful idea because "we will never know for sure whether a given idea is true," and "you cannot aim at something, cannot work to get it, unless you can recognize once you have got it.")[45] In fact it seems perfectly plausible to attempt to understand how things are without believing that one can know it with certainty, or that one can know everything about it, or that one can know it "noumenally" (whatever that might be taken to mean). We can try our best to get our opinions right, where that means giving the most accurate account of how things are, while also knowing that we cannot have certain knowledge, that we might be wrong or limited, and even sometimes being fairly aware of just how wrong or limited we are.

Indeed the attempt to get our opinions as right as we can, while recognizing the limits of our knowledge, underlies a wide variety of our practices and beliefs. In scientific practice it is (to mention only two examples) at the root of the use of the null hypothesis and of statistical confidence levels. Beyond the sciences, it appears, for instance, in the idea of standards of proof used by courts (which may take property from one person and give it to another on the basis not of certain knowledge, but of having slightly greater confidence in that decision than its opposite), by government agencies (which may take potentially life-saving products off the market or allow potentially dangerous ones on, being aware that they have no certain knowledge and often being aware of just how little they know), and by many other political-legal bodies. It appears, sometimes quite centrally, even in religious beliefs, as in the apophatic tradition, and in the complex idea of religious faith. And so on. Although some have argued that in such cases what is at issue is not truth, but justification (or that there is nothing more to truth than justification),[46] in none of these is the standard of justification comprehensible except in terms of the aim of trying to get things as right as we can under various constraints, including the condition of uncertainty.

In addition to illustrating how truth may function as a regulative aim even when it is acknowledged that it cannot be absolutely known, these examples point to the fact that various practices, institutions, and systems will differ both with respect to the *kinds* of truths with which they are concerned and the *standards* for assessing truth-claims that they employ. What those standards should *be*—and occasionally, but more rarely, what kinds of truths ought to be of concern to the enterprise—will, of course, often be matters of debate. (What should be the standard of proof for holding in military custody noncitizens alleged to have committed terrorist acts overseas? How much evidence of efficacy and safety should be required for approving a new cancer drug? Should it be the same as the standard for approving a new antiwrinkle drug? How great must the evidence be for the human contribution to global warming before we undertake various measures to reduce it?) Neither those debates—second-order debates about what I shall refer to as "truth-practices"—nor the particular judgments that are made in accordance with whatever standards are adopted in those practices will be about "how things are" absolutely. But it is a mistake to jump from this to the conclusion that these do not therefore concern in part (although certainly they concern only in part)[47] truth. They concern precisely how to act in particular contexts when we wish to be guided as best we can by "how things are" while recognizing that our knowledge of that is limited. There may not be much that can be said in general about the particular judgments that will need to be made in accordance with whatever institutional standards are adopted. But the determination and interrogation of the standards themselves involve broad political judgments, and the questions that these raise are among the most important of those likely to be neglected in a public discourse skeptical of truth-talk.

In considering the challenge to evolutionary theory, the first such question must be just what kind of truth-claim that challenge involves. That is not as obvious a question as it might appear.[48] The argument from religious neutrality, for example, is not an argument that proceeds from empirical science, but from religious authority; it cares about empirical scientific findings only insofar as it runs into them. To be sure, from this clash arose the movement that called itself "creation science" and that took as its project establishing the scientific credentials of creationist belief. But the science there was quite clearly an outgrowth of religious faith, and its conclusions foregone. The case of intelligent design is more complicated, although at least the founder of that movement, Phillip Johnson (whose own orientations are principally religious) described his approach to the problem in the following way: "Our discussion today is over whether belief in Darwinism is compatible with a meaningful theism. When most people ask that question, they take the Darwinism for granted and ask whether the theism has to be discarded. I think it is more illuminating to approach the question from the other side. Is there any reason that a person who believes in a real, personal God should believe Darwinist claims that biological creation occurred through a fully naturalistic evolutionary process? The answer is clearly 'no.'"[49] An internal memo (reportedly written by Johnson) of the leading think tank of the intelligent design movement began by lamenting that "scientific materialism" had undermined of the idea that "human beings are created in the image of God," went on to list the host of evils that has supposedly flowed from that (including moral relativism, the rejection of personal responsibility, and the mistaken view that society could be "perfect[ed]" through "coercive" government regulation), and described the purpose of the Discovery Institute's Center for the Renewal of Science and Culture as "nothing less than the overthrow of materialism and its cultural legacies. Bringing together leading scholars from the natural sciences and those from the humanities and social sciences, the Center explores how new developments in biology, physics and cognitive science raise serious doubts about scientific materialism and have re-opened the case for a broadly theistic understanding of nature."[50] A later document, which sought to downplay the religious character of the intelligent design project, nonetheless held that the three primary purposes of the Center were "(1) to support research by scientists and other scholars . . . critical of neo-Darwinism . . . , (2) to explore the larger philosophical or world-view implications of the scientific debate about design, . . . and (3) to explore the culture implications of competing philosophies of science."[51]

Such statements suggest that, as with the creationist objection to evolutionary science, at least much of the *motivation* for the intelligent design research project comes from the perceived implications of evolutionary theory for certain philosophical and religious views. What is at stake, Johnson and the Discovery Institute have frequently argued, is the conflict between the idea of a purposive universe and the claim of philosophical materialism, according to which "all of reality can be reduced to, or derived from, matter and energy alone."[52] However, many evolutionary scientists have repeatedly insisted that, although committed to "methodological materialism" or the search for explanations of purely physical phenomena in exclusively material causes, the physical sciences do not take a position on philosophical materialism; indeed a number of evolutionary scientists have personally denied a belief in philosophical materialism, often in association with their own religious views. Insofar as the concern of intelligent design is thus with philosophical materialism, it is one that can be pursued entirely outside of the science curriculum.[53] Whether or how it should be taken up at all within the public school curriculum is, of course, a legitimate matter for public debate. But if it is decided that it should be addressed by introducing students to a variety of competing views and approaches, this is—or at least a good reason for it would be—because it is thought that the organized political community ought not to be committed to any particular truth-position on the question of philosophical materialism or committed to any particular method for answering such a broad and multifaceted question.

This, however, brings us back to the more central question, the one that has been at the heart of the controversy: the question of what to teach about the *scientific* origins of complex life. It brings us back to that question through the question of the relationship between the concern with the *effects* of evolutionary theory and the *science* of it. While some have held that the intelligent design movement is a desperate, bad-faith, or ignorant attempt to save a worldview by positing a scientific account that has no plausible basis in any empirical evidence—this is, indeed, the view that has been taken by all of the courts that have addressed the issue[54]—intelligent design advocates have commonly explained the connection between their concern with the effects of evolutionary theory and the scientific claims for it in a different way. They have argued, in short, the following:

1. The evidence for the wholesale proposition that all biological structures beyond the most primitive are products of evolutionary development is not proven by the evidentiary record, but rather the evidentiary record is filled with massive "gaps."[55]
2. The research project of mainstream biology is governed by a particular worldview, scientific materialism, which (taking that term now to refer to methodological materialism) is itself supposed rather than proven.
3. The supposition of materialism precludes certain kinds of hypotheses for filling in the gaps.
4. Those who share a different cosmological orientation will naturally want an alternative research agenda to explore both

    a. those cases in which there is evidence that biological structures *could not* have come about through evolutionary means,

    b. those cases in which the presently available evidence does not provide definitive support for either evolution or intelligent design, and, therefore,

  5. in both of these cases, intelligent design ought to be presented at least as an alternative to evolutionary theory in the science curriculum.

Evolutionary scientists have often accepted the second and third of these claims, while responding to the other claims largely along three lines. First, while acknowledging gaps in the evidentiary record, they have argued that some gaps in the direct evidence are inevitable given the impossibility of preserving all evolutionary changes, but that in light of the time periods involved, the evidence, both direct and indirect, for a vast number of macro- and well as micro- evolutionary developments is overwhelming. Second, and relatedly, they have argued that the evidence for evolution and its mechanisms has been so powerful in so many specific cases as to justify its status as the reigning model for explaining all complex biological traits and to justify the confidence that further evidence will reduce (although probably never eliminate) the gaps in the evidentiary record. Third, they have sought to show, both logically and by analogy to known evolutionary developments, that the affirmative claims of some intelligent design advocates that certain features of organisms could be explained *only* as a consequence of design are mistaken.[56]

It is difficult to see how to resolve the challenge of intelligent design, and specifically the claim that the tradition and good of pluralism demand (as it is commonly put by intelligent design advocates) "teaching the debate," without some consideration of truth. But while it is tempting to think that if truth is to come into play here it must do so as a judgment about whether evolutionary theory or intelligent design describes the "world as it really is," or even about which best accounts for the available evidence, this is not so. The first of these puts the question in an impossible form, while the second puts it in a form that, as a practical matter—that is, as a *political* question to be resolved through democratic processes—is only somewhat less impossible and certainly nightmarishly daunting. As the Harvard evolutionary biologist and geneticist Richard Lewontin once wrote in a different context, the problem for "democratic self-governance" of trying to evaluate scientific claims is that "given the immense extent, inherent complexity, and counterintuitive nature of scientific knowledge, it is impossible for anyone, including non-specialist scientists, to retrace the intellectual paths that lead to scientific conclusions about nature. In the end we must trust the experts and they, in turn, exploit their authority as experts and their rhetorical skills to secure our attention and our belief in things that we do not really understand."[57] The problem is that the only persons who are competent to evaluate the evidence are part of the very scientific community that the critics argue is improperly biased.

However, the question of what to teach in the public schools need not, in fact, be resolved at this first-order level. While intelligent design advocates have often claimed that a respectable minority of scientists share concerns about "Darwinism," and while there are indeed very significant debates within the evolutionary sciences concerning the character and mechanism of evolution,[58] there is an extraordinary consensus within the scientific community about the strength of the evidence for evolutionary development. (Indeed so strong is that consensus that to teach the question of the origins of complex life as though there were a serious split in the scientific community on the basic proposition of evolution would be to misrepresent the state of the field.) The question for *political* institutions, then, should be understood as a second-order question: of whether to teach exclusively the overwhelming scientific consensus. *That* question is still very much about truth, for it requires political institutions to take a position on the character of what I have called the "truth-practices" of science: the ways the scientific community has evaluated competing truth-claims.[59] But it does not require those political institutions to endorse the consensus view as "the truth of how the world is."

The advocate for intelligent design, however, will insist that even *if* it were decided that evolutionary theory should be taught as the exclusive explanation for the origin of complex life where the scientific consensus is that the evidence strongly supports evolution, and even *if* it were decided (on the basis on the consensus view) that the affirmative intelligent design argument from "irreducible complexity" should not be taught, intelligent design should at least be given equal space with evolution as a hypothesis for filling in the "gaps"—that is, where it is agreed that there is no solid evidence to show that biological structures are the consequence of evolutionary developments. (While evolutionists might well be content just to leave these areas alone insofar as the teaching of the origins of complex life in the public schools in concerned, intelligent design advocates may respond that teaching evolution as the exclusive account of the origin of complex life while ignoring these evidentiary gaps will only reinforce the evolutionist view as the only explanation for the origin of all complex life forms, and that the only neutral position is thus to present both the evolutionist and the intelligent design hypotheses about the gaps.) As proponents of intelligent design may well remind us, there is no shortage of examples of scientific "truths" coming to be upended, either as false or (as for example, famously with Newtonian physics) as partial truths that took themselves for the whole, and there is plenty of history to confirm for us the dangers in extrapolating too far from the available evidence. To teach evolution as the exclusive account of the origin of *all* complex life forms on the ground in part that there is no better *materialist* explanation is, they will argue, scientifically dishonest and a product (2 above) of a materialist bias. In making just this point, Phillip Johnson quotes Lewontin himself, who wrote (though again not in the context of evolutionary theory), "It is not that the methods and institutions of science somehow compel us to accept a material explanation of the phenomenal world, but, on the contrary, that we are forced by our *a priori* adherence to material causes to create an apparatus of investigation and a set of concepts that produce material explanations, no matter how counter-intuitive, no matter how mystifying to the uninitiated. Moreover, that materialism is absolute, for we cannot allow a Divine Foot in the door."[60]

In contrast, then, to the wholesale claim that a commitment to pluralism requires teaching intelligent design as an alternative to evolution even where there is a scientific consensus that the evidence for evolution is strong, this claim to teach intelligent design "in the gaps" of the evidence is much more narrow. And on the face of it, it is a much stronger claim. But the nature of the question that it raises is ultimately not so very different. It *would* be different if the issue were the first-order truth-question of what the universe is actually like, or even what it is actually like as far as we can tell. But at a second-order level, the question posed for political judgment is, once again, not "how things are," but how far to teach science according to the internal truth-practices of that institution as it now exists. With respect to the specific challenge of intelligent design, the question is whether the teaching of science ought to continue the project at the core of the modern scientific tradition of searching for materialist explanations, or whether, as intelligent advocates have proposed, "the ground rules of science . . . [should] be broadened so that supernatural forces can be considered."[61] The answer that we give to that question need not be a judgment about truth in the abstract.[62] But we cannot answer it, or answer it well, without concerning ourselves with truth at all. We will hardly do justice to what matters to us about the question if we were to try to resolve it by appealing merely to, say, the fact of "our practices or traditions" or to what is "useful." The question, after all—or at least the question as most people are concerned about it—is about how to give the best account available of how complex life forms have come to be; and if we opt for a science based on "adherence to material causes" and for keeping out the "Divine Foot," this is not just because it is a prejudice of ours, but because we regard it as (to use Burke's phrase) a just prejudice of ours. (Johnson misreads Lewontin, I think, in taking him to be claiming the first of these rather than the second.) That prejudice may itself rest on a kind of faith. But it is a faith about how to get at the most truthful account available to us, and it is only on the equation of truth with certainty that it will be thought that because it is a faith it cannot also be about truth. Political institutions need not claim to be able to answer the question of "how things are," but they cannot avoid deciding how far to share that particular faith and how far to endorse in public schools the practices by which science as it is now generally practiced seeks to give the more accurate account of the world. If we choose to teach the origins of complex life as an open debate, we de facto reject the view of the scientific community that creationism or intelligent design is not a plausible scientific account of how complex life came to be. If instead we choose to teach the scientific consensus, we de facto reject certain religious and philosophical claims about the scientific origin of complex life. Which of these we choose will have to depend quite simply on whether or not we regard the account offered by the evolutionary sciences as the best one available to us, and the truth-practices of those sciences as the best approach available to us, in respect to the questions that they ask, of how the world is.

If the organized political community decides to endorse the scientific consensus, it does not, however—or at least it need not—thereby reject "pluralism" and our pluralist traditions in favor of "truth." For while the advocates of teaching multiple explanations rest their case in part on a conception of pluralism and on an interpretation of our traditions—in short, that respect for both requires that official political institutions refrain from acting in ways that have the *effect* of denying certain religious or philosophical doctrines, the dominant alternative view, and the one that (at least with respect to religious views) most public bodies have in essence adopted, also rests on a conception, but a different conception, of what pluralism should be understood to require, and on an alternative reading of our pluralist traditions. (It relies as well, as we have already discussed, on a particular understanding of the tradition of science.) On this view, respect for pluralism of opinion does not require official institutions to refrain from adopting or endorsing scientific truth-practices and accounts that happen to conflict with religious or philosophical views, but instead requires those institutions to act without *consideration* of the impact on those views. And this "without consideration of" condition cuts both ways. On the one hand, it denies that a sufficient reason to refrain from endorsing scientific practices and accounts is the mere *fact* that they conflict with religious or other supernatural views. But on the other hand, it insists that the *point* of those practices and accounts cannot be to take a position on those views. Underlying this is a recognition of the diversity of the kinds of truth-questions, the diversity of paths for pursuing them, and the diversity of ways "the world opens up," and correspondingly a recognition of the limited domain of science, the limited scope of its truth-practices, and the limited claim of the accounts of the world that it offers.

*   *   *

I have taken us fairly deeply into the debate over the teaching of evolution in order to illustrate, principally, two ideas. The first and most general is that when truth comes into political life, it need not do so in the image in which it is too often imagined: of the imperial conqueror slashing and burning its way to total domination of all that lies before it. Questions of truth will often most productively arise instead in the context of particular institutions: in the second-order question of how to go about trying to give an accurate account of how things are in light of the institution's particular aims and traditions and constraints (including constraints on knowledge), and in the first-order judgments that are made through those practices. And when questions of truth are pursued with an appropriate recognition of their institutional context, they need not stand in opposition to pluralism, but may instead be part of a robust pluralist politics.

The second, more specific idea concerns a particular form of pluralism, although one that is of special importance in political life—the pluralism of opinion—and a particular question that political institutions will sometimes have to face: when to take a position that conflicts with other deeply held opinions. I have meant to suggest that there is no uniform answer to this question, that the answer that is given in particular cases will often involve choosing *between* conceptions of pluralism rather than for or against pluralism in general, and that the answer that is given will commonly depend at least in part on whether the contested account arose through particular institutional truth-practices that we are committed to maintaining.

The Press

The example of the debate over the teaching of evolution involved decisions of official political institutions, principally school boards, legislatures, and courts. But not all political institutions are official, and as a second illustration I want to show very briefly how these same kinds of questions arise in a somewhat different form in the context of a nonofficial institution that plays an important political role: the press.

I have already mentioned the press several times in passing, and there is good reason for that: at least among nonofficial institutions, there is perhaps none whose contribution to political discourse is more significant than that of the press, and more vital than that of a press that is independent.[63] The meaning of the phrase "independent press" is not, however, self-evident, and those who share the abstract ideal of an independent press can well disagree as to how it should be understood and what it requires. But the answer that we give to that—the shape, that is, that we hope the press would have—will depend, in part, as I shall argue, on considerations of truth, and more specifically on judgments about the proper character of practices through which the press seeks to offer truthful accounts of the world. It is not (once again) that the appeal to truth will by itself provide all the answers. It is rather that we cannot get very far without any reference to it.

Earlier I referred to Arendt's somewhat cursory discussion of journalism in "Truth and Politics" and her tendency to characterize its role in terms that rely on what I suggested was a too simplistic notion of factual truth— "brutally elementary data" that no reasonable person could deny. But even that modest view of the role of the press entails an important claim about what "independence" must mean in relation to the press. To see it clearly, we need only contrast it with a conception that, while rarely defended explicitly, has too often seeped into the contemporary press's sense of what it means to be responsible. This latter conception involves a particular notion of pluralism: like the conception of religious pluralism with which I began the prior discussion, it maintains that respect for the plurality of political opinion requires the press to refrain from reporting too vigorously in ways that might have the effect of denying or undermining partisan truth-claims or partisan conflicts. Such a view is, as I have said, rarely endorsed explicitly by the main-stream press, and it is certainly not a principle that any press outlet follows consistently in practice. But in recent years—whether as a result of a loss of confidence in the idea of truth, a defensive reaction to partisan criticism, pressure from powerful political officials and private interests, changes in the ownership structure of the press, or some combination of these and other tendencies—much of the "responsible" press (I leave aside here press outlets that have gone the other way and have consciously aligned themselves with a partisan agenda) has, it seems, been increasingly reticent about offering independent review of issues that are on the public agenda and about vigor-ously pursuing stories that are not, where doing so might affect the outcome of partisan debates.[64] (One glaring example of the former is the extraordi-nary tendency of the American press to rely on competing partisan quotes to characterize political events and facts, even facts as basic as the content of legislation, official reports, and other publicly available documents, rather than offer its own independent review.)

Against this conception of press "neutrality" stands a view that is very similar to the second conception that we examined in the evolution debates: that the responsibility of an independent press is not to avoid acting in ways that *affect* partisan conflict, but rather to pursue the truth in accordance with certain internal practices and standards that are independent of partisan con-siderations generally, including that of the partisan impact that the disclosure of truth may have. There are, to be sure, some important differences between the question of state neutrality toward religion and the issue of press neutral-ity toward partisanship. But at least one of these weighs more heavily against the idea of neutrality measured by effect in the case of the press. We do not normally ask of the scientific community that it take a particular interest in a matter *because* it is a matter of religious contention. In contrast, however, we do expect the press to report on matters that are on the public agenda, and this will often mean addressing questions precisely because they are matters of partisan dispute.

To speak of the press's responsibility to the truth is, however, immediately to invite the objection that there is no simple "truth" waiting to be disclosed. We will quickly be reminded not only that there are a virtually infinite num-ber of "facts" that could be reported, and that the question of what "stories" to cover thus requires an editorial decision, but also that once that decision is made, there still must be a story *told*, and that—in contrast to the standard journalistic cliché about "getting the story"—"reporting" is never a matter of getting a story that is there, but always a matter of telling a story *about,* and so forth. This objection is not unlike that which we encountered with respect to science—that it cannot represent the world "in itself"—although it is an objection that is far stronger here. For while the point in the case of science has to do with the limitations of the conceptual world, the work of the press is much more fundamentally limited by the resources of time and space, and because of this the choices that it makes are (or ought to be) manifest even to it. Whether or not, then, one regards any particular editorial decision as the right one, it will often be clear enough that there are other reasonable possibilities available.

Yet as in the case of science, the question of truth here is not whether the press can report the world just "as it is," but about whether, when the press reports about the world, it should be guided by the attempt to give a truthful account, and if so, what the character of its truth-practices ought to be. Most will think that the answer to the first question is yes, and that that involves minimally a commitment not to report what it knows or has good reason to believe to be false. But this is hardly enough. The commitment to truth (as Bernard Williams, for one, has argued at length) includes the disposition of wanting what one says to be *accurate,* and that virtue requires more than not lying or even (what is not at all the same thing) saying what one believes; it often also requires an agent to take active steps to seek out information.[65] Now, the question of *what* information the press should seek out is not itself simply a question of truth; indeed what it requires primarily is a judgment about what is of public importance. But further questions will necessarily arise from that judgment—such as, to pick out just two, how many resources to devote to investigating a particular issue,[66] and what kinds of information in one's possession to report. (Certainly the common preference of the press for publishing whatever facts it has most easily at hand over the kind of investigation that would produce more probative facts, when the means for doing the latter are available, is demanded neither simply by a commitment to truth or by a concern for the public interest; there are times when it may reasonably be thought preferable for the press to withhold publication of certain facts—for example, the mere fact that such-and-such was asserted by an anonymous government source acting in the interests of the administration—at least until its truth-claims can be investigated.) These questions are also not exclusively questions of truth. (They are not questions of truth at all in that particular first-order sense in which that term is sometimes understood: they are not, that is, questions about an absolute, nonperspectival representation of the world. They are nonetheless, in part, questions of truth.) But they are questions that ought to be guided in part by a broad commitment to giving the most accurate account available, and the more specific answers that various press outlets give to them will thus help constitute the character of their truth-practices.

These kinds of questions are not limited to the reporting of "brutally elementary" facts. Indeed conceptually prior to any judgment about what "news is fit to print" (or, less arrogantly, which news to fit in print) is a judgment about what kind of information about the world should count as "news." Brutally elementary "factual truths" are, when they are of public importance, often among these. But there are other kinds of truths—it makes no difference whether or not we refer to them as "facts" in a broader sense—with which the press must, at least arguably, be concerned, and once again the truth-practices of the press (or particular press outlets) will be constituted in part by the judgments they make about what those are and what evidentiary standards should be employed in reporting on them.[67] Should the press concern itself with trying to discern and report on the motivation of government officials? Should it take at its word an administration's claims about its aims and agendas, or should it seek to uncover ulterior agendas?[68] To what extent should the press independently evaluate the veracity of the claims made by public officials? To what extent should the press allow the news agenda itself to be shaped by public officials or candidates or other strategic actors, and to what extent should it contribute to shaping that agenda? What responsibility does the press have during election seasons to raise issues that it has good reason to know will be on the political agenda after the election, even if candidates do not find it in their interests to raise them?[69] What responsibility does the press have to provide background information that is necessary for evaluating the claims of public officials or candidates?[70] Such questions as these—and these are obviously just a tiny sample—are not themselves questions *of* truth, in the sense that they are not questions whose answers are (or must be) truth-claims. But they are nonetheless questions *about* truth; specifically, they are questions about the kinds of truths with which the press should be concerned, or put differently, about the nature of the press's responsibility to disclose "how things are." And though they concern truth in this way, they are questions for which "action" (at least in the ordinary sense of that term) and "decision" are very much "involved." Like the associated question of what issues deserve public attention, these questions about what kinds of truths ought to be the subject of that attention are very much political (which is not to say partisan) questions; they are judgments, that is, about how to intervene in political life.

These important kinds of second-order questions, about the role that the press ought to play in reporting on matters of public concern, are not only about truth, but they are questions that cannot be give adequate treatment without understanding them as, in part, about truth and about what it means to report on the world truthfully. They are questions that are integral to the project of making "the city" and the plurality of opinions that partly constitute it "more truthful," and they are questions that deserve much more systematic reflection than they have received—both inside and outside of the press.[71] But they are questions that are likely to be either distorted or neglected in a political (and academic) culture that is suspicious of all talk of truth and that associates truth-talk with the antipolitical claim to certain and absolute knowledge. The idea that confronting these questions of how to make our politics more truthful will "take care of itself" if we only "take care of freedom" has it exactly backward: political freedom depends on various truth-practices, and the quality of that freedom depends on the seriousness with which we engage these kinds of questions.

*   *   *

Criticisms of truth-talk in political life have commonly fallen along one of two lines. In the first, the aim of the criticism is the very concept or category of truth in political discourse; truth, it is said in this line of argument, is simply the wrong kind of criteria for political decisions. In the second, more pragmatic line of argument, the aim of the criticism is not the idea of truth per se but the attention to it, which is said to be unnecessary, unhelpful, and even pernicious in its effect on political life. I have argued here that, with respect at least to certain kinds of questions, both of these lines of criticism are overstated. I have meant to show, first, that there are sensible questions of truth, beyond the important concern with not lying, that are, on an ordinary understanding of that term, political questions. Second, I have meant to suggest why these questions deserve our attention and why a political community that neglects these questions is likely to be worse off for it.

I have been suggesting that, *pace* Rorty et al., we cannot do without considerations of truth in our political life, but also that, *pace* Arendt, questions of truth cannot be limited to establishing the boundaries within which politics takes place. Truth matters to politics, but what kinds of truth matter and how they matter are themselves political questions. And those questions, I have tried to show, are often bound up with questions about the structure and practice of political institutions. As I have emphasized throughout (and as ought to go without saying), the attention to truth and to truth-practices will not *resolve* all or even most political controversies. This is so for a number of reasons, importantly among them (a) that attention to truth and truth-practices does not of itself resolve questions of truth; (b) that the question of what character various truth practices ought to have is itself a political question; and (c) that as with most political controversies more is involved than just questions of truth. Nonetheless, in addressing the ongoing and fundamental democratic challenge of how to organize ourselves as a political community, part of our concern must be how to foster institutions in which questions of truth are treated responsibly and not wantonly sacrificed to other considerations.[72]

I have said that these questions deserve more of our attention, but I have not yet said anything about who that "our" is. It includes primarily, of course, members of political communities acting in their capacity as such, and it includes political institutions, official and unofficial, with responsibilities to the political public. More locally, "our" can refer also to public intellectuals and members of the academy, including those engaged in that broad activity known as political theory. For some political theorists—and for some members of the humanities more generally—it will not include them in that capacity, either for reasons of specialization or because the kinds of institutional questions with respect to which problems of truth are likely to arise are simply not, for them, part of the aim of that activity. Yet at those times in which the quality of our public discourse has been at its richest, it has often been in part through the contribution of intellectuals who are in a special position to participate in public dialogue without having to take up the stance of narrow partisanship, and who are able to bring to bear on questions of public concern a historical and conceptual breadth that is too often otherwise missing from our political discourse. Earlier I criticized Arendt's insistence that questions of truth can be properly pursued only outside of the realm of politics in general. But if rather than politics we speak of the realm of everyday partisan conflict, Arendt was surely right in her suggestion that the academy, insofar as it maintains its "disinterested pursuit of truth"—by which I take her to mean, in the language that I have used here, insofar as its own truth-practices remain independent of partisanship—has an important role to play in political life, and that its most fruitful contributions will be made from outside the partisan arena. (Arendt herself exemplified that kind of contribution in her topical writings, in which—much more so than many of those who self-consciously write under her influence—she did not shy away from engaging with public issues of the day, and yet approached those from a vantage point removed not only from partisan agendas, but also from the narrow discourse in which those issues were often treated in political debates. In those writings she often displayed a courage that would have been nearly impossible for one bound to an electoral constituency or to the judgments of public opinion.)[73] Among the contributions to the quality of our public discourse that might come from that quarter is an engagement with the problems, as they will appear in a variety of forms and contexts, of how to pursue the good of plurality without giving up on the task of making the city more truthful; of how to be at home in our traditions without giving up the responsibility of making them better; and of how to respect that "which men cannot change at will" while being aware of the limitations of our knowledge.

Chapter 2

Truth and Politics

Linda M. G. Zerilli

> The really frightening thing about totalitarianism is not that it commits "atrocities" but that it attacks the concept of objective truth: it claims to control the past as well as the future.
> —George Orwell

A WRITER WHO made the problem of truth central to his literary and non-literary work, George Orwell controversially captured the opinion of his generation of thinkers when he identified truth as the major casualty in totalitarian regimes. But if totalitarianism spelled the death of objective truth, the threat to truth was not restricted to totalitarianism. Most scholars of Orwell's day blamed relativism, both historical and cognitive, for the rise of totalitarianism and the slowness of the allied forces to recognize the extent and nature of the threat.[1] Relativism, as Peter Novick has argued, was seen by scholars during World War II as the equivalent of cultural and political suicide for Western liberal democracies: "Philosophers were urged, in the words of Arthur Murphy, to 'surrender the shallow indifference about ultimate truth of the debased "liberalism" of our recent past.'" Relativism was "debilitating," Novick said, for it "robbed [the American] people of their convictions and their will to fight." As another critic put it, cultural relativists naïvely "assumed implicitly that there is a kind of pre-established harmony of cultures that makes it possible for all to coexist in a pluralistic cultural world."[2] A consensus emerged among many liberal and conservative intellectuals that Western liberal democracies needed to affirm certain values as beyond dispute.

Needless to say, the idea that citizens in liberal democracies should put aside their differences of opinion and defend the "core values" of their society is alive and well today. In our post-9/11 political context, talk about the "clash of civilizations" has been used to undermine belief in the possible global coexistence of diverse cultures and to suppress plural opinions and political dissent within liberal democracies themselves. More to the point, the disdain for objective truth that Orwell ascribed to totalitarian societies but not to liberal democratic ones must seem misplaced if not naïve. As the scandals surrounding the American-led invasion of Iraq demonstrated, such disdain is hardly unique to totalitarian societies. The certainty with which the Bush administration declared that Saddam Hussein had weapons of mass destruction, ignoring the counterevidence produced by its own intelligence agencies, turned out to be just the beginning of a U.S. government–sponsored program of mendacity.

In light of this recent past, it is easy to understand why citizens would fear that truth is quickly becoming a casualty of liberal democratic regimes, not just totalitarian ones. And it is also easy to understand why official investigations concerning the truthfulness of those who claim to speak in our name would provide a strange solace. Although holding public leaders accountable for the veracity of their statements is surely important and indeed essential to our belief in representative government, the question arises as to whether democratic citizens are in a position to do something with the truths that come to light as a result of such investigations. The thinker who helps us to pose and perhaps answer that question, I suggest, is not George Orwell but his contemporary, Hannah Arendt.

Although Arendt shares Orwell's concern about the fate of factual truths in totalitarian regimes, her response to the political catastrophes of the twentieth century is not to insist on the defense of objective truth as such but to emphasize the ability to make political judgments. In contrast to Orwell and those scholars of her generation who decried relativism, Arendt worried about what the insistence on a singular idea of truth would mean for democracy. In "Truth and Politics," for example, she famously sets persuasive opinion against compelling truth and declares the former to be the proper mode of discourse among citizens.[3] Plural opinions are the stuff of political judgment, she argued, not absolute truth.

Arendt's account of truth as hostile to plurality and all things democratic has led well-known critics such as Jürgen Habermas to declare her understanding of political judgment to be fatally flawed, for it offers no way to ascertain the truth of statements or adjudicate competing validity claims. According to Habermas, Arendt opens a "yawning abyss between knowledge and opinion which cannot be closed with arguments."[4] If we are interested in critically thinking through the politics of truth in contemporary liberal democracies, Habermas might ask, why turn to a thinker who seems to dismiss the demand for truth as deeply antipolitical?

When it comes to truth and politics, perhaps we—and I include myself here—have not given Arendt a fair reading. In previously published work, I tried to show that Arendt addresses the question of validity that occupies her critics, with one important caveat: she does not think that validity is the all-important task for political judgment—the affirmation of nonsovereign freedom is.[5] But I took for granted—or at least I did not adequately question—the idea that Arendt holds truth to be at odds with politics. That is why she turned to Kant's account of aesthetic judgments in the third *Critique*, I argued, for it posits a special kind of validity—what Kant called subjective validity—without an appeal to knowledge or truth. And though I would still hold (and shall argue below) that freedom rather than validity or truth is the problem that animates Arendt's entire effort to foreground the importance of the democratic capacity to judge, I want to question the central claim of her critics, namely that she excludes the problem of truth from the political realm.

I have three reasons for questioning the idea that Arendt excludes the question of truth. First, as we shall see, Arendt was not indifferent to but deeply concerned with the loss of truthfulness in political life. Not only is the obliteration of truth in public life a definitive feature of totalitarianism, just as Orwell holds, but the truthfulness of statements made by citizens or their representatives is of paramount concern in a democracy, as our current political situation makes acutely clear.

Second, if we consider that other famous Heidegger student, Hans-Georg Gadamer, and his well-known critique of Kant's "radical subjectivization" of aesthetics, we are provoked to ask whether the exclusion of truth and knowledge from politics might lead to a further sedimentation of the idea that science (and its method) is the sole claimant to and arbiter of truth and knowledge.[6] Like Gadamer, Arendt had good reason for resisting the idea that there is only one form of truth, namely that which demands the strictest criteria of proof. For such a definition, rooted as it is in the development of modern science, would grant human practices such as art and politics and human sciences such as aesthetics and political theory their special place, while depriving them of any real authority or significance.

Third, if we deny that political claims, whatever else they are, are also claims to knowledge and truth, have we not foreclosed the possibility that such claims make demands on us that may in some ways be like but also quite unlike the demands made by truth and knowledge claims in other domains of life, such as science and even aesthetics? Perhaps the question is not whether we make such claims in politics—clearly we do—but what it means to make them, to hear them, and whether, once they enter the political realm, claims to truth can survive.

In this essay, I want to revisit Arendt's account of the relationship between truth and politics. I do so not only with the aspiration of intervening in the reception of her work but also, especially in the final section, to show her account's relevance to the political issues just described. Qualifying certain aspects of my published work on Arendt, my argument will be that foregrounding the problem of freedom rather than the rational adjudication of validity claims as the central work of democratic political judgment does not lead Arendt—nor should it lead us—to exclude the question of truth from the political realm. Rather, it leads her—as it might lead us—both to call into question the idea that proof is our sole access to truth in the political realm and also to reflect on the distinctive character of truth-claims in politics and their entanglement in what Plato rejected as unworthy of serious reflection due to its inherently contingent and plural character, namely opinion.

Although Arendt's critics are right to say that she holds politics to be the domain of plural contingent opinions, not singular timeless truths, they are mistaken when they accuse her of setting truth and opinion fully at odds with each other. This critique assumes that Arendt excluded truth from the political realm because she had no alternative notion of truth to the Platonic one, with it characteristic contempt for all things worldly and contingent. By "alternative notion of truth" I mean not only a hermeneutic notion of truth (discussed below), as it was developed by Heidegger and later by Gadamer, but a public notion of truth that Arendt (in her own idiosyncratic way) takes from both Socrates and Kant. This notion of truth, as we shall see, requires more than a "discourse ethics" because it involves more than the ability to make public arguments and ascertain the validity of statements; it involves more than the ability to distinguish warranted public opinions from strategically manipulated ideology that animates Habermas's normative political project.

The problem that concerned Arendt and that ought to concern us is not only how to determine the truth of statements but also how to transform those truths into "publicly acceptable facts," to borrow Mark Danner's phrase.[7] As we shall see, there is a difference between determining the truth content of those who claim to speak in our name and turning our knowledge of what is true into something politically significant. This next step will take us beyond the problem identified by Habermas—how to redeem validity claims—and toward the problem identified by Arendt: how to develop a public sphere in which citizens could not only tell the difference between warranted public opinion and ideology, but could turn what they know to be true into something politically significant, citizens who could acknowledge what they know and draw the political consequences, so to speak.

The Truth of Opinion

Let us begin by turning not to "Truth and Politics" but to a less famous essay by Arendt, "Philosophy and Politics."[8] Here we discover that, *pace* her critics, she does not accept the founding Platonic opposition of truth and opinion and then seek merely to revalue the subordinate term (opinion) in Plato's account of absolute truth. Far from simply revaluing opinion in the ineradicable opposition between truth and opinion that Plato bequeathed to political philosophy, Arendt tries to develop instead the Socratic idea of what she calls "the truth of opinion." She does so in order to undercut the difference that Plato drew "between those who know and do not act and those who act and do not know," for this "Platonic separation between knowing and doing" obliterates freedom and plurality; it is "at the root of all theories of domination" and a conception of politics as *Herrschaft,* or rule.[9]

Reading Socrates against Plato, Arendt observes that the "opposition of truth and opinion was certainly the most anti-Socratic conclusion that Plato drew from Socrates' trial" ("PP" 75). In Arendt's reading, Socrates' life and teaching contravenes this central Platonic opposition.

> Although it is more than probable that Socrates was the first who had used *dialegesthai* [dialectic] (talking something through with somebody)

systematically, he probably did not look upon this as the opposite or even the counterpart to persuasion [as both Plato and Aristotle did], and it is certain that he did not oppose the results of this dialectic to *doxa*, opinion. To Socrates, as to his fellow citizens, *doxa* was the formulation in speech of what *dokei moi*, that is, of what appears to me. This *doxa* had as its topic not what Aristotle called the *eikos*, the probable, the many *verisimilia* (as distinguished from the *unum verum*, the one truth, on one hand, and the limitless falsehoods, the *falsa infinita*, on the other), but comprehended the world as it opens itself to me. It was not, therefore, subjective fantasy and arbitrariness, but also not something absolute and valid for all. The assumption was that the world opens up differently to every man, according to his position in it; and that the "sameness" of the world, its commonness (*koinon*, as the Greeks would say, common to all) or "objectivity" (as we would say from the subjective viewpoint of modern philosophy) resides in the fact that the same world opens up to everyone and that despite all differences between men and their positions in the world—and consequently their *doxai* (opinions)— "both you and I are human." ("PP" 81)

On the one hand, Arendt emphasizes the idea that opinion, far from being merely subjective, is the source of truth and knowledge, the basis for making claims with validity, the very origin of what we would call "objective" and the Greeks called *koinon*, common to all. On the other hand, she holds that opinion, though in no way merely subjective, is not universal and valid for all. But what can it mean, really, to say that *doxa*, or opinion (understood as the articulation of what *dokei moi*, the "formulation in speech" of the way the world opens up or shows itself to me), is at once the source of everything we hold common or objective and not universally valid for all?

At this point we could invoke Socratic dialectic as the "method" through which opinion attains objectivity by being articulated as generalizable or universal ("It appears to me as it appears to all others").[10] The danger here, however, lies precisely in thinking about Socrates' interrogative practice of maieutic (the art of midwifery) as if it were a "method," that is, a means for attenuating if not eliminating the "personal" or "subjective" elements in any practice of knowing and verifying knowledge claims through rational argumentation and the giving of proofs. In that case dialectic would yield certainty and be based on (or teach) the proper subsumption of particulars under universals (just as Plato understood it, in Arendt's view). Opinion would differ from truth as the failure of this process of subsumption.

According to Arendt, Socrates' effort "to make the city more truthful by delivering each of its citizens of their truths" proceeds neither by means of subsumption nor by leaving opinion behind. To be delivered of one's truths is not to vanquish the particular or be fully released from the subjective limitations of one's standpoint; it is not to be delivered of one's opinions, as if opinion were the opposite of truth and the person most delivered of his or her truths were the one without any opinions. Rather, it is to find, by means of public debate, what in one's opinions is true. There is no truth on Arendt's Socratic account that is not also an opinion. We never arrive at the point where we have established the "visible hallmark which marks truth from opinion" that Plato so anxiously sought but never found. It is not that any particular opinion can never be declared truthful (or not), but rather that there is no absolute criterion (or method or procedure) that would allow us to separate opinion from truth once and for all. But if the search for truth in opinion does not end with a (Platonic) declaration of the absolute difference between truth and opinion, how does one know that the opinion one holds is true?

In the view of Leo Strauss, who also turns to Plato's Socratic dialogues to discuss the relation of opinion to truth, there is no way to find the truth in opinion once we relinquish absolute standards, for how would we seek and recognize what is true if we did not already know what is true? How could we properly subsume particulars if we had no universals under which they could be recognized as true, that is, as belonging to a specific concept? We cannot determine whether a particular action is just if we have no standard of justice by which to recognize what qualifies as just and what not. "To judge soundly one must know the true standards," declares Strauss.[11] As most people in modern liberal democracies are no longer in possession of such yardsticks (as a consequence of value pluralism and historicism), he argues, it is left to the political philosopher who seeks truth "to replace opinion about the nature of political things by knowledge of the nature of political things."[12] The key word here is "replace," for opinion is not to be preserved but overcome in the quest for truth. Opinions guide the ascent to truth in Strauss's reading of the dialogues, but they are mere "fragments of the truth, soiled fragments of the pure truth."[13]

Strauss would have the political philosopher find truth in Plato's Socratic dialogues, but the curious thing about those dialogues, as Arendt remarks, "is that they are all aporetic." She explains, "The argument either leads nowhere or it goes around in circles. To know what justice is you must know what knowledge is, and to know knowing you must have a previous, unexamined notion of knowledge. . . . Hence [in *Meno* we read], 'A man cannot try to discover either what he knows or what he does not know. If he knows, there is no need of inquiry; if he does not know . . . he does not even know what he is to look for.'"[14] In his creative rereading of the dialogues, Ernesto Grassi, another Heidegger student, also remarks on their fundamentally "aporetic" character. Like Arendt, Grassi points out that the search for truth appears to take for granted that we already know what truth is, for how else would we recognize truth when we found it? Even if we were to grant that the search for truth must have as its condition knowledge of truth, says Grassi, "the search itself seems pointless, then why would we search for something we already know?"[15] But Grassi also suggests that the dialogues show something else: the aporetic character of the search for truth does not hold for truth as such, which is what Arendt seems to assume, but only for a certain conception of truth, namely an objectivist (or philosophical) conception of truth. The aporia does not hold for the notion of truth that belongs to the idea of being (*das Seiende*) as becoming (*das Werdende*), which Heidegger emphasized in his return to the ancient texts. As becoming, being is both present and absent, and thus it is something for which we can search without already knowing what we are searching for. The question of truth is a matter neither of correspondence nor of subsumption but of appearance: why things show up for us as they do (*sich-zeigen*).[16] And if we recall that for the Greeks opinion (*doxa*) is the formulation in speech of what appears to me (*dokei moi*), we can begin to see how opinion and truth might be more intertwined than a certain reading of Plato allows.

Taking up Heidegger's critique of truth as correspondence and his attempt to develop the ancient idea of truth as *alètheia*, Grassi attempts to explain how things appear by redefining the problem of the logos in Plato's Socratic dialogues as "the originary act of *légein* [*ursprünglichen Aktes des 'légein'*]" (*VL* 44).[17] Grassi wants to emphasize logos—speech, the word, reason—in a particular way: as an endless process, an ongoing act through which human beings gain access to being, to what is primordially given, and in this way create a "world" in the Heideggerian sense. In order to emphasize the idea of an ongoing and never-ending process, Grassi uses the verbal form of "logos," *légein*. This *légein* act, as the Greeks (including Plato and Socrates) understood it, is the originary act of "separating, differentiating and at the same time collecting, uniting, [and] binding [an otherwise chaotic sensible universe]" (*VL* 44). Only through such an act does the sensible world attain objectivity for human beings.

"Does it [*légein*] have one form or many, and how are they differentiated?" asks Grassi (*VL* 62).[18] In a variety of works Grassi tries to distinguish the different forms of *légein*.[19] In *Vom Vorrang des Logos*, the text currently under discussion, he distinguishes (albeit in a highly schematic manner) three forms of *légein* and thus of appearance (*sich-zeigen*): philosophical, aesthetic, and political *légein*. Important for our purposes here is not only the difference he draws between the philosophical *légein*, which is based on discerning universality, and the aesthetic *légein*, which is concerned with the particular, but also his insistence that the question of truth cannot be posed properly unless we distinguish between the different registers in which things appear and the different kinds of necessity that pertain to these different registers.

"We have to ask whether out of the constraints of logic [*aus der logischen Nötigung*] a world of art ever emerged; or whether out of the constraints of logic a political reality ever originated," comments Grassi (*VL* 214). And if the answer in both cases is no, does this mean that there is no truth in art or in politics? Like Gadamer, Grassi refuses to limit the notion of truth in this way. The ground of truth does not have the objectivist form that both logical truth and the philosophical truth advanced by Strauss's Plato must have. Truth is a question not of how things are in and of themselves but of how they appear to us, and how things appear depends in turn on the register in which they appear and the form of *légein* (e.g., philosophical, aesthetic, or political, to name but three) with which things appear. Citing Machiavelli as the paradigmatic theorist of political *légein*, Grassi argues that this, like every other form of *légein* cannot be reduced to the other forms, for each form is independent of all the others in its particular way of generating our sense of reality. To stay with the example of political *légein*, our notion of truth in the political realm is independent: though it may share with the other forms of *légein* certain features (e.g., politics is concerned with the particular just as aesthetics is, says Grassi), political *légein* is autonomous. Those who fail to see this will never understand Machiavelli but will accuse him of all that "goes under the sign 'Machiavellianism'" (*VL* 210).

Citing the tragic attempt to impose Plato's philosophy in Sicily, Grassi does not exclude the possibility that forms of *légein* that are alien to politics could be or have been imposed on the political realm. The political actor who loses sight of the direct historical situation in which he finds himself, who falls victim to the poetic or conceptual way of seeing things, transforms the political future into one guided by the maxims of aesthetics or philosophy and thereby begets a misdeed, says Grassi (*VL* 210). Like Arendt, then, Grassi warns against the introduction of standards of truth into the political realm that are foreign to it—foreign not because truth has no place in politics (as a certain reading of Arendt holds), but because things appear differently in politics, that is, they have a different sense of necessity and are meaningful for us in ways that are not identical to how they may appear when seen as philosophical, scientific, or aesthetic objects. There is, to be sure, traffic among these realms and forms of *légein*, but each form is irreducible to the others.

Grassi helps us to see that there might indeed be a form of truth in politics that is unique. This truth is not aporetic, for it is not objectivist. Contra Strauss's reading of the dialogues, we do not have to "know the true standards" in order to make judgments (subsume particulars under rules) about reality. Even if one were to grant that such standards are necessary for philosophical knowledge (which Grassi also refutes), politics is autonomous. Insofar as the Socratic project to find the truth in opinion takes place in the political realm, as Arendt will show us below, we have good reason for resisting the introduction of standards or criteria that do not apply there. Thus we shall have good reason to be suspicious of thinkers who would assimilate politics to philosophy (or to science) and demand of political claims the same measure of truth. Likewise we shall have good reason to refute the idea that politics, if it does not meet philosophical (or scientific) standards of proof, is not concerned with truth.

If the aporia of truth described earlier pertains to an objectivist (philosophical) conception of truth but not to truth tout court, as Grassi has shown us, we have all the more reason to pursue the Socratic quest for the truth in opinion, for such truth would not be based on our possession of universals under which to subsume particulars, as Strauss would have us believe. The Socratic quest to find truth in opinion is distinguished from Plato's notion of moving from opinion to truth in ways that are inseparable from the realm in which the quest for truth takes place. First, to discover truth in opinion one must move among the holders of opinion, that is to say, one's peers or equals, hence in the political realm. By contrast with Plato, for whom truth is—and indeed must be—a solitary affair, Socrates holds that truth emerges in public. The public space is not—or not always—the place to speak a truth one already knows but the condition of finding truth in one's own opinion. Socrates' practice of maieutic, the art of midwifery (by which one brings oneself and others to find the truth in their opinion), argues Arendt, "was a political activity, a give and take, fundamentally on the basis of strict equality, the fruits of which could not be measured by the result of arriving at this or that general truth" ("PP" 81). This activity is based on the conviction that "every man has his own *doxa*, his own opening to the world." Socrates must ask questions; he cannot know beforehand how the world appears to each of his fellow citizens. "Yet, just as nobody can know beforehand the other's *doxa*, so nobody can know by himself and without further effort the inherent truth of his own opinion" ("PP" 81). So the kind of truth that is relevant for politics, we might tentatively conclude, requires publicity.

There is another important way in which Socrates' search for the truth in opinion differs from Plato's search for absolute truth. As Strauss makes clear, in Plato's view opinion is something to be replaced by knowledge, whereas for Arendt's Socrates opinion is the bearer of truth. Socrates' style of questioning is deeply critical but not "relentlessly negative," as Villa interpreting Arendt asserts, for it does not just destroy opinions but reveals what in them is true.[20] What else can it mean to find the truth in opinion, unless we settle on the purely negative or skeptical definition and say that the truth Socrates discovers in opinion is that in opinion there is no truth? But surely this is not the definition Arendt has in mind when she writes, "For mortals [in Socrates' view] the important thing is to make *doxa* truthful, to see in every *doxa* truth and to speak in such a way that the truth of one's opinions reveals itself to oneself and to others. . . . [Socrates], in opposition to the Sophists, had discovered that *doxa* was neither subjective illusion nor arbitrary distortion but, on the contrary, that to which truth invariably adhered" ("PP" 85).

To see in every *doxa* truth is different from seeing in every *doxa* error, which is what the negative definition just described suggests. Furthermore the truth Socrates helps his fellow citizens to find in their opinions is not what is left over once all the errors in their *doxa* have been revealed. That this truth in opinion is not philosophical truth (that is, the absolute truths that form the rules under which the subject as "man in the singular," seeking only to be in agreement with himself, may subsume particulars) is clear, but it is a form of truth nonetheless. To be the gadfly, as Arendt explains, is not to play the role of the philosopher who rules on the basis of knowing truth from opinion; rather, it is "to make the citizens more truthful" ("PP" 81), to help them find what in their opinions is true. Let us now examine what is at stake for the political conception of truth we are trying to develop in an approach that seeks out and emphasizes what is true in opinion and not—not simply—what is false.

The Prejudice against Prejudice

If we turn to Gadamer's reading of Socrates, we can better grasp the kind of knowledge that is at stake in the quest for the truth in opinion. Like Arendt, Gadamer identifies the Socratic art of questioning as key. The ability to ask questions, he writes, is also the ability to keep these questions from "being suppressed by the dominant opinion. *A person who possesses this art will himself search for everything in favor of an opinion. Dialectic consists not in trying to discover the weakness of what is said, but in bringing out its real strength.* It is not the art of arguing (which can make a strong case out of a weak one) but the art of thinking (which can strengthen objections by referring to the subject matter)" (*TM* 367, my emphasis).

The art of questioning, in other words, seeks out the truth in opinion (the formulation in speech of the "it appears to me"); it takes for granted that truth resides in what we say, in language. Not all we say is true of course, but (contra Plato) what is true is spoken. Like Arendt, Gadamer rejects the psychologistic and subjectivist interpretation of opinion, the formulation in speech of the "it appears to me." If we think about this "it appears to me" too much in terms of the "me" (i.e., the "subject") and too little in terms of the formulation in *speech* (i.e., language) of what appears (i.e., the world), we slide into just this psychologistic conception of opinion, which leads us to think, in turn, that we need a "method" that will keep at bay our opinions, for they are the "subjective" element that hinders our quest for what is "objective."

We can grasp why this idea of opinion as subjective misunderstands what we do when we engage the opinions of others by way of the following example. When we read a letter (describing, say, an antiwar rally in Washington), Gadamer explains, we "see what is communicated through the eyes of our correspondent, but while seeing things through his eyes, it is not his personal opinions, but, rather, the event itself that we believe we ought to know by this letter. In reading a letter, to aim at the personal thoughts of our correspondent and not at the matters about which he reports is to contradict what is meant by a letter."[21] Should the description turn out to be a wildly inaccurate account of events, we might then be prompted to understand it "by recourse to a supplementary psychological or historical point of view," comments Gadamer. Although such situations surely can and do arise, we normally take for granted that what the text "really transmits to us is the truth. This confirms that the primordial significance of the idea of understanding is that of 'knowing about something' and that only in a derivative sense does it mean understanding the intentions of another as personal opinions" ("PHC" 135).

Although Gadamer appears to set "knowing about something" at odds with "personal opinions" here, I take him to mean what is conventionally meant by "personal opinions," namely that which is subjective and makes no claim to truth or knowledge. For Gadamer (as for Arendt), then, it is a mistake to think about the formulation in speech of how the world appears to someone as "mere opinion," that is, as something purely subjective.[22] This formulation in speech of how things show up for us is no private language but an expression of common sense, of what I share with others by virtue of belonging to a particular sociohistorical culture.[23] Gadamer helps us to question again the stark opposition that Plato drew between knowledge and opinion. An opinion (as expressed, for example, in a letter) makes, and is received as making, a claim to truth. Just because I can hold opinions that I (or others) may later declare mistaken does not mean that those opinions are purely subjective, as if the way the world appears to me is how it appears to me and to no other (i.e., my world is private). "Thus we come back to the original conditions of every hermeneutics: it must be a shared and comprehensible reference to the 'things in themselves'" ("PHC" 135). Without such a reference, argues Gadamer, no common, unified meaning, no truth, could possibly be aimed at or emerge.

According to the hermeneutical conception of knowledge advanced by Gadamer (following Heidegger), understanding has an anticipatory structure: every act of understanding presupposes preunderstanding, the elements of which are one's *Vorurteile*, prejudices or prejudgments. These "absolutely fundamental anticipations, that is, anticipations common to us all," is what Gadamer calls "tradition." "Hermeneutics must start from the fact that understanding is related to 'the thing itself' as manifest in the tradition, and at the same time to a tradition where 'the thing' can speak to me," he writes ("PHC" 135).

How things speak to us through tradition can be seen in the structure of preunderstanding just mentioned, composed as it is of prejudices. Prejudice, which comes from the Latin *praejudicum,* or "judgment in advance," is "an opinion formed beforehand." A central achievement of Gadamer's magnum opus, *Truth and Method*, is "to fundamentally rehabilitate the concept of prejudice and acknowledge the fact that there are legitimate prejudices" (*TM* 277). This is another way of saying that some prejudices or opinions are true, that is, they speak to the way things really are. Once we grant that there is such a thing as legitimate prejudices, says Gadamer, we can see that "the fundamental epistemological question for a truly historical hermeneutics [is this] . . . : what is the ground of the legitimacy of prejudices? What distinguishes legitimate prejudices from the countless others which it is the undeniable task of critical reason to overcome?" (*TM* 277).[24]

Arendt's account of prejudices takes up this fundamental insight into the *Vorurteilstruktur* of understanding and the questions it raises. In her view, politics is clearly concerned with "dispelling prejudices, which does not mean that politics is about an education in becoming prejudice free, or that those people, who concern themselves with such enlightenment, are themselves free of prejudices."[25] In Arendt's account, the rationalist method of dispelling prejudices often misses its mark. Such a method, premised as it is on "the prejudice against prejudice," to borrow Gadamer's felicitous description of the Enlightenment legacy, fails to grasp that prejudices are the basis (i.e., they have the anticipatory structure described above) for all knowledge and understanding. "No man can live without prejudices," argues Arendt, for no one is in the position of being able "to judge everything anew" (*WIP* 17).

And yet sometimes we are called upon to judge anew, namely when we are confronted with something we have not encountered before. In these cases, rare though they may be, prejudices may be more disabling than enabling for democratic politics. We late moderns are called upon to judge anew, in Arendt's view, largely because of the catastrophic political events of the twentieth century, which have revealed that tradition, far from being the source of continuity that it is in Gadamer's work, is characterized instead by a radical break. Arendt's claim that modernity is so characterized leads her to see in prejudices more of a threat to critical thinking and judging than Gadamer, though he is certainly attuned to the problem, might be able to address. If "political thinking is rooted in the capacity to judge," as Arendt asserts (*WIP* 19), then prejudices (*Vorurteile*) are not only enabling elements of understanding but also potentially disabling for democratic politics: prejudices are prejudgments that can substitute for (the practice of making) judgments (*Urteile*) based on current experience, and in a context characterized by the radical break just described, they often do. As shared prejudgments that appeal to what "one says [*man sagt*]," that is, to common opinion, prejudices can count on the (mostly implicit) agreement of others.[26] "If one wants to dispel prejudices, one must first discover the judgments that they contain, that is, one must identify what in them is true [*Wahrheitsgehalt*]. If one bypasses this [step], entire battalions of enlightened speakers and entire libraries of pamphlets will achieve nothing," asserts Arendt (*WIP* 19).[27]

I have suggested that that are certain affinities between Gadamer's hermeneutic account of truth and prejudice and Arendt's political account. But what if anything is distinctive about the attempt to find truth and dispel prejudices in the political realm? And would we want to talk about this task in terms of the Socratic quest for truth, the truth in opinion that we have been discussing? Does not politics introduce concerns that suggest that such a task is not—not simply—a general philosophical question about how to distinguish legitimate from illegitimate prejudices as we distinguish truth from untruth, which is more or less what both Gadamer's philosophical hermeneutics and Habermas's discourse ethics, in their different ways, suggest?

Although Arendt adopts key aspects of the hermeneutic conception of truth, what is particularly important is the idea of a specifically public understanding of truth so conceived. Arendt follows Kant as well as Socrates in arguing that critical thinking and the search for truth require publicity. Questioning the received liberal understanding of free speech and thought as "the right of an individual to express himself and his opinion in order to be able to persuade others to share his viewpoint," Arendt remarks, "This presupposes that I am capable of making up my mind all by myself and that the claim I have on the government is to permit me to propagandize whatever I already have fixed in my mind."[28] By contrast with this view, Arendt emphasizes the importance of the public space less as the place where already formed opinions are expressed and defended and more as the very condition of their formation, articulation, and circulation in a broader process of critical thinking and judging. It is through this process of opinion formation that facts come to have truth for us in a politically significant sense. Facts of concern for politics that lack a robust public realm in which to make sense of and articulate them as opinions are like meaningless particulars, things we may "know" but fail to acknowledge or accord meaning in any politically significant sense. And it is for that reason that such facts are also endangered. As we shall now see, even the exposure of deception or outright lies is unlikely to have real political consequences if the public realm in which to debate them is weak or deficient.

Freedom Saves Truth

Turning now to Arendt's discussion of truth as a problem in the modern political context, we find that what concerns her is less the rational truth sought by Plato than the factual truth of events. The "politically most relevant truths are factual," writes Arendt—and they are also the most endangered, vulnerable to human mendacity and the pursuit of political interests ("TP" 232). Like Orwell, Arendt is concerned about the fate of factual truth in totalitarian regimes, but her idea of how to save truth is different from his and from that of most intellectuals of her generation. This difference is not immediately obvious, however. Discerning precisely where it lies will help us avoid repeating the critical judgment that Arendt opposes truth to politics, as if she forbids us to make truth-claims in the political realm or as if truthfulness were not important in political life.

If we carefully reread "Truth and Politics," the essay that has earned her the charge of being hostile to truth-claims in the political realm, we find Arendt advancing several ideas that seem to endorse Orwell's asso-ciation of totalitarianism with the destruction of objective historical truth. Arendt agrees on the need to distinguish and protect factual truths from the interpretive pen of the historian and the self-interested manipulations of the politician. She raises the hermeneutical fact-value question, "But do facts, independent of opinions and interpretation, exist at all?," and an-swers, "Even if we admit that every generation has the right to write its own history, we admit no more than that it has the right to rearrange the facts in accordance with its own perspective; we don't admit the right to touch the factual matter itself" ("TP" 237–38). For example, the fact that "on the night of August 4, 1914 German troops crossed the frontier of Belgium" is one among those "brutally elementary data whose indestructibility has been taken for granted even by the most extreme and most sophisticated believers in historicism" ("TP" 239).

"Since everything that has actually happened in the realm of human affairs could just as well have been otherwise, the possibilities for lying are bound-less," writes Arendt ("TP" 257). When not denied or twisted in some way, facts become mere matters of opinion—as if it were a matter of opinion that "Germany invaded Belgium in August 1914" ("TP" 249). Arendt worries that historical facts can be subject to the kind of historical rewritings described in *Nineteen Eighty-Four*, in which the existence of undesirable historical actors and events are extinguished by "stuffing truth down the memory hole," as

Orwell put it.[29] Such was the fate "of a man by the name of Trotsky, who appears in none of the Soviet Russian history books," comments Arendt ("TP" 231). But she also distances herself from thinkers like Orwell and their idea of objective truth. The relativistic stance toward objective truth that he decries is, in Arendt's view, an inescapable risk that attaches to the very contingent nature of factual truth and, even more significantly, to human freedom.

As "factual truths are never compellingly true," argues Arendt, lying is not something that befalls speech from the outside, as it were.[30] It is not the exception to the rule of the claim to truthfulness that, say, Habermas identifies as definitive of human communication. Whereas Habermas would say that lying is a "strategic form of communication" that surely occurs but that is parasitic on and a deviation from speech oriented to genuine understanding, Arendt would argue that the possibility of lying inheres in the very character of factual truth itself, namely its irreducible contingency. "From this [contingency] it follows that no factual statement can ever be beyond doubt—as secure and shielded against attack as, for instance, the statement that two and two make four," writes Arendt ("LP" 6). To makes matters even more complicated, the possibility of lying—"which enables us to *say*, 'The sun is shining,' when it is raining cats and dogs"—is, in Arendt's account, an irreducible feature of human freedom: "If we were as thoroughly conditioned in our behavior as some philosophies have wished us to be," she writes, "we would never be able to accomplish this little miracle" ("TP" 250).

Recognizing the entanglement of the question of freedom in any talk of truth, Arendt argues that the problem with factual truths arises when they are presented either as if they were necessary and incontestable, like logical truths (e.g., two plus two equals four), or as if they were relativistic and no more debatable than subjective matters of what is agreeable (e.g., "I like canary wine," to take Kant's famous example). On the one hand, Arendt insists on the sheer stubbornness of facts, their resistance to manipulation; if anything, facts are antipolitical, for they tend to be asserted in the manner of rational truths, which, in her view, compel us and preclude all debate. On the other hand, facts are highly vulnerable: far from "being beyond agreement, dispute, or consent," they survive as meaningful for human beings only to the extent that they are talked about.[31] "The political attitude toward facts must tread the very narrow path between the danger of taking them as the results of some necessary development which men could not prevent and about which they can therefore do nothing and the danger of denying them, of trying to manipulate them out of the world" ("TP" 259).

More precisely, facts are not only vulnerable to being denied by human beings, but they can be used to deny human freedom whenever they are presented in the manner of logical truth, with its specific sense of necessity. The problem of factual truth, then, is not only that it is vulnerable to mendacity, but also that we tend to see such truth in the mode of necessity. Factual truth is crucial to the political realm, but the political challenge is how to affirm it in a manner consistent with human freedom. In Arendt's view, it is not the truth that sets you free, to cite a philosophical and religious commonplace; rather, a love and practice of freedom saves truth.

Saving truth requires that we take the risk of freedom, even though freedom (i.e., contingency, not necessity, rules in human affairs) also presents grave risks for truth. This gives rise to a paradox of truth for politics. For Arendt, the possibility of lying attaches to the irreducible contingency of factual truths and to human freedom, but one needs at once to affirm truth and contingency. Any affirmation of truth that denies contingency would risk destroying freedom, and with it the distinctive nature of truth in the realm of human affairs, namely that it could have been otherwise but was not.

From Knowing (Truth) to Acknowledging (Truth)

If we now turn to what Arendt calls "the relatively recent phenomenon of mass manipulation of fact and opinion," the paradox deepens ("TP" 252). As the Pentagon Papers show, "image-making as global policy" led to the creation of theories that were totally independent of the very facts that the U.S. government itself had paid "intelligence analysts to collect" ("LP" 18, 20). "In this 'Alice in Wonderland' atmosphere," writes Arendt, facts and decisions existed in a "nonrelation" ("LP" 20). "The facts I have in mind are publicly known, and yet the same public that knows them can successfully taboo their public discussion" ("TP" 236). The facts or truths that everyone knows but refuses to acknowledge publicly present a significant problem for democratic politics, a problem that is not easily solved by attempts to establish normative procedures by which to "redeem" validity claims.

If we consider the search for Saddam Hussein's fabled weapons of mass destruction, we can see what is at stake here. "As we now know," writes Mark Danner, "the Iraqis had in fact destroyed these weapons, probably years before George W. Bush's [October 2002] ultimatum [that Iraq destroy its WMD or face war]: 'the Iraqis'—in the words of chief weapons inspector

David Kay—'were telling the truth.'"[32] We also know that Kay's reporting of this truth had little political purchase. As "the Downing Street memo" indicates, "by July 2002 at the latest, war had been decided on; the question was how to 'fix,' as it were, what Blair will later call 'the political context'" ("SWW" 5).[33]

"What exactly does the Downing Street memo and the now numerous related documents that have since appeared, prove?" asks Danner.[34] Judging by the anemic, indeed indifferent reaction of the (mainstream) American press (which never even bothered to publish it), the story the memo tells is old hat, "nothing new" ("Reply"). When not ignored, the memo was viewed as being of little significance. As an example of this indifferent reception, Danner cites an article by Michael Kinsey about the memo. "Fixing intelligence and facts to fit a desired policy is the Bush II governing style," and if Bush had fixed the facts, it would be a politically significant scandal, says Kinsey. But, he continues, nothing in the memo reports actual decision makers saying they were "fixing the facts." Therefore, so Kinsey's logic goes, since they did not actually say "Let's fix the facts," we have no "proof" that they were fixing the facts: the memo proves nothing ("Reply"). In light of Kinsey's own characterization of Bush's political style as one of deception, how are we to interpret this puzzling refusal to come to the obvious conclusion? Danner asks, "One might ask what would convince this writer, and many others, of the truth of what, apparently, they already *know*, and get them to *acknowledge* that they already know it?" ("Reply," my emphasis).

Danner questions whether further evidence would have been able "to make a *publicly acceptable fact* out of what everyone now knows and accepts" ("Reply," my emphasis). Failing a tape recording of President Bush saying he "wants the facts fixed," remarks Danner, it appears that no such publicly accepted fact is possible. Needless to say, the discovery of the proverbial smoking gun guarantees nothing. (Was it really Bush on the tape? Maybe someone imitated his voice. Or maybe he was set up by the Democrats. Or maybe he was joking. And so on.)

I said earlier that the facts or truths that everyone knows but refuses to acknowledge publicly present a problem for democratic politics that is not solved by procedures for redeeming truth-claims. Not only is the impure domain of politics not especially "open to the possibility of 'redemption' under the normal claims of validity," as one critic of Habermas puts it, but the issue that concerns us here is not even how to establish the truth of statements.[35] The issue, rather, is "how to make a publicly acceptable fact out of what everyone . . . knows and accepts." To make a fact publicly acceptable, I suggest, is different from proving or being called upon to prove that a fact is true. It is to make the truth of a fact meaningful in a politically significant way. From knowing something to be the case it does not follow that I acknowledge that something is the case, just as from knowing that I am late it does not follow that I acknowledge that I am late, as Stanley Cavell succinctly puts this fundamental difference between knowing and acknowledging.[36] Even if we agree with Habermas and others that claims to truth always demand argumentation to warrant them, we are still left with the question of what remains after all the reasons have been not only given but accepted.

The problem I am trying to describe here might also be put in terms of what happens when a truth is revealed in the absence of an exchange of plural opinions about what might be true. One of the more curious aspects of the journalistic reporting and the public reception of the Downing Street memo was not only that its revelatory properties were questioned (as they were by Kinsey) but that, for the most part, it was simply ignored. As Danner observes, "It is a source of some irony that one of the obstacles to gaining recognition for the Downing Street memo in the American press has been the largely unspoken notion among reporters and editors that the story the memo tells is 'nothing new.'" It contains nothing new, or so it is said, because the larger story that the memo (of July 2002) tells had already been reported by the Knight Ridder agency in two articles dated October 11, 2001, and February 13, 2002, namely that President Bush had already decided to oust Saddam Hussein and had ordered the CIA, the Pentagon, and other agencies to develop a set of covert strategies to achieve that goal. Like reports on the memo after it, those Knight Ridder articles were for the most part ignored. But the truly strange thing here, argues Danner, is this: "A story is told the first time [by Knight Ridder] but hardly acknowledged because the broader story the government is telling drowns it out. When the story is later confirmed by official documents, in this case the Downing Street memorandum, the documents are largely dismissed because they contain 'nothing new'" ("Reply").

Although I share Danner's concern with deciphering the logic of contemporary journalistic reporting on the Iraq war, the problem of what "constitutes a fact" or of how journalists can "actually prove the truth of a story" far exceeds the narrow frame of journalistic practices. The political problem we face here concerns not so much the ability to actually prove something is true, for that ability, I would argue, is parasitic on the very thing that the proof is meant to adjudicate or settle: the plurality of opinions. Indeed what the curious tale of the Downing Street memo indicates is the hollowness of truth in the absence of a context of plural opinions and their exchange, for it is only in such a context that truth, when it is revealed, can reveal something to us as citizens, and further that we as citizens can reveal other aspects of the common world with the knowledge or, better, acknowledgment of that truth.

If I am right to suggest that plural opinions are the condition of not only knowing but acknowledging something as true, perhaps this helps to make sense of Arendt's brief but highly significant discussion of "representative thinking" in the third section of "Truth and Politics." Often cited as one of her earliest formulations of the capacity to judge, Arendt's discussion of representative thinking emphasizes the importance of taking into account the standpoints of other people when forming an opinion. The issue, then, is not simply the existence of plural opinions but the capacity to take them into account when forming one's own opinion or judgment. We might now say that if Arendt's response to totalitarianism and the assault on truth was not to insist on objective truth but to stress the capacity to make judgments, it may well have been because she recognized that it is only through opinions (taking account of or acknowledging them, that is) that truth in the political realm can survive.

Should we now ask of Arendt "Is there to be no truth in politics?," we might imagine her answering, "On the contrary, there is truth in politics; however this way of expressing truth is not simply a matter of being in agreement with oneself, but of thinking from the perspective, and anticipating the agreement, of everybody else. This notion of truth reveals something, for it shows us what we have in common. And such truth can not only survive in the political realm but can survive without destroying the plurality of opinions that are its original home. To search for the truth of opinion, as Socrates did, is to recognize this fundamental insight."

What does all this mean for the truth deficit in our current political context? One might say that as important as it is to expose lies and demand truth from those who claim to speak in our name, we also need to be able to do something political with those truths, to be able to make them into publicly acceptable facts—and this involves the ability to make judgments. If Arendt emphasized the importance of an active citizenry debating plural opinions and paid little attention to the mechanism with which to adjudicate such debate, it was not, I suspect, because she excluded truth-claims as such from the political realm but because she recognized that truth-claims that are redeemed but not acknowledged (in the ways I've been discussing) have short lives. According to Danner, what remains is the "world of 'frozen scandal'—so-called scandals, that is, in which we have revelation but not true investigation or punishment," that is, citizen action that finds its end point in criminal proceedings or judicial decisions. Although Arendt would not see the end point of citizen action in law, she would surely agree that we should not confuse the politics of exposure and scandal with a vital democratic polity.

Chapter 3

Truth and Disagreement

Robert Post

THE FINE AND instructive essays by Jeremy Elkins and Linda M. G. Zerilli seem inspired by the thought that American politics in the past decade has become intolerably indifferent to truth. Elkins insists that "we cannot do without considerations of truth in our political life." He urges that we "foster institutions in which questions of truth are treated responsibly and not wantonly sacrificed to other considerations." Zerilli fears "that truth is quickly becoming a casualty of liberal democratic regimes, not just totalitarian ones." Concerned with "the truth deficit in our current political context," she longs for a form of "citizen action" which, whether or not it finds its specific "end point in criminal proceedings or judicial decisions," is "able to make [truths] into publicly acceptable facts." Apparently both Elkins and Zerilli are driven to their subject by the distortions and mendacity that in their view have pervaded recent politics, including, most conspicuously, the Bush administration, "perhaps the most contemptuous of truth of any in American history," according to Elkins.

I share the concerns that motivate Elkins and Zerilli. But the rub of politics is that what reeks to us of deception and dishonesty to others epitomizes political truth. Millions of Americans genuinely support the assertions, values, and actions that we might regard as duplicitous. The depth of this disagreement leads each side to experience the other as mendacious and deceitful. I suspect that Elkins and Zerilli seek to rehabilitate the value of truth because they believe that it may offer a way to ameliorate the intensity of this impasse. Common ground might emerge if both sides sought fidelity to truth; this common ground might in turn diminish the otherwise vivid differences that now make us appear so dishonest to each other. The search for truth could lead us to a shared "world" equally open to those who were repelled by, for example, the politics of the Bush administration and to those who found it exemplary.

Hannah Arendt is frequently interpreted to repudiate this effort to mix truth with politics. She observes in her famous essay "Truth and Politics" that truth is fundamentally antipolitical. She writes, "Seen from the viewpoint of politics, truth has a despotic character."[1] Truth is singular and compels agreement, yet politics requires plurality and disagreement. Arendt thus concludes that "every claim in the sphere of human affairs to an absolute truth, whose validity needs no support from the side of opinion, strikes at the very roots of all politics and all governments."[2]

Both Elkins and Zerilli are concerned to rescue Arendt from the charge that "she excludes the problem of truth from the political realm" (Zerilli). They each turn to "a less famous essay by Arendt, 'Philosophy and Politics'" (Zerilli). In that essay Arendt praises Socrates' attempts "to make the city more truthful by delivering each of the citizens of their truths."

> The method of doing this is *dialegesthai*, talking something through, but this dialectic brings forth truth *not* by destroying *doxa* or opinion, but on the contrary reveals *doxa* in its own truthfulness. The role of the philosopher, then, is not to rule the city but to be its "gadfly," not to tell philosophical truths but to make citizens more truthful. The difference with Plato is decisive: Socrates did not want to educate the citizens so much as he wanted to improve their *doxai*, which constituted the political life in which he too took part. To Socrates, maieutic [the art of helping others to find the truth in their *doxai*] was a political activity, a give and take, fundamentally on a basis of strict equality, the fruits of which could not be measured by the result of arriving at this or that general truth.[3]

According to Arendt, Socrates sought to summon political truths that were plural, not singular. His effort was to bring out the truth in every man's "*doxa*, his own opening to the world." "Absolute truth, which would be the same for all men . . . cannot exist for mortals. For mortals the important thing is to make *doxa* truthful, to see in every *doxa* truth and to speak in such a way that the truth of one's opinion reveals itself to oneself and to others."[4]

Arendt stresses that a man's *doxa*, his opinion, is "neither subjective illusion nor arbitrary distortion"; it is not "something absolute and valid for all." *Doxa* is a view of the world that "opens up differently to every man, according to his position in it."[5] The truth of *doxa* is therefore perspectival. It is also fragile. Arendt is explicit that "the search for truth in the *doxa* can lead to the catastrophic result that the *doxa* is altogether destroyed, or that what had appeared is revealed as an illusion. . . . Truth therefore can destroy *doxa*, it can destroy the specific political reality of the citizens."[6]

Neither Elkins nor Zerilli believes that politics can tolerate truth "of the apodeictic sort," which compels agreement "as a matter of certainty" (Elkins). Both embrace the kind of perspectival truth that Arendt explores in "Philosophy and Politics." Yet this embrace seems in tension with their underlying project. If truth in politics is perspectival, how can it establish the shared world that Elkins and Zerilli plainly seek? How can it overcome the jagged divisions that divide us? Why turn to the philosophical idea of "truth" as a remedy for deep disagreement if the only relevant account of truth remains itself plural?

The fear is that the "truth" that Elkins and Zerilli locate in "Philosophy and Politics" may leave us where we began: with the hard fact of disagreement among dissimilar *doxai*. Men may inhabit a common world, but they continue to see it from different perspectives. Good faith controversies over truth may be more honorable and forthright than mere cynical struggles over power, but they may also be more intense and deadly. Even accepting as accurate Elkins's and Zerilli's perceptive revisions of Arendt, why should the turn toward truth dampen political conflict rather than sharpen it? Why would it make us any less likely to experience as dishonest those whose *doxa* differs fundamentally from ours?

In his essay, Elkins responds to this tension by constructing a complicated and ingenious thesis that shifts the analytic focus away from the political truth that Arendt describes in "Philosophy and Politics" and toward what Elkins calls the "truth-practices" of particular institutions. He begins with the premise that modern society cannot endure without some commitment to truth. The premise is not controversial if it is understood to apply to simple factual truth. No contemporary society permits harmful false facts to be published without legal regulation. Arendt herself writes, "Freedom of opinion is a farce unless factual information is guaranteed and the facts themselves are not in dispute. . . . Factual truth informs political thought."[7]

Yet Elkins carefully formulates his premise to make a broader and more controversial argument. He believes that modern society must affirm truths that are not of a simple factual nature. He observes, for example, that state-designed school curricula typically affirm complicated theoretical truths, like those of evolution, and he notes that a press that is indifferent to complicated political truths about the causes of the Iraq war would quickly prove inadequate to democratic needs. He asserts that modern society needs a concept of truth that is not limited to elementary, apolitical facts so that, "*pace* Arendt, questions of truth cannot be limited to establishing the boundaries within which politics takes place."[8]

Elkins believes that truth-practices of this kind need not foreclose political plurality. When the values of truth are properly situated within institutions, they "need not stand in opposition to pluralism, but may instead be part of a robust pluralist politics"; understood in this way, truth does not come "into political life" as "the imperial conqueror slashing and burning its way to total domination of all that lies before it." Elkins argues that a healthy political system requires such institution-specific truth-practices because "political freedom depends on various truth-practices, and the quality of that freedom depends on the seriousness with which we engage these kinds of questions."

Elkins extensively analyzes two examples of institutional truth-practices—public school curricula and press political coverage—and he suggests that each can be improved if we better understand the proper relationship between truth and politics. He is ultimately concerned that "the notion that truth and politics belong in separate realms can easily have the effect of discouraging further thought about that very crucial political question of *how* political institutions ought to confront competing claims about how things are."

Elkins's complicated thesis thus consists of (at least) four distinct propositions:

1. Particular institutions that are necessary for a successful polity must incorporate truth-practices that entail far more than the mere commitment to factual accuracy.
2. Such institution-specific truth-practices do not undermine the plural *doxai* that both Arendt and Elkins regard as necessary for politics.
3. It is important to alter "a political (and academic) culture that is

suspicious of all talk of truth and that associates truth-talk with the antipolitical claim to certain and absolute knowledge" (Elkins) in order to foster and nourish these truth-practices.

4. It is important to alter "a political (and academic) culture that is suspicious of all talk of truth and that associates truth-talk with the antipolitical claim to certain and absolute knowledge" (Elkins) in order to improve the quality of our politics.

The first proposition seems to me correct. There are many spheres of social life in which complex decisions must be relied upon as true. If a doctor harms a patient by incorrectly diagnosing her disease, the patient is entitled to sue for malpractice. The doctor cannot defend the suit on the ground that he was following the relative truth of his own *doxa*, that he was simply pursuing the way that the world happened to have opened out to him. The doctor will be held to the standards of the medical profession, which means to the truths that the medical profession presently avows. Medical truths concern far more than elementary matters of factual accuracy; they routinely turn on complex questions of judgment.

There are innumerable circumstances in which society must analogously rely on the provision of expert knowledge. Lawyers and architects, scientists and corporations will all be held legally accountable for the truth of their complex assertions. And society itself will suffer potentially grave consequences if it seeks to override what Elkins calls the "particular institutional truth-practices that we are committed to maintaining." Trofim D. Lysenko fatally damaged Soviet biology by prohibiting Soviet biologists from investigating genetics on the ground that Marxism required that all forms of behavior be explained by environmental influences.[9]

The corollary of Elkins's first proposition is that institutions that society holds accountable for truth also must at times suppress the plural *doxai* of free politics. Wherever and whenever an institution adopts truth-practices of the kind Elkins describes, the free play of opinion must ultimately be consolidated into a singular determination of truth. When a court pronounces the guilt or innocence of a defendant, it truncates political debate in favor of a decisive verdict. The legal verdict is far more complex than an elementary factual determination, and it carries authority because it is empowered to designate one particular view of the world as correct.[10] Wherever institutional truth practices are enforced, as for example by the setting of a singular school curriculum or by the publication of a particular newspaper editorial, plural *doxai* are *pro tanto* suppressed.

I agree also with Elkins's second proposition. I have in fact advanced analogous arguments in the context of First Amendment jurisprudence.[11] The idea is that a general framework of democratic politics requires both a realm of political freedom, within which the expression of plural *doxai* is protected, and particular institutions, within which particular truths are established. Such institutions are themselves necessary for the flourishing of the democratic polity taken as a whole. In my own work theorizing the First Amendment, I have used the term "public discourse" to designate the forms of communication necessary for the conduct of democratic politics.[12] The First Amendment has been interpreted to require that public discourse remain free for the expression of the diverse views of political actors.[13] The First Amendment has also been interpreted to allow the routine regulation of speech outside public discourse so that specific organizations can enforce their own distinct truth-practices.[14]

Within public discourse, for example, courts assert that "under the First Amendment there is no such thing as a false idea."[15] Outside of public discourse, by contrast, courts will permit lawsuits for medical or legal malpractice for false opinion. The Constitution thus authorizes states to enforce the truth practices that express the best available medical or legal professional standards. Although standard First Amendment doctrine holds that "there is no constitutional value in false statements of fact," within public discourse courts apply doctrines like "actual malice" or "fault" in order to avoid punishing speakers for mere factual error.[16] Outside of public discourse, as for example in the area of commercial advertising, courts freely enforce the requirement of simple factual truth.[17] In effect, therefore, the structure of First Amendment doctrine confirms Elkins's thesis that truth can be enforced in many institutional domains without compromising the capacity of society to protect the free and plural expression of opinion within the political arena.

Elkins's third proposition causes me some hesitation. It is not clear to me that a scholarly suspicion of the compatibility of truth with politics is of fundamental significance for the maintenance of truth-practices within particular institutions. Consider the practice of medicine. Medicine is not an arena of politics; plural *doxai* are not permitted. Doctors must apply medical truth, as the medical profession understands truth. The fidelity of doctors to medical truth is not in the least influenced by the beliefs of scholars or citizens about the relationship between truth and politics. These beliefs are largely irrelevant to what doctors do. Wherever institutions vigorously pursue their own healthy truth practices, analogous conclusions would seem to hold.

The two examples that Elkins discusses in detail do not suggest a contrary conclusion. Elkins is concerned that the press has "been increasingly reticent about offering independent review of issues that are on the public agenda," relying instead "on competing partisan quotes to characterize political events and facts, even facts as basic as the content of legislation, official reports, and other publicly available documents, rather than offer its own independent analysis." He believes the press has "too often" come to believe "that respect for the plurality of political opinion" should, as a matter of responsibility, re-strain its efforts to report "too vigorously in ways that might have the effect of denying or undermining partisan truth-claims or partisan conflicts." Misun-derstanding the connection between truth and politics, Elkins suggests, has led the press to regard its proper role as that of a transparent medium whose function is neutrally to convey the views of public actors. Elkins would rather that the press adopt a different role. He would like the press to become an independent speaker empowered to offer its own objective description of the world.

Whether the press should stress the value of neutrality or of objectivity is a complicated question that would seem to turn on many factors. Large-scale media have strong incentives to remain safely neutral because such a role shields them from the risk of alienating members of their audience who might disagree with the media's own "objective" point of view were they to express it. Many argue that a press that monopolizes channels of communica-tion *ought* to regard itself as a public carrier that transparently transmits the speech of political actors to ordinary persons; they fear that public opinion would be distorted in favor of the perspectives of wealthy media owners were a monopolistic press to attempt to advocate for its own independent views. Surely it is debatable whether media ought to follow the lead of networks like Fox News that explicitly exploit their ratings to push the truth of their own *doxa*. Whether democracy is better served by media like Fox News or instead by media that adopt a more modest account of their own mission is an open and much debated issue.

To establish his third proposition, Elkins must convincingly demonstrate that the tendency of the press to prioritize the value of neutrality over that of objectivity is explained by the press's misunderstanding of the proper rela-tionship between truth and politics. He must imagine the press as beguiled by misinterpretations of Arendt into believing either that truth is irrelevant to politics, so that the value of objectivity is not an available option, or that political truth is despotic, so that objectivity is not an attractive option. Either explanation strikes me as implausible. I believe it is far more likely that the press is tending toward the role of neutral medium either because of practical incentives or because of normative beliefs about its own proper role morality. These are more likely to influence the practical decisions of press organizations than the misadventures of political theorists.

The same point can be made with regard to the second example Elkins chooses to elaborate, which involves the question of whether schools ought to teach that evolution is a controversial theory rather than a biological "truth." Supporters of intelligent design advocate that schools teach "the debate" (Elkins) about evolution, and Elkins seems to me exactly right to argue that this is not a choice between following and not following a truth-practice. It is instead a choice about "how far to teach science according to the internal truth-practices of that institution as it now exists" (Elkins). This choice can be intelligently illuminated only by reference to the pedagogical mission of schools. It is thus at root a question of the proper purposes of public education. I do not understand how academic perceptions of the relationship between truth and politics has anything much to do with the question of how schools ought to teach scientific materialism. The question would seem instead to turn on specific considerations, such as the social value of science, the appropriate connection between public education and science, the proper place in a secular state of religion and of education about religion, and so on.

Even if the implementation of specific institutional truth-practices may not be much affected by improving our understanding of the proper relationship between truth and politics, Elkins in his fourth proposition argues that the health of our political dialogue might very well be enhanced. If politicians understood themselves to be arguing about the truth of a common world, for example, their disagreements might ameliorate and become more respectful. But it might also be that their disagreements become sharper and more intense. Tolerance for plural *doxai* might be reduced.

If I interpret him correctly, Elkins does not address this question. He proposes instead a justification for his fourth proposition that is more indirect and subtle. He contends that if political actors understood the importance of institution-specific truth-practices, if they understood that these practices were neither arbitrary nor despotic, they might better engage "that very crucial political question of *how* political institutions ought to confront competing claims about how things are" (Elkins). Political actors, in other words, could better comprehend how government should relate to institution-specific truth-practices. Elkins argues that affirming the proper relationship of truth to politics would illuminate "a particular question that political institutions will sometimes have to face: when to take a position that conflicts with other deeply held opinions. I have tried to suggest that there is no uniform answer to this question, that the answer that is given in particular cases often involves choosing *between* conceptions of pluralism rather than for or against pluralism in general, and that the answer that is given commonly depends at least in part on whether the contested account arose through particular institutional truth-practices that we are committed to maintaining."

In one sense Elkins's claim seems unexceptionally true. The better political actors understand the nature of institutional truth-practices, the better decisions they will reach about how government ought to situate itself vis-à-vis these practices. But if we resituate Elkins's claim in the initial problem that motivated his intervention—in the problem of deep political disagreement that produces the experience of mendacity—then his claim seems less convincing. As Elkins himself recognizes, the proper deployment of institution-specific truth-practices is itself a political question, a question about which there can be deep disagreement. Political attitudes toward science are so divergent that they produce the experience of dishonesty among antagonists. I do not understand how this experience will be reduced if political actors come to understand that scientific truths need not be despotic within politics although they may be dispositive within science. So long as plural *doxai* must be protected in the political arena, and so long as the political appropriation of institution-specific truth-practices remains itself a political question, it is not clear how a better understanding of the actual relationship between politics and institution-specific truth-practices will reduce the rancor and alienation that presently afflict our political system.

In contrast to Elkins, Zerilli does not shift her attention to institution-specific truth-practices. She instead focuses relentlessly on the significance of truth within the political sphere. She argues that although truth in politics "is a matter neither of correspondence nor of subsumption but of appearance," so that political truth always involves "an ongoing and never-ending process," political truth can nevertheless become a ground that brings persons together in common judgment. Zerilli uses the concept of "public space" to attempt to bridge these two disparate accounts of political truth.

Zerilli believes that the "public space is not—or not always—the place to speak a truth one already knows but the condition of finding truth in one's own opinion."[18] Public space is "the very condition" of the "formation, articulation, and circulation" of opinions "in a broader process of critical thinking and judging. It is through this process of opinion formation that facts come to have truth for us in a politically significant sense." The "politically significant sense" of truth that Zerilli wishes to emphasize can emerge only from the practical relationship between a speaker and her audience. In politics, truth entails the "acknowledgment of that truth" (Zerilli) by its audience. Zerilli uses the concept of a "publicly acceptable fact" to designate what happens when a political truth is acknowledged in the appropriate sort of way: "Facts or truths that everyone knows but refuses to acknowledge publicly present a problem for democratic politics that is not solved by procedures for redeeming truth-claims. . . . To make a fact publicly acceptable, I suggest, is different from proving or being called upon to prove that a fact is true. It is to make the truth of a fact meaningful in a politically significant way."

Zerilli uses "the curious tale of the Downing Street memo" to illustrate how political truth requires acknowledgment, not merely valid assertion. By emphasizing the connection between truth and acknowledgment, she links political truth to the exercise of judgment and adjudication. It is not clear, however, what she means by judgment or adjudication. Zerilli refers to Danner's call for "true investigation or punishment," which is to say "citizen action that finds its end point in criminal proceedings or judicial decisions" (Zerilli). And of course legal action is most certainly a form of social judgment that presupposes claims of truth and acknowledgment.

Yet law is an institution in which decision is paramount. Law must condemn or exonerate depending upon the truth of an indictment. Precisely for this reason truth in law does not involve "an ongoing and never-ending process." Truth in law is decisive and singular rather than plural and evolving. Truth in law is thus the opposite of truth in politics. Legal truth in the end always aspires to transcend the diverse *doxai* of citizens. In practice this means that legal truth reflects the *doxai* of those who control the law.

Those who control the law dream that law expresses the agreement of all.[19] To the extent that we share in this agreement, we experience law as a refuge from the continuous controversy of politics. If agreement in fact exists, law is the quintessential institution for enshrining our common truth. But it is a mistake to believe that law can create such agreement out of political thin air, that in its own name and on its own authority law can reliably and automatically summon political concurrence. Perhaps great political trials, as for example those that accompany the transition from dictatorship to democracy, may temporarily consolidate political meanings by endowing them with legal authority.[20] But legal authority is evanescent; it dissolves as soon as it becomes entangled in the profane give-and-take by which political meanings are reclaimed, domesticated, and dispersed in the disagreement of ordinary citizens.

So while law does indeed "make the truth of a fact meaningful in a politically significant way" (Zerilli), it does so at a steep price. Law is designed within itself to foreclose the ongoing and never-ending process that for Zerilli constitutes the political space necessary for "not only knowing but acknowledging something as true." It is perhaps because of this price that Zerilli cannot quite bring herself explicitly to endorse Danner's call for legal investigation and judgment.

Instead she chooses to attribute to Arendt a possible answer to the question of how there can be truth in politics. Zerilli imagines Arendt asserting that "truth in politics" is a matter "of thinking from the perspective, and anticipating the agreement, of everybody else. This notion of truth reveals something, for it shows us what we have in common. And such truth can not only survive in the political realm but can survive without destroying the plurality of opinions that are its original home. To search for the truth of opinion, as Socrates did, is to recognize this fundamental insight."

In this short passage Zerilli effortlessly steps from a world that we have in common to a common perspective on that world. She glides rapidly from "the plurality of opinions" to the anticipation of "agreement." If indeed we live in a world in which the plurality of *doxai* resolves itself into the singularity of agreement, we shall inhabit a polity of truth and acknowledgment. But if we are not so fortunate (or unfortunate), if disagreement persists, the hope of agreement will not save us, nor will any concept of political truth that Zerilli develops.

In the end, Zerilli offers an account of truth in politics that is contingent upon our capacity accurately to anticipate agreement. The account is alluring because the dream of agreement is enticing. But when we awake, as we always do, we shall face the shocking disharmony of politics. The tempting anticipation of agreement will lapse into the ongoing and never-ending search for political truth. Inevitably we shall at times experience the cacophony of that search as mendacity and dishonesty. Inevitably we shall at times experience it as a failure of acknowledgment, a failure to take in the significance of facts or opinions, so that we seem endlessly to "confuse the politics of exposure and scandal with a vital democratic polity" (Zerilli). Sadly, the cure for this sour experience seems to be the cure for politics itself.

Chapter 4

"Speaking Power to Truth"

Wendy Brown

> We hold these truths to be self-evident . . .
> —Thomas Jefferson

> It depends on what the meaning of "is" is.
> —William Jefferson Clinton

"NO ONE HAS ever doubted that truth and politics are on rather bad terms with each other," Arendt begins her essay on the subject. As these fine papers by Elkins and Zerilli illustrate, the truth-politics relation is not only old and vexed but has a protean and inconstant shape and refers to quite diverse corners of the field we call political. In the West, it could be said to make its first written appearance with the Greek tragedians' accounts of political knavery and Thucydides' narrative of the Peloponnesian wars, at whose nadir, it will be remembered, "words lost their meanings," a loss that heralded the demise of Athenian democracy. A different relation of truth and politics acquired sharpness and infamy in Plato's *Republic,* where the poets were banned for their provocative misrepresentations, yet truth could rule only if shrouded by a great and consequential lie. In antiquity, still another order of the truth-politics problem emerged in Aristotle's quarrel with Plato over the type of knowledge appropriate to the science and practice of politics. So already in this early moment in Western history, truth in politics is sometimes contrasted to lying, sometimes to opinion, sometimes to secrecy, sometimes to collective deliberation, sometimes to historical fit, sometimes to semiotic slide, sometimes to distortion, sometimes to religion, poetry, or myth. Things only grow more complicated when the Enlightenment makes a fetish of truth, science, and reason, and an emerging liberalism struggles both to comport with this fetish and to escape it in the name of subjective freedom and individual judgment. The truth question in politics also adheres differently to the is and the ought; the former is contoured not merely by perspectivalism and interpretation but by power's dissimulating nature, while the latter, as Elkins and Zerilli stress, is contoured by the phenomenon of human plurality, the importance of opinion and judgment, and truth's potential despotism.

This said, Elkins and Zerilli (following Arendt) understand democracy to face a particular and paradoxical set of enemies on the truth front. On the one hand, there is the damage done to democracy with lies and overt deceptions by personages or regimes of power—what we might call the Nixon problem. On the other hand, there is the danger of governance by truth—the Plato problem, the moral agenda problem, the religion problem, but also the rationality and even technocracy problem. The first signals corruption in general but also the specific sort subverting the necessary subordination of the state to the will of the people. The second signals suppression of the open-ended debate and judgments about "the good" that democracy must epistemologically presuppose and practically cultivate. Thus democracy is imperiled by untruthfulness in power and by the rule of truth. Similarly democracy is endangered by scorn for facts but also by the dominance of facticity, by refusal of reason and by rule of reason.[1] All of this Elkins and Zerilli unfold in compelling and erudite detail.

Both papers also suggest that the poststructuralist emphasis on the imbrication of truth and power did not so much produce a new problem for truth in politics as uncover an old one. If, as Nietzsche and Foucault had it, the will to truth is never independent of a will to power, if reigning truths are always regimes of power and power always instantiates a truth of its own, and if, at the same time, truth inevitably denies its imbrication with power, it is no surprise that the problem of truth is especially thorny in the political realm. Indeed this nest of difficulties for truth would almost make one want to give up on it. Yet Elkins and Zerilli both insist, knowing that truth is not absolute or unimplicated in power, that all accounts are perspectival, incomplete, and framed by discourse, that truth does not substitute for judgment, and that a simple concern with truth cannot even broker educational policies on science and religion—none of this eliminates our wish, even our demand, for truthfulness in putatively democratic political life. We were galled by G. W. Bush's pretext for invading Iraq because it was a deliberately conjured and consequential fiction, just as we were galled by Nixon's role in the Watergate scandal because it was a compound deceit: a crime, a cover-up, a lie about the cover-up. More than galled, we regard this kind of duplicity as destructive of the very fabric of democracy, as searing violations of the trust at stake in representative government.

And yet we have to wonder whether and why these extreme and noxious breaches of truth would be more dangerous to democracy than what I will be considering here as the *ordinary dissimulation of ordinary power*. Could it be due, in part, to the revelation performed by these extremes of the inherently dissimulating nature of political life and its lack of consonance with democratic conceits about authenticity, transparency, and proceduralism? That is, might we fulminate about the blatant and criminal lies because such fulmination stabilizes a norm of power's truth and transparency at odds with power's very nature? Does obsessing about lying politicians suppress the larger challenge they pose to the fiction that democratic politics is or can be a field of truth? Might even the cynical declaration "All politicians lie" function to restrict the reach of the problem? That is, might a preoccupation with lying facilitate a disavowal of the unique, and perhaps uniquely distressing, character of the field with regard to truth? Putting the matter the other way around, do we, as Zerilli suggests at the conclusion of her paper, confuse "the politics of exposure and scandal with a vital democratic polity"?

Zerilli's focus is on the difference between surfacing the truth from political lies or deceptions and doing "something political with those truths," which involves making judgments. But if the preoccupation with lying distracts the populace from what I will suggest is the toughest nugget in the truth-politics relation, I wonder if the preoccupation with criteria for judgment does not constitute a parallel distraction for political theorists. Thus even as both Elkins and Zerilli probe with subtlety and intelligence the democratic conundrum about pluralism and truth, this very probing veers and deflects from the problem of how truth and power relate and operate in ordinary political representations.

Close attention to a rhetorical feature of Arendt's "Truth and Politics" reveals a similar veering and deflection. In that complex essay, Arendt repeatedly raises a question she does not answer, nor even pursue at length, namely, "whether it is of the very essence of truth to be impotent and of . . . power to be deceitful," or, as she puts it elsewhere in the text, "wanting to find out what injury political power is capable of inflicting upon truth," and still elsewhere, "the suspicion arises that it may be in the nature of the political realm to deny or pervert truth of every kind."[2] While Arendt plumbs the matter of truth's impotence in politics, and even builds her conclusion on it, she leaves largely unexplored—as do most other political theorists—the question of why power dissimulates.[3]

The rhetorical structure of both Zerilli's and Elkins's papers imitates Arendt's foray into the truth-politics problem. Each starts with the problem of political lies and duplicity but then slides to the question of criteria, locales, institutions, or cultures appropriate to judgments, opinions, and decisions about normative political issues: Who are we or ought we to be? How are we to think or deliberate about a particular problem? What is to be done? Each shifts from the problem of representing power truthfully to the problem of making normative political truth-claims. What accounts for this slide? Why do reflections on the nature of truth and untruth in politics often end up being dodgy about power?

A strong theoretical focus on power's relation to truth, whether by Thrasymachus, Machiavelli, Hobbes, Nietzsche, or Schmitt, inevitably generates anxiety for democrats, especially of the liberal variety. Little wonder: close attention to power's relationship to truth produces two problems for the liberal democratic imaginary. The first is that truth carries a will to power, is brought into being by power, and operates as power. The second is that power inherently dissimulates; to endure, it cannot appear naked but must be dressed in a costume of some sort. Combined, these problems generate two effects at odds with democracy understood as ruling ourselves in common. On the one hand, politically governing truths are never transparent; we are necessarily ruled by powers that are subterranean and difficult to surface, hence difficult to know let alone handle in common, that is, to democratize. On the other hand, the truth about power is only politically operative as resistance or protest; power's truth vaporizes as soon as it is in office. Power's truth can be revealed, but power does not speak its own truth as part of its operation. Indeed the popular notion of "speaking truth to power" carries a tacit recognition of this asymmetry.

Liberalism, itself a discourse of power and hence implicated in these difficulties, largely eschews them. For the most part, liberal democracy carries the Enlightenment presumption of truth's autonomy from power and also tends to cast political power as contained by state actions and functions. Consequently, liberal democrats' main worry about power's truthfulness pertains to the motives and acts of politicians and political institutions, the independence of the press, and the problem of corrupting influence on officials or agencies. Liberalism does not much acknowledge the will to power *in* truth or the truth generated *by* power, but rather takes truth to be the province of science, reason, and facticity, all of which work with an idea of truth discovered rather than produced. Moreover to the extent that social contractarianism formulates power as a transferable substance contained in legislative, juridical, or executive functions, it does not feature power's inherently dissimulating tendencies. Rather, in the social contract power is conferred by the people to its representative institutions, and corruption occurs when this transferred power is exploited for the interests of those in office. End of story.

Within the models of both power and truth subscribed to by liberalism, there is no inherent reason for power to have an inherently fraught relationship with truth. Political power may have temptations in the direction of deceit or disguise, but it can, in good faith, commit itself to full disclosure. Hence Jimmy Carter came to office following the Watergate scandal promising that he would "never lie to the American people," just as Obama followed on the secrecy and deceptions of the G. W. Bush presidency with an express commitment to make decisions and formulate policy based on facts, law, and deliberation and with as much openness as possible.

The irony here is that, apart from liberalism, much of canonical Western political theory has taken as its task the unmasking of power's operations and effects. Especially but not only for critical theory, the powers governing and organizing collective life are regarded as requiring artful theoretical excision of them from tissues of concealment or complex ideological constellations. Sometimes what is required is the theoretical articulation of powers altogether absent from conventional political discourse, for example disciplinary power; at other times, theory delineates power's canny (mis)representation of itself, a (mis)representation that is a crucial dimension of power's palatability, stability, and effectiveness. Either way, the very enterprise of critical political theory could be said to be premised upon the inherent subterfuge, the nonmanifest nature, of the power or powers conditioning and governing collective life. Indeed if power were self-revealing and carried in the ordinary vernacular, what would there be to theorize? What would critical theory surface or reveal?

By the natural subterfuge of power, I mean something more precise than what is comprised by the familiar claim, whether in its Platonic, Machiavellian, Marxist, or Arendtian inflection, that politics takes place in the realm of appearances and draws extensively on theatrical motifs and effects. The analogy of politics to theater does not quite capture the matter concerning us at the moment. The emphasis on appearance stresses the linguistically rhetorical and spatially staged elements of political life, the constitution of political events and relations by action and interpretation rather than principles, fundaments, or structures, and the inappropriateness of tracing political effects directly to motives or of drawing on nonpolitical formulas for political understanding or action. The problem of power's inherent self-concealment is a little different. To my mind, no political theorist has ever offered an adequate explanation as to why, but power cannot be radically exposed without wilting. Or as Foucault suggests in volume 1 of *The History of Sexuality*, "Power is tolerable only on condition that it mask a substantial part of itself. Its success is proportional to its ability to hide its own mechanisms. Would power be accepted if it were entirely cynical? For it, secrecy is not in the nature of an abuse; it is indispensable to its operation."[4] Foucault is describing more than power's need for legitimacy in social and political life, for there is no necessary reason why all power would have to dissimulate to be legitimate, and indeed there are types of power whose legitimacy cannot be said to rest on the dissimulation they nevertheless undergo. Rather Foucault's point is the stronger one (however weakly developed): that masking and dissimulation are a crucial part of power's power. Power simply cannot act openly or nakedly—*truthfully*—without suffering a decline. Thus the paradox of all realist thought, which imagines itself to mirror epistemologically the frankness of its object, is that it resorts to a different metaphysics for grasping its object from that which is imputed to its object.

Nowhere is power's dependency on dissimulation more palpable than in the operation of power Foucault has taught us most about, that of the regulatory norm. Norms govern precisely by appearing to be unrelated to power and instead to derive from and circulate in the order of nature or common sense. Thus norms of gender and sexuality, but also norms of scholarly inquiry or civil speech, or of medical or military practice, appear natural and true rather than contingent or policed in their everyday operations. While they are generated by power and operate as power, they appear—if they can be said to appear at all—only as the ordinary terms and parameters of spheres of activity they govern and subjects they constitute. Norms rule by seeming to be neither normative nor ruling.

The necessity and inherency of a mask for power is as pertinent to large historical constellations or arcs of power, such as those traveling under the sign of rationalization, discipline, or capitalism, as to more specific normative regimes. If the nature of capital's power was revealed on the surface, Marx would not have had to write *Das Kapital*, and certainly not as a mystery story in which its secret is discovered and in which the reader is invited to go behind the curtain to see how the wheels really turn. (Nor would bourgeois economists need recourse to micro- or macroeconomic abstractions to explain the dynamics of capitalism.) If disciplinary power and biopower made themselves manifest, Foucault would have had only to name rather than excavate, genealogize, and theorize them. If the process Weber identified as rationalization was apparent to the naked eye, no *theoretical* work would be needed to comprehend its generative source, operations, trajectories, and effects.

Power's dissimulation is not limited to class or other inegalitarian societies; it is a requirement of the successful and sustained deployment of power itself.[5] Nor is its subterranean operation confined to that which governs without human direction or will. As Weber argued, even the power of charisma appears as emanating from special gifts and relations to the deities. Again, although none of the great power theorists explains why, power must dissemble not only to be tolerated but to be effective; it must deflect from its operations and fashion itself as nonpower. Thus do conventional formulations of power as simple, blunt, and crude radically misunderstand (and no doubt perpetuate the failure to explore) the generativity, intricacy, and mystery of their subject.

If the life blood of politics is power, and if power cannot speak its own truth without undoing itself, then politics is not and cannot be a field of truth. Even speaking truth to power is, in a certain sense, a parapolitical act, one that aims to expose an object in the political field from outside that field. Arendt makes a similar argument: "To look upon politics from the perspective of truth . . . means to take one's stand outside the political realm."[6] But the fact that it remains outside the political fray does not condemn this act to impotence or uselessness. To the contrary, it underscores the importance of intellectual criticism, whether academic, public, or journalistic, that engages in such acts. Still, we ought not confuse these acts with political truth—an oxymoron because power cannot tell its truth—of political power. Rather, as not only Arendt but Elkins also argues in his essay, the work of telling power's truth is gadfly work, appropriate for those who have deliberately taken some distance from politics, precisely as the original gadfly did and as have honest theorists and critics since Socrates. Should we, however, find ourselves making a more direct bid for political position, let alone hegemony, should we find ourselves inside the political arena, we will not and cannot continue speaking truth to power. We will instead be consigned to speaking power's most basic truth, which is that it cannot speak truly without undermining itself.

No degree of commitment to rationality, reason, transparency, proceduralism, Christian or Buddhist virtue, and above all to the political ethics with which much of the humanities now busies itself can overcome this feature of politics. This is because none can solve the power problem, though each in its own way attempts to subordinate power to some other element; each attempts to subdue or dethrone politics with an alien element. Still, if power cannot speak truly and truth is always imbricated with power, we are not therefore condemned to speechlessness about lies, deception, religious disavowals of science, cover-ups, or ideology. Rather we must continue to speak of and against all these things, and even do so within a discourse of truth that purports to be the opposite of what it is exposing. Such a discourse participates in what Foucault called the "game of truth," a game that has no outside and no end point. It is this game of truth, a coinage that upends truth's premises of solidity, sincerity, and fundament, that may come closest to what Elkins refers to as the idea of truth "necessary for our political life."

PART II

Authority and Justification

Chapter 5

Cynicism, Skepticism, and the Politics of Truth

Andrew Norris

THE RELATIONSHIP BETWEEN truth and democratic politics has never been a particularly easy one.[1] The large role played by rhetoric and, in the modern world, political advertising in the generation of the will of the people or the consent of the governed makes it difficult for a democrat to insist upon strict veracity in public discourse. This difficulty is compounded by the fact that the *demos* as a whole, unlike at least some elites, is not always well-educated enough to consistently discern when such rhetoric or advertising is systematically misleading or misrepresentative. But if it is little surprise that truthfulness does not usually figure as one of the prime virtues of democratic politics, we can hardly conclude that it is unimportant or inessential. The history of American politics offers more illustrations than we might care to have of the dangers of disregarding the need for truth and truthfulness in our politics. Some of these are relatively trivial, such as Sarah Palin's repeated claims that the health care reform championed and signed by President Obama will lead to the institution of "death panels," or Newt Gingrich's claim that Obama is a dedicated socialist who seeks to fulfill his father's supposed anticolonial legacy. Others are matters of life and death; the role of political mendacity in the history of American wars of aggression such as the Mexican War, the Vietnam War, and the second Iraq War is particularly significant and disturbing.[2] That such mendacity has enjoyed the success it has obviously depends

upon a variety of factors, few of which are constant. To take only the most recent of the latter examples, the Bush-Cheney administration's success selling
false claims about weapons of mass destruction to large swaths of the American people was in part the result of the continued reluctance of the mainstream press to compromise its allegedly impartial position by questioning
the veracity of the executive branch's factual claims (that is to say, the press's
apparent assumption that facts as well as values are "relative"); the fact that
the public after 9/11 looked for (or allowed themselves to be convinced that
they were looking for) a "strong leader" to defend them from terrorist attacks;
the fact that, for a significant part of Bush's time in office, all three branches
of the federal government were controlled by his own party; the fact (which is
only apparently in tension with the previous point) that the executive branch
has steadily amassed more and more power vis-à-vis the legislative, reducing
public deliberation and with it the possibility of public scrutiny of the actions
of elected officials; and the related, unprecedented surge in government secrecy associated in particular with Vice President Cheney.[3] Add to these the
insidious effects of American patriotism and the traditional awkwardness of
fit between the demands of truth and those of democratic politics, and one
might begin to find Bush and Cheney's relatively successful run with political
dishonesty rather unsurprising, as dreadful as its consequences have been.

And yet questions remain. When we are lied to in private life, we generally respond with anger or even outrage.[4] Honesty is a central good for most
of us, a necessary part of a worthwhile relationship and a necessary virtue of
a respectable person. How is that so many Americans—and so many political theorists—did *not* respond with that anger to the lies told by Bush and
his spokesmen and associates, or by Johnson and McNamara in the Tonkin
Gulf affair? Institutional reasons such as those listed above do not seem to account for this; there is a cultural aspect involved as well. It is not simply that
the press failed to challenge and interrogate the administration's claims; it is
also that at this point so many of us expected and still expect so little in the
way of truth or truthfulness in politics. What Orwell observes of Winston's
lover Julia in *1984* is true of all too many of us Americans: "She only questioned the teachings of the Party when they in some way touched upon her
own life. Often she was ready to accept the official mythology, simply because
the difference between truth and falsehood did not seem important to her."[5]
How else to explain the widespread lack of interest in, say, the debacle over
weapons of mass destruction? Plain lies were greeted either with a shrug of
indifference or a defense of the "sincerity" of the emotion or conviction of the

actor—as in, "Bush really *believed* in what he was doing" (and hence was not responsible for what he was *saying*, which is at best an epiphenomenon of the larger "project")—as if sincerity could do the work of accuracy, or as if one could be truthful without taking care that one spoke the truth.[6]

There are various explanations in turn for this sort of indifference. Cynicism about politicians and the possibilities of politics is an important one, and it is an endemic problem in a democracy where the identity of "the people" who rule and hence the identity of the common good are both constitutively in question. The problems this produces are seriously exacerbated when the people attempt to rule themselves by means of a hopelessly compromised welfare state torn between the demands of capital and those of social justice and stability.[7] It is all too easy for contemporary Americans to conclude, first, that aside from its military branches, the state is a failed institution suited only for those poor souls who cannot "buy out" into the private sector, and therefore that the notion of a vibrant public realm structured by extensive public institutions is fanciful and archaic, if not dangerous; and, second, that appeals to the common good—particularly those liberal appeals that propose the use of the tainted welfare state—are inevitably partisan and not to be trusted.[8] This suspicion all too easily leads to the familiar inversion of Clausewitz, whereby politics is war conducted by other (nonviolent) means, and as such a realm in which anything is fair—even, if not especially, manipulation by "public relations" and outright lies.[9] Of course, as people become habituated to the deceit of one group, it can easily become more difficult for them to trust that group's opponents as well. Deceitful politicians, as it were, drag everyone else down with them, making reasonable public deliberation of their false claims less and less likely. "It's all just propaganda" and "I don't know who to believe" become more and more reasonable responses to political attacks that, in turn, become more and more frenzied. That today this all takes place in a culture saturated by corporate advertising that a child of twelve greets with knowing, ironic incredulity only exacerbates the process.

Such cynicism is not the only possible source of the indifference many feel toward the revelation that we were misled into war. Another is skepticism: skepticism not just about the claims of politicians, but about our ability to ground political claims in general. Here we move to a set of concerns that are particularly important to political theorists, though they play a significant role in the wider political culture as well. Both cynicism and skepticism are deeply entwined with the origins and history of modern political theory, the first most closely associated with Machiavelli's celebration of an amoral politics of manipulation, and the second with the epistemological bases of Hobbes's initiation of post-Aristotelian political science.[10] Of the two, skepticism is far more likely to figure prominently in a contemporary political theoretic position, in part because it is obviously a philosophical position, whereas cynicism is almost a rejection of philosophy, and in part because it is simply the more attractive position of the two.[11] In particular, many political theorists argue that skepticism is not simply a correct account of our epistemological position, but an account that, properly grasped, encourages and enables genuinely democratic politics. There are many versions of this argument, from those of Richard Rorty, Stanley Fish, and Paul Feyerabend to those advanced by some followers of Carl Schmitt and Hannah Arendt, but the basic structure is generally the same: politics, it is said, is an agonistic struggle over "essentially contested concepts," one that will be severely compromised by any turn away from the *doxa* of public opinion toward the "coercive" force of truth. The freedom of individuals to develop in the way they choose and our collective ability to fashion a vibrant public life are both encouraged, not discouraged, by an acceptance of the limitations of proof, foundation, and knowledge in politics. In short, the Sophists were closer to a genuine appreciation for the dynamics of democratic political life (viz., authentic political life) than the truth-obsessed Plato, whose *Republic* and *Statesman* could offer only the apolitical "guidance" of a master or a master class. There is obviously a great deal to be said for this argument, and I am in general quite sympathetic to it. But the history of political mendacity in this country should give us pause here. Can a politics of opinion afford to put agonal conflict before truth in this way?

It may be only a slight exaggeration to say, as Arendt was fond of saying, "Truthfulness has never been counted among the political virtues."[12] (Though it is a striking omission for someone who describes the Romans as "perhaps the most political people we have known" that Arendt here ignores or forgets Cicero's discussion of the central importance of *fides* in his *De Officiis*.)[13] Public policy differs fundamentally from private policy in that the responsible party often makes decisions of greater consequence in a situation where violence is more likely, and in which—particularly in a democracy—he or she has an obligation to protect the interests of a great number of other people. There is therefore much greater chance of conflict between competing values (such as truthfulness and the protection of the citizenry) and, often at least, greater need for relatively quick resolutions of such conflicts in which one or more value is seriously compromised.[14] But it remains true that, as

Arendt also emphasized, truth in public life is "the chief stabilizing factor in the ever-changing affairs of men," and when too cheap a price is put on it, the possibility of orienting ourselves and making reasonable political judgments is seriously undermined.[15] As Arendt puts it in one of the most moving passages in her work, the political sphere "is limited by those things which men cannot change at will. And it is only by respecting its own borders that this realm, where we are free to act and to change, can remain intact, preserving its integrity and keeping its promises. Conceptually, we may call truth what we cannot change; metaphorically, it is the ground on which we stand and the sky that stretches above us."[16]

Arendt's own focus in this regard is on the figure she names "the truthteller," whom she argues is "outside the political realm—outside the community to which we belong and the community of our peers."[17] Here I think she fails to adequately appreciate the need for "truth telling" by political agents as well as the historians and spectators who judge them. Arendt is anxious to protect a political realm devoted to the free expression of the plurality of perspectives that is the public. In such a realm, opinion or *doxa* rather than truth is at issue, where *doxa* is "the formulation in speech of what *dokei moi*, that is, what appears to me." In the ancient polis "this *doxa* had as its topic not what Aristotle calls the *eikos*, the probable, the many *verisimilia* (as distinguished from . . . the one truth . . .) but comprehended the world as it opens itself up to me."[18] One's *doxa* may well require clarification and expression, and Arendt praises Socrates for trying "to make the city more truthful" by "reveal[ing] *doxa* in its own truthfulness."[19] But even "truthful" opinion remains perspectival, relative, and free. In contrast, for Arendt, truth in its "*mode of asserting validity* . . . carries within itself an element of coercion."[20] Confronted with a claim to truth, even a posteriori, historical truth, my assent is demanded, not "wooed" from me.[21] Arendt would seem to be influenced here by her immersion in ancient Greek philosophy, and, for all of her criticisms of Aristotle, the distinction she makes between knowledge and necessity on the one hand and opinion and contingency on the other bears striking similarities to that established by him in the *Posterior Analytics*. It is less clear how closely it corresponds with our own experience. It may be true, to take Arendt's example of a factual, historical truth, that the statement "In August 1914 Germany invaded Belgium" is, "once perceived as true and pronounced to be so, . . . beyond agreement, dispute, opinion, or consent"—though I imagine some historians might well argue the niceties of the point.[22] But it seems a misuse of the word to describe this as *coercion*. In what way am I constrained by or in my acceptance of this truth? And if this is constraint, what would my freedom look like? Presumably it would involve my being able to "dispute" and hence "consent" to the statement. But in general, when I do disagree with truth-claims, I do (or at least can) contest them. And when I do not, I do not. Hence any freedom lacking here would seem to be my ability to do what I don't want to do.[23] Unless, that is, Arendt is thinking of cases where we grudgingly agree to the truth of a given statement: "I have to admit, many of my fellow citizens believe that the Second Amendment guarantees an individual who is unaffili-ated with any 'well-regulated militia' the right to own and openly carry sub-automatic weaponry." But it seems more accurate here to say that the world is not as I would wish it to be, than to say that the *statement* "Many of my fellow citizens believe that the Second Amendment guarantees . . . the right to own and openly carry subautomatic weaponry" coerces me. Even if that particular ("constative") statement were not uttered, I would still be depressed.

Arendt seems to assume that the free expression of our perspectives and opinions on the world precludes any (political) appeal to truth. But does it? No doubt, we will sometimes exchange opinions in Arendt's sense without ap-pealing to standards of truth or falsity. But it is difficult to imagine a sustained serious discussion of political matters like the Mexican-American War or the Vietnam War or the second Iraq War that entirely refrained from such an ap-peal, or that became coercive for that reason.[24] The appeal to objective truth is opposed to dogmatism as well as skepticism.[25] Because truth is determined by what is the case, where what is the case is in most instances independent of any particular individual's will, anyone making claims that purport to be true can be wrong. Hence my commitment to truth is a commitment to a situation in which others judge my claims as I judge theirs. This is not authoritarian, or coercive, but egalitarian.[26] If, for example, I claim that North Vietnamese forces launched an unprovoked attack upon an American warship in the Tonkin Gulf, and there is no external constraint upon you (I am not in a position to threaten your job, place you under government surveillance, etc.), the claim as such does nothing to coerce you, but stands there awaiting your objections. *I* may mislead you, and by doing so undermine your freedom, but the sentence does not. If in modern representative politics we did not make and contest such claims, and take care to make them accurate, it is impossible to see how we might govern ourselves—though easy perhaps to see how others might rule us. As Bernard Williams reminds us, dishonesty in a democracy undermines the freedom of those who are addressed and manipulated: "Democracy (in its modern, consti-tutional, forms) is valued, to an important extent, in the name of liberty. . . . The falsification or suppression of information is an important limitation of liberty in itself and impedes the exercise of liberty in many areas. . . . Liberties . . . get their point, in good part, from the possibility of effective action, which implies true information."[27] It is simply impossible for democratic citizens to rule themselves and achieve (political) autonomy if they are manipulated and lied to by the people who act (and, often, gather information) in their name. Truth is of fundamental importance to a democratic polity, and dishonesty is not something that can be taken lightly.

And yet, as we have seen, it often is, both by political theorists and by citizens in general. I suggested above that one reason we as political theorists might fail to adequately attend to the importance of truth in politics is a commitment to a rhetorical, agonistic politics that embraces skepticism. If politics is not a matter of rational (parliamentary) disputation but of agonistic struggle, we are better off abandoning the vain attempt to ground political movements in a universalizable, rational account of the (post-)Kantian free will. Democratic politics should accept that the values and relations by which it identifies itself are, of necessity, particular and contestable: democratic politics is the politics of the *demos*, the people, not of aristocrats, monarchists, or fascists. And the differences between these camps or, better, political identities, are not ones that can be rationally eluded or negotiated. Politics is essentially a matter of conflict, and the sooner democratic activists and theorists recognize this, the sooner they can begin to meaningfully engage with their opponents. The acceptance of this position does not of itself determine one's attitude toward politically motivated dishonesty. Indeed I imagine that most of its proponents are as disgusted as I am when they recall Polk's and McNamara's and Cheney's dishonest manipulating of the American people into war. However, we should recognize that the turn away from political rationalism to a politics of conflicting identities and value systems hardly encourages a sustained attempt to consider the importance of "truth telling" for politics. Hence, to take a prominent example of a theorist advancing this sort of position, when Ernesto Laclau writes an article on discourse for the Blackwell *Companion to Contemporary Political Philosophy*, the word "truth" does not even appear.[28] And when he and his erstwhile coauthor, Chantal Mouffe, describe their central concept of *antagonism* as an *experience* and *discursive form* "in which what is manifested is . . . the final impossibility of . . . any 'objectivity,'"[29] one can conclude that the prospects for truth in politics will be fairly bleak. If objectivity is impossible, what sort of truth can we have?

Objectivity is here said to be impossible because there are no absolute foundations to our political claims. There is always another tortoise under the elephant, another opportunity to ask "Why?" to any given justification. In the end, one must simply *decide*. What is crucial is to maintain the freedom for people to decide for themselves. In Laclau and Mouffe's view, such freedom will never achieve the purity of autonomy, as any decision is made in conditions of historical struggle to achieve or maintain hegemony that limit the various options available. But freedom remains the focus—as in classical liberalism, which also takes as a primary concern the securing of the liberty of citizens to pursue their own good in their own way. Poststructuralism's antifoundational argument fits naturally with those forms of philosophical skepticism that undermine the possibility of demonstrating the superiority of one political choice over another. (It is not for nothing that Derrida's enormously influential "Force of Law" essay takes its subtitle from [Pascal's consideration of] Montaigne's skeptical reflections on the customary, contingent nature of legal justice.)[30] Though skepticism is often taken to be a conservative philosophical position implying, as it does, that there are no knowable grounds for opposing the status quo, when it is coupled with a modern emphasis on self-expression and self-assertion it quickly takes on a more radical, voluntarist valence.

The connection between poststructuralist political theory and skepticism is perhaps clearer in the case of Mouffe than of Laclau. Indeed, Mouffe is a particularly instructive example of a political theorist confronting the choice, sketched out above, between the agonistic conflict of a rhetorical politics and the attempt to regulate the politics of opinion by appeal to truth. Although she, like most poststructuralist theorists, usually phrases her arguments in ontological rather than metaphysical, semantic, or epistemological terms, she points toward a connection between the ontological and the epistemological when she accepts Claude LeFort's suggestion that the advent of modern democracy is "made possible" by "'the dissolution of the markers of certainty.'"[31] This liberating dissolution allows for and encourages an emphasis on passion, affect, and practices. Mouffe enlists Wittgenstein in this regard, arguing that the political significance of his later work is that it allows us to justify and understand this move from certain knowledge to passionate practice. "Wittgenstein's very important contribution to the elaboration of a non-rationalistic approach to political theory" is to help us see that politics is a matter of ways of living that cannot be reduced to a commitment to either the truth of any set of propositions or a set of procedures that sort out propositions into acceptable and unacceptable classes.[32] In Wittgenstein's late engagement with skepticism, "we find," she says, "many insights which can be used to envisage how allegiance to democratic values is created not through rational argumentation but through an ensemble of language-games which construct democratic forms of individuality. Against the current search . . . for a legitimacy that would be grounded on rationality, Wittgenstein's view that agreement is reached through participation in common forms of life, as a form of '*Einstimmung*' and not '*Einverstand*,' represents a path-breaking perspective."[33] Mouffe's celebration of political conflict "puts the emphasis on the types of *practices* [defining different political groups] and not the forms of *argumentation*." Deliberative democrats who emphasize political argumentation are not just inadequate, but actually "*counterproductive*."[34] I have already argued that Arendt is wrong to suggest that the appeal to truth in political contexts is coercive or destructive of those contexts. But Mouffe's appeal to Wittgenstein enlists one of the most important voices in contemporary philosophy, and her engagement with his antifoundationalism introduces epistemological questions much more subtle than those canvassed above. At the same time, it sharply highlights the issues that concern us, presenting us with theoretical contrasts that are more decisively distinguished than is often the case. For these reasons, and because of Mouffe's own very considerable importance as a democratic theorist and the extensive influence she has upon other political theorists, it will be worth our while to evaluate how well her position satisfies either the criteria of the Wittgensteinian position she celebrates or the exigencies of political life. Given the complexity both of Mouffe's own position and of her appropriation of Wittgenstein, doing so will require a detailed analysis that shall largely occupy us from here on.

*   *   *

In her most sustained discussion of Wittgenstein, the chapter "Wittgenstein, Political Theory and Democracy" from *The Democratic Paradox*, Mouffe focuses on the late notes collected in the posthumously published volume, *On Certainty*.[35] As their title suggests, Wittgenstein's topic in these notes is the concept of certainty, not the related but distinct concept of the rationality of discourse. I infer from the fact that Mouffe nonetheless takes Wittgenstein's arguments to support her own that she accepts the connection I have made between these two concepts. While Mouffe's focus is on the question of "how allegiance to democratic values is created," the fact that she takes inspiration from Wittgenstein's account of skeptical, philosophical debate and language use in general means that her account of this fairly specific point will rest upon a more general account of how statements come to be accepted as being true. In turning to Wittgenstein as she does, Mouffe implies that the question of political identity formation and attachment is a species of this larger genus. Hence, though she does not speak of truth, falsity, and honesty, this does not imply that these concepts are irrelevant to her political theory, but that they are unimportant in it—a quite significant difference.

Mouffe focuses on two passages from *On Certainty* that are among the most widely cited by political theorists, paragraphs 611 and 612: "When two principles really do meet which cannot be reconciled with one another, then each man declares the other a fool and a heretic." And "I said I would 'combat' the other man—but wouldn't I give him *reasons*? Certainly: but how far would they go? At the end of reasons comes *persuasion*."[36] The apparent implication, and the inference Mouffe draws, is that Wittgenstein supports, if not embraces, a brand of political disputation in which conflicting views confront one another without any possibility of rational adjudication. As Mouffe writes immediately before citing these lines, repeating the claim from the volume's introduction cited above, "Agreement is established not on significations (*Meinungen*) but on forms of life (*Lebensform* [*sic*]). It is *Einstimmung*, fusion of voices made possible by a common form of life, not *Einverstand*, product of reason—like in Habermas."[37] Mouffe's repeated references to Carl Schmitt's views on the need for political homogeneity are the obvious reference to the notion of the "fusion of voices."[38] Equally clearly, the collapse of *Einverstand* into *Einstimmung* and of reason into persuasion (*Überredung*) means that "truth telling" will have little independent claim upon us as a political virtue.

Less obvious is the care with which Mouffe presents this Wittgensteinian endorsement of her conception of "the political." Without indicating why, or even that she has done so, each time she cites these lines she cuts out the last line of *On Certainty* 612, which reads, "(Think what happens when missionaries convert natives)."[39] Given her desire to appropriate Wittgenstein for political and political theoretic purposes, one might think she would enthusiastically embrace this rare reference on his part to politics. The reason she does not has everything to do with the nature of the reference: it is hard to imagine how one might portray "the fusion of voices" of missionary work in, for example, the conquest of the Americas as exemplary or indicative of the nature of "the political" as such. This would have the effect of conflating the encounter between fellow citizens with that between missionary and "native," silently rendering all "ordinary" politics extraordinary. It is no coincidence that it is precisely this that characterizes the tradition of political thought within which Mouffe operates. Just as Machiavelli and Hobbes take extraordinary events—the coup d'état and civil war, respectively—and place them at the center of their political thought, so Schmitt, upon whom Mouffe draws so heavily, asserts the primacy of the decision on the exception over the rule of the normal.[40] Embracing Wittgenstein's example would not just make this explicit, but point as well to the unattractive consequences that follow from it. Hence Mouffe's silent omission of these lines.

Nor is this the only omission Mouffe has made. In the lines she cites, Wittgenstein writes, "I said I would 'combat' the other man." Mouffe does not indicate when Wittgenstein said this, nor in what circumstances he did so. This is not surprising. Wittgenstein is referring back to *On Certainty* 608 and 609:

Is it wrong for me to be guided in my actions by the propositions of physics? Am I to say I have no good ground for doing so? Isn't precisely this what we call a "good ground"?

Supposing we met people who did not regard that as a telling reason. Now, how do we imagine this? Instead of the physicist, they consult an oracle. (And for that we consider them primitive.) Is it wrong for them to consult an oracle and be guided by it?—If we call this "wrong" aren't we using our language-game as a base from which to *combat* [*bekämpfen*] theirs?

Here again we see the extreme nature of the dispute Wittgenstein is imagining—a dispute Mouffe seeks to present as exemplary of politics as conducted between fellow citizens. Are we really to believe that a Mouffe-style radical democrat's debate with a conservative fellow citizen is structurally the same as that between someone who accepts the authority of modern physics and someone who does not? I don't mean to deny that this *may* sometimes be the case. Indeed we may come to such a pass all too soon, and those Americans who deny the reality of human evolution on the grounds of biblical revelation and who seek to impose their belief in the literal truth of the book of Genesis upon our children may well be harbingers of a conflict such as that described by Wittgenstein. But to suggest that this is run-of-the-mill politics would deny the crisis toward which American politics sometimes seems to be heading.[41] Recognizing the depth of this potential crisis requires acknowledging that this sort of challenge to the theory of human evolution is a challenge to the authority of science, not an intrascientific debate between the advocates of alternative scientific theories.[42]

It might seem that Wittgenstein disagrees with this when he notes in *On Certainty* that some very well-educated people still believe in the biblical story of creation.[43] Does this not point toward a conflict that education and science can neither foreclose nor resolve, and that determines their real meaning? But Wittgenstein's recognition of the evident fact that some well-educated people are devout Christians hardly commits him to the view that the biblical story that God created man in His image on the sixth day is an alternative *scientific account* with a research agenda centering on testable hypotheses. This is perhaps clearer in his "Remarks on Frazer's *Golden Bough*," where he argues that anthropologists (and scholars such as James Frazer who follow them) have an arrogant and impoverished view of "primitive" societies. His point here is not that such societies are practicing their own form of science, which is as good as ours. Indeed quite the opposite: he is adamant that though worthy of respect, such foreign cultures are *not* scientific and are not *trying* to be so. Frazer's central error, on Wittgenstein's account, is to present "the magical and religious notions of men . . . as mistakes [*Irrtümer*]," as if religion and magic were primitive and inadequate forms of science and technology.[44] In *On Certainty* he returns to the question of what can and cannot count as a mistake and asks, "Can we say: a mistake [*Irrtum*] doesn't only have a cause, it also has a ground? I.e., roughly: when someone makes a mistake, this can be fitted into what he knows aright." And later he gives an example of an error that is *not* a mistake: "If I believe that I am sitting in my room when I am not, then I shall not be said to have *made a mistake* [*mich geirrt*]."[45] To be in the grip of this sort of delusion is something quite different from, say, getting lost in downtown Philadelphia because one mistook Walnut Street for Chestnut Street.

Mouffe writes as if Wittgenstein claimed that all of our beliefs were neither true nor false—something he plainly denies.[46] On her account, what I believe looks like a matter of my choice, as if I could *decide* on the question.[47] And it is true that in *On Certainty* 362 Wittgenstein asks, "Doesn't it come out here that knowledge is related to a decision?" Indeed we find something similar in the *Philosophical Investigations*: "'What you are saying, then, comes to this: a new insight—intuition—is needed at every step to carry out the order "+n" correctly."—To carry it out correctly! How is it decided what is the right step to take at any particular stage? . . . It would almost be more correct to say, not that an intuition was needed at every stage, but that a new decision was needed at every stage."[48] But Wittgenstein returns to this question less than ten pages later and undercuts this initial "decisionist" account: "'But this initial segment of a series obviously admitted of various interpretations (e.g. by means of algebraic expressions) and so you must first have chosen *one* such interpretation.'—Not at all. A doubt was possible in certain circumstances. But that is not to say that I did doubt, or even could doubt."[49] Moreover, even in the cases under consideration, what is being chosen is at best a move that alters as it applies an existing rule, not a form of life as such. The model whereby forms of life or systems of reference are themselves objects of choice fits better with the positivist picture than it does with Wittgenstein's postpositivism, as Michael Williams argues in *Unnatural Doubts: Epistemological Realism and the Basis of Scepticism*:

> In important ways Wittgenstein differs from Carnap. For example, he does not suppose that we *decide* to talk about physical objects. This is surely correct: our way of looking at the world is the "inherited background" against which we distinguish between the true and the false, not something we picked out of a range of alternatives [referring to *On Certainty* 94, cited above]. Indeed, Carnap's view borders on paradox: for what "framework" are we thinking in when we decide between competing frameworks, pragmatically or otherwise? Wittgenstein's does not: if the framework totters, our ability to think goes with it.[50]

When the world totters we may be open to adopting new and different ways of being. At those times we may be said in some sense not to know what is true and what is false—to live, as it were, beyond truth and falsity. It is unlikely that this shall be so across the board. As Williams emphasizes, even the choice, such as it is, for a new framework must be made on the basis of the form of life we now occupy and within which things are true and false. Wittgenstein characterizes change between forms of life as different as a society resting upon practices of magic and a society resting upon modern science as a "conversion."[51] It is here that persuasion (*Überredung*) as opposed to conviction (*Überzeugung*) is appropriate—not, as Mouffe implies, in quite ordinary political disagreements.

In Wittgenstein's example of a conflict between those who accept modern physics and those who reject it in favor of a system allowing for divination by oracles, the *practices*, and not just the opinions, of the parties differ radically.[52] Mouffe uses Wittgenstein's language of conversion to describe "a radical change in political identity."[53] She does so because she assumes that differences between political identities are best understood as different practices, forms of life.[54] It is not clear that this is consistent with Wittgenstein's conception of forms of life, or what it would even mean. Wittgenstein says famously that "to imagine a language is to imagine a form of life."[55] Do Americans of different political persuasions speak different languages in anything but a metaphoric sense? Clearly, something like this will be true only in cases of radical differences, and perhaps only of radical parties. But what about when we reach different answers to questions like the following: In the end, doesn't security trump liberty? In time of war, do we really have time for extended debate on the issues by the legislature as opposed to "efficient," quick executive decisions? Doesn't the Constitution guarantee free speech for everyone, including international corporations? Is our society united around a shared common good, or is it an aggregation of individual property owners who share little more than the common use of the government to protect their property rights? Ought we to tax the rich or the poor, or to abandon social security? Is decent health care in a prosperous modern society a right or a privilege? It is such choices, made as they are in particular circumstances, that will determine the strength and nature of our commitment to democratic values. And the answers to them neither depend upon nor imply the "fact" that the differing parties speak different languages or differ in their practices so radically that we could speak of them occupying different forms of life. Mouffe blurs the distinctions here when she describes "allegiance to democracy" as being "more in the nature of what Wittgenstein likens to 'a passionate commitment to a system of reference. Hence, although it's belief, it is really a way of living, or of assessing one's life.'"[56] Mouffe does not alert her reader to the fact that these lines from the posthumous *Culture and Value* are a tentative appraisal of "a religious belief [*ein religiöser Glaube*]."[57] It is true that some political movements have the force of religious conviction. It is hardly meaningless to speak of political theology. But not all politics is political theology, and, *pace* Mouffe, Wittgenstein gives us little reason to think it is.

Mouffe is quite right that our political allegiances are often influenced by a broader sense of who we are. For instance, it is clear that many people in America did not mind being misled by Bush in part because they felt that Bush was *one of them*. As John Micklethwait and Adrian Woolridge make clear in their sympathetic account of the modern right in America, Bush's success in selling the war on Iraq owed much to the fact that his moralism, unilateralism, and insistence on a decisive response to 9/11 chimed with already present propensities in the American right.[58] This cuts both ways, though: consider *why* Bush and Cheney sought to convince Americans that Iraq was involved in the attacks of September 11 and that it directly threatened America with weapons of mass destruction. It is in part at least because people believed claims such as these (as opposed to simply "share perspectives such as these") that they identified with Bush and Cheney and with the particular image of America they promote.[59] Indeed few people, if any, ever directly ask themselves, "Shall I be a democrat or not?" It simply isn't that kind of question.[60] The questions that people *do* ask, such as those listed earlier, may perhaps simply be "decided upon." But more often they will be appraised at least in part on the basis of the facts of the matter. Here questions of truth and falsity are unavoidable. Mouffe's critique of "political rationalism" leaves almost no room for this practice. She aims to show that, contra Rawls and Habermas, liberal democracy is not "the model that would be chosen by every individual in idealized conditions."[61] But though she refers regularly to the idea of *practice*, there is no account of the actual practices in less than ideal conditions whereby people develop a commitment to political ideals and institutions, or of the questions that are raised there. This accounts for the fact that, as James Wiley has correctly noted, in her focus of the conflict between different political identities and views Mouffe appears to "forget that the goal is not so much to 'convert' opponents, as it is to persuade third parties which side to believe."[62]

Mouffe's version of democracy shares a widespread assumption that democracy is purely a matter of will and the identity of the will. This leaves her and those who follow her with few options when it comes to identifying sites where the *demos* of a modern nation state might express itself. Consider in this regard Gopal Balakrishnan's account of the way Schmitt might aid "radical democrats." On his account, as on Mouffe's, who "the people" are is itself the subject of an ongoing antagonistic struggle for hegemony, and not something that might be defined independently: "It is only in the struggle between parties vying for hegemony over 'the people' that the latter is mobilized as an agent, and becomes something more than the empty signifier of an imagined community." This struggle needs to be publicly enacted for the people to be constituted and to express itself. "Schmitt suggested that a political system is authentically democratic to the extent that it is open to periodic 'emergencies' in which people can swing into action as an independent legislative power. Demonstrations, gigantic rallies and general strikes are events which keep alive, and in motion, the original constituent power of the people. Democracy takes on its real meaning in the exceptional situation."[63] "Gigantic rallies," however, are not hopeful sites for reasoned deliberation in which the *demos* sorts out true and false claims. At the very least this suggests that the sort of radical democracy for which Balakrishnan calls will be largely incapable of effectively governing itself or of distinguishing when a war is truly necessary and/or in its interest.[64] Indeed even in those cases where various groups simply have to "fight it out," fighting it out will obviously cover a lot of very different things, from zero-sum political conflict to civil war, but in no case will truth be of no value whatsoever. As the wars in Vietnam and Iraq remind us, even in the case of war there needs to be sufficient knowledge of the facts of the matter to avoid catastrophic error.[65] Here too our various claims must be as accurate as possible. In part for this reason, "gigantic rallies" are often organized and led by elites.

Mouffe is, as I noted above, an extreme example. While theorists such as Richard Rorty, Stanley Fish, and Paul Feyerabend echo her mix of untempered skepticism and leftist politics, other theorists of agonistic democracy such as William Connolly and Bonnie Honig are hardly as dismissive of the necessary role played by truth and its virtues in a healthy deliberative polity in which different policies and conceptions of life, justice, and freedom contest one another.[66] That said, one does not find extended discussions in their work of that role or of the institutions that make it possible, such as the press, public education, and the academy.[67] One can hardly fault someone for what he or she did not write. But the worry is that, in our anxiety to avoid the dangers of an overly rationalistic politics and a naïve positivist celebration of technique and scientific expertise, we have left ourselves poorly positioned to appreciate the nature of the challenges democratic politics now face. While we clearly need, say, the ethic of generosity for which Connolly calls, we also need to recognize that neither public deliberation nor individual judgment can effectively guide us in the absence of a shared commitment to truth. The lies told by American politicians are not, as Mouffe suggests, legitimate moves in the democratic contest for influence and self-expression, but threats to the health of that contest. If we are shy about asserting this, it may be because we focus on the ways the appeal to truth has been abused, and attribute that abuse to that appeal. Appeals to truth and scientific inquiry are hardly absent from the history of racism, colonialism, or sexism. But the problem with, say, the Tuskegee Syphilis Study was not with science or the pursuit of truth, but with the disgusting lack of concern with the rights and well-being of the men who were allowed to languish under the effects of a disease that might have been treated.[68] That truth is a value and that a tempered respect for the independence of scientific inquiry helps preserve it hardly implies that there are not other values, or that they might sometimes trump that of truth. Likewise, the fact that appeals to truth are often bound up with an arrogant, overbearingly proprietary moralism does not imply that it is arrogant or moralistic to appeal to truth.[69] Contra Mouffe, a democratic will is a complicated, mediated thing, requiring not just solidarity and passionate commitment, but also honest and truthful deliberation and the institutions that make such deliberation possible. In dangerous times like our own, this is something that we, as citizens and as political theorists, neglect at our peril.[70]

Chapter 6

Democracy as a Space of Reasons

Michael P. Lynch

The Space of Reasons

A familiar complaint by those who defend creationism is that the opposition's views are no more or less founded on reason than their own. Science, the thought goes, rests on its own principles, unproven "yet Sovereign," as Cardinal Newman once put it. If there is a point here, it is this: scientific opposition to teaching biblical stories of creation in schools naturally assumes scientific standards of justification. Those standards can themselves be open to question. Using scientific standards to defend them would be circular. Consequently, it would seem that we must admit that science itself rests on some assumptions not scientifically proven. And this, some believe, licenses the conclusion that rationally speaking, science is no better off than the Bible.

There are numerous problems with this argument, not the least of which is that the conclusion does not follow from the premises. But the point I am interested in at the moment is not the argument's flaws but its implicit structure. Its form is essentially that of the ancient skeptical problem of the criterion, which runs like this: Any claim of knowledge assumes some rational standard, some criterion, some method for sorting truth from falsehood. But how do we know the assumed standard is correct? Appealing to the same standard is circular, but appealing to another standard won't help—for the same question will arise again. Reasons require standards, and standards require reasons.

From these premises the ancient skeptics concluded that we could never know anything. We moderns and postmoderns have been more sanguine. We are more inclined to simply accept that "justification comes to an end," as Wittgenstein puts it, so that we are left with what Hume called Custom and Habit, with the way things have always been done. This appeals to our sense of ourselves as realistic and practical, as it suggests that the proper response to skeptical arguments is to acknowledge the groundlessness of our believing, roll up our sleeves, and go on from there.

But go where, exactly? In the face of a skeptical challenge to provide a noncircular defense of our standards, it sometimes seems as if we have a choice of only two directions: either accept that all standards of truth are equally valid, or plant your flag, declare that there is an objective standard (your own, naturally), but admit that reason is never going to reveal what it is.

Skepticism is sometimes discussed by philosophers as if it were an abstract mathematical problem, free from the taint of any practical matter. But as the debate over creationism illustrates, skeptical arguments have a long history of being used as weapons in political debates and subsequently in debates over political theory. In particular, skeptical arguments continue to play a foundational role in opposition, from both the left and the right, to a conception of democratic politics according to which, as I'll put it, democracy is a space of reasons.[1]

To say that democracy is a space of reasons is to say that the practice of democratic politics requires the practice of giving and acting for reasons. That is, in the democratic state, disagreements between citizens ought to be handled in the arena of reason alone, and arguments legitimizing uses of state power must be backed by reasons. And crucially, the "reasons" spoken of must, where possible, include reasons for believing what is true, as opposed to including only reasons for believing what will win us the election, make us rich, or damn our enemies. In short, to think of democracy as a space of reasons is to see the ideals of democratic politics as requiring a commitment to the rational pursuit of the truth.

Many have come to think that this conception of democratic politics is naïve or incoherent. I think it is neither. As I see it, the idea that democracy is a space of reasons is integral to the very idea of democratic politics. In this essay I defend this idea from two objections that naturally arise from our contemporary responses to skepticism. Broadly speaking, one objection emerges from the political right, and the other from the left. Yet they have more in common than they at first appear. The two objections are not only motivated by a similar skeptical stance, but each leads to a similar result: to justify a profoundly undemocratic form of dogmatism.

Reason as a Poor Guide

It is one of the little ironies of history that skeptical arguments are rarely more popular than with true believers. As Richard Popkin and Terence Penelhum have demonstrated, skeptical arguments have a long history of being used to support conservative religious and political viewpoints.[2] A particularly striking illustration of this is the Anti-Reformation writing of Montaigne, who saw ancient skeptical arguments as showing that it is best to accept without argument the prevailing tradition of one's community (Catholicism in his case). What we learn from the problem of the criterion, Montaigne argued, is that "man's plague is the belief that he has knowledge. That is why ignorance is so highly recommended by our religion as appropriate for belief and obedience."[3] Human reason, he insisted, was stained and flawed; it could not be trusted: "There cannot be any principles for men, unless the Divinity has revealed those principles to them; all the rest . . . is nothing but dreams and smoke. For those who argue by presuppositions, one must suppose, on the contrary, the very axiom about which one is arguing."[4] Montaigne was hardly alone in thinking that reason should be replaced by faith. As Pierre Bayle would put it, a century after Montaigne and in a very different political and religious context, reason is a "guide that leads one astray. . . . It can be compared to some powders that are so corrosive that, after they have eaten away the infected flesh of a wound, they then devour the living flesh, rot the bones and penetrate the very marrow."[5]

Montaigne's point is that skepticism shows us not that we know nothing, but that we don't know anything through reason. Only through unreasoned acceptance of a set of standards does salvation, not just spiritual, but political salvation, lie. The political worry, voiced explicitly by Montaigne, is that the way of reason leads only to strife and discord. Peace is possible only if man goes about "abandoning and renouncing his own means, and letting himself be raised and lifted up by purely celestial ones."[6]

This brings us to the first of the two promised objections to the idea that democracy is a space of reasons. Deliberately simplified, it is this: If reason, as Bayle believes, is a poor guide that always leads us astray from the truth, then basing one's political system on reason alone is not only unwise, it is impossible; the game of giving reasons can never be freed from an unreasoned foundation. Like it or not—and we might as well like it—we must accept some standards on faith.

This general line of argument, particularly in a form in which the standards in question are ethical or religious in character, has had a wide impact on conservative political thought. Yet importantly, both Montaigne and Bayle were not just talking about ethical standards; they were also talking about our epistemic standards, our standards for determining whether a belief is true or false. The popular defense of creation science mentioned above is an example of this thought in action. The creationist wishes to cast skeptical doubt on the reliability of the scientific method by pointing out that the scientist too must suppose "the very axiom about which [he] is arguing." Consequently, the scientific and creationist views are on a par, epistemically speaking. We have to accept either standard on faith.

Yet the conclusion of the argument raises an obvious question: If we have to just accept some standards on faith, which standards do we accept? Montaigne's answer, echoed in various ways and to various degrees by Burke, Hayek, and Oakeshott, is to trust in the calming authority of tradition. Trust the standards inherited from the past.

There are a number of things one might say about the suggestion that tradition is the ultimate arbiter of standards. Here I will be concerned only with epistemic standards, and I will limit my remarks to the following simple argument: The unreasoned acceptance of how things have always been done is dogmatism by another name. Dogmatism is undemocratic. So the idea that tradition is an ultimate epistemic arbiter has no place in democratic politics.

Prior to elaborating on this point, a few qualifications. First, the charge that dogmatism is undemocratic would hardly bother many, like Montaigne, who've made the above skeptical argument, simply because being democratic is not a value they share. But that view is not my present concern, which is not democratic politics, but a particular conception of it. Second, my complaint is not about the value of tradition. There is of course something to be said for tradition, for custom and habit. As social conservatives and progressive communitarians alike have noted, traditional ways of doing things may well embody the collective wisdom of generations. And a defense of tradition needn't be dogmatic in character; Montaigne's, for example, ultimately was not.

The issue isn't tradition, but the use of tradition as the ultimate epistemic arbiter. An ultimate epistemic arbiter is, first, a stopping point, an authority that all other epistemic reasons must obey. But second, it is itself not subject to epistemic appraisal. That is why it is an arbiter. An epistemic arbiter is an arbiter precisely because it sits outside of the epistemic game. Consequently, to treat tradition in this way, to see it as the nonepistemic ground for reasons, is to treat it as something that is beyond reason, as something that cannot be rationally assessed. And as just noted, the defender of the conservative skeptical argument crudely summarized above seemingly has no choice but to regard tradition in just this way. After all, the whole point of the skeptical argument is that skepticism shows us that every standard can be questioned, and thus ultimately we must appeal to something that is neither itself supported by reason nor needing defense against the complaints of reason. And that, surely, is dogmatism.

It is also a stance contrary to democratic politics, as the following elaboration of the simple argument demonstrates. To engage in democratic politics is to see one's fellow citizens as rational, autonomous agents worthy of equal respect under the law. Part of what it is to be an autonomous agent is to be capable of making judgments about what one ought to believe. Judgments about what one ought to believe are thus made on the basis of reasons. I fail to respect you as a fellow judge of what's true if I were to refuse to give you a reason for some claim against you should you ask for one. Likewise the state respects you less than it should if it were to refuse to give a reason for some use of political power. And crucially, the reasons in question cannot be reasons in the sense that my holding a gun to your head is reason for you to do what I want. Political claims on you cannot be ultimately or solely justified, in a democratic conception of politics, by simply wielding power, for again the imposition of a claim is not a justification for why it ought to be imposed. Rather, I should try, wherever possible, to give you reasons that my view of the facts is closer to the truth than your own. For where I could give you such reasons, but fail to do so, I fail to treat you as an autonomous, rational being capable of judging what to believe. Contrapositively, if I respect you as a fellow judge, I give you truth-conducive reasons when and where I can. Otherwise I may be preventing you from accessing the full evidence available and, in effect, even making the judgment for you. And in doing that, I do not respect your autonomy. In sum, to the degree that we cease giving reasons for our beliefs to each other, to the degree that we allow our disagreements to be resolved and our government decisions to be made without adequate reasons, to that degree we are ceasing to conceive of ourselves as equal participants in a democratic enterprise.[7]

As I see it, this argument, even in this simple form, is convincing against the idea that tradition should be treated as the ultimate epistemic arbiter. But there is more to say about the conservative attack on the idea that democracy is a space of reasons. So far we've criticized only the proffered alternative: the idea that tradition is the ultimate authority. We haven't yet dealt with the skeptical argument itself. Prior to doing so, it will be helpful to turn to the second of the two main objections to the idea that democracy is a space of reasons.

Consensus over Truth?

If the first objection is that reason is a poor guide, the second is that it is a fine guide, just not to the truth. The democratic space is a space of reasons, but reasons aimed at consensus.

There are several ways to reach this conclusion. First, one might argue that the reasons we give in political argument cannot be reasons for believing that some moral or political position is true, because to maintain the truth of one's position over another's is to violate the cardinal liberal principle of toleration. Thus our public reasoning ought to be aimed at consensus. Second, one might argue that true beliefs cannot be the aim of justification in any event, so the point is moot; consensus is the only aim available.

The first point is typically associated with Rawls's later period. It is motivated out of a direct confrontation with what Rawls himself called the paradox of public reason, the idea that the liberal cannot defend her own view by appeal to the "whole truth" and yet at the same time maintain that the government must tolerate, so far as possible, differing views of what sort of life is the best to lead.[8] This was a charge frequently leveled against Rawls's earlier work by communitarians from the left and conservatives from the right.[9] Rawls's response was to argue that the sort of reasons we must supply to each other in the democratic space are political, not "metaphysical" in character. Our purpose in giving such reasons is, at least in part, to produce an "overlapping consensus."[10] This goes for the liberal political philosopher as well as everyone else.

The overall nature of Rawls's view is of course exceedingly complex. I won't try to do it justice here, but will confine myself to a single point of Rawlsian political philosophy broadly conceived. That point is that, properly understood, aiming at consensus need not be inconsistent with aiming at the truth per se. Consequently, Rawlsian political theory is, at least in this respect, completely compatible with the idea that democracy is a space of reasons.

Rawls's point, crudely, is that in defending our political views, we should appeal only to those principles we all can accept. Note the "should": his point is clearly not that we cannot aim at the truth, nor that there is no such thing as objective truth at which to aim, but that the principle of toleration (together with the associated virtues of civility) require that democratic political justifications use premises that are widely accepted.

This of course makes a lot of sense. As Jean Hampton put it, "No matter what our religion, moral beliefs, or metaphysical commitments, if we are to work together in one system of cooperation, we have to have a 'common currency' for debating and settling disputes or our society will be in ruins."[11] Our political reasons must trade in that currency; that is, they must be given against a common background of standards against which we measure what counts as true and what counts as false. It is disrespectful, not to mention entirely ineffective, to try to convince someone to accept your claims by way of reasons he will not recognize as reasons. But of course this fact is entirely consistent with its being the case that the common reasons we all do recognize as reasons are reasons for thinking that some belief is true. In political argument, I ought to give reasons that others accept as reasons. But that does not require that those very reasons aim only at acceptance. After all, if acceptance is all that matters, there are many means more effective than reason. It is not "reasons" that I should be employing at all, but rhetoric, big sticks, and clever television ads. But that is not the Rawlsian's point. As I understand them, Rawlsians would be the first to endorse the sort of argument given at the end of the previous section: We need to appeal to reasons to justify our political views because only then do we respect each other as citizens, no matter what our different views on the good life. And if I respect you, I will endeavor to give you, where possible, reasons for believing what is true. When I do so, I treat you as an autonomous, rational agent as opposed to a tool to be manipulated. That in turn means that the principle of toleration, far from prescribing our aiming at the truth in political argument, supports it. Indeed that same principle, not to mention the practical facts, requires that the reasons we give to each other in civil discourse for believing that some proposition is true be reasons that most of us can recognize as reasons for believing it to be true. So it is not that truth isn't the ultimate aim of our practice of political justification; it is just that we limit the stock from which we draw.

In my view, then, the later Rawls does not provide an objection to the idea that the democratic space is a space of reasons in the sense of "reason" that aims at the truth. But given our discussion in the previous section, it might be thought that I've missed the forest for the trees. Might not the real issue for the Rawlsian liberal be not whether political reasons are aimed at consensus or truth, but her undefended reliance on her own conception of reason? The serious charge is that the liberal too is committed to her own faith: the faith in a particularly "scientific" standard of reason. For as the problem of the criterion seems to show, if the reasoner cannot give reasons for her standard of reason, she must admit that her worship of said standard is only that: worship of a standard accepted on faith. So she too must admit that reason always ends up standing on what is not reason, and therefore that the democratic space cannot be the space of reasons after all. Democracy is rather firmly within the sphere of faith.

Thus we find ourselves back at the first objection, as one might well have thought we would. For it is one thing to argue that democratic politics requires a common currency of rational standards; it is another thing to say what those standards are without begging some question or other.

The most direct way to answer this challenge would be to provide epistemic reasons for adopting our particular epistemic standards. Thus, in the style of Descartes, one might try supplying a "metastandard" for showing that some of our standards are more epistemically justified than others. Such a metastandard would serve as the self-securing foundation for all our other epistemic standards, and thus for our beliefs in general. Alternatively, one might, with the externalist, dismiss the skeptical argument as resting on an unwarranted assumption.[12] That is, one might dismiss the assumption that in order to be epistemically justified in employing an epistemic standard, one must be able to justify that standard by appeal to reasons. Perhaps it is enough that the standard be justified, whether or not we can justify it in the way demanded by the skeptic.

I will not attempt either sort of answer here. For even if neither answer were to work—that is, even if we cannot hope to give a noncircular epistemic reason for trusting some epistemic standards over others—that doesn't mean that there are no reasons of any sort to take some standards as among the common currency.

Indeed one might think that what one needs here are practical reasons, not epistemic or theoretical ones. After all, the question here is at root practical: Which standards of reason ought we to include among the common currency for our political discourse? Moreover, including an epistemic standard among the common currency of our political discourse presumably commits us to politically privileging that standard. To politically privilege a standard is to see it as worthy of being taught in the schools, institutionally protected, and assigned more weight in political discourse. These are practical matters.

As I see it, far from acting as an objection to the idea that democracy is a space of reasons, the Rawlsian framework suggests how we might approach this practical question. Call it the argument from the epistemic original position.

Imagine that we are charged with coming up with reasons for politically privileging some epistemic methods for forming beliefs over others in some society w. Candidates will include methods such as deduction, induction, sense perception, reading palms, and consulting sacred texts. Our deliberations must operate under the following constraints. First, we cannot, in our deliberations, presuppose that any method is more reliable for producing true beliefs than others in w. That is, we must operate under the assumption that consulting the sacred texts may well be as reliable a method of belief formation for the inhabitants of w as sense perception. In effect, our deliberations must take place under the assumption that skepticism is true: all methods for forming beliefs are as reliable as others because none is reliable. Second, just as we cannot, in our deliberations, assume that one method of belief-formation is more reliable than any other, so we cannot assume that one metaphysical picture of the world is any more accurate than others. By a "metaphysical picture" I mean, admittedly somewhat loosely, a view about the ultimate structure and nature of reality. Thus we cannot assume that, for example, naturalism is true, nor that, for example, Christian theism is true. Third, we know that we will eventually inhabit w. And fourth, we don't know all the methods we will—because of upbringing, education, religion, and so on—wish to employ ourselves in w.

Forced to come up with some reason to politically privilege some methods under these admittedly abstract constraints, it would seem to be in our self-interest to favor those methods that, to the greatest degree possible, are repeatable, adaptable, public, and widespread. Repeatable methods are those that in like cases produce like results. It would be in our interest to favor repeatable methods because such methods could be used over and over again by people with different social standings. Adaptable methods are those that can be employed on distinct kinds of problems and that produce results given a variety of kinds of inputs. It would be in our interest to favor such methods because we don't know what sort of problems we'll face in w. Public methods are those whose effectiveness could, in principle, be judged publicly; that is, it is not the case that only one person is its sole judge of effectiveness. It would be in our self-interest to favor public methods because we don't know if we'll be lucky enough to be that one person in w. Finally, widespread methods are those that many people can employ. It seems rational that we would privilege methods with these features simply because by doing so, we would maximize each of our chances to both use and assess the use of the privileged methods. In this sense, such methods could be called democratic.

But aren't we participants in the epistemic original position ourselves using various methods (such as a priori and causal reasoning) to arrive at our conclusion about w? Obviously we are, and we may be using other methods as well. But the situation described is not one where the participants are without epistemic methods, nor is it one where we (participants) must share epistemic methods. It is one where we are asked to decide, using whatever methods we have available and acting under the relevant constraints, which methods should be politically privileged in w. The methods that are so privileged are those that will form the content of our epistemic standards and principles.

One might object that the conservative skeptic was asking for some reason to believe that certain standards of reason are true. Our argument gives something else. It gives practical reasons for adopting some standards over others. Above, I replied that this may be the best we can do. But I think a stronger point is in the offing. Given the present dialectical situation, it is perhaps not only the best we can do; it is what we should do.

Our previous considerations led us to the conclusion that to engage in democratic politics, we must respect each other as fellow judges. And where we respect each other as fellow judges, we should, where possible, defend our claims both with reasons that we each recognize as reasons and with reasons aimed at the truth. In the present situation, the very issue at hand between the conservative skeptic and the liberal is whether reason (and in particular, certain standards of reason) can be employed in the service of truth. So to invoke those standards to give an argument for why those standards are truth-conducive would be to fail to employ reasons that the conservative skeptic would recognize as reasons.[13] If we are to satisfy the demand to respect each other as fellow judges, we should appeal to the common currency of our self-interest to justify why we should privilege certain standards. By doing so, we not only give reasons, but we give reasons that can be recognized as reasons. As I've already argued, this does not mean that we shouldn't also supply truth-conducive reasons for thinking that reason is truth-conducive. Nor does it undermine our claim that democracy requires that we respect each other as fellows judges of what is true and false. What it does mean is that, paradoxically, if we are to respect the skeptic as a fellow judge of the truth, we ought to appeal to reasons he recognizes as reasons, and because of that fact, here those reasons should not be reasons for judging something to be true.

I should also add that my point here is not to argue which specific methods would emerge from the epistemic original position, although I very much doubt that "consulting past customs" or "reading the sacred text" would be one. My point is that even in the face of skepticism, we can give reasons for conceiving of the democratic space as the space of reasons. The reasons are practical, not theoretical, but they are reasons all the same. If we are to treat each other as autonomous agents worthy of equal respect, we must engage in the process of giving and asking for reasons for what we ought to believe. And the reasons we employ—at least those we employ on the public stage—must be the result of methods that are themselves democratic in character. Where we don't give reasons for our beliefs, or where we use methods for producing reasons that are secretive and isolated, the province of only the few, we risk not only incoherence; we risk falling out of democratic space altogether.

The Unseen Target

Let's take stock. I've outlined two main objections to the idea that democracy is a space of reasons. The first is overtly skeptical: it maintains that because reasons always come to an end, politics, including democratic politics, must presuppose certain unreasoned standards. Thus in practicing democratic politics, even the liberal must presuppose certain standards, such as the very standards of reasoning she privileges in political argument. In reply, I've pointed out that we *can* give reasons for the standards of reasoning we privilege. Some standards are worth privileging simply because they are themselves democratic in character. Moreover the chief alternative— to simply accept some standards on faith and tradition—is itself deeply undemocratic.

The second objection accepts that democracy is a space of reasons, but rejects the idea that the reasons in question are reasons to believe what is true.

We've seen that Rawls's later work supplies no support for this idea. But as I mentioned above, there is another route to this objection.

According to Richard Rorty, the social practice of justifying our opinions to each other neither needs nor requires what he considered the "transcendent" goal of truth. The only thing that transcends a social practice, Rorty thinks, is another social practice. As such, it doesn't help to say that truth is the aim of such practices: "I know how to aim at greater honesty, greater charity, greater patience, greater inclusiveness and so on. I see democratic politics as serving such concrete, describable goals. But I do not see that it helps to add 'truth' . . . to our list of goals, for I do not see what we shall do differently if such additions are made."[14] Consequently, the question of truth is irrelevant to democratic politics. He explains, "The grounding premise of my argument is that you cannot aim at something, cannot work to get it, unless you can recognize it once you have got it. . . . We shall never know for sure whether a given belief is true, but we can be sure that nobody is presently able to summon up any residual objections to it, that everybody agrees that it ought to be held."[15]

As I understand it, Rorty's argument is essentially this: Truth cannot be the target of our justificatory practices—of inquiry, so to speak—because we can never know whether our beliefs are true. And a target we can't know whether we've hit is no target at all. Yet we can know whether "everybody agrees" with a belief. Therefore, agreement or consensus is the aim of inquiry, not truth.

The argument is curious on a number of fronts. First, why isn't it possible for me to know "for sure" whether my beliefs are true? The Pyrrhonian skeptical argument provides an explanation, but an explosive one. If that is the sort of skepticism that is driving Rorty's argument, it becomes even more curious why he thinks he can know for sure that "everybody agrees" that a certain belief ought to be held. What about this is so immune from doubt? Indeed for most beliefs that I am sure are true, I am not at all sure that everyone agrees they are true. After all, "everyone," even if it is just "everyone in my culture" or even "everyone in my culture who looks and speaks like me," includes quite a lot of folks. Figuring out that everyone agrees with me, or even would agree with me with regard to even the most mundane beliefs, is not easy.

But of course Rorty isn't playing the radical skeptic. The reason that Rorty thinks it is impossible to ever hit the target of truth is not because of skeptical interference but because the target itself is fundamentally flawed. His point is that the sense in which I and others think that truth is the goal of reason and justification must be a bloated, metaphysical, dubious sense of truth. It involves, as he elsewhere makes clear, a commitment to a looking-glass view of the mind, a view of the human according to which our thoughts, when correct, are mirrors of nature. In short, Rorty thinks that the conception of reason and justification I've been defending in this essay assumes an objectionable correspondence theory of truth. And his point is not just that we can't know whether our beliefs correspond to the world, but that this should show us that the entire notion of truth as correspondence is incoherent and unhelpful.

This is a better argument, more interesting and more plausible. But it is not persuasive. Two faults in particular stand out. The first is a semi-technical point about the viability of correspondence theories of truth. Rorty is correct, in my view, that traditional correspondence theories of truth are not viable. They take truth to be a relation between beliefs (or sentences) and facts, conceived of as entities over and above the more familiar objects and properties that populate our environment.[16] Such things seem metaphysically suspicious, made-to-order truth-makers for our beliefs. But one can keep the core thought behind correspondence theories without quantifying over facts. This is exactly what contemporary theories of mental representation do. According to such theories—the dominant paradigm in cognitive science—beliefs represent objects as having certain properties, where the "representation" in question is akin to the way a map represents the landscape. That representation is accurate (read: true) just when that belief does have that property. Beliefs are therefore true by virtue of how accurately they map the world around them, but that world is not a metaphysically mysterious world of "facts," but the world of mountains and molehills that we already know.

This theory of the mind is not so easy to dismiss, simply because of the success cognitive scientists enjoy employing it. Moreover it retains a core thought behind the traditional correspondence theory of truth, namely that true thoughts accurately represent the world.

The second fault with Rorty's argument is that the idea I'm here defending—that the practice of giving and asking for reasons is aimed at forming true beliefs—doesn't actually presuppose the correspondence theory or its contemporary cousin. It is, in fact, entirely consistent with a thinner definition of truth, according to which we don't need to do deep metaphysics to understand what makes a true belief different from a false one. Understanding what true beliefs are, on this view, involves simply understanding what they do, their role in our cognitive economy. True beliefs are those that play the true-belief role. Part of that role is being objective in a very obvious sense: To believe what is true is for things to be as one believes them to be (as opposed to being as one hopes they would be, for example). Another part of that role is to serve as the goal of our scientific and everyday inquiries: True beliefs are those that, other things being equal, we aim at when asking and answering questions. By grasping the role of true beliefs, one grasps the concept of truth. Metaphysics comes into play only when we ask what in fact plays the truth-role for particular kinds of beliefs, what properties particular kinds of beliefs must have to play the true belief-role. And importantly, it is entirely consistent with this conception that beliefs with very different properties might play that role. Some beliefs might play the role when they accurately represent the physical world; others might play the role when they cohere over the long run with our other beliefs. These are metaphysical matters that go beyond our ordinary understanding of truth.[17]

There is nothing in the conception of reason I've been employing in this essay that requires anything more than the functionalist view of truth just described. For the soul of that conception of reason is the simple idea that justification—reason-giving—aims at the formation of true beliefs, not the formation of beliefs "everyone agrees ought to be held." For even the thin functionalist definition I just gave implies that the set of true beliefs and the set of beliefs everyone agrees ought to be held need not be the same.

This brings us back to Rorty's curious argument. For once truth is understood in the more minimal, functionalist way, it is again no longer clear why we can't aim at believing what is true. Sure, if to be true, a belief must always mirror a mysterious world of mind-independent facts, we might raise our eyebrows. But this is not the sense of objectivity required. A belief is true, in the sense defined, just when things are as they are believed to be. And it is not clear why, independent of the general skepticism we've already dismissed as not in play here, I can't aim to have beliefs that are precisely of this sort.

Indeed it is difficult to see how we can avoid aiming at true beliefs in the functionalist sense. For when I aim to believe anything, including that "everyone agrees with me," to use Rorty's example, I aim to believe what is, not what seems to be. And the obvious reason for this is that there is a tight analytical relation between truth and belief. To believe that p, as opposed to hoping that p, or fearing that p, or doubting that p, just is is to hold it to be true that p. So insofar as I aim to believe, I aim to believe what is true. And again, one can make this point without having to buy into representationalism about belief.

All that is required is the humble platitude that to believe a proposition is to hold it to be true.

In discussing these matters, it is helpful to distinguish between the ultimate end or value that governs a practice and the more immediate aims that are justified in light of this ultimate value. The former is the light, however faint, by which the practice steers; the latter are the direct goals practitioners typically aim to achieve. In saying that true belief is a goal of inquiry, we take it to be an aim of inquiry in the first sense. One thing we can agree with Rorty about is that an individual inquirer rarely has anything so high-falutin as truth as a conscious aim in her everyday life. Even when she does, she cannot achieve that end directly. One does not simply will oneself to believe. Rather, we pursue truth indirectly, by pursuing evidence that supplies us with reasons for belief. Indirect or not, however, it is truth that supplies the point of this enterprise and that distinguishes it from merely pursuing that which will rally others to our cause or flatter our opinions. Reasons for a belief are reasons because they are means to the further end of truth. Thus justification—reason-giving—is distinct from truth precisely because it is a means to it.

Rorty sometimes seems to concede that there is a point here. But he thinks that all it amounts to is that "true" has what he calls a "cautionary" use. We use the word in this way, he says, to remind ourselves that what may be justified to one audience may not be justified to another, "to remind oneself that there might be . . . objections that have not yet occurred to anyone."[18] It is certainly good to remind ourselves of this fact. But the reason I think it is good is because some of those objections might turn out to be right—and my view may turn out to be wrong. Admitting that we can be wrong is admitting that what we believe is the case, and what we can justify to each other as the case, needn't be the case.

This is not how Rorty sees it. On his view, when we justify our political views—say, for example, when we argue that people of the same sex have a right to marry—we should not see ourselves as trying to argue for what is true. Rather, when using arguments that appeal to rights, we should see ourselves as identifying with a "community of like-minded persons—those who find it natural to act in a certain way."[19]

Yet come tomorrow, our like-minded friends may no longer be so like-minded. They may come to think that it is more useful to believe that we should start restricting what books people read, or the ideas they think. If so, then they will be justified in the Rortian sense in abandoning talk about rights. Such talk would no longer allow us to express our solidarity. Rorty would agree that this would be tragic, but that is all. It wouldn't be wrong except in the sense that he wouldn't agree with it. But this, I submit, is not what we have in mind when we talk of rights, nor is it what we have in mind whenever we offer arguments for our political views, whether they involve rights or not.

Concluding Observation

I began this essay by distinguishing two objections to the idea that a democracy is a space of reasons. My chief aim has been to refute these criticisms. But I'd like to conclude with a more general point: that, whatever their differences, the overall theoretical positions implicitly supported by those objections are markedly similar. And that, I think, should give us pause, not only because the positions in question are untenable but because it is a sign that something has gone gravely wrong in a debate when the extremists on either side end up agreeing with one another while still insisting on their disagreement.

Rorty's views on these matters, for example, are strikingly close in certain respects to those of the conservative skeptics discussed above. According to those skeptics, reason gives out and faith takes over. We have no choice, they say, but to dogmatically accept our own traditional first principles without having any tradition-independent reason for thinking they are more true than rival principles. Likewise Rorty. Rorty (honestly and bravely) describes his view as a "cheerful ethnocentrism" and remarks, "There is nothing to my use of the term 'reason' that could not be replaced by 'the way we Western liberals, the heirs of Socrates and the French Revolution conduct ourselves.' I agree with MacIntyre and Michael Kelly that all reasoning, both in physics and ethics, is tradition-bound."[20] Of course, Rorty might protest that unlike the conservative skeptics, he is not claiming that his liberal traditions can actually be known to be true by faith. But this seems to me a feeble protest if we are to take the idea that "reason" is just another word for "accepted by the tradition in which I live." It is a feeble protest because, as Rorty himself liked to say, a distinction that makes no difference is no distinction at all. And it is hard to see the practical difference between a defense of tradition based on faith and a defense of tradition based on, well, nothing. In both cases, we have given up on the open-minded pursuit of the truth, given up on reason, given up, we might say, on democracy.[21]

Chapter 7

Truth and Democracy: Theme and Variations

William A. Galston

Introduction: The Argument in Brief

All political systems need truth to some extent. Democracies need it in a special form—namely, easily available and widely dispersed. And they need it for a special reason: democracies cannot function without public trust, which depends on the public belief that officials are competent to ascertain relevant truth and committed to presenting it candidly. This does not means that democratic officials are always obligated to declare the truth, because doing so may sometimes undermine other important objectives, such as national security. It does mean that truth-telling enjoys a strong if occasionally rebuttable presumption.

Some of the truths relevant to practice are substantially context-independent and enjoy wide agreement. But many practical truths are hard to obtain, for two reasons above all. Some are embedded in contested theories (about the economy, for example), and others involve predictions about the effects of proposed policies on complex human systems. For both legal and deliberative purposes, therefore, some standard short of certainty is required. Our argument about where the bar should be set rests on values other than truth.

Two considerations complicate the relation between truth and democracy: truth does not trump democratic legitimacy, and democratic governments cannot dictate truth. A law enacted on the basis of false assumptions is not ipso facto illegitimate; conversely, no democratic government may intervene in processes of truth seeking to shape politically convenient findings.

*   *   *

"What is truth?" Pontius Pilate famously asked. We may argue among ourselves about the answer. But we are not permitted to be divided within ourselves. As individuals, we cannot rightly use one conception of truth for scholarly or artistic purposes and another in civic life.

Political Truth

What is the relation between truth and democracy? I approach this question from an unusual vantage point. Trained as an academic political theorist (a field in which I continue to participate), I have also spent considerable time in practical politics. For this reason, among others, I find it impossible to treat the relation between truth and democracy as a theoretical question. We, or at least I, must begin with practice and then attend to the theoretical issues that reflection on practice may raise. So let us begin where we are.

The Iraq War has done to postmodernist skepticism what the Vietnam War did to moral relativism. Four decades ago, academics and social critics discovered that they could not avoid making claims about what was right and wrong; today they have discovered the same thing about truth and falsehood. (Colbertian "truthiness" just isn't good enough when matters of life and death are at stake.) We can argue all we want about competing conceptions of truth and the criteria for assessing it. While we do, the proposition that "Iraq had weapons of mass destruction in 2003" will still be false.

The late Harold Pinter recognized this. He began his 2005 Nobel lecture by quoting something he wrote in 1958: "There are no hard distinctions between what is real and what is unreal, nor between what is true and what is false. A thing is not necessarily either true or false; it can be both true and false." Nearly five decades later, Pinter found himself forced to modify his position: "I believe that these assertions . . . do still apply to the exploration of reality through art. So as a writer I stand behind them but as a citizen I cannot. As a citizen I must ask: What is true? What is false?" In that spirit, he goes on to catalogue a number of factual claims used to justify the American invasion of Iraq, remarking after each, "It was not true."

At the end of this essay, I will contest the proposition that we can have one conception of truth as an artist (or philosopher) and a different one as a citizen. For current purposes, the key inference from the Iraq example is that at least some politically significant truth-claims are not embedded in fungible conceptual frameworks. Not all facts are "essentially contested." We share a commonsense conception of what "Iraq" means, and also of what constitutes a weapon of mass destruction. We can argue at the margin, of course. To explain why we found no WMD within the borders of Iraq, some observers suggested that Saddam Hussein's government had shipped them to Syria as tension with the United States mounted. If that claim had been verified, Iraq would have been guilty as charged, despite the fact that it had no chemical, biological, or nuclear weapons within its territory.

This is an easy case, to be sure, but hardly a trivial or unrepresentative one. In everyday political life, controversies often hinge on matters of fact: Did a public official tell X to fire Y? How many heroin addicts are there in a particular city? Did a public program reach its intended beneficiaries, or were the resources siphoned off by others along the way? Garden-variety factual propositions influence political power when they function as minor premises in practical syllogisms whose major premises are not in dispute. For example, a law may distinguish between permitted and forbidden grounds and procedures for firing an employee. In this context, the factual finding that an official ordered a subordinate to fire someone might warrant the conclusion that the official had acted wrongly and *ultra vires*.

Other kinds of empirical assertions are harder to evaluate. Consider a time-honored staple of education reform: We need better teachers. In the near-tautological sense—we need more teachers who can help students learn as well as the best teachers now do—the proposition is unimpeachable. Although it is true, it is not useful, because it lacks action-guiding force. Even if we agree on the standards for distinguishing better from worse teachers, we are as yet unable to specify the indicators or characteristics that we could use to pick them out before we hire them. The truths we need are at a lower level of abstraction.

This point is even more obvious when empirical assertions bring the distinction between concept and conception into play. We cannot assess propositions of the form "This war would be in the national interest" until we put a specific conception of the national interest on the table. If someone says "A more democratic world would be a world safer for America, and this war will help create a stable democracy in the heart of the Middle East," we are then in a position to assess a number of empirical assertions. What is the evidence that more democracy always, or usually, serves U.S. national interests? How sure are we that we can use force to plant democracy in these particular circumstances?

Even if empirical propositions are specific enough to be tested, it is by no means clear that we will be able to do so successfully. Assessing truth-claims that contain assertions about causal relations poses tremendous challenges. Still, political practice forces us to confront them. "What should we do?" is the core question of practical politics. The problem, which Aristotle was perhaps the first to explicate, is that answers to this question always rely on factual hypotheses whose validity is hard to assess ex ante. During the 1996 debate on welfare reform, Senator Daniel Patrick Moynihan, one of the Senate's leading experts on the subject, charged that we would have large numbers of children sleeping on heating grates if the proposal passed. If that prediction had turned out to be true, it would have constituted a compelling argument against the legislation. During the 2008 debate about shoring up the nation's financial system, critics of Treasury Secretary Henry Paulson's proposal said that it would not accomplish its intended purposes—again, a compelling reason (if true) not to use $700 billion in that manner. Although that intervention did stave off a possible collapse of the U.S. and global financial system, we still do not know whether it will enable us to avoid an extended period of Japanese-style stagnation in which weakened banks that keep devalued assets on their books are reluctant to make new loans.

The difficulty of assessment does not disappear if we ask, down the road, whether we should keep on doing what we previously decided to do. The easiest case is when the problem we set out to solve remains in full force. Clearly, what we are doing is not working, and the argument for changing course is potent. But it is not irresistible; it is always possible to argue that if we simply stay the course, our perseverance will be rewarded. At some point, the latter argument loses plausibility; after years of insisting that our strategy in Iraq was working or would work, President Bush conceded that it was time to try something different.

Consider another example: President Obama's economic program. Two facts are not in dispute: that it was designed in part to reduce unemployment, and that at this writing (August 2010) it has not yet done so. Everything else is vehemently contested. The program's supporters argue that without it, unemployment would have been much worse: the problem with the prescription was inadequate dosage, not the drug itself. Its detractors counter that the program rests on a flawed diagnosis and that increasing the dosage will only waste money and make things worse. Behind this controversy lie competing theories of how modern market economies grow and create jobs.

Interpreting success is often no easier. The question then becomes, What would happen if we stopped doing what we are now doing? To answer this question, we have no choice but to dig deeper in an effort to understand why events have taken a turn for the better. If the 2007–8 surge in Iraq succeeded only because American troops interposed themselves between hostile forces who remain implacably opposed to one another, then the odds are high that removing American forces will re-create the status quo ante. On the other hand, if the surge created a breathing space during which the Iraqi combatants moved toward a new modus vivendi, then the orderly phased withdrawal that President Obama is carrying out will leave recent gains more or less intact.

We cannot know for sure which of these theses in true. Indeed the demand for certainty is incompatible with the requirements of politics. In practical life there is no escaping the need to assess truth-claims on the basis of information and arguments that will leave us well short of certainty. In every situation there is a point of equipoise between the extremes of randomness and certainty at which further inquiry will not make us less uncertain, a point at which "look before you leap" shades over into the "paralysis of analysis." Unfortunately there is no algorithm that locates that point—one of many reasons why politics is an art rather than a science.

This uncertain relation to certainty affects not just politics, but every practice. In U.S. criminal law, the standard for conviction is a finding of guilt "beyond a reasonable doubt." Given the vagaries of evidence, this turns out to be a demanding criterion. And not by accident; because depriving the innocent of liberty or even life is regarded as a graver wrong than exonerating the guilty, the standard deliberately tilts toward underinclusion rather than overinclusion. In civil cases, by contrast, where property rather than life or liberty is usually at stake, the bar is set lower: not the absence of reasonable doubt but only the preponderance of the evidence is needed to find for one party against the other.

There are political analogues to the distinction between civil and criminal law. If the consequences of failure are unlikely to be grave, one might undertake a diplomatic initiative with only a modest empirical basis for optimism. But if the stakes are high, if the question is one of war and peace, or the death of thousands of individuals, or serious and widespread economic deprivation, then the evidentiary standard should be much more demanding. For example, the argument in favor of dropping atom bombs on Hiroshima and Nagasaki rested on two premises: the alternative was a land invasion of the Japanese home islands, which would have cost even more lives; and there was no other alternative that would have convinced the Japanese government to surrender. The counterargument was that if the United States had announced and then staged a demonstration of the bomb off the coast of Japan, the more reasonable elements of the imperial government would have seized the initiative and brought the war to a conclusion. (The counter-counterargument was that if the test failed, the United States would have been left with only one bomb, and the Japanese would have been emboldened to resist even longer.)

Amid this uncertainty, one thing is clear: decision makers should have faced this choice with a heavy heart and the realization that they might turn out to be mistaken, whatever they did. President Truman's statement that he slept soundly after making the decision to drop the bombs suggests he harbored more certainty than the facts warranted. Odd as it may sound, there may be an "ethic of uncertainty" that makes doubt and humility a moral requirement in the conduct of public affairs. Whether leaders are required to put doubt and humility on public display is another question altogether.

Truth and Politics, Truth and Democracy

The alert reader will have noticed that up to now, I have said almost nothing about democracy. That is no accident. Many of the ways truth matters in political life apply to all regimes, not just to democracies. Certain kinds of truth are a means to every end, because false beliefs increase the chance of failure. If you take a midwinter walk on an ice-covered lake in the belief that the ice is a foot thick and it's only an inch, the consequences will be unpleasant as well as unexpected. The reverse is also the case: if you accept unduly pessimistic beliefs about the world, you may well refrain from doing things that would have succeeded, and your adversaries have an incentive to make you believe the worst. (It now appears that Saddam Hussein resisted international inspections because he was trying to bluff his neighbors into believing that he was better armed and more dangerous than he turned out to be.)

Not only democratic governments, but also tyrants determined to subdue other nations need accurate assessments of their own military capabilities and those of their adversaries. Often tyrants fail because their subordinates are too terrified to tell them the truth. A characteristic pathology of tyranny is the ruler's belief that because he has imposed his will on his subjects, he can bend all reality to his own purposes. What begins in hubris ends in megalomania.

This dangerous deformation is found everywhere, of course. One claim in favor of democracy is that dispersing power serves as a check on hubris. The need to assemble a winning coalition forces even the most arrogant statesman to pay attention to the opinions of others. As the will is chastened, information increases and judgment is refined. At least that is the hope. In practice, democracies can make big mistakes, and not always because government has manipulated the people into false beliefs. Popular majorities, and majorities of their representatives, can sometimes convince themselves to believe what is not true and to act on that belief.

Also common to all forms of government is outright resistance to truth. One source of resistance is organized interest groups who understand that they will lose out if certain truths come to shape public policy. These groups try, often successfully, to obscure the truth with plausible rhetoric and selective half-truths. Often culpability is more widely shared, however. Former Vice President Al Gore has famously labeled global climate change an "inconvenient" truth. And so it is, not only for special interest groups but for all of us, because taking it seriously would require us to change the way we live. Human beings tend to resist change per se, especially change that calls on us to sacrifice something we value. This can give rise to a politics of fantasy, a determined effort to ignore an unpleasant reality.

The problem goes even deeper. Taking truth seriously will sometimes require an entire people to acknowledge its complicity in a mistake, even a grave misdeed. To a remarkable extent, Germans have accepted responsibility for the crimes of the Nazi era and have reshaped their political, educational, and cultural institutions to ensure that such a thing never happens again. This is unusual, however. To this day the Japanese continue to resist acknowledging what they did to the Chinese during the 1930s and to the enemy soldiers they captured during World War II. It took Americans nearly half a century to apologize and make restitution for the incarceration of Japanese Americans after Pearl Harbor, even though the allegations used to justify this step were disproved long ago.

Truth and Leadership, Truth and Citizenship

Aristotle's typology of regimes suggests what observation confirms: some governments that are not democratic may nonetheless care about the interests of their people, not just their own preservation. (Compare the government of Singapore's former president Lee Kwan Yew with the government of North Korea.) To promote the public interest, it is not enough to be well-intentioned; leaders must possess the requisite skills and knowledge. Effective leadership requires a constant effort to acquire information and to evaluate its reliability. A leader who does not do so is unlikely to succeed. More than that, he has not met a basic moral requirement of office: the political equivalent of the lawyer's "due diligence" standard.

In explaining a policy fiasco, it is not enough for a leader to say "I did not know." The question is whether he should have known, whether he did everything that could reasonably be expected to acquire the information that might have made the difference between failure and success. President George W. Bush has often been described as incurious, as making decisions based on gut instinct rather than the patient effort to assemble facts and assess their implications. If this is true (and future historians may determine that it is not), it would represent a culpable shortcoming.

It is this requirement—to make every reasonable effort to acquire the truth on which policy should rest—that makes the case of former secretary of state Colin Powell so difficult. The Bush administration assigned to Powell the task of presenting the U.S. case for war against Iraq to the United Nations Security Council. Powell knew that his speech would be pivotal, and therefore subject to detailed scrutiny. According to several published accounts, he rejected a White House draft as factually flawed and instead went to CIA headquarters, where he remained for four days poring over intelligence files and consulting with senior intelligence officials.[1] This was not enough to save Powell from delivering a speech whose central allegations turned out to be false, a speech he himself has called a "blot" on his record.

It is at this point that interpretations diverge. Powell's defenders argue that no one could have done more, that much of the CIA's raw intelligence data rested on the testimony of Iraqi defectors of dubious reliability, many of whom had their own political axes to grind. In addition, they claim, the materials Powell was able to review did not adequately reflect dissenting views within the agency. Another position is that though he gave an honest representation of what he took to be the truth, he did not push hard enough to get to the bottom of the matter. If he had, he would have known that experts in his own department had poured cold water on the claim that the famous shipment of aluminum tubes proved that Saddam Hussein had restarted his nuclear weapons program. (The tubes turned out to be components, not of centrifuges to enrich uranium, but rather of conventional rockets.) For our purposes, the point is that this disagreement takes place within a shared moral understanding: that due diligence requirements for ascertaining policy-relevant truth do exist and do apply to public officials.

Not all offices are created equal, of course. Some have wider responsibilities and greater freedom of action, and the content of due diligence norms varies accordingly. Lower level State Department officials would not have had the same broad access to CIA data that their secretary enjoyed. The best they could do was assess the information they were able to obtain, which they did (in many cases quite accurately, as things turned out).

Consider a very different case. For years, scandals in child welfare services have rocked the District of Columbia. In several high-profile cases, foster parents have abused, neglected, and even murdered the children in their care. Questions inevitably arise: Whose responsibility was it to know what was going on? Did child welfare workers diligently work to monitor the children in their jurisdiction, did they fall down on the job, or were they doing the best they could with insufficient resources and caseloads so large that they could not possibly give individual cases the attention they deserved? This final alternative, for which independent observers have adduced considerable evidence, would imply that the fault lies with the government (and ultimately the people) of the District for failing to provide the funding and staffing levels needed to monitor the foster care system. The truth we need for responsible governance is seldom cheap and easy to obtain. In most cases, governments must make substantial investments in the people and institutions needed to ferret out the truth, often from sources with strong incentives to conceal it. In democracies, the people themselves must accept this fact, and its fiscal consequences. If they do not, they are complicit in policies that are made and implemented without the facts these policies need to function effectively.

We have reached, unsurprisingly, an important distinction between democracies and nondemocracies. In democracies, the people have distinctive responsibilities, not only to sustain institutions that can provide the truth that officials require for effective governance, but also to acquire the information that citizens need to make wise decisions in their own right. While this proposition smacks of a high school civics class, it is more than a bromide. If citizens do not make even a modest effort to become informed, they will be vulnerable to manipulative appeals based on emotion and moralism.

In late 2008 the U.S. financial system was in crisis, with capital eroding and confidence waning. The people were understandably upset that the government had allowed matters to deteriorate to that point, and also furious that they were being asked to put taxpayer dollars at risk. While their desire to punish the guilty was predictable, it got in the way of a basic fact: even if your neighbor's house catches fire because he stupidly smoked in bed, letting it burn down is not in your interest. The essential idea is that the interests of individuals who want to buy cars and homes on credit are linked not only to their neighborhoods, but also to the fate of large, remote economic institutions whose leaders have distinguished themselves for shortsightedness, greed, and hubris. This is not to say that the plan the Bush administration initiated and the Obama administration largely continued was the best response. But trying to punish the guilty without addressing the systemic crisis would have been the worst. While the people's initial impulse to do just that reflected their leaders' failure to explain the stakes with clarity, it also represented their own failure to stop, read a few newspapers, and learn the basics. How else could they sensibly hold their representatives accountable?

This example suggests a broader point, so obvious that it is often overlooked. Because democracies disperse decision-making power, access to reliable information must be dispersed as well. This means that government and other centers of concentrated power should erect the fewest possible barriers to the acquisition of such information. It means, as well, that accurate information must exist along with mechanisms that distinguish it, nonrandomly if not infallibly, from inaccuracies, half-truths, and outright errors. The Internet now offers everyone access to primary data and full texts. It also multiplies beyond measure the babble of competing voices and undermines the power of gatekeepers who once took it upon themselves to exercise control over the quality of information that went out via print and the public airwaves. It is an open question whether, on balance, this momentous technological change will yield a net gain for democracy—that is, whether, over time, citizens will be more or less likely than in previous generations to approach politics armed with the basic information they will need to make democracy work.

Drawing on John Dewey's analogy between democratic publics and communities of scientific inquiry, some argue that democracy has an inherent orientation toward truth. This is too optimistic. The analogy between democracy and the market seems closer, and we all know about market failures, not to mention Gresham's Law, which offers a parsimonious explanation of most electoral campaigns. As Bernard Williams points out, "free scientific inquiry" is not a free-for-all, but rather a "managed market" with high, carefully policed barriers to entry. The competition to seek the truth takes place only among those who have been certified as competent truth-seekers.[2]

The political marketplace in the United States is much less managed than it once was. As a result, more people can express themselves more freely and communicate their views to others. This does not necessarily mean progress toward a politics of truth. Although the relation between freedom of expression and the acquisition of truth isn't random, it's not linear either. The disappearance of gatekeepers may broaden the range of views to which citizens are exposed, but their absence also means that there is more noise in the political system and that it is harder to prevent knaves and fools from influencing public opinion.

Some truth is managed, of course. Like all forms of government, democracies try to keep certain matters secret. Unlike other forms of government, this effort creates an essential tension. How can the people judge what they do not know? The classic answer is that their representatives will advance their interests and safeguard their liberties. As we know, it doesn't always work out that way in practice. Governments can keep secrets for bad reasons as well as good: to aggrandize power and conceal mistakes, for example. The more closely held information is, the more difficult it is for normal checks and balances to operate.

It is easy to respond with bromides such as "Sunlight is the best disinfectant." Sometimes it is; at other times it blinds us to real dangers. Democracies have enemies, and certain kinds of information can strengthen them. Truth is one thing, its dissemination another. It is not self-contradictory to want truth to guide government policy while also believing that democratic governments may appropriately withhold certain policy-relevant truths from the public. As we have learned, however, there is no simple blueprint for constructing policies and institutions that can police the boundary between justified and unjustified secrecy.

While recognizing disagreeable but legitimate necessities, we must be careful not to lose our bearings. Yes, there is a distinction between public and private morality. But in politics as well as in our personal lives, there is still a presumption in favor of disclosure. Withholding or distorting the truth always requires a justification, whereas deliberate truthfulness usually doesn't. Despite their flaws, democratic governments are more likely to end up honoring this presumption than are other regimes, a not insubstantial argument in favor of democracy.

Truth and Trust

One thing is clear: no matter how open our government may be and how committed we are as individuals to civic responsibility, democratic citizens cannot possibly know what we would need to evaluate every proposal that comes before us. We have no choice, then, but to follow the lead of those we regard as trustworthy, those we believe know what we do not and honestly convey their knowledge to others. Politics can be a realm of truth only when we trust those who are worthy of trust. Nondemocratic governments do not care much about maintaining trust between the governors and the governed. Indeed they often employ mistrust to keep potential opponents off-balance, because they can use force and fear to enforce compliance. Democratic governance needs trust. When trust disappears, democracy collapses into a politics of suspicion.

Recent events in the United States offer sad illustration of this risk. When Treasury Secretary Paulson put his initial proposal on the table in the fall of 2008, the public was incredulous. In part, their response was moral: "You're expecting *us* to pay for *their* incompetence and greed?" In part, though, it reflected a generalized mistrust of government assertions. A typical reaction: "They said that we had to go to war against Iraq because Saddam's weapons were a threat. They were wrong then, so why should we believe them now, when they tell us that our economy faces a comparable risk? Our leaders are either incompetent or dishonest, so why should we trust them?" (One anonymous wit grimly labeled Paulson's proposal the "Authorization to Use Financial Force.")

There is a school of thought, supported by some evidence, that Colin Powell's speech reflected neither of the errors discussed above, but rather a systematic effort to twist the evidence and deceive the people. I do not know whether this is true, but the fact that so many people believe it is an indication of just how much trust has waned. It is one thing for a government to make a mistake, however catastrophic; it is another thing altogether for a government to lie, especially when the stakes are so high. "Bush lied, people died," chant the protesters. I hope they are wrong. The bad news is that so many Americans are ready to believe the worst. The good news is that they continue to believe in the distinction between truth and falsehood, and in the possibility that truth can guide political decisions.

Democracies often create institutions whose mission is to resist the tendencies of everyday politics, ferret out the truth, and make it available to the public. Some of these institutions are ongoing; for example, each cabinet agency in the U.S. government has an inspector-general with independent powers. Others are ad hoc, which need not mean that their impact is transitory. The best recent example is the 9/11 Commission, which used powers formal and informal to establish the sequence of events that led to the terrorist attacks, assign responsibility, and make recommendations to help the government ward off future incidents. Though imperfect, the Commission's report exemplified the ability of a democratic government to pursue, and act on, uncomfortable truths. It is not an accident that Tom Kean and Lee Hamilton, the Commission's cochairs, remain widely trusted by other officials and by the people.

Democratic Authority versus the Authority of Truth

As Michael Walzer has rightly argued, the writ of truth over democracy is limited. In democratic contestation, the scientist's voice is one among many others.[3] If a democratic legislature believes that human activity has no impact on global climate change and makes policy on the basis of that belief, the scientist has every right to protest in the name of truth. He can argue that the adopted policy is wrong, shortsighted, and dangerous. He cannot argue that the legislature had no right to do what it did. Truth is one thing, legitimacy another. The people have a right to be wrong, a right they often exercise.

The reverse is also true: democracy has limited sway over truth and the processes through which it is acquired. Consider the nature of democratic authority over scientific inquiry. It seems perfectly appropriate for democratic institutions to determine the distribution of resources devoted to various domains of inquiry. From the standpoint of many physicists, it may be regrettable when the U.S. government declines to invest the billions of dollars needed to construct the next-generation particle accelerator, ceding world leadership to Europe, but it cannot be said that the government has over-stepped its bounds. It is legitimate, moreover, for democratic governments to make such decisions based, in part, on their assessment of the kinds of inquiry that are most likely to sustain democratic institutions. (They may choose not to fund research that might end up underscoring genetically based inequalities among human beings.) Democracies can impose restrictions on research methods (on human subjects, for example), although these restraints may make it more difficult for research to succeed. And in certain circumstances, it may even be legitimate for democracies to restrict the public discussion of specific research results.

Distinct from all these actions is government intervention to dictate the outcome of inquiry. The quest for truth is an autonomous activity guided by its own rules. To be sure, communities of inquiry shape these rules and judge their products, but not on a democratic basis.

One of the sorriest episodes in the sorry history of the Soviet Union was the use of state power to impose the pseudo-Lamarckian views of the quack agronomist Trofim Lysenko on the whole of Soviet biology. Plant scientists of unimpeachable international standing were forced to recant their adherence to Mendelian genetics and to conduct their research on the basis of an ideologically based theory preaching the environmental determination of species change. This affair is frequently presented as the epitome of totalitarianism. But the real point is broader: Lysenko's biology would have been no better, and no more legitimate, if it had been imposed by a democratic vote after full public deliberation. The sphere of democratic politics has no rightful authority over the internal processes that guide the quest for truth in diverse communities of inquiry.[4]

Truth and Other Values

If we don't think too hard about it, it is easy to worship truth monotheistically, or at least as the god before whom none other shall be placed. Whatever may be the case in the conduct of inquiry, matters are more complicated in the arena of politics. A Jewish sage once stated that the world rests on three pillars: truth, justice, and peace.[5] In practice, these pillars may not be mutually supporting and can actually conflict. Consider the truth and reconciliation commissions used to great effect in postapartheid South Africa and to less effect elsewhere. One of the pillars, justice, is conspicuous by its absence. That is no accident: these commissions rest on the proposition that if we want peace within badly divided societies, we may have to forgo justice, at least as it is typically understood. We may choose to regard truth publicly acknowledged as a kind of justice, but the survivors of the abuse may disagree. And if they do, who can blame them?

In politics there is no guarantee that truth will always be the trumping value. In David Park's latest novel, *The Truth Commissioner*, the effort to exhume buried truths and make them public leaves a trail of destruction.[6] For nations as for individuals, life demands a complex weave of remembering and forgetting, of truth-telling and obfuscation. Hamlet asks (I paraphrase), Treat every man according to his desert, and who would escape whipping? There are great crimes in the history of every nation. Sometimes it is right to bring them to light, acknowledge them, and ask future generations to remember. At other times, insisting on the truth yields little except outrage and resentment. In some communities, achieving even a modus vivendi will require all parties to accept something less than their full measure of truth. Although outsiders may criticize them for practicing social amnesia, ordinary citizens who most of all want their children to grow up in peace are entitled to a different view.

Truth and Democratic Legitimacy

"We the people of the United States ... do ordain and establish this Constitution for the United States of America." While these words explicitly state a political fact, they implicitly advance a moral claim: the people, and *only* the people, are entitled to ordain and establish a constitution. What can justify such a claim? It is reasonable to regard the Declaration of Independence as offering at least a sketch of the answer. Note the words that frame and situate this answer: "We hold these Truths to be self-evident." If they are not, then one may well doubt that it is the right of the people, having discerned flaws in existing arrangements, to "alter or abolish [them]" and to "institute new Government, laying its Foundation on such Principles, and organizing its Powers in such form, as to them shall seem most likely to effect their Safety and Happiness."

Democratic government, we have seen, needs truth to do its business well. It also needs truth to justify the power it wields. The alternatives to truth as the basis of democratic legitimacy are unattractive. Either the people rule by force majeure, a claim that fails as soon as undemocratic leaders can mobilize power against the failing of democracy, or they rule by custom and habit—because this is the way we do things around here—a claim that fails as soon as people who want to do things differently accumulate enough power to challenge democratic complacency.

Conclusion: A Unitary View of Truth

We have reached the end neither of history nor of political theory. We may, if we choose, draw a conception of citizens as free and equal from the "public culture of a democratic society." This complacent self-inspection will hardly move those individuals (and they are numerous) who have grown up in nondemocratic cultures and who are less persuaded of the merits of democracy than we are. We must make our case to those who disagree with us, which means defending certain propositions about politics as true, or at least as more nearly true than any competitors.

This is why I doubt that in the final analysis, Harold Pinter or anyone else can adopt one stance toward truth as an artist, scientist, or philosopher, and another as a citizen. The truths science uncovers about climate change are among the propositions that should shape public policy. Philosophers who conclude that ordinary conceptions of moral desert rest on false premises about personal responsibility are obligated to bring that conclusion into practical debates about punishment and distribution. To be sure, artists who dive deep to plumb the human heart may return to the surface with ambiguous results. But the same is true in ordinary civic life. We may hypothesize that Ronald Reagan's affable distance from most human beings somehow reflects growing up with an alcoholic father, or that George W. Bush's assertive self-confidence emerged through an effort to break free of his father, or that Barack Obama's disciplined, self-contained style is the product of his struggle to construct a coherent identity. The artist and the citizen may use different strategies to investigate these hypotheses. But the truth they seek is the same.

Chapter 8

On Truth and Democracy: Hermeneutic Responses

David Couzens Hoy

HOW ARE THE concepts of truth and democracy related? On the one hand, they could well seem to be as unrelated as apples and oranges: truth is an issue for the philosophy of language to determine, whereas democracy is a political and social arrangement usually discussed under the rubric of value theory. On the other hand, the connection of truth and democracy seems self-evident: How could democracy not presuppose the truth? How could democracy function without trust in the truthfulness of our fellow citizens?

Kant gives us a useful allegory for this topic in "Perpetual Peace" (1795). In reflecting on the ideal goal of society, Kant posits that this goal would be a perfect constitution that would maximize individual freedom with the minimal amount of restraint of individual desire. He speculates in a famous thought experiment that even a race of devils, where "devil" is a technical term for a being that is concerned only with itself and its own desires, would over time approach this ideal asymptotically. His discussion leaves it open for us today to continue thinking about the type of political arrangement, democratic or other, that would be involved in the ideal constitution of this "demonocracy."

In the present context the specific question is whether these devils could do without the concept of truth. In light of that question it is interesting that Kant also argued that a society in which everyone always lied would be impossible. Presumably, therefore, even the devilish society governed by the perfect constitution would require its denizens to know the difference between truth and falsity and sometimes to speak the truth, whether or not they had any particular desire to do so. Kant's thought experiment thus implies that truth requires at least a modicum of trust, for if one did not trust one's fellow devils to be telling the truth on occasion, the social fabric would disintegrate. Kant's considered view could thus be taken to be that society and its practices of communication and cooperation would be impossible in the absence of the distinction between truth and falsity.

What my reading of Kant's allegory is meant to suggest is that truth and democracy go hand in hand. But philosophers with a transcendental bent might well want to ask about the derivation relation here, that is, which comes first, truth or trust? On the one hand, one might think that without the distinction between truth and falsity, we would lack the basis for trust. On the other hand, insofar as our minds are finite and individuals can ascertain the truth or falsity of only a limited subset of their beliefs, trust would seem to be the social basis for truth.

The three essays that the editors assigned to me approach these questions from three different perspectives. One is by a skilled analytic philosopher with a deep grounding in philosophy of language, another author has extensive practical experience in recent politics and political theory, and the third author is schooled in the Continental tradition of critical social theory, which is my own perspective as well. My task, as I understand it, is to provide an interpretive context from which to view not only the question of the relation of truth and democracy, but also these three different ways of approaching this question.

Insofar as my space is very limited, I begin with a brief sketch of how the issues look from my point of view. I then want to focus in particular on the thread of skepticism about truth in politics. I see these essays as united in the conviction that such skepticism can lead to the mistaken belief that *anything* is justifiable, which is the flip side of the nihilism that asserts that *nothing* is justifiable. I share their rejection of these two tenets. Even a race of devils could not function with a constitution built on these unprincipled principles. The question that I see running through these essays in intriguingly different ways is why that is the case.

My own perspective is hermeneutical in the sense that Richard Rorty effectively contrasted to the epistemological. That is to say, I work at the level of the theory of understanding and interpretation rather than at the level of semantic theories of truth. From my point of view, there are lots of truths: "the sky is blue," "grass is green," and "snow is white" are true if and only if the sky is blue, grass is green, and snow is white. Even if this disquotational approach to the theory of truth is rejected, I do not think that its defeat would be a problem for the kinds of questions that I want to ask. From my standpoint, the question is not about the nature of sentential truth. Truth is trivial, in the sense that there are too many truths, and that much of what we say or believe must be true.

When we use the term "truth" as in the phrase, "*the* truth," I think that we are really concerned with the distinction between these trivial truths and more significant truths. The multiplicity of the former is countered by the relative rarity of the latter. These significant truths organize truths that are taken to be important more centripetally around themselves, while less important ones are pushed centrifugally toward the periphery.

Another way to draw this distinction is to note that truth is relative to a language, or better, to an interpretation. Truths are not atoms that sit around waiting to be asserted. On the contrary, they are always uttered in a context. Contexts are not themselves true or false so much as they are appropriate or inappropriate. Contexts are, in other words, a function of the interpretation or understanding of what is at issue. Interpretations do not make statements true or false, but they do determine what can be said, that is, what can even come up for grabs as being counted as possibly either true or false. Interpretive understanding of what is appropriate or inappropriate is what provides the context in which statements can be uttered, as well as the standards or criteria for judging which utterances are true and which are false. The sense for the application of these criteria is what Aristotle calls *phronesis,* or practical wisdom.

I wish to note further the difference between, on the one hand, the use of "truth" as a count noun and, on the other, the use of the phrase "*the* truth" for something more like "the best interpretation" of all the many beliefs and truths that go into having a view or an understanding. In fact we tend to overlook a similar difference between using "interpretation" as a count noun (as when we ask, Which of these two interpretations of the text is the best one?) and speaking of interpretation as a phenomenon or activity (as when we ask, How should the text be interpreted?). In either case, we can say that a given interpretation is wrong about the text without implying that there is only one right or true interpretation.

While these issues may seem to be unrelated to questions about democratic social arrangements, there are in fact some crucial points of connection.

For instance, the hermeneutical emphasis on understanding is often taken as implying that the concept of truth is connected to the ideal of reaching agreement. Some philosophers therefore see discursive communication as presupposing the ideal telos of uncoerced consensus. The argument is that unless the ideal possibility of democratic consensus is presupposed, any communication or any cognitive inquiry would be mere appearance or sham.

Debate on this topic has revolved around the derivation relation between truth and consensus. Does consensus come before and thus determine what is true, or does the agreement of consensus follow from learning the truth? That is, in any attempt to resolve differences through rational argumentation, do we find out what the truth is by virtue of what we can agree to, or do we agree to something because it is the truth? In science there may be a strong prima facie case for the latter view, that truth is already there and is discovered only in the course of argumentation. In politics, however, the role of agreement and consensus is more pronounced. Our agreement that, for instance, water is H_2O does not make water H_2O. While this claim about the independence of the fact of the matter from any understanding of it might seem plausible for scientific terms, there are other terms for which that independence is not so obvious. Social terms such as money and love depend for their use on how they are understood, and there is no independent fact of the matter about their essence.

More radical philosophers, often referred to as critical theorists and sometimes as poststructuralists, raise a further question about the relation of truth and consensus that challenges the ideal of consensus and that potentially could even disrupt the ideal of democracy. Criticisms of consensus theories of truth are echoed in criticisms of theories of democracy that overlook the possibility that consensus may result not from true states of affairs, but from a general false consciousness. The argument is that in societies with divisive inequalities people's perceptions of what is in their real interests may be massively distorted. Divided societies, it could be claimed, produce divided minds that in turn perpetuate rather than eliminate false social consciousness.

At this point in my remarks we appear to be a long way from the issues about semantic theories of truth. Has this quick and circuitous route brought us back to the apples and oranges sense of the relation of truth and democracy with which I began? Or does it in fact show the importance of the connections between truth and democracy? Let me now pursue these questions in the terms of the three essays that the editors have assigned to me for discussion.

Michael Lynch defines democracy usefully as a "space of reasons." Democracy is the fundamental social practice of not simply acting, but of acting in concert with one another. Democratic social practice requires us to give one another reasons for our choices of how to act, and among these reasons is the particular practice of giving reasons for believing what is true. So Lynch believes that there is an essential connection between democracy and truth. Truth is the inescapable basis of democratic social practice, and there must be reasons for preferring particular methods for achieving it.

One might worry about this prioritizing of truth that if we fall short in our role as autonomous rational beings capable of determining the truth of what we believe, governmental authority might too often want to step in and make our choices for us. However, Lynch is not saying that in the absence of truth, governmental authority *must* step in. Given the difficulty of knowing what is true, such a democratic principle would permit too much governmental intervention, manipulation, and even coercion. In fact, Lynch's appeal to truth is intended to block both this practical cynicism as well as epistemological skepticism. He takes issue, for instance, with Richard Rorty's view that there is no noncircular way of giving a conclusive epistemic reason for trusting some epistemic reasons over others. Lynch suggests that finally the choice of standard for preferring some reasons to others must be the result of a method of politically privileging some standards by giving them more weight and by protecting them through social institutions. The methods for assigning this political privilege, he says, ought to be "repeatable, adaptable, public, and widespread."

The hermeneutic version of Rorty's position that I am projecting here could accept these methods insofar as they represent sufficient pragmatic guidelines for democratic social practice. The question is, should truth be added to this list? Rorty himself thought not. Rorty's argument is roughly that truth could not be the target of our justificatory practices because we can never know which of our beliefs are true, and a target that we can never know we have hit is not a target. In contrast, Lynch maintains that truth is the ground for the social practice of giving reasons, not consensus or agreement about what we believe the truth to be. He thus rejects Rorty's view that the only grounds for a social practice can be further social practices, and that the only way to justify a belief is through the solidarity of consensus. Such a view is not tantamount to skepticism, but on Lynch's view it is not strong enough to defeat skepticism, and it only serves to foster cynicism. For Lynch only the stronger view that truth grounds our social practice of giving reasons will defeat the skepticism according to which "all methods for forming beliefs are as reliable as others because none are reliable." To use the allegory I borrowed from Kant, Lynch could be interpreted as saying that only the stronger insistence on truth as the metaphysical ground of democracy can successfully block the skeptical threat of demonocracy.

This challenging debate between Lynch and Rorty is further illuminated by the practical cases in recent politics discussed by William A. Galston. Galston's concrete engagement in practical politics leads to his insightful reflections on actual examples of ways in which the insistence on truth can come into conflict with the ideals of democracy. Popular majorities, he points out, "can sometimes convince themselves to believe what is not true and to act on that belief." Although Galston is not a critical theorist, he does point out that government authority can give rise to a "politics of fantasy." A patently unpleasant reality that people would rather not face is covered over by fantasy, and they then elect representatives who tell them what they want to hear.

His experience thus makes concrete the worry that without truth, government authority may all too easily undermine our autonomy. Galston, however, cautions against what he calls a "monotheistic" worship of truth. He believes that the view that "democracy has an inherent orientation toward truth" is too optimistic. Given my earlier question about which comes first, truth or trust, the following assertion puts him on the side of those who think trust is the more basic condition of political agency: "Politics can be a realm of truth only when we trust those who are worthy of trust."

But just as the politics of truth can degenerate into a politics of fantasy, so can the politics of trust devolve into a politics of suspicion. So even though Galston recognizes the requirement on governments to "acquire the truth on which policy should rest," he also thinks that truth is only one value in politics, and that it can sometimes be trumped. For one thing, he could well be read as siding with Rorty in pointing out that political decisions are often based on beliefs that cannot be known to be true. As Galston writes, "Indeed, the demand for certainty is incompatible with the requirements of politics." He is fully aware of the pathos of the "ethics of uncertainty" whereby political decision makers must be aware of the incompleteness of their knowledge. Doubt and humility thus become moral requirements in real-time situations.

A further challenge to the monotheistic worship of truth comes when he affirms Michael Walzer's point that truth and legitimation are different issues and require different tactics and lines of reasoning. Claims of, say, scientific truth do not outweigh the democratic legislative process and its right to introduce policies based on premises that are scientifically inaccurate. "The people have a right to be wrong," he remarks, "a right they often exercise."

Here I see a different kind of skepticism working its way into the discussion. This skepticism is directed not so much against truth per se as against the very idea of politics and legitimation. Skepticism in this sense is tied to the mistaken idea that there is always some interpretation that will make any accusation of cover-up or dissimulation go away. Such a view is often attributed to hermeneutics and to poststructuralism. However, the hermeneutical insistence on the inevitability of interpretation does not entail that there is no way to assess conflicting interpretations. Some interpretations are indeed better than others. I think, therefore, that Galston is right to point to cases in practical politics where truth does not always trump other competing values. I think that Galston is equally right, as I read him, that bald mendacity should never trump anything. There is certainly a difference between saying, on the one hand, that when truth is not ascertainable, other values may have to be invoked to justify a decision, and saying on the other hand that there is a right to mask the situation with deliberate misinterpretations, or even outright lies. While some interpretations may depend on "essentially contestable" concepts on which a final consensus cannot be expected, this does not mean that all interpretations are equally acceptable.

Andrew Norris's essay shows how Galston's useful council about the practical difficulties of appealing to truth in modern democracies can lead some theorists to try to theorize democracy without appealing to truth at all. His essay thus presents and takes issue with positions at the opposite end of the philosophical spectrum from Lynch's strong insistence on truth as the metaphysical basis of democracy (with Galston's essay occupying a middle position recognizing the importance of truth as a democratic value, but one that can be trumped by competing values). The theorists in question, whom Norris labels poststructuralist "skeptics," argue that democracy is an agonistic struggle over essentially contested concepts about which there is no fact of the matter and which can reasonably divide people. In the face of such divisions politics for these poststructuralists is a matter not of reaching agreement or of forming consensus or of finding the truth about these types of concepts. Dissensus could sometimes be a better sign of democratic health than consensus. At best, politics can be said to be a matter of working out arrangements of how we can all get along even in the face of our differences.

One of the issues between Jürgen Habermas, on the one hand, and

Ernesto Laclau and Chantal Mouffe on the other was over the question of the inevitability of hegemonic differences undermining political consensus. Norris shows skillfully how the politics of trust can slide over into the politics of suspicion. Critical theory comes in degrees on a gradient between trust and suspicion. Even if skepticism is warranted in specific cases, Norris argues against Chantal Mouffe that a generalized nihilism of the sort that I identified earlier does not follow. The basis for this nihilistic attitude toward politics might seem either extremely cynical, with its view of politics as the hungry hordes seeking only power over their fellows, or else overly optimistic and idealistic, as the Kingdom of Ends inhabited by purely rational choosers.

Does the democratic ship need the anchor of truth, or should it cut itself free from truth and drift with the tides like Neurath's boat? Could Kant's demonocracy really be approaching asymptotically the perfect constitution without any concern for truth or trust, or must there be at least some recognition of the practical importance of truth and trust at the basis of present-day democratic contests? To my mind these are the urgent questions with which Norris's essay leaves us. Indeed these questions place this entire volume at the heart of both contemporary social philosophy and current practical politics. These essays are thus appearing at exactly the right moment, one where at some future point in time history might well look back and judge that an old regime of secrecy and manipulation was being left behind. Their authors provide grounds for the current hopes for the emergence of a new regime of truthfulness and openness based on trust. Whether trust has limits, and whether they can be specified, might well be the topic of the sequel to this timely volume.

Chapter 9

Too Soon for the Counterreformation

Jane Bennett

YES, GEORGE W. BUSH was a liar, but that is not all. His foul administration spread an infectious mood of mendacity, aggression, indecency, callousness, self-indulgence, and stupidity over the land. One could say that the "Bush Doctrine" that Sarah Palin was unable to identify (in her ABC interview with Charlie Gibson) consists in the affirmation of all of these practical dispositions together and not merely in the defense of preemptive violence in foreign policy. Or let us name it "Bushism," to denote an assemblage of bodies and forces that exceeds the narrow intellectual bonds of a "doctrine."

I think that moral-sensuous revulsion at Bushism is an important part of what propels Norris, Galston, and Lynch to offer their various accounts of the role of truth in democratic politics. Truth is presented in each essay as an antidote to an American public culture infused with the Bush Doctrine to the point where disinformation, military aggression, torture, indifference to the suffering of foreigners and people with little money, wanton consumption of energy and commodities, and the uninhibited urge to punish and get revenge were able to don the official cloak of virtue. Perhaps "suffused" is a better descriptor in the previous sentence than "infused," for even those who expressed a different set of affects or a different sensibility about war, the economy, nature, science, and divinity had to do so in the context of Bushism. The gist of my remarks will be to second the attempts by those three authors to draw attention to the public value of truth-telling but also to remind even more insistently than Norris and Galston do that truth alone can't cure what ails us. I'm even less certain than perhaps all three authors that a renewed public debate framed in terms of "truth" is what we need most at this point in our history—even if such a debate were to yield one of the antidogmatic versions of the concept that the authors defend. And that "if" is a big one, given the dispositional propensity for dogmatism and impatience with complexity that a large segment of the American public and the news media have displayed. All forces have their limits, and I think that the force of truth, even as what Lynch calls a "practical" rather than an "epistemic" standard of judgment, isn't strong enough by itself to turn the public culture in a more generous, intelligent, and leftward direction. As Norris acknowledges, despite his critique of Mouffe's too-exclusive focus on the role of affect, democratic will-formation is in part an *affective* process.

Each of the authors addressed here takes pains to distance himself from a notion of truth as a fixed, transparently intelligible standard for judgment. Lynch, for example, takes a "functionalist" view of truth according to which "true beliefs are those that, other things being equal, we aim at when asking and answering questions." For him, democracy requires the practice of reason-giving because this is a key sign of respect for one's fellow citizens' capacity for self-rule, and reason-giving presupposes (in the modified Kantian sense of implicitly aiming at) truth. That democracy is a good *at all* is a judgment that "the common currency" of a self-interested calculation yields. Our beliefs, concludes Lynch, are thus not "groundless" but anchored in the ideal of a fidelity to a state of affairs. Galston takes a pragmatic approach to truth, defining it simply as the most accurate information currently available about the particular policy problem at hand. Good information is a good thing when you can get it: it is "a means to every end, because false beliefs increase the chance of failure." I am drawn to Galston's thoughtful exploration of the vicissitudes of appeals to truth in practical politics, though I see more need perhaps than he does to attend explicitly to the (sometimes positive, sometimes negative, but always there) role of bodies—the moody bodies of humans but also the quirky material agency of nonhuman bodies like technologies, storms, climate, diseases, and commodities—in politics. Even with such attentiveness, of course, uncertainty will persist, for the alteration of a public mood is no science. It is, rather, a precarious and unwieldy process especially subject to unintended consequences. As Galston says, "There may be an 'ethic of uncertainty' that makes doubt and humility a moral requirement in the conduct of public affairs."

Norris attends to affect when he frames his discussion of truth in terms of the *virtue* of truth-telling, in terms of honesty. To the extent that he sticks to this framing, he can keep his eye on the political (rather than epistemological) ball: Why were so many Americans indifferent to Bush's lies and attracted to Bushism? Norris rightly points to the long and relentless (and affect-centric) campaign by the right to undermine belief in a common good and to ridicule faith in the possibility of state action issuing in something other than interference or incompetence, something like efficacious action on behalf of the public. I would like to underscore the point that faith in the power of collective action to remedy social injustice, for example, is fueled as much by *enlarged sympathy* as by the cooler affect of a commitment to truth as the giving of reasons. If the real problem is a *political mood*, then it is unlikely that either the reasoned, philosophical critiques of the epistemologies of skepticism and cynicism offered by Norris and Lynch or a higher public profile for appeals to "truth" in the news media and official pronouncements will have enough bite. Truth and truth-telling alone can't neutralize that toxic brew of mendacity, aggression, indecency, callousness, self-indulgence, and stuporousness. I'm not saying that political theory, because it takes the form of specialized discourse with a small audience, doesn't matter to politics. I am saying that political theory increases its small and indirect influence upon Bushism to the extent that it accounts for and rhetorically counters that compound mood.

Nevertheless I agree with many of the claims offered in the essays: there does seem to be a close link between having a belief and believing it to be true, as Lynch emphasizes, though there are also situations in which it is important to act as if something might be true when belief is not yet warranted; appeals to truth and falsity do seem to be unavoidable in politics and, as Norris says, "when too cheap a price is put on [truth], the possibility of orienting ourselves and making reasonable political judgments is seriously undermined." But I am especially sympathetic to Galston's pragmatic view that just because something is true doesn't mean that it will be effective in addressing a political problem. Some true propositions, writes Galston, are "not useful, because [they lack] action-guiding force." And though I endorse Lynch's view that democracy must include "the practice of giving and acting for reasons" and that reason-giving is an integral part of the civility and impulse restraint required by democratic governance, I don't agree that disagreements can be, or ever are, handled in the "arena of reason alone." I disagree because for me reason, like perception, thinking, and judgment, is itself always affect-imbued, and this affective dimension plays an indispensable role in political and ethical *action*.

Elsewhere I have explored how, for example, a mood of sensuous "enchantment" with everyday objects of nature and culture can provide the energy to move selves from the mere endorsement of a moral principle to the actual practice of an ethical behavior. In making this case, I participate in a larger trend within political theory, a kind of affective-aesthetic turn, inspired in large part by feminist studies of the body and explorations of "care" and by Foucault's work on ethical exercises in ancient Greece. Some have criticized this turn as a retreat to soft issues of "identity" at the expense of the hard matters of economic justice, rights, or democratic governance. But I agree with those who reply that the bodily disciplines through which sensibilities are formed and reformed are *themselves* political—indeed, that they constitute a whole (underexplored) field of "micropolitics" without which a principle or policy risks collapsing into mere words. There will be no greening of the economy, no redistribution of wealth, no enforcement or extension of rights, no progressive alternative to Bushism or to the Bush Doctrine unless there are also present dispositions and moods hospitable to these projects. That goes for all institutions too, with respect to the lived ethos that suffuses them. If a set of principles is actually to be lived out, the right mood or landscape of affect has to be in place.

In sum, while I agree with Norris that "a democratic will is a complicated . . . thing, requiring not just . . . passionate commitment, but also honest and truthful deliberation and the institutions that make such deliberation possible," I think it is premature to call for a counterreformation against an affective turn that has barely lifted itself off the ground. Political theorists on the left ought to try to disseminate pro-democratic moods or affective virtues, such as magnanimity, enlarged sympathy, and a tolerance for complexity. (Here I, like Rorty, have no trouble saying that democratic politics serves such concrete goals as "greater honesty, greater charity, greater patience, greater inclusiveness and so on" but wonder just how much it helps "to add 'truth' . . . to our list of goals" [Rorty as cited in Lynch].) Norris may be right that, despite the profound influence of Plato, there has been a lull in political theory's attention to "the importance of truth in politics." But I discern a rather more ambiguous relationship between progressive affects and the appeal to truth. The invasion of Iraq was enabled by a bellicose, vengeful mood seeking to attach itself to some target or other. And the quest for truth is always animated by some mood or other, for better or worse.

Chapter 10

Response to Norris, Lynch, and Galston

Martin Jay

THERE CAN BE few more predictable denunciations in the history of political discourse than those directed against the deleterious effects of mendacity and hypocrisy. When it comes to democratic politics, they are even more passionately delivered by those who argue that honesty, accountability, transparency, and trust are the bedrock premises of popular rule. Truthfulness in a politician, as the essays considered in this response demonstrate, is often associated with the more ambitious ideal of ascertaining the truth as a prerequisite to sound judgment in political decision making, which itself is often tied to rational procedures of deliberation to reveal that truth. Democracy, as Michael Lynch puts it, is therefore best understood as a "space of reasons," which can only be persuasive—or at least should be— if those reasons are expressed sincerely and conform to the truth of what is the case.

Indignation against lying in politics often bubbles over when an egregious case of it occurs, especially if it involves someone on the other side of the political divide. The most obvious recent instance, of course, is the Bush administration's dubious claims about weapons of mass destruction in Saddam Hussein's Iraq, which arouses Andrew Norris's ire (and not his alone).[1] Even more chagrining, it seems, is the world-weary cynicism of the American public, which does not share his level of outrage. For political theorists from Machiavelli to Arendt and Mouffe, who concoct excuses to justify mendacity, he has even less patience. Michael Lynch is no less determined to defend a version of democratic politics that is grounded in a clear-headed assessment and sincere expression of what is in fact the case, rather than a politics based on hope or fear. Although William Galston, the most experienced of the three in the actual give and take of politics, has a more cautious approach—"the demand for certainty is incompatible," he admits, "with the requirements of politics"—he too concludes that democratic government "needs truth to do its business well."

It would be foolish to gainsay the intuition that a politics valuing truth and truthfulness, sincerity and transparency, integrity and accountability has a great deal to recommend itself. But examined more closely, the assumptions underlying these essays, in particular those of Norris and Lynch, are somewhat troubling. First, the linkage between the truth—a concept whose definition has bedeviled thinkers from ancient times on—and truthfulness or sincerity is by no means self-evident.[2] Thus it was possible for Plato to be a fervent believer in the truth, hostile to sophistic attempts to dissolve it into rhetorical relativism, and yet countenance noble lies for an elite of rulers. Conversely, it may well have been the case that Bush and Cheney were truthful when they said they believed weapons of mass destruction were going to be found, but that ultimately the facts of the case proved to be different. The jury is still out on that issue. So there is no simple passage from demanding that our politicians speak truthfully to the verification of what is really the case in the world they govern.

Second, the claim that giving reasons is the lifeblood of democratic as opposed to authoritarian decision making does not entail, *pace* Lynch, that those reasons be rational in any full-blooded sense of the term. A Burkean who says that we should follow concrete customs and honor existing hierarchies because it has "always" been done that way is justifying his position not rationally, but historically. Although the latent argument may be utilitarian—if it has lasted, it must be functioning—no rational attempt is made to answer the obvious question: functioning for whom? Nor when she warns that a politics imposing reason on the world is likely to produce theoretically inspired coercion is a conservative refusing to offer reasons, although those reasons may be hostile to a certain version of rationality. It may be reasonable to be critical of abstract rationality, at least when the latter is assumed to be applicable to the contested terrain of values and interests that we normally call politics.

Finally, a politics that seeks to base itself on what is the case rather than on hopes and fears may well commit a performative contradiction when it claims that the essence of democracy is truth-telling and the rational search for consensus based on the better argument. For it is precisely *not* the case that any functioning democracy has actually acted this way. Democracies are just as accurately characterized by countless examples of dissembling, hypocrisy, spin, bullshit (in Harry Frankfurt's now familiar sense of the term), "truthiness," and outright lying. So paradoxically, a plea for a politics of veracity and integrity is itself a politics of hope far more than a politics based on acknowledging "what is the case." To tell the truth is to admit that truthfulness has not been, as Arendt correctly says in the well-known passage cited by Norris, one of the traditional political virtues.

Another way to make this point is that however much politics may involve statements about the past, such as Clemenceau's famous example that Germany invaded Belgium in 1914 rather than the reverse, which can be considered true or false to what really happened, it also frequently makes statements about the future, such as the politician's promise that if he is elected, real change and reform will occur, or the converse prediction that if his opponent is elected, disaster will ensue. As such, political speech is embedded in narratives that have endings still to be determined. Such speech is not amenable to simple tests of truthfulness or insincerity, and even less so truth or error, for two reasons. First, as Hayden White has persuasively made clear, all historical narratives necessarily involve a rhetorical or tropic dimension—for example, comedy, tragedy, romance, satire—which cannot simply be measured against the past "as it actually happened."[3] Second, narratives whose end we cannot foresee lack the resolving cadence that allows us to know how we should plausibly emplot them and therefore are a fortiori resistant to truth-claims in the present. Although it might be said that politics strives for consensus when it comes to such narratives—these are the collective "tales of the tribe" that bind together a political community—their success is not based on whether or not they are somehow true or even believed in by those who spin them.

To complicate the picture still further, we have to acknowledge that a great deal of political speech doesn't really assert truth-claims, or rather the mixture of constative and performative dimensions of political speech acts often privileges the latter. The rhetoric of political persuasion is not, to use a term of art favored by philosophers, "truth-apt." Take, for example, the effective slogan just used in Obama's campaign, "Yes, we can!" Clearly, this is more intended to inspire and exhort than to describe what is the case. It is not clear who is the "we," nor what it is that "we" are supposed to be able to do, let alone whether or not "we" can do it. Is Obama telling the truth when he gets his believers to chant the slogan along with him? Or is he arousing their hopes—audaciously so, as he willingly confesses—about a future that may never happen? If, as Derrida often argued, democracy is not an actual condition, but a deferred future (*avenir*) that is always still to come (*à venir*), then we cannot fully apply the criterion of truth or error to much political speech even in a democracy. Outright lying, as rhetoricians like J. Hillis Miller have argued, is a volatile mixture of performative and constative elements, perhaps even more explicitly than most other speech acts that have both dimensions.[4] It involves a desire on the part of the liar to change the world as it is, as Arendt pointed out, and as such has a future state of affairs as its center of gravity.

A still further consideration has been introduced in the work of political theorists like Ruth Grant and David Runciman, who have shown the importance of building fragile coalitions in a democracy of actors with values and interests that are rarely, if ever, fully congruent.[5] In the service of avoiding violence as a way to overcome opposition, it may be necessary to engage in hypocritical protestations of common positions, when in fact they are not really shared. That is, absent the rational consensus that is the ideal telos of democratic will-formation, a telos that is more counterfactual than real, it is necessary to pretend that solidarity exists even as all participants know that it is fragile and ephemeral. Here the players in the game are aware that the truth is not always told when former bitter rivals unite to form a front against another foe. There is trust, to be sure, but it is not always in the veracity of the partners in a coalition. Similarly, it should be added, the populace often trusts its leaders to do what is in their best interest, not to be brutally candid about everything. This trust can, of course, be miserably abused, but as in the case of friends who sometimes withhold the stark truth in the service of another laudable end, it need not be.

One final observation is in order, which concerns the political implications of privileging truth in the realm of the political. Our three authors make a strong case for truth's relevance for liberal democracies, based on presenting evidence in a "space of reasons," sincerely expressing intentions, and allowing an informed populace to decide based on alternatives that are candidly and transparently presented. Although one may claim a logical entailment, there is plenty of empirical evidence that denouncing lying and blaming it on one's opponents is not the monopoly of one political orientation. Tellingly, the infamous concept of the "big lie" was introduced in *Mein Kampf* by Hitler not as a technique of totalitarian duplicity to be adopted for sinister ends, but rather as a vile tactic used by those, such as the Jews, who had falsely denied Germany had been "stabbed in the back" in 1918.[6] And perhaps the most vociferous contemporary champion of politics as a "truth procedure" is the French philosopher Alain Badiou, an outspoken critic of Arendt's attempt to banish truth-telling as inherently monological and coercive.[7] A champion of Robespierre's war against hypocrisy, he has advocated a Maoist version of Leninism that has nothing but scorn for the Habermasian rational consensus model of communicative interaction underlying the arguments of Lynch and Norris. In short, the denunciation of mendacity and hypocrisy in politics is no guarantee that those who do the denouncing will produce the results that liberal democrats want.

PART III

Decision and Deliberation

Chapter 11

Democracy and the Love of Truth

Bernard Yack

MOST LOVERS OF truth find democratic elections rather hard to stomach. So many words, so much sound, so much fury—so little effort to improve our understanding of who we are and where we stand in the world. Periodic elections ensure that democracy remains, among other things, "an aristocracy of orators," since they hand the greatest powers to those who have mastered—or purchased—the arts of persuasion rather than to those who make the best arguments.[1] They provide an extraordinarily exciting spectacle for political junkies and journalists, the type of people whom Plato takes pleasure in deriding as "lovers of mere sights and sounds."[2] But they cannot help but disturb those who are committed, like Plato's philosophers, to using arguments to gain a better understanding of the way things are.

We students of democracy, political theorists, social scientists, and moral philosophers alike, are at least in this sense heirs to Plato's philosophers. We are by profession, and often by character and conviction, lovers of truth. We are trained and, hopefully, inclined to "want to understand who we are, to correct error, to avoid deceiving ourselves, to get beyond comfortable falsehood."[3] Even when, like so many contemporary philosophers, we deny our access to any accurate, objective account of the truth, we are compelled to do so by our desire to dispel familiar illusions about the way things are.[4]

But unlike lovers of truth in past ages, most of us are inclined by habit and convention, and often by character and conviction, to be democrats as well. As a result, we face a problem few of our predecessors ever had to confront: the tension between moral commitments to democratic politics and intellectual commitments to dispelling illusion and seeking the truth about the way things are. Like all lovers of truth, we are quite uncomfortable with democratic rhetoric and the whole spectacle of democratic elections. But unlike most of our predecessors, we feel uneasy about this discomfort, given our own democratic commitments and loyalties. This uneasiness draws us toward theories that promise to reconcile our political and intellectual commitments, for example, by reconstructing the democratic polity as a "great community" of inquirers, or by reinterpreting Socratic dialectic as a kind of democratic engagement, or by reimagining democratic deliberation as the exchange and examination of opinions rather than the rhetorical competition we have now.[5]

In this paper I argue that these efforts to eliminate the tension between our commitments to democracy and the love of truth end up doing a disservice to both. For they tend, on the one hand, to undermine the legitimacy of democratic decision making and, on the other, to subordinate the search for truth to the search for some form of mutual accommodation.

I develop this argument by means of a critique of the most elaborate and influential attempt to reconcile our commitments to democracy and the love of truth: the vision of democratic deliberation inspired by the theories of Habermas and Rawls. The advocates of this "strong version" of deliberative democracy eliminate the tension between these commitments by adapting their understanding of each to fit the other.[6] They begin by adopting the understanding of moral truth, developed especially by Habermas, according to which valid and objectively binding moral claims are the product of something like an idealized process of democratic deliberation. Then they reimagine democracy as a set of practices that seeks, as far as possible, to institutionalize this process of deliberation. I shall argue, however, that they can revise our understanding of democracy and the search for truth in these ways only by conflating the political legitimacy of democratic decisions with their moral justification. They reconcile our commitments to democracy and the love of truth by making sure that democracies "embody the idealized content of a form of practical reason."[7] But they can do so only because they have already made the search for moral and political truth embody something like the idealized content of a form of democratic deliberation.

I conclude that if we are genuinely committed to both democracy and the love of truth, we need to learn how to live with the tension between them. The vain search for means of harmonizing them diverts energy and attention from this important task.

The Aristocracy of Orators and the Sovereignty of Voters

Why does rhetoric, speech that aims at persuasion rather than the exchange and examination of information and opinions, dominate public reasoning in democracies? Why does democracy always seem to turn into something like Hobbes's "aristocracy of orators"? Because, as Michael Walzer suggests, the democratic principle of popular consent requires that "the citizen who makes the most persuasive argument—that is, the argument that actually persuades the largest number of citizens—gets [or should get] his way."[8] In order to attain even the most public-spirited ends in a democratic polity, you need to find a way of bringing a majority of people to your side. Rhetoric, as Aristotle suggests, is the art that identifies the available means of persuasion in any given situation.[9] In order to succeed in a democracy you need master the art of rhetoric or make use of the services of people who have done so. Democracy becomes, among other things, an aristocracy of orators because it seeks, not the elimination of political inequality, but the elimination of wealth, knowledge, good birth, and all other qualities except the ability to persuade the public as a legitimate qualification to unequal political influence and authority.

We tend to take for granted this consequence of the principle of popular consent, even if we do not especially like it. But this principle structures democratic deliberation in ways that, unlike the principle itself, are far from obvious. In particular, it introduces an asymmetry between speakers and voters that extends and deepens the role of rhetoric in democratic deliberation.

Voters, unlike the speakers who try to persuade them, do not have to give an account of their actions and character. They need not explain why or, where there is a secret ballot, even how they voted. And even if they do give an account of their reasons for voting, nothing they say diminishes the legitimacy of their vote. They may have chosen to vote for the best-dressed candidate or for the policy with the silliest sounding name. But that does not make their vote count any less than those cast by people who carefully weighed the virtues of competing candidates and platforms. For with regard to his vote, "the voter is sovereign, in the old and narrow sense of the word. He could rightly adopt the motto of absolutist rulers and say: '*Sic volo, sic jubeo, stat pro ratione voluntas*' ('thus I wish, I ordain, my will takes the place of reason.')"[10] Arbitrary power, if very narrowly circumscribed, survives in democracies in the democratic voter's equally distributed power over his or her vote. "One person, one vote" means that each citizen's vote carries the same weight as any other's, no matter how he or she chooses to use it. To challenge a voter's use of the franchise is to challenge the principle of democratic legitimacy itself. For it would suggest that we may measure the legitimacy of a democratic vote by something other than the choices of democratic voters.

This very narrowly circumscribed sovereignty of democratic voters over their votes helps shape the practice of democratic deliberation as we have come to know it. Far from a process of mutual accountability, it is an asymmetrical process in which some people seek the approval of the general pool of voters for candidates and their proposals. To gain this approval they have to render persuasive accounts of their choices and their virtues—even if only, like Coriolanus, by showing the public their wounds—to a public that never has to account for their own choices and virtues. The persuasiveness of these appeals is determined, as in all forms of rhetoric, by the decisions made by the people who hear them,[11] not by any intrinsic quality of the arguments that they make. So rather than analyze and correct commonly held premises, democratic speakers rely on these premises as the foundation of their arguments. And rather than spell out clearly the ways their proposals depart from currently held beliefs, they introduce changes as means of preserving already valued practices. The former is often denounced as pandering, the latter as manipulation. But the use of these rhetorical tools follows from the need to find ways of appealing to a voting public that is not held accountable to any standard for how it exercises its votes.[12] Ironically, it is the sovereignty of voters over their votes that turns democracy into an aristocracy of orators.

Moreover, by focusing so exclusively on popular consent as the source of political legitimacy, modern democracies have extended and deepened their reliance on persuasive speech. In Athens the great majority of public offices were distributed by lot rather than by election, a system that removed the selection of officials from the reach of the rhetorical competition that dominated the rest of Athenian public life. But modern democracies have abandoned the reliance on lotteries for all but the selection of juries, and they have done so because it violates the principle of popular consent that sustains their legitimacy, and not just because of its inconvenience in such large political communities.[13] We seem unwilling to leave such important decisions as the selection of public officials to the luck of the draw. We demand the right to choose our officials, which means that in order to gain office candidates must find a way of persuading us of their virtues. The distribution of power and influence to the persuasive is a consequence, not a corruption, of the democratic principle of popular consent.

Unlike hereditary aristocrats, the members of democracy's aristocracy of orators must be willing to submit themselves and their proposals to an unaccountable power—and be willing to take no for an answer. If, like Coriolanus, they are unwilling to do so, there is no room for them in this aristocracy, despite their manifest virtues and record of public service. They almost always begin with superior resources—rhetorical ability, political experience, wealthy friends, media advisers, pollsters, advertisers, hair stylists, and so on—that increase their effectiveness in persuading their listeners. And if successful, they are raised to positions of authority that the vast majority of their listeners will never approach. But in order to get from one place to the other, to transform their unequal resources into unequal authority, they have to submit their arguments to the unaccountable judgment of voters, which means they need "to pay attention to their fellow citizens and display a certain respect for their points of view and judgment."[14] As a result, even the most Machiavellian, manipulative speakers must defer to some extent to popular needs and sentiments in order to be successful in a democracy.

The prominence of rhetoric in democratic deliberation thus bespeaks rather than betrays a form of democratic accountability. But it does so in a way that is far from reassuring to the lover of truth. For the feature of rhetorical speech that establishes its affinity for democracy, deference to the judgment of listeners, also creates serious impediments to the search for truth. Judges who are protected from rendering an account of their judgments are unlikely to refine their understanding of things. Speakers who need to find ways of bringing over a majority of unaccountable judges to their side will rely upon the most widely shared opinions. As a result, democratic deliberation tends to perpetuate and extend the errors embedded in received opinion rather than refine and correct them. It may compel Machiavellian schemers to stoop to conquer, since they cannot manipulate the public unless they are ready to defer or pander to them in some way. But the gain in accountability seems to be purchased at a rather high price for any lover of truth.

The Conflation of Legitimacy and Justification

If rhetoric's dominance of democratic deliberation is a product of the basic democratic principle of popular consent, then we are going to need a new understanding of democratic legitimacy in order to eliminate the tension between democracy and the love of truth. And that is precisely what the more ambitious advocates of deliberative democracy offer us.[15] Seyla Benhabib, for example, argues that "legitimacy in complex democratic societies must be thought to result from the free and unconstrained public deliberation of all about matters of common concern."[16] Josh Cohen insists that "free deliberation among equals is the basis of legitimacy," that the basic institutions of a democracy are "legitimate insofar as they establish the framework for free public deliberation."[17] And Jürgen Habermas accounts for the "legitimating force" of democratic institutions by suggesting that "democratic procedure makes it possible for issues and contributions, information and reason to float freely; it secures a discursive character for political will-formation; and it thereby grounds the fallibilist assumption that results from proper procedure are more or less reasonable."[18] According to this understanding of democracy, "political choice, to be legitimate, must be the outcome of deliberation about ends among free, equal, and rational agents."[19] It is the process of discussion and mutual accountability that legitimates democratic decisions, rather than the number of votes that a particular candidate or proposal receives. Popular consent and all the more familiar democratic institutions derive their legitimacy from the support they lend to a free and open discussion of issues among equals. A democracy, understood in this way, is "an association whose affairs are governed by the public deliberation of its members."[20]

This new understanding of democratic legitimacy, as well as the alternative vision of democratic deliberation that it sustains, is clearly inspired by the approach to moral justification developed by Rawls and, especially, by Habermas. Indeed it is hard to imagine the recent wave of interest in deliberative democracy in the absence of these powerful new theories about the source of moral truths.[21] By encouraging us to think about justifiable moral principles as the product of a process of deliberation that ensures that we reason as "free, equal, and rational agents," Rawls and Habermas opened the door to a new way of thinking about democratic deliberation and legitimacy. As Rawls and Habermas would have us justify moral claims by imagining the results of a hypothetical or idealized process of deliberation, so their followers ask us to justify the exercise of collective power by the degree to which it succeeds in institutionalizing this ideal of deliberation among equals. Their "ideal deliberative procedure provides a model for [democratic] institutions, a model that they should mirror, so far as possible."[22]

Understood in this way, democratic deliberation seems to offer little to disturb the lover of truth. In place of the asymmetry between unaccountable voters and the aristocracy of orators who compete for their approval, we get a process of discussion in which we all hold each other accountable for our choices. In place of persuasive speech, with its ever-present combination of pandering and manipulation, we get the mutual exchange and examination of reasons. Moreover, since this ideal of democratic deliberation is based on a deliberative understanding of moral justification, the search for moral truth will proceed along a path similar to that trod by participants in the democratic process. It seems tailor-made to ease the tension between our commitments to democracy and the love of truth.

The problem with this new understanding of democratic legitimacy, and with the reconciliation that it makes possible, is that it is hard to conceive of how public deliberation can "govern" our affairs in the absence of some rule, like majority rule or unanimity, which brings it to a determinate and authoritative conclusion. Deliberative democrats like to contrast deliberative and aggregative approaches to collective decision making, the mutual exchange of opinions with the mere counting of individual votes.[23] But by itself public deliberation decides nothing. We need to invoke some authoritative decision rule—wait for unanimity, follow the majority, obey the monarch, do what the oracle tells us to do—in order to recognize the results of public deliberation, let alone be governed by them. Public deliberation informs and prepares such decisions, as do other nondeliberative processes such as bargaining, polling, and consulting oracles. But it cannot make these decisions and thus cannot "govern" our affairs.

Cohen, like most deliberative democrats, recognizes the problem and acknowledges that even in the most ideal conditions voting will be required to bring public deliberation to a determinate and authoritative conclusion. But he insists that even if we have to rely on voting to end the process of deliberation, our doing so does not erase the profound difference between an aggregative and deliberative approach to democratic decision making.[24] That is certainly true. A democratic process in which we simply count the preferences of isolated individuals will be very different from one in which there is an extended discussion of issues before a vote is taken. But by the same token, a deliberative process that we know will be decided by a majority rule vote will be very different from one that is unconstrained by such a decision rule, let alone one that we know will be ended only by the monarch's fiat or by our reaching agreement. For when we know that an appeal to popular consent will end the deliberation, even, or perhaps especially the most responsible and public-spirited among us will be inclined to speak in ways that persuade others to do what we think is right. Similarly, we will argue in a very different and likely much less public manner when we know that the final decision will be made by an absolute monarch.

Habermas and his followers want, in effect, to separate out two spheres of public discourse: the highly rhetorical and asymmetric sphere of public discussion generated by voting and the free-floating exchange of opinion among equals in the larger community that lends legitimacy to the former. But ideas never float freely in democratic deliberation. They are deeply and inevitably shaped by our awareness of the audience that must be persuaded if they are ever to govern our affairs. There is therefore simply no way for democratic procedures to carve out a sphere that "secures a discursive [i.e., nonrhetorical] character for political will-formation."[25] On the contrary, the reliance on democratic decision rules ensures the prominence of rhetorical and asymmetric speech in our public deliberations.

The advocates of "strong" deliberative democracy avoid this conclusion and continue portraying democratic deliberation as a process of reason giving and mutual accountability by conflating the political legitimacy of democratic decisions with their moral justification. Political legitimacy, as they portray it, is something conferred by following a relatively democratic process of justification, and moral justification is something that we achieve by invoking an idealized vision of democratic decision making.

Ordinarily we make a strong and clear distinction between political legitimacy and moral justification, between the judgments that we recognize as authoritative and those that we recognize as morally sound or valid. Standards of political legitimacy usually tell us to whom we need to appeal, whom we have to persuade, in order to get the political community to endorse and enforce our judgments. Standards of moral justification tell us, in contrast, how to measure the validity of moral judgments, regardless of who is or is not persuaded by them. We develop standards of political legitimacy precisely so that we can act as a political community in the absence of shared and easily applied standards of moral justification. We may develop our standards of political legitimacy by invoking a particular mode of moral justification, say, by arguing that free and equal individuals in a state of nature or Rawlsian "original position" would, if rational, choose to accept only a democratic form of political authority. But even in this case, political legitimacy and moral justification refer to two different standards: the pedigree by which we recognize the right to speak for the community (some form of popular consent) and the process of reasoning that leads us to endorse that particular pedigree.

But the advocates of the strong version of deliberative democracy erase this clear and familiar distinction between moral justification and political legitimacy. Instead they treat political legitimacy as the more or less imperfect institutionalization of an ideal of moral justification.[26] Benhabib writes, "According to the deliberative model of democracy, it is a necessary condition for attaining legitimacy and rationality with regard to collective decision making processes in a polity, that the institutions of this polity are so arranged that what is considered in the common interest of all results from processes of collective deliberation conducted rationally and fairly among free and equal individuals. The more collective decision-making processes approximate this model the greater their legitimacy and rationality."[27]

Political legitimacy, understood in this way, measures the degree to which political institutions "approximate" the ideal conditions of deliberation relied upon to determine the validity of moral claims. It derives the pedigree of political authority from the same set of standards that determines their moral correctness. "More or less legitimate" therefore also means "more or less morally correct" in this understanding of political legitimacy, just as "more or less correct" means "more or less legitimate." For political legitimacy, in this account, no longer refers to a threshold beyond which we recognize political decisions as authoritative for the community. It refers instead to the continuum of more or less justified moral claims that, it is suggested, supports the "presumption" of legitimacy that we make about democratic institutions.

Rewriting political legitimacy as "an ideal of justification" allows its advocates to construct a vision of democratic deliberation in which rhetoric is subordinated to the exchange and examination of opinions, in which we turn from rhetorical competition to a public search for the correct answers to questions of common concern. For, understood in this way, political legitimacy no longer refers us to the people who are authorized to decide how to end our deliberations, the majorities of unaccountable voters whom democratic speakers ordinarily try to bring over to their side. It refers instead to a process of discussion that reassures us of the rationality of whatever decisions we may come to in the end. The democratic standards we invoke in order to make such decisions are legitimate, from this point of view, only to the extent to which they promote and protect this process of discussion.

Now, if I am right about the way awareness of the need to appeal to majorities ensures the prominence of rhetoric in democratic deliberation, then it is hard to avoid the conclusion that democratic institutions as we know them fail this particular test of legitimacy. But let us put aside that concern for the moment and ask a broader question: Does it make sense to treat the legitimacy of democratic decisions as something that flows from their contribution to the institutionalization of a process by which we justify moral claims? I think not. No doubt, we sometimes view the democratic process, like the adversarial system of justice, as a means of weeding out irrational, immoral, and self-serving claims. But as with the adversarial system of justice, we also rely on this process as a means of coordinating our actions and making authoritative judgments in conditions where we cannot identify or agree on what the most justifiable course of action would be.

That becomes clear when we look at the different ways we invoke standards of political legitimacy, on the one hand, and standards of moral justification, on the other. We ordinarily invoke political legitimacy as a threshold concept rather than as an ideal that we are trying to approximate. When invoking political legitimacy we are trying to determine whether we can all treat a particular decision as an authoritative expression of the community, not how authoritative or how acceptable that decision may be. When, in contrast, we invoke standards of moral justification, we are very interested in degrees of justification. For the issue there is how correct or morally acceptable our judgments can be, not how to identify a common standard of legitimacy that everyone can endorse. Talking about political legitimacy as something we approach "the more collective decision-making processes approximate [a deliberative] model" of moral justification thus defeats the purpose of invoking the legitimacy of political decisions in the first place,[28] since it invites a debate about how much legitimacy is needed before we should accept democratic decisions as authoritative. Since even the most committed democrats are bound to differ on this question, these debates would probably be just as inconclusive as our public debates about the moral correctness of these decisions. Erase the distinction between political legitimacy and moral justification in this way and you might finally incite that "legitimation crisis" that Habermas has been warning us about for so many years.

As I have already noted, it is the popularity of Rawls's and Habermas's deliberative approaches to moral reasoning that has inspired this new understanding of democratic deliberation. It is relatively easy to write the practice of moral justification into one's understanding of democratic deliberation when you begin with the belief that morally valid judgments are the product of an idealized process of deliberation among free and equal individuals. And it is relatively easy to reconcile democracy and the love of truth when you think that moral truth is the product of such a process.

But we need to ask the same question about this idealized process of democratic deliberation that we posed to the advocates of its institutionalization in democratic practice: How can such a process produce anything like determinate standards in the absence of some authoritative decision rule that brings deliberation to a close? This problem is much more acute for Habermas than for Rawls, since Habermas eschews the appeal to basic standards of reasonableness that Rawls still relies on to produce determinate results from his hypothetical vision of deliberation. For Habermas, unlike for Rawls, morally valid standards are produced by genuine deliberation among free and equal individuals rather than by the judgments that we hypothesize a reasonable individual would choose if compelled to enter into such a deliberation. But why should unconstrained conversation among free, equal, and rational individuals lead to determinate and generally accepted standards, let alone rational ones? Even if we grant Habermas the ideal conditions that eliminate time and other practical constraints on deliberation, why should we think that such an unconstrained discussion would avoid the dead ends, drift, and dispersal of focus with which we are all familiar from our own experiences with undirected discussion among large groups?[29]

The answer, I would suggest, is that Habermas and his followers are imagining moral justification to be a process undertaken, like real-world democratic deliberation, to inform authoritative decisions made by some understanding of the people. As the strong deliberative democrats treat democratic deliberation as the institutionalization of a process of discussion that justifies moral standards, so they treat that process of discussion as an idealization of the conditions of democratic deliberation. They remove the practical constraints and social inequalities that keep us from deliberating freely with each other in our actual institutions, but they retain from our real-world experience the expectation that the goal of the process is the production of shared standards that we can all recognize. They expect unconstrained discussion to produce determinate moral standards because they treat such discussion as if, like democratic deliberation, it is undertaken with the goal of making choices that we can all accept as legitimate expressions of the popular will.

But there is no reason for our moral discussions to begin with such an expectation, unless we begin by writing the needs of political legitimacy into the practice of moral justification, which is precisely what I believe Habermas and his followers have done. Just as their discursive understanding of democratic deliberation is inspired by their conflation of political legitimacy with moral justification, so their deliberative understanding of moral justification is inspired by the conflation of moral justification with political legitimacy.

When we search for democratic standards of political legitimacy we are looking for interpretations of the principle of popular consent that allow us to act together without agreeing about the moral rightness of collective decisions. When we seek standards of moral justification we are looking for means of identifying what is right, not principles that allow us to act together. By imagining moral justification as an idealized process of democratic deliberation Habermas and his followers conflate these two distinct goals. The fact that I cannot gain assent from others for my moral claims tells me that my principles cannot ground the coordination of our actions by the political community, not that I am wrong. The deliberative democrats' reconciliation of democracy and the love of truth thus succeeds only by blurring this distinction between the desire to get things right and the desire to establish social order and political coordination by an appeal to the principle of popular consent.

The Tension between Democracy and the Love of Truth

The "strong" version of deliberative democracy examined here is the most elaborate and influential attempt to harmonize democracy and the love of truth. But it will not be the last. For as long as we maintain our commitments to these two ideals we will be drawn to theories that promise to eliminate the tension between them. It is therefore important to emphasize that deliberative democracy's failure to deliver on that promise is due to the character of democracy and the love of truth, rather than to any correctible mistakes in theory construction.

A commitment to democracy demands that we engage with, even defer to, the opinions of people who never have to acknowledge and account for their delusions and mistakes. It cannot tolerate the demand that everyone should be able to give an adequate account for their political judgments, a demand that searchers after truth, like Socrates examining the opinions of the

Athenian citizens, are constantly making.[30] The pursuit of truth, in contrast, demands that we discount or ignore the opinions of people whose delusions are manifest or easily demonstrated. It cannot tolerate any release from the demands of accountability. The tension between these two commitments is therefore unavoidable. You cannot eliminate that tension without seriously distorting one or both of these commitments.

Authority is the great enemy of the love of truth because it compels us to start from premises, modes of inquiry, and conclusions on the strength of their endorsement by particular individuals, rather than their ability to stand up to examination. Moreover authority compels us to persuade or find a way of replacing those individuals if we want to alter the judgments they make rather than simply expose their illusions and demonstrate their errors. If the emperor has the authority to set a community's sartorial standards, then we may have to get used to going naked unless we can remove him from power or persuade him that his new clothes are no clothes at all.

A commitment to democracy inevitably creates tensions with the love of truth because it endorses, among other things, a particular distribution of authority. Compared to merely taking the trouble to be born the daughter of the king or the son of a duke, this democratic principle of distributive justice has the virtue of subjecting the granting of authority to rational examination and argument. But it still establishes a distribution of *authority*. It still points us toward the people whom we have to *persuade* if we want to establish or alter public standards, rather than to criteria for identifying error and dispelling illusion. Democratic principles give us a chance to argue about the leadership qualifications of anyone who wants to try on the emperor's new clothes. But they measure the success of these arguments by their persuasiveness to large numbers of people, not by their ability to make manifest the nakedness of our leaders.

Pursuing the love of truth demands that we challenge democratic standards of authority no less than any other such standards. Indeed the deliberative democrats' revised understanding of political legitimacy issues just such a challenge, even if few of its proponents are willing to acknowledge that it does so. For it derives the legitimacy of democratic decisions from the process of discussion and mutual accountability that precedes them rather than from their persuasiveness to authoritative decision makers. Taken seriously, this understanding of political legitimacy would require us to challenge the votes of people who cannot reasonably account for their political choices. None of the deliberative democrats has been willing to issue such a challenge, since it would immediately bring into question his or her own standing as a democrat. They never insist that we should discount the votes of people who, to use Tim Scanlon's formulation, fail to endorse propositions that "they cannot reasonably reject."[31] But if we genuinely want to shift the focus of political legitimacy from voting to discussion and reason giving, then we have to be ready to do so. The unwillingness of deliberative democrats to issue such a challenge suggests that they are not fully committed to their proposed transformation of political legitimacy, that they continue to distinguish between the process of moral justification, where such challenges are appropriate, and the process of democratic deliberation, where they plainly are not.

The ideal of mutual accountability is a powerful tool in the pursuit of truth, since it insists that no degree of authority should free people from accounting for the claims they make about the world. And it challenges hierarchy in a way that certainly makes it seem democratic. No wonder, then, that even defenders of rhetoric against the deliberative democrats have begun to write mutual accountability into their understanding of democracy.[32] Nevertheless, as a political ideal mutual accountability has profoundly antidemocratic implications. For it demands that we ignore or discount the judgments of people who cannot adequately account for the choices they have made. It thus cannot bridge this gap between democracy and the love of truth, even if it can, quite contrary to the intentions of its advocates, raise doubts about democratic standards of political legitimacy.

Attempts to eliminate the tensions between democracy and the love of truth tend to undermine our commitment to the latter as well. For they discourage us from discounting or ignoring opinions that cannot stand up to critical examination.

We certainly need to listen to others, especially when they disagree with us, if we are interested in pursuing the truth. But if that is our goal, then we also need to stop listening to them when they show themselves unwilling or unable to correct manifest errors and delusions in their judgments. Democrats cannot and should not stop listening to such people, since their success is measured by their ability to bring the greater number of people over to their side. Lovers of truth, in contrast, have to learn how to identify and ignore mistaken and irrelevant opinion.

Democratic commitments would not pose much of a problem for the lovers of truth if, like Rorty, we were willing to treat the love of truth as nothing more than a combination of curiosity and openness.[33] For then the love of truth would draw us toward the opinions of paranoids and frauds no less, perhaps even more than the opinions of people who help us see the world more clearly. But the love of truth is inspired by dissatisfaction with inaccuracy and self-delusion, not just by curiosity and openness. It pushes us "to correct error, to avoid deceiving ourselves, to get beyond comfortable falsehood" rather than merely take pleasure in all of the curious sights and sounds the world has to offer.[34] Even if we know that we cannot fully succeed in this quest, the love of truth inspires us to unmask and leave behind opinions that misrepresent the way things are, just as Rorty seeks to unmask and leave behind what he judges to be our delusions about truth.[35]

Attempts to harmonize democracy and the love of truth, like the deliberative approach to moral justification discussed in the preceding section, make it harder for us to do this. As we have seen, this understanding of moral justification rests on a process of unconstrained discussion in which we exchange and examine each other's opinions. But no matter how much another's opinion suffers when subjected to this process of examination, we can never simply leave it behind as long as it continues to be maintained by its advocate. For the justification of moral claims in this process of discussion rests on the ultimate agreement of the participants rather than the intrinsic qualities of their opinions. This leads, in general, to the overvaluing of the whole sphere of public opinion by Habermas and his followers. But it strikes particularly hard at the refinement and correction of opinion that the love of truth requires us to pursue.

Of course, the introduction of something like the Habermasian ideal of deliberative democracy would considerably increase the respect paid to the love of truth in democratic politics. In particular, it would increase the value that democrats place on sincerity, which, as Bernard Williams suggests, is a major component of the virtue of truthfulness.[36] Indeed it is precisely rhetoric's encouragement of deceptive, manipulative, and flattering speech that leads deliberative democrats to try to remove it from democratic public speech. Freed from the competition to persuade large numbers to come over to our side, we will be much less tolerant of insincere and deceitful political speech.

But even in democratic politics, efforts to reconcile democracy and the love of truth could at times undermine the latter. For there is a trade-off between sincerity and accuracy, the passion for getting things right that represents the other major component of the virtue of truthfulness.[37] Make a cult of sincerity, as Elizabeth Markovits suggests most deliberative democrats tend to do,[38] and you will shrink from the use of rhetorical appeals to character and emotion as means of breaking through the falsehoods that surround us. Chasing the orators from the marketplace might diminish the problem of misrepresentation and self-delusion in public life, but it would also strip us of one of our most effective means of addressing that problem.

Conclusion

There is nothing to prevent us from pursuing commitments to both democracy and the love of truth. The endorsement of democratic forms of political authority entails no particular understanding of truth. And, *pace* Plato, the love of truth entails no particular understanding of political authority. But if we want to continue to pursue both of these commitments, we need to get used to the discomfort that doing so is bound to create for us.

"Democracy," as Michael Walzer elegantly puts it, "has no claims in the philosophical realm, and philosophers have no special rights in the political community." In the democratic world, "truth is indeed another opinion, and the philosopher is only another opinion-maker."[39] And in the world of truth-seekers, popular opinion is just another claim to be examined and, if necessary, discarded, by the lover of truth. Trying to live in both of these worlds is bound to make us uncomfortable at times. But it is far better to learn how to live with this discomfort than to devalue both worlds by vain attempts to bring them into harmony with each other.

Chapter 12

J. S. Mill on Truth, Liberty, and Democracy

Frederick Rosen

IN COMMON POLITICAL debate a belief in absolute values is often opposed
to relativism.[1] Those who uphold the importance of "truth" in politics are
usually on the side of the absolutists, and relativism tends to attract skeptics
who deny that truth has much to do with politics or morality. John Stuart
Mill was an unusual philosopher in adopting a historically based (and hence
relativist) system of ethics and politics, a strong commitment to individual
liberty, and, at the same time, a robust idea of truth.

His commitment to truth was developed primarily, though by no means
exclusively, in his major work, the *System of Logic* (1843),[2] and remained relevant to numerous works concerned with ethics and politics. Before turning
to the *Logic*, however, we shall first consider a passage from Bernard Williams's *Truth and Truthfulness*, which brings out in an interesting way a common misinterpretation of Mill this essay is meant to challenge. According to
Williams:

> Democracy (in its modern, constitutional, forms) is valued, to an im-
> portant extent in the name of liberty. . . . The appeal to liberty comes in
> stronger and weaker versions. The minimal version insists merely that
> government should permit maximum freedom (compatible with other
> goods, especially others' freedom), and that to deny people information

and the right to spread information both violates liberty directly, in particular the freedom of speech, and devalues liberty in other areas, since effective action requires knowledge. A stronger version of the appeal calls, as J. S. Mill did, on the value of individuals' exercising and developing their powers. Both versions of the appeal to liberty raise an important question: how far are we concerned with liberty (above all, the freedom of speech), and how far are we concerned with truth? The standard liberal assumption is that the two objectives go together, and to some extent this is true. Self-development has been understood as development in the light of the truth, and liberties do get their point, in good part, from the possibility of effective action, which implies true information. However, it does not follow that all liberty, and specifically the freedom of speech, is necessarily helpful to the spread of the truth. We cannot take for granted Mill's optimistic conclusion that maximal freedom of speech must assist the emergence of truth in what has come to be called "a market-place of ideas."[3]

This lengthy but helpful passage attempts to relate truth, liberty, and democracy with reference to Mill's thought and with reference to the commitment of liberalism generally to freedom of speech. Nevertheless one may ask, does this fairly commonplace criticism of Mill embrace the whole of Mill's approach? Did Mill believe, as Williams seems to suggest, that maximum freedom of speech "must assist" the emergence of truth? This view omits the emphasis Mill placed on logic, for it is logic that assists the discovery of truth, and liberty that simply, though importantly, keeps truth alive. Mill defined logic as "the science which treats of the operations of the human understanding in the pursuit of truth" (*CW* 7:6).[4] Such a science might change from place to place or from age to age, but logic, though also evolving, as a rational science, remains committed to the discovery of truth. Mill put it dramatically: "If there were but one rational being in the universe, that being might be a perfect logician; and the science and art of logic would be the same for that one person as for the whole human race" (*CW* 7:6).

Truth and Logic

It is important to appreciate the novelty of Mill's approach to logic and to truth in an age when great strides were being made to free logic from the scholastic tradition that in the early nineteenth century was still firmly entrenched in English universities.[5] For Mill, there was considerable merit in the scholastic tradition, based on Aristotelian philosophy, but its study had become repetitive and lackluster. Nevertheless modern philosophy, from Locke onward, tended to reject the tradition and concentrated mainly on psychology and language, and in the process minimized the importance of traditional logic.[6] For Locke, for example, traditional logic seemed to generate useless disputes of little practical benefit to society.[7]

In *Elements of Logic* (1826) Richard Whately made an attempt to revitalize the study of logic at Oxford by restating Aristotelian logic in a new context, using fresh examples and without the burdensome baggage of scholasticism.[8] This context might be described as Coleridgean, as early versions of both the *Elements of Logic* and its companion, *Elements of Rhetoric*, first appeared in the *Encyclopaedia Metropolitana*, a work inspired by Coleridge to advance progressive views that could be seen as emerging out of traditional thought and institutions.[9]

Mill was an enthusiastic reviewer of Whately's book on logic, and his review represented his first major essay in this field (*CW* 11:1–35).[10] Among the ideas and arguments to which Mill was drawn was Whately's defense of the syllogism, which was important both in traditional logic and for the discovery of truth (see *CW* 11:33). The whole thrust of modern philosophy and science was to dismiss the syllogism as irrelevant to the pursuit of truth, as the conclusion (e.g., Socrates is mortal) was considered already present in the premise (e.g., all men are mortal). The rejection of Aristotelianism by modern philosophers usually included the dismissal of the syllogism almost in passing, in favor of an emphasis on induction. Francis Bacon was generally credited with initiating this shift in focus to investigating nature by means of induction. Mill, however, argued that Bacon did not reject the syllogism, but simply criticized the scholastic philosophers in the Aristotelian tradition for being poor investigators of nature, that is to say, for neglecting inductive logic (see *CW* 11:12ff). Mill then proceeded to argue that the syllogism enabled one to discover new truths, even though these truths were implicit in the premises of the syllogism. He pointed to numerous fields, from geometry to mechanics, where the syllogism had been used to discover new truths. In the *Logic* Mill retained the syllogism and also created a new theory of inductive logic. In addition, he developed features of Aristotelian thought, such as the theory of logical fallacies, in which he adopted the traditional fallacies and then expanded the whole genre in a novel and striking manner.[11]

In the *Logic*, as in the early essay on Whately, as we have seen, Mill took the view that logic was concerned with the pursuit of truth. He acknowledged that many writers on logic believed that it was wholly concerned with an art of reasoning or thinking (see *CW* 7:4–5). For Mill, no such art could stand alone, as all arts were connected with various sciences, and logic had to be regarded as a science as well as an art. This science, like all others, had to aim at truth, in this case, universally true laws of thought and reasoning.

We might gain some insight into Mill's emphasis on truth in logic by considering those whom he regarded as his opponents. In the *Autobiography* he referred to the *Logic* as providing "a text-book of the opposite doctrine" to the "German, or *à priori* view [early draft: "German or ontological view"] of human knowledge and of the knowing faculties" (*CW* 1:232–33). Mill's doctrine, in contrast, "derives all knowledge from experience, and all moral and intellectual qualities principally from the direction given to the associations." Mill's opposition to the "German, or *à priori* view" was deeply felt. He went on to declare:

> The notion that truths external to the mind may be known by intuition or consciousness, independently of observation and experience, is, I am persuaded, in these times, the great intellectual support of false doctrines and bad institutions. By the aid of this theory, every inveterate belief and every intense feeling, of which the origin is not remembered, is enabled to dispense with the obligation of justifying itself by reason, and is erected into its own all-sufficient voucher and justification. There never was such an instrument devised for consecrating all deep seated prejudices. And the chief strength of this false philosophy in morals, politics, and religion, lies in the appeal which it is accustomed to make to the evidence of mathematics and of the cognate branches of physical science. (*CW* 1:233)

Mill clearly believed that the task of the *Logic* was to oppose this doctrine and even "to expel" it from mathematics and physical sciences through his own system of logic. In the *Logic*, however, he was far less combative. Logic, he declared, was "common ground on which the partisans of Hartley and of Reid, of Locke and of Kant, may meet and join hands" (*CW* 7:14). Doubtless, there would be disputes between the successors of these figures, but such disputes could be resolved. Even metaphysics needed to use the tools of logic to deal with the themes that fell within the scope of its enquiries. When metaphysics proceeded, like other sciences, to require evidence to establish a position, it was forced to draw inferences from evidence. To accomplish this, "logic becomes the sovereign judge" as to whether the inferences were properly grounded or whether or not other inferences should be considered (*CW* 7:14).

For logic to become "the sovereign judge," however, it had to base itself on truth. Other philosophers were prepared to recognize the importance of logic, but in their view its province was limited to that of achieving consistency in argument rather than truth. Mill ascribed this view to Henry Mansel and, particularly, to Sir William Hamilton, who either held that logic had no concern with truth or that it was subordinate to other studies or sciences that did have these concerns. Mill called their conceptions of logic "formal logic" (see *CW* 11:367), which consisted mainly of syllogistic logic that considered only the consistency of arguments from premises to conclusions. It rejected the possibility of a general theory of evidence, which Bacon had envisaged (see *CW* 11:368). For Hamilton, each science contained its own criterion of truth, and he denied that there could be some general theory of evidence applicable to all enquiries (see *CW* 11:369).

Mill did not reject formal logic, or what he called at times the logic of consistency (see *CW* 7:208). He regarded it as a small, though important part of the logic of truth. He also pointed out that the study of the logic of truth, which rivaled in complexity and difficulty the study of mathematics and many sciences, would be open to and attract only a few superior minds in any generation. Formal logic, however, was separable from logic as a whole and could be introduced into education at a much lower level. It aimed at removing obstacles to the attainment of truth by functioning in a negative manner and pointing out fallacies and inconsistencies (see *CW* 11:370). Formal logic thus retained its connection with truth, though it could be taught, as it was, almost as sporting exercises.

In his essay on education, the *Inaugural Address Delivered to the University of St. Andrews* (1867), Mill restated these ideas in a new context. Here we again find the emphasis on logic as being concerned with truth ("Logic lays down the general principles and laws of the search after truth") and closely related to mathematics and physics (*CW* 21:238). He also distinguished between ratiocinative and inductive logic, with the former "already carried to a high degree of perfection by Aristotle," and the latter, more difficult, requiring a knowledge of the inductive sciences. All logic is praised, including ratiocinative logic, roughly equivalent to what he earlier had called formal logic.

But in this work on education he dwelled more on this aspect of logic and its importance in society. Discovering and pointing out error is mainly a negative function designed "not so much to teach us to go right, as to keep us from going wrong" (*CW* 21:328). "Logic," he continued, "is the great disperser of hazy and confused thinking: it clears up the fogs which hide us from our own ignorance, and make us believe that we understand a subject when we do not." For those who disparaged school logic, he wrote, "Take the trouble to learn it. You will easily do so in a few weeks, and you will see whether it is of no use to you in making your mind clear, and keeping you from stumbling in the dark over the most outrageous fallacies" (*CW* 21:329).

Socrates

These allusions to keeping one from going wrong, curing ignorance, and preventing one from stumbling in the dark lead us to the importance of Plato's Socrates in Mill's account of logic. Although most discussions of the history of scholastic logic include Aristotle and Thomas, one seldom finds many of Mill's contemporaries (or ours) going back to Socrates. Yet Mill's logic is almost unique in its being grounded in an understanding of the Socratic elenchus.[12] He wrote in the early draft of the *Autobiography* that "the Socratic method . . . is unsurpassed as a discipline for abstract thought on the most difficult subjects. Nothing in modern life and education in the smallest degree supplies its place" (*CW* 1:24). Even as a boy, he was persuaded of its importance: "[The Socratic method] took such hold on me that it became part of my own mind; and I have ever felt myself, beyond any modern that I know of except my father and perhaps even beyond him, a pupil of Plato, and cast in the mould of his dialectics" (*CW* 1:24).

Mill did not refer to the Plato of the transcendent forms, but to Plato's Socrates in the early dialogues, where a negative dialectic revealed the ignorance of the most confident and learned of his interlocutors. Mill was strongly impressed by Plato's picture in the *Gorgias* and *Republic* "of the solitary and despised position of the philosopher in every existing society, and the universal impression against him, as at best an useless person, but more frequently an eminently wicked one" (*CW* 11:399).[13] He adopted George Grote's arguments that while Plato might have despised the Sophists, because they were more concerned with appearances than with reality, and took money for their services, they were not the real enemy. The real corruptors of the young were not the Sophists, but "their families, their associates, all whom they see and converse with, the applauses and hootings of the public assembly, the sentences of the court of justice. These are what pervert young men, by holding up to them a false standard of good and evil, and giving an entirely wrong direction to their desires. As for the Sophists, they merely repeat the people's own opinions" (*CW* 11:400). Mill not only adopted Grote's view of the importance of the Sophists to public debate and the role of Socrates in this debate, but in a review of Grote's posthumously published study of Aristotle, he acknowledged the importance of Aristotle's *Sophistical Refutations* in the development of an important aspect of logic and in the pursuit of truth. Even though Aristotle's work was a study of the art of arguing for victory rather than for truth, Mill saw nothing wrong with such public debates so long as they took place within established rules. Furthermore he believed that Aristotle regarded such exercises in dialectical argument to be valuable in the pursuit of truth. Quoting from Grote, Mill gave three reasons for this belief (*CW* 11:508). First, the debates constituted a kind of mental exercise that was valuable and stimulating. Second, the debates put one in touch with the ordinary opinions held by other members of society. Third, such dialectical debate influenced science and philosophy, encouraging one to look at both sides of questions and to determine which answers were true and which were false. Mill believed that Aristotle's method in dialectical argument "was greatly in advance not only of his own time, but of ours": "His general advice for exercise and practice in Dialectic is admirably adapted to the training of one's own mind for the pursuit of truth. 'You ought to test every thesis by first assuming it to be true, then assuming it to be false, and following out the consequences on both sides.' This was already the practice of the Eleatic dialecticians, as we see in the *Parmenides*" (*CW* 11:508). In Mill's view Aristotle's account of dialectic also took one directly back to the Socratic elenchus.

Socrates and Liberty of Thought and Discussion

One of the most striking arguments in *On Liberty* (1859), in which Socrates was invoked, arose from Mill's defense of liberty of expression.[14] Mill was concerned with the lack of attention paid to truth in the way most people, even those who were willing to entertain dissenting opinions, formed their views and enforced them on others. He noted that they tended to be diffident about their own opinions and were happy to accept those held by "the world," or by that part of the world with which they came into contact. Few were troubled by the fact that this acquiescence in the views of others led to a kind of relativism, as opinions differed in various parts of the world—"The same causes . . . make him a Churchman in London . . . [and] a Buddhist or a Confucian in Pekin"—or in different ages (*CW* 18:230).

The legal or popular enforcement of these opinions involved an assumption of infallibility, and it is worth noting that such an assumption went hand in hand with what might be called an indifference to truth. The deaths of Socrates and Jesus were terrible events on which we look back with horror. But Mill believed that those who carried out these crimes were not evil people but "men who possessed in a full . . . measure, the religious, moral, and patriotic feelings of their time and people: the very kind of men who, in all times, our own included, have every chance of passing through life blameless and respected" (*CW* 18:236). What was missing in these "ordinary" people was a serious concern for the truth, which initially involved a recognition that they might not know the truth and hence could not act with any infallible certainty. According to Mill, for people to act on the basis of their opinions with regard to truth, they should accept, as a condition of doing so, a complete liberty of challenging their opinions (see *CW* 18:231ff). This condition should apply whether or not the received opinions were false or true. If they were false, then freedom of expression would enable people to have access to the truth. If they were true, Mill believed that freedom of expression would enable the truths to be living truths and not dead dogmas. Mill regarded received truths as particularly dangerous. They lulled the mind into a passive acceptance and almost a vacancy of understanding, in which the truth was forgotten or never reconsidered. In some cases, he argued, accepted doctrines remained "outside the mind, incrusting and petrifying it against all other influences addressed to the higher parts of our nature" (*CW* 18:248).

Mill's approach to truth was a crucial part of his doctrine of freedom of expression. His admiration of Socrates was as much due to Socrates' insistence on the search for truth as on whatever truths Socrates uncovered in his searches (except, perhaps, for the main one, that he knew nothing). Nevertheless Mill was never optimistic that truth would prevail over error; after all, Socrates and Jesus died for truth (*CW* 18:235–36). Mill could write, "On any matter not self-evident, there are ninety-nine persons totally incapable of judging it, for one who is capable; and the capacity of the hundredth person is only comparative; for the majority of the eminent men of every past generation held many opinions now known to be erroneous, and did

or approved numerous things which no one will now justify" (*CW* 18:231).
But just following this pessimistic view of the human condition, he posed a
different question, which seems somewhat at odds with his view of ninety-
nine of a hundred persons and, strikingly, provided an answer apparently
at odds with it: "Why is it, then, that there is on the whole a preponderance
among mankind of rational opinions and rational conduct? If there really
is this preponderance—which there might be unless human affairs are, and
have always been, in an almost desperate state—it is owing to a quality of the
human mind, the source of everything respectable in man either as an intellectual or as a moral being, namely that his errors are corrigible: (*CW* 18:231).

Mill's sudden ascription of rationality in mankind reveals an important
duality in *On Liberty* and in his thought generally. On the one hand, the great
thinker must be free to follow his intellect wherever it led. The person who
thought for himself and did not give up was superior to those who held only
opinions, some possibly true and others possibly false, due to an indifference to the truth. But, as we have seen, Mill was not satisfied only to provide
liberty of thought and discussion or liberty generally for a few great people:
"Not that it is solely, or chiefly, to form great thinkers, that freedom of thinking is required. On the contrary, it is as much and even more indispensable,
to enable average human beings to attain the mental stature which they are
capable of. There have been, and may again be, great individual thinkers, in a
general atmosphere of mental slavery. But there never has been, nor ever will
be, in that atmosphere an intellectually active people" (*CW* 18:243). His argument regarding "an intellectually active people" takes us back to the *Logic* and
to the Socratic dimension in numerous other works. The study of elementary
logic and, particularly, the study of logical fallacies reveal a Socratic dimension to this intellectual activity. It is within the grasp of most people to question the opinions they have accepted, and with an understanding of the elements of logic and argument to discover their ignorance and its significance.
With freedom of expression it is also within their grasp to look for truth and
to keep truth alive, so long as they retain this knowledge of their ignorance
and the belief that their errors are corrigible.

Mill was also restating in this context his distinction in the *Logic* between
formal logic, or the logic of consistency, and the logic of truth. The former
was an important part of the latter, and could play a significant role in the
great Socratic enterprise of making people aware of their own ignorance and
the need to pursue and maintain truth. In opposition to the view set forth by
Williams, quoted above, we can see that for Mill it is not liberty that assists

the emergence of truth, but that the pursuit of truth (even if confined to the recognition of one's ignorance) that assists the emergence of liberty. For each person there is potentially a Socratic moment when an acknowledgment of ignorance allows one to pursue truth. This pursuit then requires liberty of thought and discussion to be successful. To possess liberty without a Socratic moment leads nowhere, except perhaps to an endless pursuit of variety and novelty, as entertainment or something worse substitutes for truth.

Democracy

It is well-known that Mill was highly ambivalent about the virtues of modern democracy and, like Tocqueville, was critical and fearful of the tyranny of the majority. But despite his fears regarding democracy, he became a strong admirer of ancient Athenian democracy as depicted in Pericles' famous funeral oration.[15]

Prior to Grote's magisterial *History of Greece* there were few champions of ancient Athenian democracy, which, after all, had condemned Socrates, who remained a major hero of the Victorian period and, additionally, was known as a critic of democracy.[16] Most historians of Greece followed Plato, Aristotle, Xenophon, Lysias, and Isocrates, and favored Sparta over Periclean Athens, as did Rousseau and other philosophers.[17] It is important to appreciate the significance of Grote's history of Greece for Mill's thought. Grote referred to the emphasis Pericles placed on liberty of thought and action not only from legal restraints but also "from practical intolerance between man and man, and tyranny of the majority over individual dissenters in taste and pursuit."[18] In a remarkable passage Grote elevated Periclean Athens above all modern states, including modern democracies, in the liberty it granted to individuals. For Grote, Pericles' funeral speech both encouraged a wide diversity of tastes and sentiments and reflected this encouragement within Athenian democracy.[19]

Grote was well aware that his praise of Periclean Athens required him to provide an account of the life and death of Socrates that was compatible with it. Just as with Mill, Socrates was a philosophical hero for Grote, and both emphasized the significance for later thought of Socrates' negative method.[20] Grote had also corrected the general opinion of the Sophists as corrupt and subversive, and he did not hesitate to link Socrates with the best (particularly those who encouraged liberty of thought and discussion) among the Sophists.[21] As for the Athenian condemnation of Socrates, he wrote, "In any other government of Greece, as well as in the Platonic Republic, Sokrates would have been quickly arrested in his career, even if not severely punished; in Athens, he was allowed to talk and teach publicly for twenty-five or thirty years, and then condemned when an old man. Of these two applications of the same mischievous principle, assuredly the latter is at once the more moderate and less noxious."[22]

Mill accepted this new version of Greek history with enthusiasm (see *CW* 24:867–75, 1084–88; 25:1121–28, 1128–34, 1157–64). He twice reprinted the passage on Pericles that Grote had written (as well as quoting at length from Pericles' funeral oration as it appeared in Thucydides), and referred to the passage as a valuable contribution to a "vital question of social morals" (*CW* 11:319–20; 25:1129–31). He wrote, "In the greatest Greek commonwealth, as described by its most distinguished citizen [Pericles], the public interest was held of paramount obligation in all things which concerned it; but, with that part of the conduct of individuals which concerned only themselves, public opinion did not interfere: while in the ethical practice of the moderns, this is exactly reversed, and no one is required by opinion to pay any regard to the public, except by conducting his own private concerns in conformity to its expectations" (*CW* 11:319). In most modern European states vigorous self-assertion on the public stage was not encouraged. Not only was submission and obedience the norm in public life, but Mill also noted the tendency for individuals to conform in private life to the expectations of society. By emphasizing the example of Periclean Athens, Mill was first pointing to the importance of a free and vigorous public sphere in which there was full debate of ethical and political issues. This public sphere then enabled the private sphere to be free as well, insofar as it was left to its own devices.

Mill was mainly concerned here with the public sphere of modern societies in which the tyranny of the majority in its "collective mediocrity" had begun to assume power (*CW* 18:268ff). He found this majority, however powerful in limiting liberty, nonetheless passive and susceptible to being led by others. He particularly criticized Carlyle's idea of hero worship, in which the "strong man of genius" would undoubtedly be corrupted in the process of exercising power (*CW* 18:269). Mill sought instead a society that embraced individual liberty and allowed and encouraged individuality to flourish, as did Athens with its acceptance of Socrates for seventy years. Mill wanted to oppose the "tyranny of opinion" in his own society by the encouragement of eccentricity. As he wrote, "Eccentricity has always abounded when and where strength of character has abounded; and the amount of eccentricity in a society has generally been proportional to the amount of genius, mental vigour, and moral courage which it contained. That so few now dare to be eccentric marks the chief danger of the time" (*CW* 18:269). The cultivation of individuality thus depended on individuals of strong character and genius daring to be eccentric, but to dare to be eccentric depended in turn on a public sphere that encouraged such eccentricity to develop. Without the Periclean perspective Mill believed that the cultivation of eccentricity would seriously diminish and, with it, the existence of liberty throughout society.

As we have seen, Mill's conception of Periclean democracy encouraged liberty in both the public and private spheres. But to say that Mill's conception of democracy was based on liberty is to state only half (or even less than half) of the story. Let us contrast Mill with Bentham, whose theory of constitutional democracy was well-known to Mill and, on some important issues, was rejected by him.[23] Bentham (who tended to write of representative *democracy* rather than simply of representative *government*, as Mill did) believed that his theory of constitutional democracy was based on liberty. The liberty that was relevant here was civil liberty, whereby the law prevented others from interfering in one's life and activities, and one should be free to think and act freely so long as one did not harm others. Bentham came to believe that civil liberty could not establish the security an individual required without constitutional liberty, because it could not on its own secure the individual from the corruption and tyranny exercised by government itself. The only way to establish constitutional liberty, as an extension of civil liberty, was to provide institutions to remove from power those rulers who threatened it. This was to be achieved by representative democracy, including a widespread and equal suffrage, the use of the secret ballot, and freedom of expression.[24]

It is worth noting that Bentham was as concerned with truth as was Mill. He wrote extensively on logic and on evidence, but his theory of democracy was based on liberty rather than truth.[25] A well-run representative democracy would, of course, give those dedicated to the search for truth the liberty to do so, and government officials were to be educated in their fields of expertise, but democracy would not be based on some attempt to embody the pursuit and representation of truth in its very institutions.

Mill's idea of representative government was entirely different, and was based on a diffusion of the Socratic elenchus, via the negative and critical dialectic, throughout society. This diffusion took various kinds of active character in the population and directed them toward establishing and sustaining representative institutions. For Mill, human beings were for the most part active beings, but unless their critical faculties were awakened, they tended to accept the prevailing opinions of their nation and their generation. A growing knowledge of one's ignorance could first crack the shell that enclosed the human mind in received opinion. Liberating the individual mind to question such opinions and to challenge the utility of established institutions in turn encouraged active character in families, society, and government. Mill believed that in most societies the level of such development of active character was not sufficient to create and maintain representative government. In a few, such as Britain and the United States, it was. Thus Socratic self-awareness of ignorance, plus a psychological disposition to be active, plus the development of active character could lead to representative democracy and the institutions that might support it, such as the open ballot.

It is possible to argue, as Williams seems to do, that Mill is nonetheless basing democracy on a different notion of liberty than that employed by Bentham and the earlier generation of radicals. Williams depicts this liberty in terms of "individuals exercising and developing their powers," but he then finds it inadequate to believe that freedom of speech will deliver the truth involved in the exercise of human powers. I have already suggested that for Mill it is not liberty that assists in the emergence of truth, but truth, via the Socratic dialectic, that assists the emergence of liberty. Furthermore this truth-based liberty works only indirectly in politics, as it is mainly confined to the sphere of "ethology" and the cultivation of active character in society. It is important to note that, unlike philosophers such as Aristotle and Montesquieu, Mill did not develop a typology of political constitutions. Following Comte, he looked to a historically based social science, but one that, unlike Comte, assumed that societies were capable of "improvement." The details of this "improvement" would be unique to the society under consideration, and Mill's emphasis on national character reflects this focus.[26] Active character in turn may or may not develop into democratic political institutions, so that Mill's emphasis on the development of the individual's powers may not lead to democracy at all.

In *On Liberty* Mill did not dwell on politics to any extent, as he was concerned with liberty in society. At the end of the essay, however, he referred to a form of government for which he had earlier coined the term "pedantocracy."[27] In an early letter to Comte, Mill had written, "The majority of an educated class may well be less disposed than any other to be led by the most advanced minds in its midst; and since this majority would doubtless be composed, not of great thinkers, but simply of scholars or scientists lacking true originality, there could result only what one finds in China, a *pedantocracy*" (*CW* 13:502).[28] The context of Mill's remark was his acceptance of Comte's arguments for the separation of the temporal and spiritual powers that would prevent some kind of rule by philosophers or educated bureaucrats in a Platonic, St. Simonian, or other utopian form of rule by intellectuals.[29] For Mill, the allusion to "pedantocracy" in *On Liberty* was closely connected with his estimation of the kind of bureaucratic regime existing in China, where virtually all liberty was extinguished (see *CW* 18:308). As he wrote elsewhere, "If the lettered and cultivated class, embodied and disciplined under a central organ, could become in Europe, what it is in China, the Government—unchecked by any power residing in the mass of citizens, and permitted to assume a parental tutelage over all operations of life—the result would probably be a darker despotism, one more opposed to improvement, than even the military monarchies and aristocracies have in fact proved" (*CW* 20:270).[30]

He also referred to this kind of rule as "a perfection of despotism" (*CW* 20:274). In *On Liberty* itself he evoked the Chinese mandarin, who was "as much the tool and creature of a despotism as the humblest cultivator" (*CW* 18:308). This material in *On Liberty* was concerned with the extent to which government interference might assist with the development of individual liberty in society. As Collini has pointed out, this discussion might easily be confused (and was confused) with a debate over individualism versus collectivism.[31] But Mill was arguing here, more profoundly perhaps, that rule by an educated elite, even a liberal elite, apparently in favor of helping people to possess and enjoy liberty, might easily degenerate into despotic rule. For this very reason we would do well not to seek "improvement" through government but through the maintenance of groups of educated people outside government able and willing to criticize and challenge the ruling bureaucracy.

For Mill in *On Liberty* the opposing term to pedantocracy, if he possessed a constitutional typology, might be Athenian democracy under Pericles. The key feature of this form of rule was less its commitment to democracy than its commitment to a private space in which the Socratic elenchus and its cultivation could take root. It is possible to see the *Considerations on Representative Government* (1861) as an attempt to establish modern liberal democracy on the foundations of Athenian democracy,[32] but such a view abstracts the regime from the context, on which Mill insisted, of particular societies evolving historically. The *Considerations* was clearly written for Britain in the 1860s, and despite ingenious attempts to see in it some relevance to later politics and other societies, Mill's doctrine, unlike that of *On Liberty*, has resisted most attempts at reincarnation. Perhaps, as I have argued elsewhere, the *Considerations* is linked more with a "method of reform" than with a typology of constitutions, as a way to bring together liberals and conservatives to pursue reform in an ideologically divided society.[33]

Liberalism

The status of Mill as a liberal, and what kind of liberal he was, has been hotly debated over the past fifty years. Alan Ryan has written of *On Liberty,* "*That* it is a liberal manifesto is clear beyond doubt; *What* the liberalism is that it defends and *how* it defends it remain matters of controversy."[34] Ryan's point is undoubtedly true, and Mill's *On Liberty* is deeply embedded in current debates about liberty as well as in the history of liberalism.[35] Nevertheless one might easily argue that how Mill saw himself as a liberal in his nineteenth-century context and how we see Mill today are considerably different, because liberalism itself has evolved. But Mill is as much a part of the evolution as its historical source, and his ideas appear and reappear in numerous contexts. The passage from Williams, to which we have returned on several occasions, almost innocently ascribes to Mill a view to which Mill himself might not have subscribed. I have emphasized Mill's concern with truth, not just in the *Logic,* but in *On Liberty* as well. In a letter to Alexander Bain written in 1859, just after the publication of *On Liberty,* Mill rejected Bain's interpretation of his position and emphasized the importance of truth: "The 'Liberty' has produced an effect on you which it was never intended to produce if it has made you think that we ought not to attempt to convert the world. I meant nothing of the kind, & hold that we ought to convert all we can. We *must* be satisfied with keeping alive the sacred fire in a few minds when we are unable to do more—but the notion of an intellectual aristocracy of *lumières* while the rest of the world remains in darkness fulfils none of my aspirations—& the effect I aim at by the book is, on the contrary, to make the many more accessible to all truth by making them more open minded" (*CW* 15:631). Mill continued by asserting that only in the matter of religion was he not prepared to convert the world to all of his views but only "really superior intellects & characters." As for the rest, he would prefer "to improve their religion than to destroy it," which might occur if his views were fully revealed at that time (*CW* 15:631).

The "sacred fire" to which Mill and Bain are dedicated is that of truth, and liberty of thought and discussion is a way of extending a concern for truth to a wider group in society. Mill's reservations regarding religion are not reservations about freedom of worship, but about the extent to which people generally in Britain were prepared in the 1850s to have their deepest views on religion challenged by Mill. He had clearly hoped that one day he would be able to reveal the truth to all, that is to say, that British society would be able to put his position regarding truth and religion to good use and not merely react negatively against Mill himself.[36]

At the outset of this essay I noted that although Mill was a relativist, he held to the importance of truth in society and for the individual. This adherence to truth did not mean that truths concerning the individual and society could not change from time to time and from place to place. On the contrary, unless this change took place, stagnation in science and politics might occur. A commitment to truth also embodied a belief that there were new truths to discover, that natural and social science evolved, and improvement in all aspects of human life and understanding was possible. Nevertheless, to favor liberty without any concern for truth (as some liberals might argue today) would not make much sense to Mill. The foundation of his liberalism, as we have seen, is in logic, but it is fair to acknowledge that he regarded some developments in logic to be as great a threat to the pursuit of truth as its apparent disregard by later liberals. For the logic Mill favored was one inspired by the Socratic elenchus, and even in his lifetime this approach was threatened by highly technical work in mathematical aspects of logic.[37] When Mill began writing on logic, he found that it had been dismissed by many as irrelevant to truth, and the same may be said nowadays, though for different reasons. To appreciate Mill's liberalism requires us, almost as archaeologists, to recover the Socratic dimension in his logic and to show its connection with liberty in numerous areas of ethics and politics.

Chapter 13

Can This Marriage Be Saved? The Relationship of Democracy and Truth

Rogers M. Smith

IF I USED to be even partly right, the perceptive reflections on democracy and truth provided by Bernard Yack and Frederick Rosen do not bode well for the American Political Science Association, and perhaps not for humanity more generally. Years ago I argued that the leaders of the discipline of political science in the United States had always professed that they were equally dedicated to pursuing truth via science and to serving American democracy, and disciplinary leaders like Robert Putnam continue to make that case today.[1] I thought then that political scientists needed to acknowledge that pursuing truth and serving American democracy were not always the same thing, and these essays sharpen recognition of the gaps between those endeavors.

Frederick Rosen contends that John Stuart Mill did not believe that liberty of thought and expression would necessarily lead to truth, so much as Mill thought that the critical exchanges he saw as intrinsic to the search for truth would help preserve liberty. Democratic debates can be one arena in which valuable critical exchanges take place, and in Mill's eyes it is good for people to be brought into such exchanges in any arena. But as Rosen notes, Mill did not really think most people in most societies were really capable of contributing much to competent representative government. So in Mill the quest for truth supports liberty but not necessarily democracy.

Bernard Yack places truth and democracy even further apart. Democracy solves the problems of how necessary authoritative decisions can be reached in societies with conflicting views and interests by privileging the majority of voters, who need not base their votes on truth and whose votes often must be won by rhetorical appeal to their misconceptions, not via truth. The search for truth, in contrast, requires challenging majority beliefs and even the legitimacy of democratic decision making itself. If we try to conflate the endeavors of democracy and truth seeking, either by seeking to turn democratic debates into academic seminars or by letting vote totals persuade us what is really true, we may well make it impossible either to reach authoritative democratic political decisions or to make progress toward grasping truth.

I believe that Rosen is not only correct in his reading of Mill, but that Mill was largely right about the relationship of the quest for truth to achieving and maintaining human liberty, and that Yack is also correct in his core claim that there is an ineradicable tension between democratic standards of political legitimacy and pursuing truth. Yet it is wrong, I think, to conclude that modern efforts to wed democracy and truth, like those long pursued by the American discipline of political science, represent at best arranged marriages of convenience. I believe they are instead, in the language of the certificates given by state regulatory commissions to public utilities, matters of public "convenience and necessity." Like the "necessary and proper" clause in Article I, section 8 of the U.S. Constitution, this apparently redundant phrasing leaves room for interpreting "necessity" not as something that absolutely must exist for the good in question to be achieved, but as something that is so often and so strongly conducive to attaining that good that what is deemed a "necessity" ought to be more or less permanently in place. I am saying, in short, that although they are not only distinct but in profound tension, in practice and in the long run the endeavors of democratic decision making and intellectual truth seeking benefit each other so much that we should almost always strive to keep them together, more so than perhaps these papers would prompt us to do.

The one point at which I demur at Yack's formulations of the relationship of truth to democracy is when he writes that invoking truth seeking standards of moral justification to criticize the legitimacy of political decisions "defeats the purpose of invoking the legitimacy of political decisions in the first place, since it invites a debate about how much legitimacy is needed before we should accept democratic decisions as authoritative." He is not wrong, to be sure, that such debate delays completing the task of reaching what can be widely accepted as a legitimate political decision, and so it cannot serve as a replacement standard for legitimate decision making. But even on important public issues, getting to the "yes" or "no" that 51 percent provides is not our only concern. And precisely because democratic decision making is often a matter of persuading people that a particular decision best expresses their prejudices, it is valuable to have as a recurrent feature of democratic politics debates over whether, taking all pertinent moral and political considerations into account, we should really regard a particular democratic decision as legitimate or authoritative. If, as Yack later notes, "the introduction of something like the Habermasian ideal of deliberative democracy would considerably increase the respect paid to the love of truth in democratic politics," that strikes me as on balance a good thing—fully accepting his caveat that sometimes emotional rhetorical appeals do a better job of building support for desirable decisions. In so arguing I am not disputing Yack's contention that we cannot ever wholly harmonize democratic decision making and the quest for truth but must instead learn how to live best with the tensions between them. I am instead contending that we live best with those tensions if we keep them alive, using truth seeking to challenge democratic decision making, instead of treating the two activities as properly quite separate, as some of Yack's formulations might be read (I think misread) to suggest.

But if truth seeking is on the whole good for democracy, is democracy on the whole good for truth seeking? Rosen's Mill (and mine) did not particularly think so. It was, again, the mutually beneficial relationship of truth seeking with free thought and expression that most concerned him. And though some forms of free thought and expression are required to some degree by commitments to democracy—people must at a minimum generally be free to write their choices for candidates on ballots and to announce themselves as candidates—considerable intellectual and expressive freedoms can exist in nondemocratic societies, while democratic majorities sometimes act to suppress some such freedoms, legally or more often sociologically. And when democracies thus limit freedoms of thought and expression, they inevitably limit some forms of truth seeking.

But here, as in so many other regards, if democracies are highly imperfect, all the other forms of government seem so much worse. To be sure, sometimes an enlightened monarch may be at the helm. Many kinds of scientific research can and have flourished under undemocratic regimes, ranging from Stalinism to Islamic clerical governance. But in general, hereditary aristocracies, one-party or one-person dictatorships, theocracies, and other such undemocratic systems are all likely to propagate whatever mythologies they are deploying to justify their rule (even to themselves) and to suppress all inquiries that have the potential to be critical or debunking. And as Rosen notes, even Mill himself, who could contemplate extra votes for the highly educated, nonetheless opposed a "pedantocracy" in which only the educated would govern, "unchecked by any power residing in the mass of citizens." A mandarin-style pedantocracy was more likely to produce despotic bureaucratic groupthink than continued progress toward either greater truth or greater liberty. To be sure, democratic politics generally do not and cannot display anything like serious Socratic elenchus, in which conventional popular opinions are subjected to rigorous criticism. Instead, as Yack points out and as Mill well knew, most democratic debate panders to or manipulates such opinions. But still, on most topics a diverse modern electorate has a range of opinions, and on many most people have no opinions. As a result, the more open and robust processes of democratic contestation are, the more likely it is that its participants will find a wide range of inquiries potentially useful to them, either in challenging opponents or in persuading people to form opinions on matters they have not previously considered. Democratic politicians and citizens are therefore likely to accept, albeit sometimes grudgingly, a society in which a wide range of inquiries takes place—and among these can be some relatively rigorous quests for truth.

So even though they are at heart very different, I believe democratic decision making and truth seeking need each other, more than in their most passionately self-realizing moments either cares to admit (which is to say, theirs is a marriage of convenience and necessity but, much of the time, not of passion). I write this out of concern that an undue focus on their differences might lead us to neglect rather than strengthen the contributions each can make to the other. At the same time, I agree with Yack that it is unwise to seek to collapse one into the other, and I also continue to think that too many American scholars, at least, still unconsciously assume they always go hand in hand or, even worse, consciously contend that there are ultimately no real tensions between them. At best, both those unconscious assumptions and the conscious contentions express beliefs that we know more than we actually do know about how democracy and truth can best be realized. At worst, as these essays bring out, they work to hamper the contributions that the tensions between democratic governance and the quest for truth have the potential to make to each other.

Chapter 14

Democratic Politics and the Lovers of Truth

Nadia Urbinati

PHILOSOPHERS NEVER LOVED democracy. Yet their scorn of the government of the many kept alive the interest for democracy throughout the centuries and was an invaluable source of knowledge of that unique democratic experiment that was Athens. Consolidation of democracy in contemporary Western societies seems to have interrupted philosophy's ancient hostility toward democracy. Today, Bernard Yack reminds us, philosophers are also democrats. Does this mean that modernity was able to sanctify the marriage of truth and majority rule? No, it does not. Indeed the unusual fact of contemporary philosophers who are also democrats reverberates with a paradox: like their Greek ancestors, they too are convinced that truth is not a matter of opinion and vote counting, yet they believe that thanks to its constitutional transformation democracy has become the safest place for freedom of thought and the political system most friendly to philosophy. The hidden hope beneath the new alliance of philosophy and democracy, Yack explains, is that the latter would be transformed and enjoy moral as well as political legitimacy. Constitutional democracy makes liberty more secure; it guarantees free expression, exchange of opinions, and the right to change one's mind in the search for better solutions or solutions more consistent with democracy's own principles. In the long run, this *commercium* of ideas (John Stuart Mill used to compare the public space with "a free market of ideas") would affect citizens' minds, making them aspire to more than just procedurally legitimate decisions, and in fact to a truthful convergence between what is right and what gains their consent. From democracy of persuasion to democracy of conviction: this is the ambition of contemporary democratic philosophers, of Jürgen Habermas, to a lesser degree John Rawls, and moreover their commentators and followers.

Yack's critical argument points in particular to Habermas's "strong version" of deliberative democracy. Indeed, to paraphrase Cicero's description of Socrates' role in Athens, we might say that through public deliberation Habermas has brought reason down from the heavens of pure theoretical deduction and set her in the city, thus compelling his fellow citizens to ask questions about life and morality and answer them with reliable and rational accuracy. Deliberation is an extended process of public justification, an exercise in intellectual honesty, reciprocal recognition of one another, dignity and equality, and a sign of true autonomy. Clearly, any decision that fulfills these criteria is universalizable and able to speak for humanity as a whole, not merely the will of the specific community that made it. The moderns seem capable of achieving what the Athenians couldn't: a democracy that is inspired by a truly universalistic and egalitarian perspective.

It is not hard to predict that this achievement is primed to have enormous consequences. For sure, it may encourage an expansion of the meaning of democracy from politics to morality, and moreover from a state-based government to a cosmopolitan or supranational ideal order. Today democracy is not simply the name of a form of government; its meaning is unavoidably *prescriptive,* enriched by a moral content that ascribes to participation and people's self-determination an ethical, educational, and cognitive purpose. In the end, democracy is the name of a holistic project, not simply a matter of popular consent; in fact it is patently disassociated from consent. This is the theoretical and political project that Yack criticizes because, he argues, in order to be fulfilled, it must disclaim (as it actually does) the "prominence of rhetoric in democratic deliberation," because rhetoric creates serious impediments to the search for truth and tends "to perpetuate and extend the errors embedded in received opinion rather than refine and correct them."

Bernard Yack believes, rightly, that today's lovers of truth are reconciled with democracy not because they think philosophy is or can become democratic, but because they think democracy can be made capable of honoring its procedures of deliberation as the "idealized content of a form of practical reason," not simply as strategies for coping peacefully with the risk of conflict.[1]

Yack criticizes this epistemic trend because he thinks it does a "disservice" to both philosophy and democracy, both truth and politics. In making his counterargument, he does not question the rationalist version of philosophy that the epistemic trend conceals. Instead he seems to accept this version when he suggests that democratic politics is opposed to truth. He seems to deduce the incompatibility of philosophy and democracy from a conception of philosophy that retains a rationalistic temper. From here another important consequence comes. In order to stress the antideliberative character of politics and democracy, Yack questions democracy's self-consistency as a political system that, precisely because it is based on opinions and vote counting, praises overall the ability to persuade, an ability that in addition is not equally distributed, and actually needs not to be equally distributed for electoral selection to be meaningful. To be sure, Yack does not propose anything like a full vision of democratic politics in his chapter; instead he puts forward some welcome critical reflections of the dominant discourse of deliberation in political theory. Let us follow his train of critical arguments.

To oppose the holistic trend in contemporary deliberative democracy, Yack emphasizes the tension between popular will (and politics more generally) and the truth: "I conclude that if we are genuinely committed to both democracy and the love of truth, we need to learn how to live with the tension between them." Against deliberativist theorists, he invites us to resume the classical dualism between truth and democracy and accept the bare fact that power and deception are more at home in politics than are sincerity and truth. Against them he does not argue that political deliberation is autonomous of truth because it employs reason to make judgments about general convenience rather than truth or falsity. It seems to me that to make such an argument, he would have to elaborate a different conception of truth and conclude not that politics is opposite to truth, but that politics employs reason and knowledge in order to achieve a goal that is not cognitive but practical. I am persuaded that this would be an interesting road to take in order to rethink the relationship between politics and philosophy. This relationship should aim at giving politics dignity without making it an exercise of arbitrary power, also because in the latter's case any distinction between forms of government and of decision making would be impossible. As I shall argue below in the part of the chapter I devote to Frederick Rosen's analysis of Mill's notion of truth, this outcome can be achieved provided we abandon any rationalist approach to philosophy and make truth a pragmatic work of critical questioning of our and others' beliefs and judgments in the attempt to adjust our society to the democratic promises we have made to ourselves as citizens.

But in starting from the opposition between truth and politics, Yack makes a much more radical argument than simply accepting "the tension between democracy and the love of truth" as he promises. Indeed he argues that in a democracy, political deliberation is structured so as to "perpetuate and extend ... errors" since it is embedded in "received opinions." Politics produces the opposite of what philosophy is about; but contrary to what contemporary democratic philosophers think, we have no alternative but to live with this contradiction. Actually, as I anticipated above, Yack goes further: he broadens the distance between rhetoric and democratic decision by arguing that orators must follow general opinion if they want to win people's consent. Hence not only is rhetoric naturally distant from truth, but it is not the real master of the political game either. The democratic master of the stage is popular opinion, an absolute sovereign that makes the orators court the people, not the other way around. To be listened to, orators must condescend to expressing people's wants rather than try to orient or shape them. "Deference to the judgment of the listeners" is the inner logic of democratic deliberation, not equality or reciprocity.

According to Yack, there are two main consequences of having opinions and rhetoric at the foundations of democracy. The first pertains to the nature of politics. Politics carries a negative connotation (Yack uses the adjective "Machiavellian" to describe "manipulative speakers") that democracy is unfortunately unable to amend. Indeed deference to the judgment of the listeners is deafness to both reason and democratic principles. It is the evidence of the arbitrary character of political decisions, any decision, including democratic ones. Yack's answer to the epistemic ambition of contemporary democratic philosophers seems to bring us straight back to Thrasymachus' proto-Machiavellian's argument against Socrates the rationalist: politics is arbitrariness; justice is the power of the strongest or the winner. Not only does democracy not change the nature of politics, but it makes politics even more deceptive because its ideological reference to equality and liberty makes people believe, wrongly, that democracy is able to dignify politics by purging it of arbitrariness.

The second and intertwined consequence is perhaps more radical because it goes straight to equality, the core principle of democracy. In sketching a comparison between ancient and modern democracy, Yack tries to prove not only that democratic practice is deceptive, but that it is not founded on political equality, as it would seem. Since its Athenian inception, he explains, democracy was meant to be a neutralization of social and economic factors in the distribution of political power. It did not, however, imply the neutralization of all factors, certainly not "the ability to persuade the public as a legitimate qualification to unequal political influence and authority." Contrary to the ambition of the democratic philosophers, irrationality and inequality linger at the core of democracy. Elections have actually exacerbated these two defects. Indeed in abandoning lottery for election, democracy has fatally aggravated the endogenous factor of rhetorical inequality because it has subjected it to the arbitrary choice of the secret voting act. Much more than ancient democracy, contemporary democracy pivots on popular consent and rhetoric. The problem is that the rhetoricians' "deference to the judgment of listeners" does two things: it makes accountability an empty word and creates "serious impediments to the search for truth." In sum, democracy is constituted by inequality, arbitrariness, and the perpetuation of mistakes.

The place of decision in democratic politics is the crucial issue here. Deliberative democracy theorists are aware that elections are hardly reconcilable with truth and circumvent them by stressing that what gives moral legitimacy to democratic procedures and institutions is the process of discussion that precedes the voting act. Deliberative democracy, Yack rightly observes, downplays the role of decision and gives priority to the informal process of discourse; its aim is to prove that because democratic decision making is open to revision, the process of critical understanding and deliberation reflects the character of democracy much more closely than voting does. To amend the deliberative theory of democracy, Yack overturns this argument: he restores the central role of decision and identifies democracy with the voting act. This allows him to prove that the deliberative view is unrealistic because the "moral legitimacy" that discussion prompts in the system has no authoritative power: "By itself public deliberation decides nothing." Preparing for and informing decisions with a broad process of discussion offer no guarantee that voters will be influenced by good reasons precisely because voting is wholly arbitrary and unaccountable. As Adam Przeworski says, "Voting is an imposition of a will over a will."[2] The "new" or moral understanding of legitimacy that theorists of democratic deliberation propose is purely hypothetical and politically irrelevant.

Yack's claim that political theory should pay more attention to decision is well taken and welcome. But how are we to judge the conclusion he derives from this reasonable critique? It seems to me that Yack rests his case against deliberative democracy on a revival of a minimalist view of democracy and political realism, a view that is based on effectual truth (elections) and deems as fictitious any reference to the informal political process that occurs outside the institutions.[3] Moreover this view presumes a juridical view of sovereignty as authoritative will and makes voting, the act of the will, the only uncontroversial data democracy's legitimacy relies upon.

The identification of democracy with "the force of numbers" has traditionally attracted skeptics and also detractors of democracy. After having derided the idea that government can be resolved as a numerical issue, Vilfredo Pareto wrote, "We need not linger on the fiction of 'popular representation'—poppycock grinds no flour. Let us go on and see what substance underlines the various forms of power in the governing classes. . . . The differences lie principally . . . in the relative proportions of force and consent." For Pareto, number is indeed a means to use force through consent, and democracy is the most effective way to achieve the goal a tyrant longs for but cannot get since he does not have the power of numbers on his side.[4] Along this line of thought, Giovanni Sartori wrote years ago that voting is what counts in democracy, and citizens do not learn how to vote by voting. No matter how rich and articulate, the open arena of discussion does not change the arbitrary character of voting.[5] Yack seems to restore this line of thought against deliberative theorists.

Yack has good reasons to insist, against deliberative theorists, that in stressing the *process* of deliberation they neglect the *moment* of decision. Yet the dilemma remains. If elections alone qualify democracy, then it is hard to find good arguments against the critics of democracy who, from the left to the right, set out from time to time to unmask the role of the people as a mere myth. It would be just as hard to devise criteria to detect and obstruct the oligarchic degeneration and corrupting practices of representative institutions. The very proposal to extend the meaning of democratic politics to include the informal discursive character of a pluralistic public sphere of associations, political movements, and opinions risks looking like an ideological refurbishment, functional to the new communicative strategies for elite selection. Indeed it is a fact that, as Yack reminds us (following Bernard Manin), only the elected have both deliberative and decision-making power, unlike the citizens, whose freedom to discuss and criticize proposals and policies does not ensure that their opinions will affect the legislative setting.

Although well posed, these criticisms are neither new nor entirely convincing. To begin with, it is not clear why to reject the holistic pretense of deliberative theorists we should resume a Schumpeterian electoral democracy, and moreover why to question the hegemonic role of moral justification in politics we should resort to a denormativized political realism and assume that politics is deception and naked power (no matter whether by democratic voting or absolute monarch's decision). As a matter of fact, both moves would make all critical discourse powerless. Undeniably, if we reduce the norm of democracy solely to the election of representatives, we are left with little to say about our political regimes. If our democratic societies are simply and necessarily elected aristocracies driven by the power of the listeners, political theory is stuck between the proverbial rock and a hard place. It can either capitulate to positivistic behaviorism and the science of public opinion surveys, or become a hopeless lament of our political condition. The former makes a critical vision literally inconceivable; the latter deprives a critical vision of any strength since there is nothing worth criticizing in a world congenitally lacking in politics. A denormativized realism would invariably become the only theoretical dimension of our political discourse.

Yet the realist claim for a disenchanted objectivity notwithstanding, the electoralist paradigm reflects a political attitude that is not ideology-free or neutral. It suggests, quite explicitly, what citizens and political theorists should do and what they should abstain from doing. In this sense, it is highly prescriptive because it tacitly assumes that citizens should not judge representative institutions from the perspective of normative democratic premises since these are at best ideals with no connection to reality, and at worst strategically deployed ideological discourses. Finally, it tacitly assumes that political theorists should not go beyond an analytical understanding of the way institutional and electoral mechanisms function if they are to avoid slipping into ideology. Since democracy cannot make promises it is inappropriate to accuse it of betraying promises. How could we demand that our governments act in a way for which they were not designed? How could we criticize our political leaders and representatives? Whereas deliberative theory risks making criticism a moral exercise, the realist solution risks exsiccating all critical perspective. Can we find a way out of the cul-de-sac alternative of either an enervating reduction of politics to a discursive exercise of justification or a minimalist rendering of democracy as the act of voting and of politics as arbitrary power for the sake of victory?

Let us briefly examine Yack's resolving of democracy to decision or voting. This proposal rests on a divorce between deliberation and decision (a solution that has recently been put forth also by Philip Pettit, although for the opposite goal, that of narrowing the scope of the latter and expanding the former's).[6] It is true that from a juristic conception of sovereignty what makes a democratic decision authoritative is the "force of numbers." Yet deliberation or the "open market of ideas" is not without an impact on voting decisions; democracy denotes not simply the sovereign act of the will but also the free and even conflicting exchange of opinions and views that precedes and follows that simple act. Modern democracy is *diarchy of will and judgment, not monocracy of the will.* Certainly judgment has an indirect influence, yet it is part of democratic politics (and popular sovereignty) as much as voting. When speaking of contemporary democracy we are referring to a kind of democracy that is hardly comparable with the ancient one. The difference does not simply lie in the election versus the lottery. The difference consists instead in the political process that elections put in motion and that links the place where decisions are made (state institutions) with the place in which problems are raised, brought to the attention of the public, and discussed (the general public arena). Direct voting (what Condorcet called "immediate democracy") can be represented as a discrete series of decisions. We can think of this as *pointillist sovereignty.* But when politics is organized according to electoral terms and the political proposals the candidates embody, opinions create a narrative that links voters through time and make prospective accounts of the entire society, its aspirations and problems.[7]

This explains why opinions (and rhetorical speeches) never have equal weight, not even in the hypothetical case of two different opinions receiving the same number of votes. If the weight of opinions were equal, the dialectics between opinions, and between opinion and voting itself, would make little or no sense. Voting is an attempt to give ideas weight, not to make them identical in weight.[8] Ideas and opinions are not like dispersed atoms or accidental entities in the mind of the voters. As opinions, they must have been formed and developed by men and women together who experience a combination of economic, social, and cultural factors. Association and communication, either scattered or organized, are essential in the formation of opinions, electoral issues, and the selection of candidates. The "counting of votes is the final manifestation of a long process" in which all participate in different ways and with different prospects of influence and impact.[9] Yet to be aware of this complex phenomenon that is voting we should pay attention also to representation, which is not an ancillary institution but the institution that has contributed to making opinion and media central (in good ways and bad) in modern democracy, something the ancients did not have, as the perspicacious Mill noticed. It is a pity that Yack does not pay attention to this democratic device and the multifarious roles it plays in the making of modern democracy. Representation can hardly be understood if we focus only on voting.

Democratic representation is the *dynamic synthesis* of two forms of representation: electoral or formal, and virtual or ideological. It is a medium in the unifying work of opinion formation, filtering of interests and passions, critical assessment of policies, persuasion, and the political action people perform in the most democratic sense—directly and publicly, by talking and listening, writing and reading, associating and demonstrating, petitioning and voting, and voting again.[10] All this is to say that the link between formal and informal political process gives the originally undemocratic institution of elected representation a uniquely democratic feature and raises, when it is defective, the specter of a "crisis" of confidence in democracy.[11]

Therefore, although Yack's criticism of a surplus of justification propelled by the deliberative theory of democracy is welcome and well posed, one might feel some dissatisfaction with his strategy of splitting decision and deliberation and resolving democracy in the voting acts. If for nothing else, we might cast doubt on this strategy because it points to a kind of realist rendering of power that, though no more justifiable than the moral reasoning sponsored by deliberative theorists, risks doing a disservice to democracy because it leaves us with no criteria to critically evaluate democratic institutions' actual performance. To put it differently: Should we return to democratic minimalism in order to demystify the deliberative theory of democracy? Would it not be better to take away the myths of epistemic validity and moral improvement from political deliberation and bring back the latter's rhetorical character, as according to Aristotle's intuition (and Yack's own suggestion in an excellent article he wrote recently on deliberative rhetoric)?[12] Would it not be better to reevaluate the place of disagreement and the conflict of ideas, as proposed by Mill?

Mill proposed we defend the "Socratic Plato" against the "dogmatic Plato" and did so in order to sponsor a pragmatic and inquiry-based view of philosophy against a deductive (*more geometric*) and transcendental view. (The dualism is well expressed by Rosen: "Mill did not refer to the Plato of the transcendent forms, but to Plato's Socrates in the early dialogues, where a negative dialectic revealed the ignorance of the most confident and learned of his interlocutors.") This entails, more appropriately, that we question both the rationalist view of truth and the Thrasymachean view of politics.

John Stuart Mill advanced *in nuce* this solution, which we may call pragmatic in the sense Charles Sanders Peirce and John Dewey used the term pragmatism. These authors tried to redefine the very notions of philosophy and truth in the conviction that the deductive system relaunched by seventeenth-century rationalism was inherently inimical to democracy because it was despotic toward human experience, practical and theoretical.[13] They believed that ideas are not at the beginning, like immobile forms that impinge on us, but are working hypotheses, and that human society is not and should not be organized in the view of making individuals actualize them, either by coercion or manipulation of consent or both. (Plato suggested the creation of "beautiful lies.") Ideas, moral and ethical ideals in particular, are the object of a permanent process of inquiry and redefinition that the democratic community makes in the quotidian attempt to detect and solve the problems it faces. Mill understood that democracy ("free government") entails not merely a procedural system of decision (voting and vote counting) but also a transformation of the notion of truth as a process not solely of justification but also of construction and change of meanings.

The character of this pragmatist reinterpretation of truth is hinted at by Rosen in his analysis of the political implication of Mill's *System of Logic* and Mill's attempt "to relate truth, liberty, and democracy." Rosen's reconstruction of this crucial aspect of Mill's thought is both engaging and convincing. I would like to simply add some additional elucidation so as to stress Rosen's case (and mine).

In the early 1830s Mill started thinking of logic as a guide for evaluating evidence and asserted beliefs (or, as we would call it today, the realm of general opinions). It is interesting to note that he began working on the *Logic* while he was writing the introduction to his translation of the Platonic dialogues (and opposing, in George Grote's footsteps, the "Socratic Plato" to the "dogmatic Plato"). It was there that he first advanced the idea that the Socratic method is "an exercise in the art of investigating the truth" (rather than deducing it) to be adapted to a democratic society. As Grote pointed out, the notion of a critical function of logic linked Mill's project both to Francis Bacon's *ars artium* and to the Socratic elenchus as a tool for critical examination. Socrates "sought to test the fundamental notions and generalizations respecting man and society, in the same spirit in which Bacon approached those of physics." Socrates attained that outcome by "incessantly discussing human affairs . . . investigating—What is the just and the unjust? What is courage or cowardice? What is a city? What is the character fit for a citizen?"[14]

This was also Mill's attempt in *A System of Logic.* As he stated at the beginning of the work, he wanted to devise a method for finding out how the mind proceeds when working out an opinion or a belief. He sought to provide rules for asking questions and assessing answers, for helping to clarify the reason for disagreements and create the possibility for a new and, he hoped, more progressive stage of deliberation. To explore the connotation of a "general term" or a "classification" implies exploring the notions that shape one's moral and political positions. Like Socrates (as according to Cicero's representation in his *Tusculanae Disputationes*), Mill challenged his readers to consider the meaning of justice, marriage, happiness, equality, citizenship, virtue, and so on. Socrates, unlike the Sophists, was interested in more than his fellow citizens' conventional understanding and tried to indicate worthy goals. Equally, Mill wanted to explore what people assumed along with their general ideas and how they explained those assumptions. Thus he saw the Socratic dialectic as a work in progress that a democratic community undertakes through ongoing communication and with the help of the critical philosopher.[15]

Mill made it clear that his Socratic approach was neither an indifferent acceptance of common opinions nor a method for bargaining among irreconcilable differences. Socrates' method was consistent with what Mill thought philosophy should do, namely help clarify existing opinions or accepted truths. As Rosen puts it, "Mill regarded received truths as particularly dangerous. They lulled the mind into a passive acceptance and almost a vacancy of understanding, in which the truth was forgotten or never considered." However, precisely because Mill thought of the mind as a permanent exercise in self-surveillance against the tendency of the social environment to make it passively accept acquired opinions and beliefs, his relationship to Grote was complex. To amend Rosen's rendering of the relationship between Mill and Grote in relation to Socrates, I would thus argue that Mill distanced himself from Grote's interpretation of Socrates as the best among the Sophists and the identification of Socratic dialectic with only elenchus. Mill's relationship to his father may help illuminate his distance from Grote's Socrates.

Mill's critique of his father's polemical use of dialectics as a "collision of ideas" and his discovery of Friedrich D. E. Schleiermacher's Socrates in the years of his mental crisis were crucial steps in his reinterpretation of the role of dialogue as a process of clarification in view of acquiring a new habit toward truth, not merely denouncing or opposing existing opinions.[16] The elenchus was meant to be a "restless polemic against dogmatism" and an instrument for ascertaining the consistency of opinions, as Grote also thought. Thus both Grote and Mill pinpointed the difference between elenchus and the eristic, but Grote (unlike Mill) did not explain what made Socrates a "missionary of the examined life" rather than simply a critical examiner of others' opinions. Although he succeeded in capturing the methodological difference between Socrates and the Sophists, Grote failed to perceive the difference between Socrates' own truths and those of a dogmatic philosopher. He did not give his readers sufficient reason for embracing Socrates' truth as opposed to that of some other.[17] In sum, Mill made an important distinction between discussion oriented toward victory and discussion oriented toward conscious conviction (or self-criticism), between eloquence for the sake of public speech in deliberative contests in which decisions were to be made (as in Parliament) and informal dialogue among citizens out of the desire for self-searching and opinion formation.

Mill's practical philosophy of modernity envisioned an "active engagement in open argument . . . for the sake of developing the habits of inquiry and self-examination and the virtues needed for success in the business of making a life for oneself."[18] Injustices would be acknowledged when they were perceived as problems, that is, when people developed rational objections to them and asked for justifications. What, for example, constitutes the complex relationship of marriage? The patriarchal model is the result of a long and complicated social construction of identities for men and women that seem natural because their historical origins have been forgotten. The task of the critical philosopher (and the democratic citizen as well) is to deconstruct the traditional definition of marriage into its constitutive elements, thereby denaturalizing and problematizing it. The final step is to reveal the common denominator that allows people to reform the institution of marriage.

Mill wanted to overturn people's tendency to take the way they lived or what they thought for granted. He wanted them to become the guardians of their own lives and resist domination, whether direct or indirect. As Stuart Hampshire has argued, problematizing issues entails taking away from our opinions and beliefs the aura of naturalness that they acquire through their reiterated usage.[19] The question is thus *not* one of truth versus opinion, but of opinions that open themselves to a public and free questioning process versus opinions that resist any critical inquiry. The function of philosophy as critical examination and clarification is after all a way to put it in a friendly relation with democracy, whose procedures of decision presume a permanent legal changeability because they presume human fallibility and conflicting views along with the awareness that emendation is always possible.

This casts light on the place of equality in modern democracy and brings me back to the issue with which I began this commentary. All contemporary democratic constitutions and political practices, judicial and legislative, reflect two perspectives on equality: as legal equality (equality before the law) and the equal political right citizens have to support or oppose laws or government policies (largely in order to redress what they perceive to be real or potential inequalities, and hence injustices). All constitutions inscribe the legal equality of individuals and citizens regardless of gender, economic status, race, religious affiliation, or belief. (Some constitutions also contain articles *claiming* to promote equality by removing socioeconomic and cultural obstacles that de facto impede or disfigure it.)[20] One possible interpretation of these two perspectives on equality is that democratic constitutions acknowledge the fact that, although formally equal, citizens are not, and perhaps will never be, actually equal. As such, they presume and actually endorse a politics of antagonism or conflict over and for the realization of the democratic promises ingrained in the constitution. In other words, "achieving membership within a political community is not necessarily the same thing as achieving *equal* membership."[21] Constitutions of representative democracies do two things: they legislate (and thereby limit) political agency and government activity, and they define goals (enhancing and preserving equality) that stimulate political agency and participation. Furthermore they use norms of legal equality to regulate political action. In that they inscribe politics as the terrain that protects and promotes equality and constitutions that anticipate political conflict and antagonism.

A democratic constitution establishes the norms that regulate political action *because* it presumes political activism and contestation; in a word, it foresees a conflict between different interpretations of which decisions are needed and when, and also the challenge to any achieved majority, in relation to which any voting decision appears to be lacking understanding and in this sense never fully legitimate. Yet for a democratic constitution to survive, no election or voting decision is and must be the last one. The democratic process defies rationalism precisely because it does not have a time in relation to which rationality can be assessed once and for all. Undoubtedly people's votes can be, and many times are, blatant evidence of their irrationality or lack of information or incompetence. Yet given the constitutional regulation of votes' temporary effectiveness, at what time would lovers of truth decide to interrupt the political process and proclaim the verdict of falsehood? The question is certainly rhetorical because no philosophy can in all honesty give an uncontroversial answer of this kind. Thus it is not by making politics irreconcilable with knowledge (and declaring it a work of arbitrariness) that democracy can be emancipated from the tyranny of truth, but by reinterpreting truth as a process of searching and emending, dissenting and conflicting, a process that closely resembles democratic politics.

PART IV

Truth and Public Reasons

Chapter 15

Truth and Public Reason

Joshua Cohen

In 1958 I wrote the following:

"There are no hard distinctions between what is real and what is unreal, nor between what is true and what is false. A thing is not necessarily either true or false; it can be both true and false."

I believe that these assertions still make sense and do still apply to the exploration of reality through art. So as a writer I stand by them but as a citizen I cannot. As a citizen I must ask: What is true? What is false?
   —Harold Pinter, Nobel Prize lecture (2005)

Political constructivism does not use (or deny) the concept of truth; nor does it question that concept, nor could it say that the concept of truth and its idea of the reasonable are the same. Rather, within itself, the political conception does without the concept of truth.
   —John Rawls, *Political Liberalism*

DEMOCRATIC POLITICS COMPRISES, among other things, public discussion about laws and policies on the basis of reasons of justice.[1] How large a part is not my concern here. I assume that such reasoning, mixed with bargaining and hectoring, confession and accusation, self-pity and compulsive self-display, provides some part of democratic politics. Focusing on this deliberative part, I want to consider the role that the concept of truth might properly play in it.

I will defend two conclusions about that role.

First, the concept of truth, and judgments and assertions deploying that concept—including judgments and assertions that apply the concept to basic principles of justice—have a legitimate role to play in public, political argument. Here I endorse Pinter's view in his Nobel lecture about the place of truth in the reflection of citizens (not his comments on the artistic license to violate the law of noncontradiction) and disagree with Rawls's claim in *Political Liberalism* that a political conception of justice "does without the concept of truth."[2]

Second, the conception of truth that plays a role in public justification should be political. A "conception" or "understanding" of truth is a set of claims about truth, though not offered as an analysis of the concept.[3] By a political conception of truth, then, I mean (very roughly) a set of claims about truth—for example, that truth is distinct from warrant, and that it is important—that is suited for the purposes of political reflection and argument in a pluralistic democracy, characterized by doctrinal disagreements. I will explain later the special aim and distinctive content of a political conception of truth. Suffice it to say here that the aim is to present a view of truth that suffices for public reasoning and could reasonably be endorsed by the adherents of conflicting doctrines, which may themselves employ richer conceptions of truth, for example, the view that truth consists in a correspondence of truth bearer and fact, or in some sort of idealized justification.

A political conception of truth is thus a genuine conception of truth,[4] although less committal than the conceptions that have traditionally occupied philosophical attention and that have deep roots in our practices of making and defending assertions (including logically complex assertions), in our reasoning, and in ordinary understandings about the content and correctness of thoughts. Because a political conception is less committal it bears some similarity to antimetaphysical, "deflationary" theories of truth. Those theories are inspired by the redundancy theories of Frege and Ramsey, according to which the content of the claim that a proposition is true is the same as the content of the proposition.[5] Their main thrust is that truth is not a philosophically deep idea, and that the concept is fully captured by the infinitely many instances of the truth schema (T):

(T) The proposition that p is true if and only if p.[6]

Deflationary theories thus deny that truth is correspondence, or warranted assertibility, or consensus in inquiry's ideal limit, or a cheerfully solidaristic backslap. In denying these claims, such theories are conceptually deflationary, and thus to be distinguished from the evaluatively deflationary view that truth is not something to which we should attach great importance. A political conception cannot endorse an antimetaphysical, conceptually deflationary theory. That endorsement is not needed for public reasoning and would put the political conception needlessly at odds with religious or philosophical views that comprise more ambitious conceptions of truth. Endorsing an antimetaphysical deflationism would make the political conception of truth unacceptably sectarian. Instead, a political conception aims to be nonmetaphysical rather than antimetaphysical.

Two points of clarification before proceeding. First, while disagreeing with Rawls's claims about truth, I endorse the ideal of public reason.[7] According to that ideal, political justification, at least on certain fundamental questions, should proceed on a terrain of argument that can be shared. In the case of democracy's public reason, the shared terrain comprises values that can reasonably be shared by people who regard themselves as free and equal, despite irreconcilable doctrinal disagreements and disagreements about justice. Although I find the idea of public reason compelling, I disagree with Rawls's claim that the concept of truth finds no place in it. That claim makes the idea of public reason unnecessarily contentious, as if it were committed to the view that the truth about justice does not matter. It also makes the idea of public reason hard to understand, because it proposes to leave the concept of truth behind while preserving notions of belief, assertion, judgment, reason, and objectivity, all of which are essential to an idea of public reason. In making his case for putting truth aside, Rawls suggests that we face a dilemma: that we can have truth or public reason, but not both. My aim in presenting a political conception of truth is to show that this is a false dilemma and that we can have both. The political conception of truth, then, is presented as part of a defense of the idea of public reason.

Second, I emphasize that the political conception is not, to borrow a phrase from Rawls, "political in the wrong way." A political conception of truth does not say that a proposition is true just in case it solves our problems or is part of a broad consensus. Still less does it say that a proposition is true just in case authorities say that it is true, or it confers advantage on the power-ful. Such Thrasymachean theses about truth and politics are best understood as critical claims about how the term "true" and its cognates are used. They derive their critical edge from the fact that they do not express conceptions of truth. Instead, they present the charge—understandable to anyone who has the concept of truth, troubling to anyone who cares about it—that "true" is systematically applied to propositions in virtue of their satisfying a condition that does nothing to make them worthy of belief.[8] The political conception is not political in virtue of tracing cognitive appraisals to an exercise of au-thority or the effects of power. It belongs to a very different conception of the political, and is classified as political because it can reasonably be endorsed as common ground for the purposes of consequential collective decisions.

To defend my two claims, I start by sketching the background of Rawls's idea that public reason "does without the concept of truth." Second, I discuss why it is hard to understand the idea that public reason leaves truth aside. To clarify the puzzlement, I distinguish four views that diminish the place of truth in political argument: the No Concept view (Rawls's position), No Truth Bearers, No Substantive Judgments, and No Big Deal. Third, I sketch a political conception of truth and offer an account of what having such a conception available in public political argument comes to. Fourth, I criticize three arguments that might be offered in support of the No Concept view that truth does not belong to public reason. Finally, I distinguish the idea that public reason does without truth from an evaluatively deflationary view that I call the "cultural proposal." Drawing on this cultural-political distinction, I suggest that a political world that does without the concept of truth is missing something important.

Truth and Public Reason

The intellectual context for the discussion is provided by Rawls's idea of a specifically political liberalism. The phrase "political liberalism" may have the air of a pleonasm. Liberalism has always been, inter alia, a political outlook, defined by an emphasis on personal freedom, religious tolerance, open inquiry, the rule of law, social mobility, and, in its modern formulations, democratic politics.

The point of the phrase, then, is that the liberal political outlook has also often been presented as the political department of a broader philosophical position, mixing an ethic of self-direction, religious latitudinarianism, suspicion about the normative force of tradition and authority, and metaphysical and epistemological modesty. But as, for example, the twentieth-century Catholic accommodation to modernism illustrates, a liberal political perspective can derive support from other philosophical starting points, including religious views that downplay autonomous choice in favor of substantively correct decisions, regard tradition as a deposit of evolving insight, are metaphysically and epistemologically ambitious, and see religious commitments as providing less latitude and greater density of demands.[9] Presentations of liberal political commitments that tie them to a general philosophical liberalism may therefore impose unnecessary barriers to a broad embrace of liberalism. To the extent that such presentations take hold in the political culture, they may work to intolerantly exclude people from the political public sphere. Political liberalism aims to free the formulation of liberalism as a political outlook, so far as possible, from that wider set of philosophical and religious commitments, and thus to "put no unnecessary obstacles in the way of . . . affirming the political conception."[10] Moreover it would honor the value of tolerance and the ideal of the political arena as a space of public reasoning open to equal citizens.

Rawls's concerns about truth emerge from this background. To explain how, I need to say a little more about why political liberalism might seem a forceful response to doctrinal conflict, particularly in a democratic society.

The trouble with truth begins, then, with doctrinal pluralism, the pluralism of incompatible "comprehensive doctrines": views about the world, the place of human beings in it, the appropriate ways to acquire an understanding of the world, and the way that human beings should accordingly live their lives. Doctrinal pluralism is not the only political problem: conflicts of interest—or of ethnicity, race, or nation—are not, at root, doctrinal. Moreover doctrinal conflict is not only a problem. As Mill and others have observed, it can work as a basis of social learning, as we pool information drawn from the varieties of human experience and reflect in light of thoughts and patterns of conduct that we would never otherwise have entertained. Too, doctrinal conflict may be seen as having some intrinsic attraction, as an expression of the scope of human possibilities.

Doctrinal pluralism is also a problem, however, and presents a distinctive challenge in a democracy. Democracy is not simply a matter of living together, but, ideally at least, a society of equals, whose members decide together how to live together. People who disagree fundamentally, however, have trouble occupying a common ground on which they can justify to one another those joint decisions.

One response to this trouble is to try to characterize such a common ground of political justification. I will call this democracy's public reason. Democracy's public reason is a terrain of political reflection and judgment that equal persons, drawn to conflicting doctrines, can reasonably be expected to occupy and endorse as a basis for addressing public issues. The essential point here is that common ground, if it is available at all, requires that the content of public reason is restricted relative to the doctrines endorsed by members.

For example, concepts of self-realization, associated with the view that there is an essential human nature that consists in the possession of certain self-governing powers, and of salvation, associated with the idea of a transcendent God, are not available to public reason. Moreover Rawls thinks that the concept of truth is unavailable.

This claim about truth is not founded on any general philosophical doubts about truth, nor on general doubts about the place of normative notions in public reason. Ideas of rightness, justice, reasonableness, correct judgment, and objectivity all have a proper place in public reason. Rawls's concern is specifically about public reason and truth, and he locates this concern at the heart of his account of political liberalism and public reason.[11] When Rawls first proposed the idea of a conception of justice that would be "political, not metaphysical," he defined a political conception as one that avoids claims about truth: "The aim of justice as fairness as a political conception is practical, and not metaphysical or epistemological. *That is*, it presents itself not as a conception of justice that is true, but one that can serve as a basis of informed and willing political agreement between citizens viewed as free and equal persons" (emphasis added).[12] Later formulations of political liberalism remained emphatic about steering clear of the concept of truth.[13] "Political liberalism," Rawls says, "rather than referring to its political conception of justice as true, refers to it as reasonable instead." Moreover political liberalism "has an account of objectivity" that is connected to an account of "reasonable judgment" and suffices for the purposes of public justification, and "may leave the concept of a true moral judgment to comprehensive doctrines." Perhaps most fundamentally, political liberalism "does not use (or deny) the concept of truth; nor does it question that concept, nor could it say that the concept of truth and its idea of the reasonable are the same. Rather, within itself, the political conception *does without the concept of truth*" (emphasis added). Reasonableness, not truth, is the "standard of correctness,"[14] and the objectivity of judgments about justice is characterized without reference to the notion of truth. In response to Habermas's claim that political liberalism cannot avoid issues of truth, Rawls forcefully replies that people will "certainly . . . continue to raise questions of truth and to tax political liberalism with not discussing them. In the absence of particulars, these complaints fall short of being objections."[15]

Rawls's point, I emphasize, is that the concept of truth is unavailable. (Later I will contrast this No Concept view with a few other views that are skeptical about a role for truth in political argument.) Thus we cannot, while operating within democracy's public reason, make claims about the nature of truth (and whether it has a nature), about its importance, or its relationship to justification, objectivity, and reasonableness. Nor can we make assertions about the truth of any elements of our views, including our comprehensive doctrine, or our views about justice, or our understanding of how the society works.

Consider, for example, justice as fairness, with its two principles of justice. Assume that justice as fairness is one of several reasonable conceptions of justice that would win support among citizens in a democratic society. The idea, then, is that it would be appropriate in political argument to think or assert that justice as fairness is reasonable—indeed the "most reasonable" conception of justice—and thus to use its principles in judging political arrangements.[16] Yet it would be an inappropriate departure from the norms of public reason to assert its truth, and inappropriate, in one's capacity as a citizen assessing laws and policies, to think that justice as fairness is true and act on the basis of that thought. More particularly, it would be inappropriate to affirm the truth even of the proposition—uncontested among the competing reasonable conceptions of justice—that individuals have a right to liberty of conscience. And this would be inappropriate even though it is entirely in order to assert that people have a right to such liberty as a matter of justice, that it is reasonable to believe that they have a right to liberty of conscience as a matter of justice, and that that thesis about the right to liberty of conscience is objectively correct in virtue of being reasonable.[17]

Advancing claims about truth is, then, needlessly divisive: it undermines public reason and conflicts with the equal standing in public, political argument that democracy promises. "Once we accept the fact that reasonable pluralism is a permanent condition of public culture under free institutions, the idea of the reasonable is more suitable as part of the basis of public justification for a constitutional regime than the idea of moral truth. Holding a political conception as true, and for that reason alone the one suitable basis for public reason, is exclusive, even sectarian, and so likely to foster political division."[18] Rawls does sometimes hint, if only indirectly, an alternative view. "Rational intuitionism," he says, "conceives of truth *in a traditional way* by viewing moral judgments as true when they are both about and accurate to the independent order of moral values" (emphasis added).[19] Rational intuitionism, which Rawls associates with Cudworth, Clarke, Grotius, Pufendorf, and Locke, is a species of nonreductive moral realism, treats our moral thought as an exercise of theoretical reason, and is arguably an ingredient in much natural law theory.[20] His remark about a "traditional way" of understanding truth and an independent order of values suggests that it endorses a correspondence theory of truth, and the phrase "a traditional way" suggests that other conceptions of truth are available. If there is such an alternative, then it might have a role in public deliberation.[21]

Moreover such a conception might fit with the spirit of political liberalism. Political liberalism distinguishes comprehensive doctrines, which include moral ideas that guide people in all aspects of their lives, from political conceptions, which comprise moral ideas and values expressed in political judgments. I will not try to characterize the distinction here. Suffice it to say that ideas with a role in comprehensive doctrines can also play a role in political conceptions, if those ideas are given a "political" interpretation, as with political conceptions of justice, the person, objectivity, reasonableness, autonomy, and liberalism itself. The political conceptions are intended, roughly, to play a role when citizens reason together about political affairs. Thus a political conception of persons as free says, for example, that no particular ends are mandatory or obligatory from a public point of view, that obligations a person has in virtue of his or her moral or religious outlook do not have public standing as obligations, and that civil standing does not shift with shifts in fundamental aims, no matter how much or how deeply a person's self-conception is bound up with those aims.[22] This political conception of persons as free is meant to be available to adherents of views that endorse distinct and incompatible philosophical conceptions of the free person, as autonomous self-legislators with a will sensitive to reflective judgments, or as created in God's image, subject to His laws, and free when in willing compliance with those laws. Similarly, a political conception of liberalism as assigning equal liberties to all is meant to be available to both proponents and critics of the moral-liberal view that individual, reflective self-direction is essential to a good life.

Why not, then, a political conception of truth, understood as a conception of truth suited to play a role in democracy's public reason? Rawls did not pursue this path. Perhaps he thought that the concept of truth is unavoidably metaphysical, originally owned by Platonists, and passed along to their rational intuitionist descendants. As applied to moral thought, he might have supposed that truth comes packaged with the rational intuitionist's notion of an independent order of values. Or perhaps he thought that the alternatives are either a correspondence theory, a coherence theory, an antimetaphysical deflationism, or some other unacceptably philosophically demanding theory. In any case, he proposed to "leave the concept of a true moral judgment to comprehensive moral doctrines."

I think that Rawls is mistaken, and that affirmations of the truth of propositions about justice are a perfectly legitimate part of democracy's public reason. To address the animating concerns about the tensions between truth and public reason, however, we need a political conception of truth. To understand why, it will help to say more about Rawls's proposed response to these tensions, and why that response is deeply puzzling.

Doing without Truth

How could we "do without the concept of truth"? Truth is of course a controversial idea. Yet however it is best understood, the concept of truth—like concepts of cause, object, fact, reason, and evidence—is deeply rooted in our thought and reasoning. Truth is intimately linked to the notions of belief and meaning, both fundamental in an account of thought. Thus beliefs are said to "aim at" the truth, in that truth is their standard of correctness; correspondingly, coming to believe that p is not true is typically "fatal" to the belief that p. Moreover because truth is the standard of correctness for beliefs, while we may come to believe that p without deliberating about whether p (is true), when we deliberate about whether to believe that p, we try to determine whether p (is true).[23] As for meaning, Donald Davidson has observed that we often figure out what someone's utterances mean by assuming that he is saying something true, at least when he is saying something about publicly observable surroundings.[24]

The notion of truth is also fundamental in our understanding of reasoning. Thus truth is tied to judging, in that judging whether p is closely connected to judging whether p is true (judgment is the "acknowledgement of the truth of a thought"); to assertion, inasmuch as asserting is commonly understood to involve presenting the asserted content to others as true ("What distinguishes [truth] from all other predicates is that it is always asserted when anything at all is asserted"); to assuming that p for the sake of argument, in that when we assume that p we assume that it is true; to reasons for believing, which are reasons for believing true; and to ideas of a logical consequence, as a proposition whose truth is assured by the truth of other propositions, and of deductive argument, whose special virtue is to be truth-preserving.[25] Truth is connected as well to norms of thought and interaction that call for accuracy in representation, sincerity in expression, consistency, "getting it right," and being attentive to how things are and not simply how we wish them to be.[26]

These observations are all familiar. I register them to distinguish the concept of truth from a variety of other concepts that public reason might arguably do without. Suppose someone proposes that public reason avoid concepts of salvation, or self-realization, soul, personal autonomy, purity, courage, or honor. Whatever the merits of such abstention, we have some idea of what is being proposed. We can imagine what it would mean to conduct political justification without recourse to such concepts. In contrast, the idea of locating a common ground of political reflection and argument that does without the concept of truth—like doing without the concept of an object, or cause, or thought, or reason, or inference, or evidence—is hard to grasp. Truth is so closely connected with intuitive notions of thinking, asserting, believing, judging, and reasoning that it is difficult to understand what leaving it behind amounts to.

Keep in mind that what is at stake here is the concept of truth, not a theory of truth. It is easy to see reasons for avoiding philosophical controversy about truth: whether the truth of a proposition consists in its correspondence with a world of facts that exist determinately and independently, or consists instead in the beliefs on which ideally conducted inquiry would ultimately converge; or whether, as the minimalist theory claims, grasping the concept of truth consists in being disposed to assert instances of the truth schema, or the Heideggerian, that truth is the disclosure of being.[27] Such disagreements may be seen as needlessly divisive because they invite controversies that are politically idle. What matters is what we think is right or just, not what we think the truth of normative propositions consists in.

There are good reasons for steering democracy's public reason clear of such philosophical controversies and leaving it to competing traditions of thought to add their own philosophical interpretation of truth to public discourse (if they have such an interpretation). Similarly, they may add different interpretations of the nature of justice to a public understanding of justice, or different accounts of the competence of reason to a conception of the politically reasonable. But the fact that there is more to be said about justice does not exclude considerations of justice from public reason: disagreements between empiricists and rationalists about the nature and powers of reason do not exclude a conception of the politically reasonable, and disagreements between Kantians and rational intuitionists about objectivity do not keep the idea of objectivity out of public reason. So too the fact that there is more to be said about truth does not provide a rationale for excluding truth.

What could it be for the shared public terrain of argument to do without the concept of truth? I have expressed some puzzlement about this, but skeptical attitudes about the place of truth in political argument are familiar. Is it really so puzzling? To explain why it is, I want to distinguish the idea under consideration—I will call it the No Concept view—from three other skeptical views: that truth has no role because no truth-apt claims are in play (No Truth Bearers); that truth-apt claims are in play and the concept is available, but we should refrain from applying it to substantive political claims (No Substantive Judgments); and that truth-apt claims are in play, the concept is available, and there is no problem applying it to substantive normative judgments, but it is of no real interest (No Big Deal). The distinctions will help to clarify the view and the puzzlement.

No Truth Bearers

The idea that democracy's public reason does without the concept of truth must be distinguished, first, from a noncognitivist view of political discourse, akin to the views taken by classical, metaethical noncognitivists about evaluative discourse generally (though rejected by many contemporary noncognitivists). According to the classically noncognitivist emotivist, for example, the concept of truth has no application to normative discourse because no truth-apt claims are being made.[28] Statements with the surface form of assertions that are made in normative discourse are devices for emotional appeal, rhetorical manipulation, and badgering.

If we say, with a variant of classical noncognitivism, that political argument is a matter of decisions (say, deciding on friends and enemies, and expressing the decisions) or expressions of attitude (cheering for your side, shouting at the other) or using words to provoke behaviors, then the concept of truth would arguably have no hold. Despite the surface forms of political discourse—apparently asserting logically simple propositions and embedding them in logically complex ones ("If slavery is not unjust, then nothing is unjust," or "If the fetus is a person, then abortion is morally wrong"), seeming to reason to and from those apparent assertions—it would not involve claims that could be either true or false. Saying that a political conception does without the concept of truth, then, would be like saying that cheerleading does without the concept of truth. You do without the concept because you are not trafficking in anything to which the concept applies. Of course, cheers often have the form of assertions. But when cheerleaders say "We are number one" in the final minutes, with the team down 46–0, no one thinks that they are really expressing the belief that theirs is the best team.[29]

Whatever the merits of this view, it is not public reason. Rawls proposes to leave truth out, but not because he is endorsing an interpretation of political argument in which no claims are being made that are apt to be either true or false. Although public reason is to do without the concept of truth, it is an exercise of practical reason, of reflection and judgment: "So if the idea of reasoning and judgment applies to our moral and political statements, as opposed simply to our voicing our psychological state, we must be able to make judgments and draw inferences on the basis of mutually recognized criteria and evidence; and in that way, and not in some other way, say by mere rhetoric or persuasion, reach agreement by the free exercise of our powers of judgment."[30]

My point about the truth-aptness of claims made in the domain of public reason can be put more strongly. The reason that the concept of truth has no place cannot be that the claims made by a political conception are not truth-apt; those claims must be truth-apt, even if the political conception itself somehow abjures the concept of truth. They must be, if there is to be a common ground of argument under conditions of doctrinal disagreement. To deny the truth-aptness of the claims made on the terrain of public reason would offend against the essential idea of public reason. That is because the very propositions advanced in public political argument, even if not taken as or presented in that context as true, might be judged true by the religious or moral doctrine affirmed by a citizen.

Consider an example. Suppose I endorse a Catholic natural law view. I will say with *Dignitatis Humanae* that it is true that citizens have a right to religious freedom. But also, with *Veritatis Splendor*, I will say that "the splendour of truth" is the foundation of morality and political justice, that there is a "moral obligation, and a grave one at that, to seek the truth and to adhere to it once it is known," and that there is an "inseparable connection between truth and freedom—which expresses the essential bond between God's wisdom and will." Moreover, with the conviction that Christ is "the way, the truth, and the life," and, resisting the temptation of "detaching human freedom from its essential and constitutive relationship to truth," I will hold that the truth of the (political) proposition—that individuals have a basic right to religious freedom—follows from the truth of an account of human dignity founded on the doctrine that human beings, created in God's image, are bound by His laws.[31] If that is all correct, then the political claim expressed on the terrain of public reason—that there is a right to religious freedom—must be truth-apt. It must be capable of being true or false, because that very proposition can be judged to be true from the standpoint of Catholic doctrine and is said to be derivable from the underlying truths about human dignity.

It would conflict with the essentials of public reason to deny any of this: to deny that the proposition that individuals have a right to liberty of conscience is true, or to deny that its truth follows from the basic truths about the right way to live as fixed by natural law. Lacking the concept of truth, a political conception used for public reasoning can issue no such denial. At the same time, the Rawlsian proposal is that the very proposition about religious liberty that the natural law adherent affirms as true and as a consequence of more fundamental truths is available for assertion in political reflection and argument, available to be used as a premise in reasoning. The natural law adherent is simply not permitted to say everything he or she believes about that proposition—in particular, not to say that it is true and a consequence of more fundamental truths.

In short, Rawls's proposal is to endorse a cognitivist understanding of political conceptions of justice and political argument on which notions of judgment, reasoning, and argument are fully in play, while denying the availability of the concept of truth within such conceptions. The concern is specifically with the concept of truth, and the reason for leaving it out cannot be that political discourse traffics in something other than truth bearers. Someone might offer that rationale for the view that truth has no place in political argument, but not if he thinks of political argument as an exercise of public reason.

No Substantive Judgments

A second view is that the contents of political conceptions are truth-apt, the concept of truth is available, and certain kinds of judgments using it are permissible, but in public reason we are to abstain from making substantive moral or political judgments using that concept. David Estlund appears to attribute this combination of views to Rawls. The attribution is, I think, mistaken, but characterizing the view will help in clarifying the No Concept view.

Estlund summarizes Rawls's view this way: "Truth is held to be neither necessary nor sufficient for a doctrine's admissibility [in public political argument]."[32] But the claim that the truth of a proposition is neither necessary nor sufficient in licensing appeal to it in public argument—if understood as an assertion within public reason—belongs to a very different view from the one that Rawls endorses and that we are exploring. Asserting that truth is neither necessary nor sufficient requires having the concept of truth available. It is thus quite different from neither holding truth to be necessary nor holding truth to be sufficient for a doctrine's admissibility, which does not require the concept.

Consider a parallel. It is one thing to say that a view holds that conduciveness to salvation is neither necessary nor sufficient for the rectitude of conduct. It is quite another to say that it neither holds that salvation is necessary nor holds that it is sufficient. You can endorse the first only if you have the concept of salvation. You can, however, consistent with holding neither, lack the concept. So a public understanding of justice for use in public reason does not hold salvation to be necessary nor hold it to be sufficient for rectitude. Yet it would be a serious misunderstanding to say that it holds that salvation is neither necessary nor sufficient. Lacking the concept of salvation, the public understanding makes no judgments about it at all.

If public reason works without the concept of truth, then, it cannot hold that truth is neither necessary nor sufficient for admissibility as a premise in political argument, much less make any claims about the truth or falsity of substantive propositions of political justice. In effect, Estlund urges a modified political liberalism, which has the concept of truth available, affirms that truth is neither necessary nor sufficient for admissibility in public justification, also affirms as true the proposition that reasonable acceptance is necessary for admissibility, but does not apply the concept to substantive moral and political claims. Adding this proposition about reasonable acceptance would be a natural extension of a view that has the concept of truth available and holds truth to be neither necessary nor sufficient for a doctrine's admissibility. This is a very different view from the No Concept conception, however.[33]

Rawls's No Concept thesis is that public reason lacks the concept. No Substantive Judgments says that public reason has the concept but abjures substantive applications of it. I will not discuss this view further. Suffice it to say that the motivations for it are not very clear. After all, it is perfectly consistent to say both that reasonableness is necessary and sufficient for the admissibility of a consideration into public reason—for its use in public justification—and to say that it is permissible to present substantive moral and political claims as true. Once truth is available, it is not clear why it should be cabined in the way suggested.

No Big Deal

A third view, normative-political positivism, accepts a role for assertions of truth and falsity in political argument. It says, as distinct from No Truth Bearers, that the contents presented in political argument are (at least sometimes) truth-apt. It says, as distinct from No Substantive Judgments, that the application of the concept of truth to substantive moral and political judgments is legitimate. Because of the normative positivism, however, truth does not play a substantial role in political reflection and argument.

To appreciate the point, consider Hobbes's claim that "the authority of writers, without the authority of the commonwealth, maketh not their opinions law, be they never so true": *auctoritas non veritas facit legem.*[34] Hobbes's thesis is about legal validity, not about justice. The idea is that legal validity is fixed entirely by an act of authority, and not at all by moral rectitude. I think it is a useful, deflationism-inspired anachronism to think that Hobbes expresses a point about the independence of legal validity from moral rectitude in convenient shorthand when he says that truth does not make the laws. He might have said: If lying is right, that is irrelevant to legal validity; if lying is wrong, that is irrelevant; if stealing is right, that is irrelevant; if stealing is wrong, that is irrelevant; if kindness is nice, that is irrelevant; if kindness is not nice, that is irrelevant; and so on, ad infinitum. Instead, taking semantic flight, he generalizes over all propositions of any content, and says that truth does not make the laws.

That position is legal-positivism, which is consistent with the view that there are natural standards of rectitude to be used in evaluating laws.[35] But

Hobbes was arguably (only arguably) led to his legal-positivism from positivism about justice itself: *auctoritas non veritas facit justitiam*. As Hobbes says, there are no unjust laws because, antecedent to the sovereign's lawmaking activity, there is no just or unjust distinction for laws to be answerable to. So when Hobbes says that truth does not make law, he means that legal validity does not depend on truths about rightness. But that is in part because there are no normative truths available prior to authority that might enter into determinations of legal validity. If that is indeed the rationale for legal-positivism, then it follows as well that the truth—that is, truths about what is just and unjust, right and wrong—cannot figure in assessing valid laws as just or unjust because the justice-making facts too are exercises of sovereign legislative authority.

Once more, in semantic ascent, we might report this view by saying that truth does not make justice. Nevertheless the concept of truth can be used in assertions about propositions concerning the justice of valid laws. There is no trouble affirming that the proposition that theft is unjust is true, no more trouble than in affirming simply that theft is unjust, or that theft violates the law. What makes theft unjust is that authorities make laws defining and enforcing property rights. Nothing beyond that illegality is needed to make theft unjust and therefore to make the proposition that theft is unjust true. As a result, claims about the truth of propositions concerning justice are available in political argument, even though truth does not make the justice of the laws.

Truth is available for the normative-positivist, then, but its relevance is limited. The limits come not from the conception of truth as a device for expressing generalizations, but from the positivist view that justice is fixed by the social facts of sovereign enactment. That view limits the force of worries about whether our views about justice are true, about whether we have it right about justice. The concern is intelligible. I might think that I have been misinformed about the laws in a jurisdiction, and so wonder whether my beliefs are true. Once I know what the social facts are, however, in particular, what the authority has decided, I have no basis for further concern about whether justice is what I suppose it to be.

Drawing these points together, we have four views in play, each interpreting the general idea that, roughly stated, truth is not important in political argument:

1. No Concept: Though public, political justification is an exercise of

reason and the contents presented are truth-apt; the concept of truth is not available.

2. No Truth Bearers: The concept of truth has no application because the contents presented in normative political discourse are not truth-apt.

3. No Substantive Judgments: The contents are truth-apt, and the concept is available, but the concept is to be left on idle when it comes to substantive issues of justice.

4. No Big Deal: The concept is available and exercisable, but does no significant work because it is simply available to report the results of exercises of authority that are not constrained by norms of justice (or any other norms).

Rawls, I said, in effect suggests that we face a dilemma: that we can have truth or public reason, but not both. He embraces the idea of public reason as common ground under conditions of doctrinal disagreement, and concludes that we should leave truth aside. For the reasons I have been suggesting, it is hard to see how we can, however. It is difficult to understand what leaving truth aside comes to. Moreover, if political argument involves (as the idea of public reason indicates) beliefs, assertions, judgments, and reasoning, then truth also seems to be in play. Furthermore if justice is not, as the normative positivist holds, fixed by authoritative decision, then there is plausibly something important about getting justice right. Is there some way to reconcile these competing pulls?

To see how we might free ourselves from the dilemma, we need first to have an account of what is involved in the idea that the concept of truth is available to political reflection and argument.

Including Truth

I said at the beginning that political argument in democracies is in part a matter of reasoning and judging on the basis of considerations of justice. Such reasoning and judging might appeal, for example, to the principle that all citizens are entitled to the same basic liberties, to the abstract idea that a just society must treat its members as being of equal importance, and to arguments showing that a just society must secure equal basic liberties in part because securing those liberties is essential to treating members as being of equal importance. All of this, the principles as well as the reasoning, lies, I will assume, on the terrain of democracy's public reason.

What, then, would it mean to say that a conception of justice—say, a conception that includes the proposition that justice requires equal basic liberties—includes the concept of truth? The issue is not about a word, but about what it is for the concept of truth to be part of the conception. Rawls says that a political conception of justice does without the concept of truth, leaving the concept to comprehensive moral doctrines. We want to know what this "doing without" consists in, or, more precisely, what it would be to "do with" the concept.

Think of a political conception, used to formulate arguments in public reason, as a set of propositions. Let's say it includes, among others, the proposition that persons are entitled to a fully adequate scheme of equal basic liberties, that fairness is a fundamental political value, and that the original position models the ideal of fair cooperation among persons understood as free and equal. Consider a formulation of the conception in English, including the word "true" and the biconditional. Speakers, by virtue of their mastery of English, can say what propositions are expressed by various sentences; they can also say that the sentences expressing those propositions are true; and they can formulate biconditionals connecting the propositions and their truth conditions. So, for example, the sentence "Justice requires assurances of equal fundamental liberties" expresses the proposition that justice requires assurances of equal fundamental liberties, and the proposition that justice requires assurances of equal fundamental liberties is true if and only if justice requires assurances of equal fundamental liberties. So the formulation of the conception enables speakers to state and endorse instances of the truth schema: the proposition that p is true if and only if p. For example, they can say that the proposition that justice requires equal basic liberties is true if and only if justice requires equal basic liberties.

More than this is needed, however, to have truth available in public reason. To see why, consider a deflationary theory of truth, which tells us that truth is not a substantial property—not, for example, a relation of correspondence between a truth bearer and an independent order of facts—and that the truth schema tells us all there is to be said about the concept of truth. I assume that that schema is not itself in dispute between deflationary theories and their opponents. The point of contention is whether the schema exhausts the concept, of if there is anything more to the concept or nature of truth than is captured by the schema (or by a truth-definition that entails instances of the schema).

Consider, in particular, a version of the deflationary theory that says, among other things, that the truth schema, itself unexplained by any deeper theory, fully explains everything about the property of being true; that a grasp of the concept of truth consists in a disposition to affirm all the instances of the truth schema; and that truth is not a substantial property and lacks a nature. Moreover it says that the sole point of having a truth predicate is to be able to express generalizations, for example, to say that everything that Einstein said is true, or that all propositions of a certain form are true, or that the truth of normative propositions is not relevant to legal validity.[36] If you hold such a minimalist theory, then you will think that having the phrase "is true" and all the sentences that can be used to express instances of the truth schema is—assuming competent speakers, who are disposed to affirm all instances of the schema—what having the concept of truth in the political conception consists in.

Neither minimalism of this kind, nor any other form of deflationism, however, can provide the account of what it is to have the concept of truth in the political conception. Although the instances of the schema and inferences deploying it can be part of democracy's public reason, the minimalist theory of truth cannot be, and for two reasons. (Parallel considerations apply to other forms of deflationism.)

First, minimalism does not say, on its face, anything about the fact that truth is important or why it might be important: that our beliefs and assertions ought to be true, that it is good that they be true. Understanding the equivalence schema and being disposed to assert its instances, but not knowing anything about the point of classifying propositions as true and false is like knowing the rules of a game without knowing that the point of games is to win. Grasping the significance of truth is arguably (I come back below to the force of this qualification) not something you understand simply by virtue of understanding that the use of the concept of truth is captured by the instances of the schema, and that mastery of the concept consists in a disposition to affirm those instances.[37] A conception of justice, even when its formulation is understood to include the term "is true" and all the instances of the schema, may nevertheless arguably be said not yet to include the concept of truth. Including the concept as part of public reason also requires incorporating some account of the point of judging claims to be true and of the classifications that employ the concept of truth. I will return to this point in a moment.

Second, and more fundamentally, minimalism is a contested theory about truth. In contrast to correspondence, coherence, and pragmatic theories, it says that truth has no nature and is not a substantial property. It thus puts public reason needlessly at odds with philosophical doctrines—say, the rational intuitionism associated with some formulations of natural law theory—that embrace metaphysically more demanding theories of truth. It says more than is necessary for the purposes of including the concept of truth within democracy's public reason. Minimalism is an antimetaphysical theory of truth. In contrast, a political conception of truth cannot, as I said earlier, be antimetaphysical. It should, however, be nonmetaphysical, which will give it significant overlap with an antimetaphysical theory: it will not make claims about the real nature of truth, or affirm that it is substantial property, or make claims about what substantial property it is. However, it needs to say less than minimalism does so that it does not impose unnecessary barriers to entry onto the terrain of public reason. (It will not deny claims about the nature of truth either.)

In short, minimalism says too much (denies too much), and perhaps says too little to serve as a conception of truth in public reason. For the concept of truth to have a place in public reason, we need both more and less. The political conception of truth needs, first, to avoid asserting any theory about the nature of truth or its lack of a nature. Such assertions impose unnecessary hurdles and seem to serve no purpose within public reasoning.

Second, the political conception needs to include at least four commonplaces about truth:[38]

> *Attitudes*:   Believing (asserting, judging) is believing (asserting, judging) true, where this slogan is understood to mean that truth is the norm governing beliefs, assertions, and judgments.
>
> *Correspondence*:   True beliefs present things as they are (they "say of what is that it is and of what is not that it is not"), and in that uncontroversial sense correspond to how things are, although it will not add (or deny) that such beliefs present things as they really are in themselves, determinately and mind-independently.
>
> *Contrast*:   There is a distinction between truth and warrant or justification, so that an account of justice, for example, may be warranted—we may have grounds for endorsing it—but not true;[39] although, to reiterate, it will not say that truth is a substantive property different from warrant, nor offer

an account of what property truth is that distinguishes it from warrant, but it will also avoid claiming that nothing informative can be said on this issue.

Value: Truth is important, and given that truth is different from warrant, that truth is important in a way different from the way that warrant is important.

I mentioned before that minimalism may say too little to serve as an acceptable political conception of truth, and I need here to clarify the point. Minimalists do not dispute these four claims, but argue that the truth predicate is a device of generalization, that our grasp of the concept consists in our disposition to affirm instances of the truth schema, and that these additional claims—for example, about the value of truth—are derivative. They are explained in terms of the truth schema: according to minimalism, everything about truth can be so explained.[40] The political conception of truth, in contrast, takes no position on whether the truth schema is "explanatorily basic" in this way: it neither affirms nor denies the minimalist's explanation. It is agreed that an adequate account of truth must in some way include the commonplaces about truth. The political conception of truth can simply treat these commonplace claims as elements in the shared understanding of truth without claiming that they are part of the concept or aiming at an explanation (or denying the plausibility of some proposed explanation). In contrast, minimalism either lacks an account of the value of truth, in which case it says too little, or offers a theory about the value of truth, in which case it says too much.

If our aim is to provide a philosophical theory of truth, then abstaining from investigating the structure of this whole cluster of claims is bound to seem unsatisfying, a dereliction of intellectual duty, or simple laziness. But that is not the point of an account of public reason. Here the aim is simply to show that the concept, on a certain way of understanding it, is available as part of a shared ground of argument. We should not exclude the concept, but we need not incorporate a philosophical theory of truth, any more than we incorporate a philosophical theory of reason when we include an account of reasonableness. We have an understanding that serves the purposes of public political argument, but does not go beyond those purposes.

Three Reasons for Keeping Truth out of Public Reason

Having sketched a political conception of truth, I want now to consider in more detail some considerations that might be advanced for excluding truth from public reason, for what I have called the No Concept view. I presented an intuitive case earlier, but want now to discuss three lines of argument, each of which exemplifies some general reason for thinking that concerns about truth do not belong to politics, at least not to the kind of deliberative politics on common ground under conditions of doctrinal disagreement associated with the idea of public reason. The first is that the "singularity of truth" makes it practically divisive, perhaps intolerant, and thus at odds with the animating concerns of public reason; the second is that the inclusion of truth encourages the idea that truth is sufficient, which in turn encourages sectarianism; and the third, that truth introduces a concern with depth that is inappropriate to public reason. Rawls and others suggest each of these three, and each has some force. But with the political conception of truth available, we can accommodate the force while also preserving public reason.

Singularity

Assertions about the truth of a view may be seen as needlessly divisive, perhaps intolerant, because of a fundamental logical property of truth, namely, that truth is singular, whereas reasonableness is plural. Thus inconsistent propositions cannot both be true, and their adherents cannot therefore all believe the truth, whereas inconsistent propositions can both be reasonable to believe, and their adherents can all hold reasonable beliefs. It is not a philosophical theory, but a commonplace about the concept of reasonableness that reasonable people disagree about certain matters. The singularity argument turns this logical distinction between truth and reasonableness into a rationale for dropping truth while keeping reasonableness.

Rawls suggests the singularity argument when he says, "Holding a political conception as true, and for that reason alone the one suitable basis of public reason, is exclusive, even sectarian, and so likely to foster political division."[41] I will return later to the phrase "and for that reason alone." Putting it aside for now, the essential point is that if I assert that my account of justice is true, and yours conflicts with mine, then I am committed to denying that yours is true. I may assert that my view is reasonable, however, while accepting that yours is too. Why bring truth in, with this potentially troubling exclusiveness? Hannah Arendt gives forceful expression to this concern, suggesting that truth-claims are divisive in ways that are hostile to political life: "Factual truth, like all other truth, peremptorily claims to be acknowledged and precludes debate, and debate constitutes the very essence of political life. The modes of thought and communication that deal with truth, if seen from a political perspective, are necessarily domineering; they do not take into account other people's opinions, and taking these into account is the hallmark of all strictly political thinking."[42]

A first trouble with the singularity argument is that truth has close competitors in the divisive singularity market. Even if truth is not in play, other standards of appraisal seem as divisively singular, but also seem unavoidable, at least on the broadly cognitivist understanding of political discourse associated with public reason. So, for example, while there are a variety of different political conceptions of justice, and though reasonableness is plural, only one can be the most reasonable conception; "most reasonable" is as singular as "true."[43] Indeed even "more reasonable" might be seen as divisive, since conflicting views can both be reasonable, but each cannot be more reasonable than the other. When, in political reflection and argument, I rely on a particular conception of justice, I must distinguish mine from others on some relevant dimension of appraisal. Saying it is the most reasonable conception (or at least more reasonable than others)—that it is more strongly supported by the range of relevant reasons—is one such distinction.

Of course, it might be argued that the fluidly continuous more/less reasonable distinction is less needlessly divisive than the rigid true/false binary. Closer inspection reveals that this observation has little force. After all, I can say that someone has it more or less right, or is close to the truth, or that what he thinks is approximately true, or more or less true, but not quite. Indeed in the spirit of nondivisiveness, I can say that it is very reasonable, even if it is not true.

A second problem with the singularity argument lies in its supposition that "is true" causes the trouble. We should resist shooting the semantic messenger. I think that justice requires equal basic liberties; you think it requires maximin basic liberties; I think that privacy is among the basic liberties required by justice, while you do not. We agree that these views come to the same thing in most circumstances, and I accept that what you think is reasonable. Still, we disagree, and we seem to disagree not simply about which view is "most reasonable," but also about what justice requires. I think that unequal liberties are unjust, even when the inequality is associated with greater liberty for those with lesser liberty. We cannot both be right, though our views may both be reasonable. I want, then, to reject the claim that the concept of truth (or the deployment of that concept) provokes disagreement. Its use, insofar as it is used in public reason, expresses the disagreement that we have.

The first two responses to the singularity argument both emphasize that we can have divisiveness and perhaps intolerance without truth. A third observation is that we can have truth without divisiveness. Consider again the passage in which Rawls suggests what I am calling the singularity argument: "Holding a political conception as true, *and for that reason alone* the one suitable basis of public reason, is exclusive, even sectarian, and so likely to foster political division" (emphasis added). The point is that divisiveness does not come from the concept of truth, with its singularity, but from thinking that there is one suitable basis for public reason. If that is objectionable, then it is wrong to think that because a conception is true, it alone has a role to play in public argument. That inference can be resisted, however, while preserving a place for the concept of truth. It makes perfectly good sense to say, "My view is true, but other views, while not true, are reasonable to believe, and what matters for democracy's public reason is reasonableness, not truth." We need not drop the concept of truth in order to drop the thesis, suggested in this passage, that the truth of a proposition is a necessary condition for its playing a permissible role in public reason, or the thesis, to be investigated next, that its truth suffices to license appeal to it in political reflection and argument.

Sufficiency Argument

The sufficiency argument, with its concern about fostering sectarianism, begins from the suspicion that the concept of truth would serve in public reason as a general license for introducing considerations that might otherwise be of suspect appropriateness. I call this the sufficiency argument because the claim is that a proposition's truth suffices to make an appeal to it appropriate in political justification.

If truth did work as a license, there would be troubles for including truth within democracy's public reason. But this provides a rationale for leaving truth behind only if we think that the concept of truth, once available, will end up serving as a rationale for treating any true proposition as a relevant consideration in political argument. Thus Rawls worries about a "zeal for the *whole truth*" and about people who think of politics as a "relentless struggle to win the world for the *whole truth*," and he emphasizes "that politics in a democratic society can never be guided by what we see as the *whole truth*."[44] But should concerns about the whole truth provide a rationale for excluding truth? Only if its inclusion leads to an endorsement of its sufficiency.

Suppose someone asserts that abortion after eighteen weeks should be stopped because, as Aquinas argued, God ensouls the fetus at quickening, thus transforming it into a living human being. Or consider the view that gay marriage should not be permitted because it violates the duality essential to God's creation, or that social insurance ought to be eliminated because the best human life is a life of personal independence at odds with social insurance that protects against life's risks. In each of these three cases, an argument can be made for excluding the consideration from democracy's public reason, because proponents cannot reasonably expect others to endorse the consideration. (I am not defending this idea here; it is part of the background to the discussion.) When presented with that case, the proponent might say, for example, "But it is true that God ensouls the fetus at quickening, and therefore true that abortion after eighteen weeks is murder. How could these truths—universal and objective—not matter in deciding what to do?"

This appeal to truth carries no weight, and the availability of the concept changes nothing. If the proposition that God ensouls the fetus at quickening was not relevant, then the truth of that proposition is not relevant. After all, the case for its being irrelevant in public justification could not depend on the claim that it is false, since that claim would defeat the point of public reason. Correspondingly, the assertion that it is true does not add anything to the case for its relevance.

This point—that if the proposition that p is not relevant, then it is true that p is also not relevant—may seem to depend on endorsing a redundancy theory of truth, according to which the attributing truth to a proposition adds nothing to an assertion of the proposition itself. That is, the argument against truth as a license may be seen as semantic: if a person who asserts the truth of some proposition says nothing more than a person who asserts the proposition, then how could the former be relevant if the latter is not? Consider a person who rejects the redundancy theory and says that when he claims that the proposition about the fetus is true he is adding something. He is asserting, he might say, that the proposition corresponds to the facts about the fetus—to how things really are—and that it is true that abortion is murder because God decided the issue, and our belief fits the facts as they are, independently of our decisions and judgments. How, he might say, could that not be of decisive relevance?

These claims indicate that the proponent rejects the redundancy theory, but add no politically relevant argument. They tell us what makes it wrong to have an abortion, from which it follows that it is true. If someone, then, argues for the relevance of truth along the lines just suggested, the answer is that if the wrong-making facts did not suffice to establish the relevance of the consideration, then the truth-making facts cannot, that the understanding of truth as correspondence does not yield any additional facts of moral importance. If God's making abortion murder was not relevant, given the constraints of public reason, then how could the additional fact of correspondence with the divine-instituted wrongness make the wrongness relevant? Truth, in short, has no power to lift an otherwise irrelevant consideration into relevance.

A similar point is familiar from other settings, and does not have to do with the theory of truth or with any judgment about the importance of the truth. Suppose I am on a jury, deliberating on a charge of theft. If I mention in the deliberations that the defendant stole my wallet, I will be ruled out of order, and it will not make any difference to insist, "But I am telling you the truth." The objection by the other jurors was to the pertinence of my claim in this setting, not its veracity. And denying the relevance of my claim to be speaking the truth does not depend on a particular theory of truth.

But these reasons for rejecting the claim that truth operates as a general license are not reasons for steering clear of the concept of truth, unless the concept itself—or the practice of using it in political argument—invites us to slide to an assumption of its sufficiency. There appears to be some temptation to make this slide. For example, in explaining why Rawls refrains from presenting his conception of justice as true, Raz says, "Asserting the truth of the doctrine of justice, or rather claiming that its truth is the reason for accepting it, would negate the very spirit of Rawls's enterprise."[45] By "accepting it," Raz must mean "accepting it as an appropriate basis for public justification." Thus interpreted, Raz is certainly right that the claim that the truth of a proposition is "the reason for accepting it"—and contrapositively, that doubts about acceptability require denial of truth—is at odds with the fundamentals of political liberalism and public reason. But if we were not tempted to slide from truth to sufficiency, why would we think that this observation provides a good reason to "refrain from claiming" that a view is true—and correspondingly, that if we have good reason to think that assertions about truth are permissible, then we ought to accept that truth is sufficient for acceptability?

The way to resist the slide from affirming the truth of concededly relevant normative claims to the view that all truths are relevant, the slide from nothing but the truth to the whole truth, is by pointing to the error in that inference, not by denying a role for truth. The inference may be tempting because of the thought that there would be no good reason to affirm the truth of a proposition in the practical setting of a political discussion if the sufficiency thesis were not true, that it would be practically idle to affirm the truth of a claim unless an affirmation of truth sufficed to establish the relevance of a claim and as a conversation-stopping rebuttal to all objections. Yet familiar reasons about the use of truth as a device of generalization show that this is wrong.[46] Consider again the jury setting. Imagine that the jury hears from a particularly convincing witness, and one of the jurors says, "I think that everything she said was true." (Assume that nothing the juror said was ruled out of order.) Alternatively, one of the jurors might say that the essential thing the jury needs to settle on is whether "Jones is speaking the truth." The other jurors agree, and that common conviction is a working premise in their subsequent deliberations. But the fact that that working premise is expressed using the concept of truth does nothing to establish the relevance of my claim to be speaking the truth when I say that the defendant robbed me.

In short, truth may be relevant without being sufficient. Our (intellectual) response to those who aim to win the world for the whole truth is not to yield the concept of truth. Instead the response is to underscore the phenomenon of reasonable doctrinal disagreement, explain the value of a shared ground of argument among equals, point out that the case for a shared ground is not founded on a skeptical or relativist outlook, and clarify the appropriate but limited role of judgments about truth on that shared ground—thus denying the sufficiency of truth.

Limited Display

The limited display argument suggests that we should leave the concept of truth out of public reason because its inclusion leads to a concern with philosophical depth that is unsuited to public reason. Suppose that everyone in a group accepts a principle of equal basic liberties, and accepts it in part because this principle would be agreed to by the members as a way to live together as equals with conflicting fundamental religious and moral convictions. They all see the principle as supported by a set of reasons— about living together as equals, about permitting conduct guided by basic convictions, about finding terms that others can reasonably be expected to accept—that, we are assuming, are accepted by all.

At the same time, the common acceptance of this argument is founded on different and conflicting doctrines about the bases of those shared reasons. Now someone might say, "I see that the principle of equal basic liberties is reasonable, and I see how the case for its being reasonable can be presented by reference to a procedure of construction that brings together the relevant reasons. But is the principle of equal basic liberties true?" This question can be interpreted in two ways. It might be understood as asking whether justice requires some other principle, even if equal basic liberties is an acceptable accommodation. Or it might be understood as asking for a "full display" of the case for equal basic liberties: not simply a case that operates on common ground but an argument issuing from more fundamental values, principles, and reasons. The argument might, for example, be founded on the idea of human dignity associated with creation in God's image, or an idea of human autonomy associated with the powers of reflective thought. The line of thought underlying full display might go like this (suggested by general norms governing assertion): In asserting a principle of justice to be true, the speaker communicates to the listener that he believes that he has some grounds for making that assertion. Moreover the speaker commits herself to presenting a justification that gives the case for the truth of the principle. But such a justification must derive the principle (or the conception of which it is a part) from true moral principles: that is, a full display of the case for it. But such a derivation—a full display—cannot be part of public reasoning.[47] Since the assertion about truth commits the speaker to the full display, and only a limited display is permissible, claims about truth should be excluded.

The second interpretation is the relevant one, and it invites four responses. First, even if we agree that asserting that p, or asserting that it is true that p, commits the speaker to offering a justification for the claim that it is true that p, it does not follow that assertions of truth invite or commit the speaker to a full display of her entire ethical view (assuming that she has one)—that the rule, in the space of reasons, is in for a penny, in for a pound. Recall that democracy's public reason is a terrain of argument, and it may suffice, when challenged, to present a case for liberty of conscience, for example, that lies on common ground, with shared premises. If the premises are assumed to be true, then nothing more is needed to make a case for the assertion that that proposition is true. An assertion about truth need not be understood as committing the speaker to presenting a full display, any more than the assertion that justice requires liberty of conscience needs to be understood that way. Even if assertions commit a speaker to presenting a justification, they need not express commitments to depth. Truth is not depth. Sometimes, as Rawls observed, the point of philosophy is "to extend the range of some existing consensus."[48]

Second, whatever commitments about presenting reasons may follow from asserting that a proposition is true presumably also follow from asserting the proposition itself. If we are required to get into excessively deep waters when we assert that it is true that justice requires liberty of conscience, we also get into those waters when we assert that justice requires liberty of conscience. If there is a culprit, it is assertion (and the norms governing it), not truth.

Third, assertions about truth may not call for any display of argument at all. Suppose Smith says that he agrees with Mill's harm principle, but not with Mill's views about equality and democracy. If Jones says in response that she thinks that more or less everything Mill said was true, I cannot see that she has advanced any claim at all about the kind of argument that can or needs to be given for Mill's conclusions—in particular, and following on the second point, that she now has a justificatory burden greater than the one she would have had if she had simply said that she agreed with various claims Mill made about equality and democracy, and not said anything about truth.

Fourth, even if claims about truth do invite a full display, there may be nothing objectionable about presenting a full display of a doctrine that leads one onto common ground. I might say that I have a case, founded on a broader doctrine that underwrites my view that a principle of equal basic liberties is true. At the same time, I am fully aware that others disagree with the doctrine and have their own reasons for endorsing the liberty principle. What we share is an understanding of what justice requires and a conviction about the truth of that requirement. I understand that others endorse that requirement and assert it to be true for reasons different from mine. A full display need not be divisive, then, but may involve my presenting my reasons for accepting the common ground we are all assumed to occupy.[49] Of course, the full display will not provide a public justification, but it may nevertheless play a constructive role.

Getting It Right

The political conception of truth, I have argued, spares us from the horns of a dilemma. It enables us to respect the limits of public reason and to preserve a place for truth. The political conception thus addresses what might be seen as a fundamental objection to the idea of public reason. I want to conclude now with some comments that will set the discussion in a wider context and clarify what is at stake.

Consider the following remarks:

1. "[Fania Pascal's] statement ['I feel just like a dog that has been run over'] is grounded neither in a belief that it is true nor, as a lie must be, in a belief that it is not true. It is just this lack of connection to a concern with truth—this indifference to how things really are—that I regard as the essence of bullshit."[50]

2. "The truth of an opinion is part of its utility. If we would know whether or not it is desirable that a proposition should be believed, is it possible to exclude the consideration of whether or not it is true? In the opinion, not of bad men, but of the best men, no belief which is contrary to truth can really be useful: and can you prevent such men from urging that plea, when they are charged with denying some doctrine which they are told is useful, but which they believe to be false."[51]

3. "[We] need to take seriously the idea that to the extent that we lose a sense of the value of truth, we shall certainly lose something and may well lose everything."[52]

Set against the background of these remarks by Frankfurt, Mill, and Williams, Rawls's claim that the concept of truth has no place in public reason may seem startling. Is political liberalism an invitation to the bullshitter's indifference to truth and falsity; to tying the hands of the "best men" from pleading the truth of unconventional beliefs; or, by losing the distinction between belief with its characteristic discipline and undisciplined wishful thinking, to losing everything? Certainly not. Rawls's point about truth and its place in public reason is less starkly at odds with the claims of Frankfurt, Mill, and Williams than these passages might suggest, and in at least two ways that should by now be clear.

First, in his defense of truth and truthfulness, Williams was especially concerned about a kind of infantilization of discourse consequent on losing the distinction between belief and wishful thinking. Yet there may be other barriers than truth to the encroachment of wishful thinking: the Rawlsian standard of reasonableness may suffice.

Second, and more fundamentally, the idea that democracy's public reason should do without the concept of truth is not the idea that "we" can do without the concept of truth, and therefore need not, in any straightforward way, provoke Williams's concern, or Frankfurt's about a culture of bullshitting, or Mill's about indifference to truth. To explain, I will call the proposal that we do without the concept of truth *the cultural proposal*. The thought is that the culture, broadly speaking, should do without the concept of truth. More particularly, suppose we accept (as the political conception says) that truth is a norm for belief distinct from the norm of justification, and that a concern for believing the truth is a concern for getting things right, for how things really are, and not simply for having warranted beliefs, even ideally warranted. The proposal, then, is that the culture would be better off—and we would be better off—if we lacked the notion of truth and the associated distinct norm in public discourse. We would be better off if concerns about the correctness of belief were correspondingly understood to be exhausted by concerns about having beliefs that are supported by the best available reasons and that help us to navigate our way in the world.

Richard Rorty's view of truth is, I think, best understood along the lines of the cultural proposal.[53] Although Rorty sometimes presented a reductive theory, on which truth is understood as acceptance in a community, or warranted assertibility, or warranted assertibility at the idealized end of inquiry (or as a jocular slap on the back for ideas we agree with), he agreed that none of these reductive proposals gives an adequate account of truth.[54] The problem with the concept of truth, on the cultural proposal, is precisely that it is irreducibly distinct from justification, that it makes perfectly good sense to ask, relative to any account of what justification is, whether a proposition that meets that standard of justification, and that we are therefore warranted in believing and asserting, is true.[55]

Because of this irreducible difference from justification, the adherent of the cultural proposal urges that we drop the concept of truth from our repertoire and aspire to a cultural world in which people regard the concern for truth—for getting it right, latching onto things as they really are—as a thankfully transcended preoccupation, like the concern about whether there are ghosts in the cellar or an incubus upstairs: "Attaining truth as distinct from making justified statements is a goal for metaphysically active inquirers. We metaphysical quietists deplore the fact that most people in our culture can be incited to this sort of activity. . . . We pragmatists hope our culture will eventually replace itself with the culture that James and Dewey foresaw." Pragmatists, Rorty says, "should see themselves involved in a long-term attempt to change the rhetoric, the common sense, and the self-image of the community"[56]—all deposits for the detritus left by decaying metaphysical doctrine. Pragmatism, thus understood, is not the thesis that truth is what works in the long run or any other run, but a recommendation that we figure out what works, get down to the business of doing it, and stop worrying about truth.

Of course, that counsel is hard to follow. Foucault says that "the question for the West" is: "How did it come about that all of Western culture began to revolve around this obligation of truth which has so far taken a lot of different forms? Things being as they are, *nothing so far has shown* that it is possible to define a strategy outside of this concern [emphasis added]. It is within the field of the obligation to truth that it is possible to move one way or another, sometimes against the effects of domination which may be linked to structures of truth or institutions entrusted with truth."[57] These hardships notwithstanding, the pragmatist urges that we soldier on.

According to the cultural proposal, concerns with truth foster anxiety about whether we have things really right, or skepticism because we might not, or despair because we do not or cannot. Those concerns reflect a failure to take a proper sense of responsibility for our convictions as our own. We would live better, freer, happier, less fraught lives if we gave up worrying about getting things really right, stopped fretting that the world might be other than what we justifiably take it to be, focused on solving problems, and—with cheerful irony—embraced our convictions and our culture wholeheartedly and without embarrassment as . . . ours. We should unburden ourselves not because we finally have found the philosopher's stone—a way to answer the skeptic, or a grip on the idea of correspondence with reality, or an understanding of precisely what substantial property distinct from warrant truth really is—and are entitled to some rest after an intellectual job well done. The critique of truth is a cultural intervention, not a philosophical argument, a recommendation for living, not a theory. We should drop the concept of truth because it does not help us get on with life's business.

Williams and Frankfurt are, I think, worried about the cultural proposal. That proposal is, however, different in three important ways from the idea that democracy's public reason lacks the concept of truth. First, public reason is about political justification, not about the culture generally. Second, in presenting a political conception as available on common ground, the idea is precisely not to take a view on the correct theory of truth or the proper attitude to it in the culture, but to assume a range of views and avoid unnecessary controversy: the political proposal begins from the assumption, suggested by the idea of doctrinal conflict, that "the public culture" is unalterably divided in its understanding of, inter alia, the nature of truth. Third, the point of finding a conception that can serve as common ground is to provide a basis for cooperation among equals on a basis of mutual respect; the cultural proposal, in contrast, appears to express a specifically romantic ideal of self-creation and rejects the concept of truth because it burdens such creation.

Suppose, then, we put aside the cultural proposal about dropping truth from the culture, not because the cultural proposal is wrong, but because it is not our topic. The disagreement at issue here is not between Rorty and Williams (or Frankfurt or Mill), but between Rawls and Pinter. Assume, then, a culture in which the concept of truth is available: some people think we have already lost this culture; others regret that they are wrong. And suppose that we are tempted to reject the Rawlsian view about keeping truth out of public reason: we agree that it is hard to understand what it means to drop the concept (unless we are also prepared to drop, among others, the concepts of belief, assertion, judgment), that a nonmetaphysical (not antimetaphysical) understanding of truth is available, and that the reasons for dropping it are not compelling. So we are prepared to keep the concept of truth (interpreted along the political lines I described earlier) in political justification, and to acknowledge that truth is different from (even ideal) warrant. In rejecting the Rawlsian proposal, aren't we still recommending the public anxiety that the cultural proposal condemns? The objection to keeping the concept of truth raised by the cultural proposal may still have force even when our focus is narrowed to the arena of public-political discourse.

It may. Should the alleged anxiety be laid at the doorstep of truth, however? Why not say instead that it comes with the territory of justice, thus with the territory of public reason?

We are concerned to do what justice requires. Anyway, that is what we say; that is what we want other people to think we are committed to; it is what we want to take ourselves to be committed to. Not simply what we think justice requires, or what we warrantedly believe it to require, but what justice requires. But caring about justice, as the political conception indicates, requires caring about the truth about justice. If a concern about justice, as I said at the outset, has a place in democracy's public reason, then so too does a concern about getting it right, that is, about the truth about justice. We of course should, while keeping a concern for the truth, steer clear of needless controversy about the nature of truth: the political conception of truth suffices to meet that aim; nothing either so extreme or so fugitive as leaving the concept of truth out is needed.

As for the anxiety that comes with the concern to get justice right: that comes with the territory of taking justice seriously. We can live with it, should not live without it, and should not enlist philosophy to provide therapy for that anxiety.

Chapter 16

The Truth in Political Liberalism

David Estlund

The Stormy Relationship of Truth and Politics

Our democratic age tempts us to think that everything is up to us. Of course, as Hannah Arendt insists, the proposition "Germany invaded Belgium in August 1914" is a permanent truth, and nothing we decide can change it.[1] So not everything is up to us. Still, that historical fact is not a truth that affects what is right, or just, or good. So it might be held that these evaluative matters are the ones that are entirely up to us. By analogy with regicide and democratic revolution we might try to cast off the bogus boss-like order of moral and political prescriptions, declaring our authority to decide them for ourselves.

Among the deepest problems for this view is that it cannot even hold together. Does it mean that there is only this one truth about what we should do, the one about our authority: "Everything (else) is up to us"? This is undeniably a claim about what we should do, imprecise but momentous. The idea that there is this truth but no others is fundamentally different from saying that everything is up to us, a claim that is thus abandoned. And still, even this less absolute rejection of truth is hard to maintain once we ask how it is that "we" shall make these decisions we supposedly have the authority to make: the decisions that constitute all the facts about what we should do, the facts that are "up to us." When Germany decided that it should invade Belgium, is the idea that this decision made it the case that indeed they should do so? Was it up to them in that way? In that case, we must say that it was right for Germany to invade Belgium. In general, the view that evaluative truths are up to us can be maintained only at the cost of embracing piles of moral absurdity.

A natural response is to say that everything about what we should do is indeed up to us, but not just any way of making the decisions is valid. So we might (with Habermas) lay out the conditions for a proper and authoritative procedure for setting the truths about what we ought to do. (Again, incidentally, is there just this one truth? Is there a timeless universal procedure-independent truth—one that would not be up to us—that says that whatever is decided in *this* way is so?) On one reading, the view might be that truths about what we should do come into existence only when these idealized conditions have actually been satisfied. On any tempting account of the conditions, however, they have never actually been satisfied. (This is certainly true of Habermas's conditions.) So the view might be, instead, that the truths about what we should do are whichever truths *would*, hypothetically, be agreed upon by us (or certain theoretical counterparts of ours) under the relevant ideal conditions. But this gives up the game. For it is *not up to us* what the outcome of such an idealized collective procedure would be. Nothing we actually decide determines the matter, and so these evaluative things would not be up to us after all.[2]

Hereafter I will assume that not everything, not even everything about what we should do, is up to us. It may yet be that some things are. It might be that under the right conditions some actual collective decisions determine what we should do, while other things are independent of our decisions. The idea of democracy incorporates both ideas: it is not up to us whether democratic principles are true; if they are true, they are true whether we think so or not, and regardless of our decisions. But according to these democratic principles, when certain things are properly decided by democratic means they newly determine what we should do. That is what it means to say they are up to us: we get to determine those facts about what we should do, but then they *are* facts about what we should do. So some truths about what we should do are up to us, others are not.

Truth and democracy, then, have a real but complicated relationship. It is complicated even more by a further truth (or so I believe) about the relationship between truth and political justification. Following Rawls, I accept that a successful justification for political coercion can take place only in terms acceptable to all reasonable points of view. Rawls and others have called this approach "political liberalism."[3] Rawls argued that we must try to devise a conception of justice that does not purport to be the truth about justice, since that is something about which reasonable views disagree. He called this substitute account a "political conception" of justice, and this idea will figure importantly below. The idea of "reasonable" points of view strikes some people as insulting to other ("unreasonable") views, but it is important to keep in mind that one of the main positions being opposed by this doctrine is that viewpoints that are mistaken, no matter how reasonable they might be, may be ignored completely. The Rawlsian denies this, and is thus *more* tolerant and liberal in an important sense. The whole point of this Rawlsian view is to give moral standing to certain viewpoints even if they are mistaken. Compared with traditional political philosophy, it vastly expands the range of views that must be accommodated in the terms of political justification. The idea that it is an exclusionary philosophy is, it seems to me, simply a confusion.

The other opposing flank holds, against the Rawlsian view, that not only the so-called reasonable points of view, but all points of view should have this same status: objections from any point of view are fatal to any proposed political justification. But no one can seriously think this. It would mean that a proposed political justification, while unobjectionable in other ways, would lose all moral force if it were unacceptable to a Nazi ideologue. If there's anything to be said for this view, I have never heard it. There is, of course, the very difficult question of which views count as reasonable and which do not. This is not likely to be settled by ordinary language use, and so an emptier, less suggestive term such as "qualified" might be more appropriate than "reasonable." In any case, I will assume that political justification must take place in terms acceptable to all qualified or reasonable points of view, a category whose boundaries are not antecedently clear. I want to build this into our picture of the relationship between democracy and truth: truths are not available in political justification (which makes up only one part of public political discourse) unless they are acceptable to all qualified points of view.

With these preliminary points in mind, I turn to several ways the question of truth arises in political philosophy, and liberal democratic theory in particular. Even more specifically, I look closely and sympathetically at three ways truth might play a larger role within political liberalism than has often been assumed. First, I explore some implications of Charles Larmore's argument that political liberalism must rest on a moral principle of respect that has its authority independently of public reason. Second, I explain and critique Joshua Cohen's proposal to bring a "political conception of truth" into political justification while staying true to the deep principles of political liberalism, a move that would give truth a role that was eschewed by Rawls. I argue that Cohen's proposal actually would introduce something other than truth: a (mere) political conception of truth. The discussion of Cohen throws into relief a feature of Rawls's view that is, though not fatal, at least awkward. The political conception of justice in Rawls cannot be seen as addressing the truth about justice, and so a society that meets the principles does not thereby count as just. It counts only as in conformity with an ersatz conception of justice, devised, for good moral reasons, to be acceptable for this role by all reasonable points of view. Third, I briefly sketch an alternative possible form for political liberalism, one that dispenses with the idea of a political conception of justice (along with the awkwardness of its ersatz character) altogether, substituting at every point the idea of the (real) truth about justice, without abandoning political liberalism's foundational principle of political justification. I limit myself to explaining the conceptual possibility of such a view, which strikes me as worthy of more thought than this occasion allows.

The Truth on Which Political Liberalism Rests

In *Political Liberalism* John Rawls raised new questions about political philosophy's traditional assumption that, like any other branch of philosophy, it seeks the truth about a list of central issues such as justice, obligation, and authority. Rawls argued that political philosophy is different insofar as it has a political role. In the light of certain fundamental principles about (roughly) the equal right of all people to be free from arbitrary coercion by the community, political philosophy itself is required to devise a set of conceptions that harmonize the ideas of authority and legitimate coercion with respect for disagreement among reasonable contending worldviews. Political philosophy is self-restraining in a certain way: one part of it implies restrictions on the rest of it. In particular, Rawls asserted what he called the "liberal criterion of legitimacy," which says that political coercion is justified only if there is a possible justification that relies only on doctrines to which there is no reasonable objection.[4] Whereas traditional political philosophy derived justifications from what it took to be deep truths about human nature, value, and religion, this fundamental principle says that such accounts fail to recognize that it is intolerant to impose a political order on people on grounds that they don't accept, so long as their objections are part of a reasonable view.

What becomes of the truth on this view, when it is controversial among reasonable views? Rawls says that he hopes political liberalism can proceed without putting anything forward as true, preferring to rely on the property of reasonableness instead.[5] His reasons for this sweeping position are not particularly clear. He says, invoking the liberal criterion of legitimacy, that the nature of truth is too controversial for political justification to take a stand on it.[6] That would only show that political justification cannot take a stand on the nature of truth, but that wouldn't preclude putting things forward as true. Certainly, in addition to controversy about the nature of truth, many truths are themselves subject to reasonable dispute, but that would be a different argument. Those truths could not, according to the principle, be invoked in political justification. But that has nothing to do with controversy over the nature of truth. It is fairly clear, then, how the principle of legitimacy would forbid resting political justification either on any truths that are open to reasonable controversy, or on any particular account of the nature of truth. But that leaves open the possibility of asserting certain things as true so long as their truth is not open to reasonable dispute. Rawls, however, suggests that political liberalism must try to proceed without so much as the concept of truth.

Political liberalism, in any case, seems to limit appeals to the truth as such, in certain ways. However, none of this is correct unless the principle of legitimacy is true. That principle does indeed seem to imply all these truth-limiting things, but that is of little interest if they are implications of a principle that is not itself true. The principle's being acceptable to reasonable points of view is neither here nor there unless there is a true principle according to which that fact about it matters.[7] This places a limit on how far truth-claims can be avoided by political liberalism: the principle that limits truth-claims must be put forward as true. If it is true, then doctrines have justificatory force only owing to their general acceptability and not owing to their truth.

There are plenty of writers who reject the whole project of political liberalism, many of them on the grounds that it keeps too great a distance from the truth. My argument in this section, by contrast, accepts and defends political liberalism, including its core principle limiting appeals to the truth in political justification.[8] I argue only that this principle must itself be put forward as true, and consider some implications. The opponents of political liberalism argue that the principle is false. We can't take up their arguments here, but it is important to see the difference.

If the principle of legitimacy must be put forward as true in a way that is prior to and independent of reasonable agreement, then it might seem as though this opens the door to the comprehensive mode of argumentation more generally. After all, if the principle is put forward as true, it can be asked what argument there is for the principle, and the answer must apparently be in the comprehensive mode. Does this show that it is impossible to wall off a domain of political argumentation that steers completely clear of any comprehensive view of value? If it all rests on the principle of legitimacy, and this principle can only rest on doctrines in the comprehensive domain, doesn't it all rest on comprehensive doctrines?

In one sense, of course, it all does. The political realm of argumentation is not meant to be philosophically insulated from all other questions (whatever that would mean). If there is no good philosophical account of the principle of legitimacy, or no good philosophical answer to objections to it (questions that are taken up outside of public reason), then this ought to put the principle in doubt. But the question is whether the *principle* could be beyond reasonable doubt, not whether there is any moral or philosophical *basis* for it that is beyond reasonable doubt. Even if there is no basis for it that all reasonable points of view could accept, that doesn't mean that it couldn't itself be accepted by all reasonable points of view. They might simply have different reasonable accounts of its basis. The fact that the liberal principle of legitimacy must be put forward by the political liberal as true in the comprehensive sense does not mean that political justification must rely on comprehensive views that are controversial among reasonable views.

Charles Larmore emphasizes the special status of the principle of legitimacy—its having an authority that, unlike that of the other doctrines used in political argument, is prior to and independent of the implications of consensus among reasonable views—by saying that it "embodies a principle of respect for persons."[9] This is a useful description of the principle because it helps us see that the relevance of reasonable consensus must itself be given by a moral principle. This is a corrective to those who think (as, for example, Habermas does) that a democratic people are not under the authority of any moral principles that the people do not somehow give to themselves. This claim itself expresses a moral principle, a certain principle of respect for persons. That principle itself cannot coherently be held to emerge from consensus among reasonable views, a consensus whose relevance precisely derives from this principle of respect.

It might seem that if we grant that the liberal principle of legitimacy rests on a prior moral principle, then we are forced to go into controversial moral territory. Is the principle of respect that underlies the liberal principle of legitimacy the province of one or a few reasonable comprehensive conceptions and foreign to others? The question is whether appealing to a moral principle of respect that grounds or illuminates the liberal principle of legitimacy necessarily goes beyond the set of doctrines that are common to all reasonable comprehensive views. Larmore says he shares the project of a "freestanding" conception of political values in Rawls's sense. So his claim is not the claim of many of Rawls's critics, that justification cannot avoid resting on a comprehensive conception of truth and value. Larmore believes that it can. His point is that this "method of avoidance" (as Rawls called it) is required by a principle that is not itself the product of a consensus among reasonable views. In this respect it is committed to something moral and true that underlies and explains the required reticence about truth on other matters. That does not mean, so far, that it is committed to anything that can't be accepted by all reasonable points of view.

Interestingly, though, Larmore says that he believes the principle is open to reasonable dispute. It is not clear to me how to reconcile this with his also holding that political justification must be "freestanding." Larmore writes, "In *Political Liberalism*, Rawls declares that a political conception is freestanding, if it looks only to the principles that should govern the political life of society. It does not present itself as applying to the political realm a comprehensive doctrine about the ends of life. . . . I share Rawls's conviction that a liberal conception of political association should be freestanding in this sense" (*Moral Basis*, 599–600). Larmore believes that the principle of legitimacy and the associated principle of respect are not things that must be accepted by all reasonable points of view; that is, they are themselves subject to reasonable disagreement. We can invoke them in political argument to the extent that our audience happens to accept them, he says, but reasonable dispute about them is possible: "Being reasonable (in my sense of the term) does not entail the principle of respect for persons. If the moral basis of liberal democracy stands free of any comprehensive conception of the good, it does not on that account become inherently universal. Its appeal can extend only so far as people happen to be committed to the principle of respect" (624). This appears to violate the principle of legitimacy:

no doctrines may be used in justification unless they are acceptable to all reasonable points of view. Larmore must either revise the principle of legitimacy, or hold that it is not itself part of justification and so escapes its own scrutiny, or keep it as it is but hold that it cannot be reasonably rejected after all.

My concern is that if Larmore is correct that it is possible for reasonable people to disagree about the principle of respect underlying liberalism, then, if the principle is true, this very principle is unavailable in liberal political justification. But if that is so, then it can hardly serve the role Larmore assigns to it, of being the moral basis of liberal democracy (613, 617, 623, 624). Here is my argument laid out more directly, that Larmore's combined positions lead to the conclusion that political liberalism is a moral failure, something he surely doesn't accept:

1. The principle of respect precludes appealing in justification to doctrines open to reasonable dispute. (Accepted by Larmore)
2. The principle of respect is open to reasonable dispute. (Accepted by Larmore)

  ———

3. (from 1, 2) The principle of respect precludes appealing to the principle of respect in justification.
4. If the justification of liberal democratic arrangements makes no use of the principle of respect, then the principle of respect is no part of the moral basis of those arrangements. (Assumption)
5. The principle of respect is the moral basis of liberal democratic arrangements. (Accepted by Larmore)

  ———

6. (from 4, 5) The justification of liberal democratic arrangements makes use of the principle of respect.

  ———

7. (from 3, 7) The justification of liberal democratic arrangements makes use of the principle of respect, and such reference is morally precluded by the principle itself.

  ———

8. (from 7) The justification of liberal democracy is a moral failure.

Of course, Larmore does not think it is a failure, so the question is which of these steps he can resist. He must either change his view about (2), and hold that the principle of respect is *not* open to reasonable dispute, or he must hold that the principle of respect can somehow be the moral "basis" of liberal democracy without being used in its justification. Or, I suppose, he could give up his view that the principle of respect is any part of the moral basis of liberal democracy.

The difficulty would disappear if the principle of respect were itself acceptable to all reasonable views. Larmore does not think that it is, but we should note that this is partly because of the way he conceives of reasonableness, departing in this from Rawls. Larmore thinks that the people whose agreement must be possible in political justification are those who think and converse in good faith, and apply, as best they can, the general capacities of reason.[10] Crucially, this does not seem to preclude any moral content. Or if it does, Larmore is clear that it is not meant to exclude views that do not accept the principle of respect itself or any such commitment to reciprocity. Larmore's principle of legitimacy, then, is a different principle from Rawls's, as similar as they are in certain ways. On Rawls's principle, if a person rejects some justification on certain immoral grounds, this might (depending on details) disqualify her view from counting as reasonable, thus disqualifying her objection from counting against the proposed justification. On Larmore's different principle, the moral quality of an objection is irrelevant to whether it blocks the justification. A person's moral views do not bear on whether the person's overall view is a good faith application of reason, and this latter issue is the one that determines whether her objection defeats the justification. In effect, more objections are decisive on Larmore's view. This is a moral disagreement between him and Rawls. The stakes are heightened by the fact that, as I have argued, if Larmore is right in this dispute, then the principle of respect cannot be used in political justification even if it is true. If Rawls is right, that problem might be avoided, since the principle of respect might itself be a common moral element in all points of view that are included in the set counted as "reasonable": the views whose objections to justification morally defeat those justifications.

How might we adjudicate this dispute? The question is: Which features must a point of view have in order that objections stemming from that point of view are, whether they are correct or not, fatal to proffered political justifications? We can't give as the answer that they must be "reasonable." The question is precisely what should be counted in that category. The dictionary and ordinary language must be put aside, since they settle no moral questions at all. "Reasonable" is a term of art here, and it is a question for philosophers what (if any) content it can be given so that the resulting principle of legitimacy is correct. It can be helpful, as I have said, to substitute the blander and less suggestive term "qualified" for "reasonable" in order to avoid being misled by the latter term's common uses. What features must a point of view have, then, in order to be qualified in this particular way? Larmore says that it must manifest good faith thought and discussion along with respect for the standards of reason that apply to all areas of inquiry, but that it need not include any particular moral position such as a commitment to respect for persons. Why hold this particular view, rather than Rawls's view that a point of view is disqualified if it lacks certain moral content, in particular a commitment to reciprocity of a certain kind? It is, as I say, a moral question which of these (if either) is correct.

Some writers have resisted building any moral content into the qualifications on the ground that this merely moves the controversy from one part of the theory to another. Call this the objection from "relocated controversy." It says that if the problem in the first place is the pluralism of conflicting views in society, you haven't avoided it merely by saying that all views are equal so long as they are morally reasonable. This is a false gesture of toleration. The views counted as unreasonable will often continue to dispute their disqualification from the class of views whose objections are decisive.

When it is said that the problem has not been avoided, this seems to mean that there remains disagreement, now relocated to the fundamental principle of legitimacy. But it would be wrong to suppose that disagreement is the problem that motivated the theory in the first place. The motivating problem was that not only is there disagreement, but some of it stems from points of view that are qualified to defeat justifications to which they can object. Not all disagreements will be disagreements between views that are so qualified. So the fact that a morally laden principle of respect will remain controversial is no problem unless it is also shown that the controversy is between qualified points of view. Which views are qualified can perfectly well remain controversial, so long as it is not controversial among qualified points of view. The project is not one of creating a de facto social peace. It is one of providing a justification for political arrangements, and this is not at all the same thing. Showing that disagreement remains does not begin to show that justification has not been provided.

Of course, if the only views that were counted as reasonable or qualified were the one or several that were correct about everything, then the project would be incoherent. The reason is that in that case there could not be such a thing as reasonable or qualified disagreement, and there would be no animating problem about justification in the first place. If we say that there is reasonable disagreement about many things and that this is a challenge to political justification, then we must mean that some views that are not correct about everything are nevertheless reasonable or qualified in a way that entitles their holders to justifications they can accept. If we can devise justifications that satisfy all such views, then we have indeed solved the problem, regardless of whether there is continuing controversy about which views have been counted as qualified and which have not. We need only satisfy the qualified ones; that status is what their qualification consists in.

The fact, then, that even people who reason in good faith can disagree about any morally laden definition of qualified points of view is no objection to such a definition or to the resulting principle of legitimacy. We are morally free to use justifications to which there are objections, just so long as the objections don't come from qualified views.

If the objection from relocated controversy doesn't succeed, then what reason remains to block moral content from the relevant notion of qualification and disqualification? It is simply a moral question which features of a point of view qualify or disqualify a point of view in the specified way. But why should we not think that certain morally objectionable points of view are, for that very reason, disqualified—excluded from the set of views whose objections can defeat justifications? This wouldn't yet mean that all morally erroneous views are disqualifying. That too is a moral question. Perhaps some are disqualifying and some are not. That is, perhaps for purposes of political justification there is reasonable disagreement about some moral matters, but not about all of them. I don't propose to answer the moral question here, but only to point out that if there is no general difficulty for including moral content in the conditions of qualification, then it is, so far, open to hold that views that reject the moral principle of respect are for that reason disqualified. This couldn't be the whole definition of qualification, or it would be empty, with nothing in it for any view to accept or reject. But so long as there are other disqualifying conditions, there could also be this one. Whatever other virtues this approach might have, it would also, as I have argued, allow political liberalism to avoid a serious problem: the threat that the principle of respect is blocked from use in political justification because it is itself open to reasonable disagreement.

In any case, Larmore and I agree that political liberalism rests on a moral basis that it does not itself generate out of the overlap of reasonable views, and that this does not vitiate the liberal principle of legitimacy that lies at the foundation of political liberalism. There is a moral truth at its basis.

Ersatz Justice: Can Public Reason Handle the Truth?

As we've seen, Rawls proposes that political liberalism should be understood as banning the concept of truth from our proper justificatory practices. Doctrines and arguments are admissible in public reason on the ground that they are acceptable to all reasonable views, not because of any claim to their being true. I have argued that the underlying principle of justification must itself be put forward as true, but that point is off-stage in this section. We now look at the implications of that principle for the use of the concept of truth in the rest of our practices of political justification. Rawls suggests that truth should make no appearance at all. Joshua Cohen points out that this is a very difficult position to maintain, for reasons I will explain shortly.[11] He proposes to introduce the idea of truth in order to solve the problems he identifies, but only in the form of a political conception of truth. I will argue that there is no real halfway house of this kind, but the issues that motivate Cohen do point to striking and important features of political liberalism that may not be properly appreciated.

What is wrong with banishing truth from our justificatory practices, according to Cohen? The problem is that public justificatory discourse evidently involves asserting things, denying other things, giving arguments for conclusions, pointing out fallacious reasoning in the arguments of others, and so on. All of these are inseparably linked to the concept of truth, at least in the minimal sense. By the "minimal" sense, he means the disquotational interpretation of truth, according to which the proposition "x is F" is true if and only if x is F. The kinds of discourse I just listed seem crucially to involve the idea of things being the way they are asserted to be, or not being the way they are denied to be, and so on, which is an element of the idea of truth. And inferential reasoning seems to require what logicians call truth-functional logic. So, Cohen concludes, we can't make any sense of what goes on in proper justificatory practice if we deprive ourselves of the very concept of truth.

As Rawls plausibly claimed, conceptions of the nature of truth are too controversial to make it into public reason, which must be beyond dispute among reasonable views. What this shows, as we have seen, is that no particular view of the nature of truth can be appealed to in political justification according to political liberalism. As Cohen rightly says, this includes even the "minimal" or "deflationary" theory of truth. It too is open to reasonable dispute. So while we may assume that the disquotational feature is a part of any reasonable conception of truth (or so I understand Cohen to assume), we must avoid committing ourselves to the controversial view that this is all there is to truth. The question is how to introduce the concept of truth into public reason while avoiding any particular controversial conception of truth.

Cohen distinguishes, in a classically Rawlsian way, between a political conception and a comprehensive conception. Applying the distinction where Rawls did not, he says, in effect: We may not use a comprehensive conception of truth, but why not a political conception? For example, despite much disagreement, all reasonable conceptions of truth seem to converge on the disquotational element. If we availed ourselves of a minimalist conception of truth for political purposes, leaving aside whether there was more to the nature of truth than just this, we would not be offending any reasonable view, and yet we would be able to accommodate the truth-aptness of the activities of public justification such as assertion, denial, and inference. We use, as it were, a fragment of the concept of truth, the fragment that all reasonable views accept. It is a fragment, available for political purposes, of the genuine truth-predicate. This parallels the way Cohen sees the idea of a political conception of justice. It is a fragment of the correct comprehensive conception of justice (whatever that conception might be). It is not the whole truth about justice, but it is a part, available for political purposes, of the true conception of justice.

I think this use of political conceptions will not work as a reconstruction of political liberalism. Consider, first, the so-called political conception of truth in Cohen's account, a conception that is meant to allow us to say of the various claims in the so-called political conception of justice that they are true. Even though no controversial conception of the nature of truth is carried along by such a statement, the statement goes too far. To see why, it is helpful to distinguish between two possible meanings when it is said that a certain conception of justice is acceptable to all reasonable views. One thing this might mean is that all reasonable conceptions agree that this is the truth about justice. Another thing it might mean is that even if they don't agree that it is the truth about justice, they each find it acceptable within their own larger view to use this conception as the framework for reasoning about justice under conditions of reasonable disagreement. Cohen's approach must assume the first kind of agreement, since only then would the elements of the political conception count as truths about justice from each reasonable point of view.

As Rawls argues (and Cohen indicates no dissent), there are multiple reasonable conceptions of justice (within a sort of family).[12] Being different, they are, in at least some respects, incompatible. It is impossible, then, to be an adherent of one of them without regarding the others as false (even if not in every particular). So adherents of conceptions other than justice-as-fairness must believe that particular conception is false. There is reasonable disagreement about whether it is the truth about justice. It can nevertheless be agreed by all reasonable views that it is suitable as a conception of justice for purposes of public reasoning in pluralistic conditions. This can be summarized as being an agreement about its reasonableness, even if not its truth. Rawls writes, "Once we accept the fact that reasonable pluralism is a permanent condition of public culture under free institutions, the idea of the reasonable is more suitable as part of the basis of public justification for a constitutional regime than the idea of moral truth. Holding a political conception as true, and for that reason alone the one suitable basis for public reason, is exclusive, even sectarian, and so likely to foster political division."[13] Since there is reasonable disagreement about the truth of any conception of justice, even Rawls's own view, justice-as-fairness, the liberal principle of legitimacy blocks that truth-claim from public reason.

Cohen points out that if we fear the sectarian significance of appeals to truth, we must also worry about the sectarian significance of claiming that a conception of justice is the most reasonable one. That too will be disputed among reasonable views. Assuming that this would be absurd, he concludes that neither concept is blocked from public reason. It is not clear what permits this move. Maybe it would be serious trouble for political liberalism if even "most reasonable" were blocked from public reason by the liberal principle of legitimacy (a question I'll come back to). But that wouldn't allow us to act as if there is no problem by just stipulating that it is not blocked. We don't have the power to decide such a thing as we choose. If there is reasonable disagreement about "most reasonable," then it simply *is* blocked by the principle that says justification may not appeal to doctrines that are open to reasonable dispute. This is a logical truth, not a theoretical decision.

How bad would it be if even "most reasonable" were unavailable in public reason? I don't see why it would be a serious problem. Rawls offers one member of the family of liberal conceptions because he believes it is the most reasonable. But there is no need to rest political justification on this feature of the conception, rather than the less controversial feature of its being, simply, reasonable. It is, as are other conceptions, acceptable to all reasonable points of view as a shared public conception of justice that is appropriate for use in public political reasoning. Which of the reasonable liberal conceptions might actually be settled on as a shared public conception of justice will depend on many things, but they all share the feature that allows political justification to rely on them: they are, if not the most reasonable, at least reasonable. So I accept Cohen's point that "most reasonable" would be as divisive as "true," but I conclude that both are banned from use in political justification. Of course, as with many other doctrines that lie outside of public reason, these predicates will have various legitimate uses in public political discourse. But, as Rawls says, in due course we must be prepared to give justifications that limit themselves to doctrines acceptable to all reasonable points of view, and claims about which conception of justice is true or most reasonable are blocked by this requirement.

There are two features of this reading of political liberalism that some might find alarming. First, as we have seen, it is hard to make sense of political discourse in public reason without treating the claims about justice as true or false. Second, if the political conception of justice is not put forward as true, then no claim is being made about (real) justice. I take them up in order.

I accept Cohen's important point that political liberalism needs some way to include the truth-linked concepts of assertion and denial, inference and fallacy, in the activities of public reasoning. This might seem to be threatened if citizens are not permitted to make truth-claims about justice (etc.) in public reason. A similar situation arises in the context of legal courtrooms, however, and the analogy suggests there is no problem after all. It is a familiar fact that the opposing parties might each find it convenient to "stipulate" that "x is F" even if they and the judge all know that x is really not F. For example, the prosecution might stipulate (or refrain from challenging) the proposition that the defendant was at home at midnight. They might stipulate this because their case will proceed without any need to deny this. At this point, reasoning in the case is to proceed on the assumption that the defendant was home at midnight. It may be asserted, inferences may be drawn from it, and so on. These are truth-linked activities. How can they go on when the statement, in court, that "x is F" is not being put forward as true? The answer is that it is understood that it shall be treated as if it were true, including all the truth-linked activities that this would normally warrant, but all governed by the understanding that it is not really put forward as true (and indeed may not be true). That "x is F" becomes one of the "facts of the case," even though it is not really granted to be a fact. For certain reasons, the participants use a certain conception (as we might put it) of the facts. They are not (or may not be) actually the facts, but they can function as an ersatz set of facts. There are interesting philosophical questions about the semantics of the utterances that take place in a context like this, but the analogy is enough, I think, to suggest that there is no obvious incoherence in combining the following two features: (1) the propositions in the conception are not put forward as true, and (2) the full range of truth-linked activities can carry on as if the propositions in the conception were true, with an understanding that this is being done for certain reasons, and that they may not really be true at all. The truth-linked activities require no more than an ersatz conception of the facts. Cohen is correct that, because the contending comprehensive views will often assert or deny some of the elements of the political conception, they must regard them as truth-apt: they must be either true or false. That is compatible with my suggestion that in the political conception (as in the trial context) they are not put forward as true, even though they must, in fact, be either true or false.

This point leads directly to the second concern I mentioned about my interpretation of political liberalism, namely that if citizens are not putting forth their claims about justice as true, then they are not really making claims about justice. There is something right about this, although this might be an exaggerated way of putting it. After all, the stipulated "fact" in the criminal case, that the defendant was home at midnight, is surely about the defendant and about midnight. It is not about some other person or time. It is just saying things about the defendant in a context where it is to be understood that they are not meant to be true. Similarly, we can perfectly well say that claims about justice in public reason, even if they are not put forward as true, are still *about* justice.

But there remains a significant concern. If, for example, Rawls's two principles of justice are not (as I claim) to be understood as put forward as true, then a society that meets the principles cannot, on that basis, be determined to be just. Again, this is right in a way, but exaggerated. After all, in the same context in which the participants are understood to limit themselves to the political conception, namely, public political argument, it would be perfectly appropriate to say that societies that meet the two principles are just. It follows logically from saying that those are the principles of justice. In that context, however, it is understood that this is not being put forward as true. With that understood, it is just the right thing to infer. Inference, as we know from the legal context, does not require genuine claims to truth.

That is why it is an exaggeration to say that societies meeting the principles in the political conception can't be said to be just. But from a philosophical point of view, what is right about it is that the context is one in which the principles are (for moral reasons) not being put forward as true, and so the inferences and so on are all governed by that understanding. The political conception does not purport to give the truth about justice, not even part of it. It might literally be false. Rawls conjectures that perhaps we should find this to be unlikely given the conception's acceptability to all reasonable points of view, but he clearly allows for it in principle.[14] The political conception of justice is a substitute for a true conception of justice for certain purposes, and so we might call it an ersatz conception of justice. Simply noting this about the view is not any objection to it, since the legal context shows that there might be adequate reasons for the use of ersatz conceptions. Many seem to think that it would be (if I am right) an awkward and undesirable feature of the view. I'm not sure I agree. It does seem fair, however, to say that while a politics governed by a political conception of justice is, as I argued above, still about justice, it does not aim at justice. This ersatz feature of the view is not entirely satisfying, I suppose, but that hardly establishes that the moral reasons that are given for resorting to a political conception are not adequate. This might very well be the best that can be done given the range of reasonable pluralism. Nevertheless in the next section I explore an alternative development of political liberalism that would avoid the ersatz issue entirely.

Beyond Political Conceptions?

I have argued that if the truth about justice is not necessarily a competent public reason, then political argument must not be addressed to the truth about justice as such, but to a political conception that can serve as justice for political purposes.[15] This requires a distinction between true justice (justice in the true or best comprehensive conception) and political justice (justice on the most reasonable political conception). An awkward implication is that political justice might not be true justice. If it's not true justice, it's not justice. If a painting isn't a true Van Gogh, it's not a Van Gogh, however well it might serve *as* a Van Gogh for certain purposes.

Many writers have rejected the whole framework of political liberalism for reasons like this.[16] The thought seems to have been that the principle that justification must be acceptable to all reasonable points of view is incompatible with the indispensible conviction that political procedures and participants aim at and address true justice. My thesis in this section is that these are not incompatible after all. Political liberalism does not necessarily preclude conceiving of politics as aiming at true justice, although in Rawls's version it does. My goal is mainly to make this abstract point, and not to advocate that particular path for political liberalism. But it will be helpful to explore this truth-oriented option in some detail.

The Rawlsian view is, in the first instance, a view about what kinds of purported justifications of political coercion are successful—that is, which ones really accomplish the moral feat of justification. (This is not at all the same as the question of which justification will actually find acceptance, or promote stability, etc.) It is only as a corollary that the view leads to principles about how citizens ought to conduct themselves in public political argument. My argument exploits the difference between these two enterprises. I accept the basic point that if a form of justification is not morally successful, then it is a natural corollary to hold that citizens ought not to offer such justifications as if they were. But this doesn't yet tell us much about what kinds of things they should or should not say. In particular, it doesn't yet imply that citizens ought not to assert what they take to be the real truth (in the comprehensive sense). It entails only that if they do so, they should not be suggesting that the truth of the view is enough to justify coercing people in accordance with it. Rawls's final view about public reason incorporates this point, laying out numerous contexts in which asserting one's comprehensive views in public would not violate his principle of public reason.[17] Rawls argued that "in due course," however, citizens must be prepared to frame their public political arguments in terms acceptable to all reasonable points of view, and this, he concluded, will be different from asserting one's own comprehensive view as the truth. I will call this "Rawls's proviso."

In order to supply a generally acceptable substitute for truth seeking, he argues that citizens, when in due course they give their real argument, are to address a suitable political conception of justice (he proposes his famous theory of justice-as-fairness for this role) rather than the truth about justice as they see it. It is this last step, the substitute of a political conception of justice for true justice, that I want to suggest may not be required. The result of the alternative I will propose would be a theory that remains faithful to the principles of political liberalism but jettisons justice-as-fairness as a political conception of justice. Justice-as-fairness would remain important, of course, but in the role Rawls originally gave to it (later rescinding this status), as a proposal about true justice. The role I will be envisaging for discourse about true justice thus goes far beyond what is implied by Rawls's proviso, and is frankly incompatible with a major component of Rawls's overall view: the need to rely on a shared political conception of justice while putting aside disputes about true justice in our public justificatory practices.

To say that there must be a publicly acceptable justification for some political action—say, for a certain law—does not directly imply that what people ought to be doing in political discourse is presenting what they take to be publicly acceptable justifications. Presumably that is one thing that ought to be done, but it is a mistake to think that political liberalism requires this as the primary mode of political discourse or argumentation. All we really know from political liberalism's principle of justification is that people ought to act in such a way that there *is* a generally acceptable justification for the resulting laws and policies. The possibility that I want to explore is that there could be such a justification for a political practice in which the predominant topic of discussion is the (real, comprehensive) truth about justice. Nothing fundamental to political liberalism is violated by citizens supporting laws or candidates on the basis of comprehensive views of the truth, so long as there is a justification that is *itself* acceptable to all reasonable points of view for imposing on citizens laws and policies that are arrived at in this way.

The fundamental tenet of political liberalism is about what counts as a successful justification, not about how to conduct ourselves in political argument. Something would indeed be wrong if the citizens offered their comprehensive doctrines as if they were adequate justifications. (This would violate the "natural corollary" of which I spoke earlier.) But that is not the only thing that they could be doing when they support laws or policies on the basis of their comprehensive views. It might seem that if someone advocates a law on certain grounds, then he is committed to saying that those grounds would be an adequate justification for that law. But consider the context of democratic voting. As a legislator I might advocate a law on the ground that, say, it would benefit some and hurt none. But I don't think that this consideration by itself would justify the law, since I think the law would be justified only if it is passed by a majority of my fellow legislators. If I think the justification is procedural in some way, then I will distinguish between two levels of reasons for or against a law. At one level the reasons are about the procedure. At another level the reasons are the ones that are to be given within the procedure. We might even say that these turn out to be reasons for different things. Only the procedural reasons are reasons in favor of the imposition of the law. The reasons given within the procedure might be said to be reasons for voting for the law, which is something quite different.

When citizens advocate a law on the basis of their comprehensive view, they are participating in the political procedure. We might interpret them as giving reasons for voting or working for certain laws or policies. The analogy with the legislator shows that it would be a mistake to assume that they are also giving what they take to be a justification for implementing and imposing the law. On that question the right sort of reasons might be procedural considerations. Now here's the important point: the right procedural justification might refer to a procedure in which participants address the truth, in the comprehensive sense, about justice. If this procedural justification is itself acceptable to all reasonable points of view, then the Rawlsian principle of justification would be fully respected.

Strikingly, this (still fully politically liberal) approach would eliminate the role for a political conception of justice. It is worth looking briefly at the development of Rawls's thought in order to distinguish this approach more clearly from his own. In *A Theory of Justice*, Rawls develops a theory of true justice—a theory of how justice might be conceived in the best comprehensive conception. Over time he comes to accept a principle of general acceptability in justification, and to realize that his case for justice-as-fairness cannot meet that requirement. At that point there are two choices. The one Rawls takes is to recast the theory of justice as a "political conception of justice," and pointedly not (any longer) as a proposal about true justice in the comprehensive sense. It is to serve as a conception of justice whose use for public political purposes is acceptable to all reasonable views that differ about true justice and much else.

The other choice, the road not taken, would have been to give an account of how a process in which people address true justice could justify the laws in a way acceptable to the wide variety of contending reasonable comprehensive conceptions (of justice, among other things). This second choice does entirely without the idea of a public conception of justice. Justice is justice. Of course, it all depends on whether there is some justification of a truth-oriented political process that can plausibly fill the bill, serving as a justification that is acceptable to all of the contending reasonable points of view.

My point, then, is an abstract one: Political liberalism as a theory of justification does not necessarily lead to the need for a political conception of justice. A second point is that there is something to be said for a procedural justification in which the arguments of participants are primarily addressed to true justice rather than to a political conception of justice. In this short space I will have only brief and tentative things to say about this, the goal being to put this question forward as one of some interest and importance.

One natural way to proceed would be to appeal to the epistemic value of appropriately structured discussion on a common topic. If (in a familiar formula) free and vigorous debate under equal and favorable conditions would tend to lead toward the correct answer, then this is one strong reason for implementing such a discursive procedure. Moreover, the origin of a political decision in a procedure with this epistemic value might be a significant source of its moral legitimacy—the moral permissibility of its enforcement.[18] I have discussed a view with this structure elsewhere, so here I will merely note an intuitively helpful analogy. In jury trials the outcome is normally thought to be permissibly enforced, even when it is mistaken (so long as there weren't procedural improprieties). Part of the moral basis for this is the presumed epistemic value of the jury trial, its tendency (certainly fallible) to lead to substantively correct decisions. If it weren't for that feature of jury trials there would surely be no moral basis for enforcing the decisions. So we are familiar with this way of thinking: the decisions are legitimate partly on the ground that they were produced by a procedure with a significant tendency to get the right answer. We might call this structure "epistemic proceduralism."[19] We might, then, dub this alternative version of political liberalism "epistemic political liberalism."[20]

Now, of course, there might be a variety of procedures with at least as much epistemic value as a democratic regime with free and vigorous expression. Perhaps there are experts, and they could rule at least as justly. But in a Rawlsian framework, where justifications must be in terms all reasonable views can accept, it is far from certain that there would be anyone whose status as an expert in the factual and moral domain of political decision could pass muster.

It is important to emphasize that the underlying theory of political justification would remain deeply Rawlsian. The normal practices of public political justification would see participants citing myriad doctrines about which there is much reasonable dispute. So, by the liberal principle of legitimacy, the arguments they would be giving could not serve as the justification they must, in due course, be prepared to give if pressed. That "due course" justification would step back and speak, in a way (so we are supposing) that would be acceptable to all reasonable points of view, of the epistemic value of a public deliberative practice in which participants press their comprehensive views about true justice.

There is much more to be said. It is enough for now to point out that there is this perhaps surprising possibility: a version of political liberalism, brooking no compromise on the fundamental principle of justification, and yet within which there is no political conception of justice at all, but rather in which justice is justice, and truth is truth.

Chapter 17

Truth at the Door of Public Reason: Response to Cohen and Estlund

Josiah Ober

> Until March, anyone could carry firearms openly into the [Virginia General Assembly]
> legislators' office building and the Capitol nearby. Then a joint committee of delegates
> and senators passed a rule requiring residents to hold a . . . permit to bring in a
> firearm. . . . People without permits will be able to check their guns at the door.
> —*Washington Post*, January 18, 2005

TRUTH AND DEMOCRATIC politics are very big topics; the papers by Cohen and Estlund are concerned with a set of analytic questions at their intersection. Before we enter the domain of public reason—a space posited by Rawlsian liberalism in which reasonable justifications are offered in favor of binding rules—must we first check our conceptions of truth (like guns without permits) at the door? Or might permits be issued allowing at least some sorts of truth-claims to be brought inside?

The fact that this clearly defined philosophical problem is situated in a larger field is signaled by the first epigraph of Cohen's paper. Harold Pinter situated his hair-raising speech accepting the 2005 Nobel Prize for Literature squarely in the terrain of truth and democratic politics. But he was concerned, not with liberal analytic philosophy as such, but with a policy of deception and its costs—with the deaths and suffering caused by democratically elected American and British leaders who, as he argued, purposefully chose to misdescribe reality. Pinter condemned systematic patterns of deception as well as particular lies: inter alia, false justifications offered by the Bush administration for the 2003 invasion of Iraq and earlier U.S. government lying in support of the murderous Contras in Nicaragua. He further condemned passive democratic citizens who tacitly accept these sorts of lies. Leaders lie to keep power, and citizens collude in those lies. This is a persistent problem for democracy. It motivated much critical writing in classical Athens.[1]

The extensive field of inquiry in which these papers are situated also accommodates practical questions about "epistemic democracy." Under what conditions might a democratic community better manage dispersed knowledge—both facts known uniquely by diverse persons and groups, and knowledge potentially held in common by all—and thereby grow more capable of fulfilling important public purposes?[2]

Cohen and Estlund each argue that the domain of public reason cannot, as Rawls supposed it could, do without a conception of truth. This important philosophical issue seems in some ways remote from the horrors perpetrated by lying politicians or the hopes fostered by more democratic management of useful knowledge. Agreement among Rawlsian liberals about the role of truth in Rawls's argument for political liberalism might seem unlikely to have much direct effect on the nightmarish nexus of power and lies that Pinter (et al.) regards as the great problem of "democratic politics and truth." Yet the question at issue is important even for those who do not regard political philosophy as intrinsically valuable. Rawlsian liberals have offered influential accounts of justice, and those accounts may affect the administration of justice. The distinction between "true" and "the whole truth" is relevant to the wider enterprise of studying truth and democratic politics; it is especially relevant to these papers about truth and justice in the domain of public reason.

The history of the question of truth in Rawls's theory of justice is neatly laid out by Estlund. In *A Theory of Justice*, Rawls made a powerful argument that justice-as-fairness is the truth about justice. That argument convinced many readers and thereby transformed Anglophone political philosophy. But in his later *Political Liberalism* and other works, Rawls revised his position. He now argued that instead of concerning themselves with the true conception of justice, liberals should focus on a political conception of justice. The new theory took account of a fact about justice-as-fairness, a fact about the world, and a foundational liberal premise. The premise is that assent is a morally essential precondition for legitimate coercion (i.e., for formal rules binding those who live together in a community). The fact about the world is that reasonable people disagree about comprehensive conceptions of justice (as well as about salvation and so on), and they will not assent to any justification for coercion that is based on a comprehensive conception that contradicts their own. The fact about justice-as-fairness is that, as long as it was held to be the truth about justice, it is a comprehensive conception of justice. If we (liberals, Muslims, Christians, et al.) insist on employing our comprehensive conceptions as the basis of deliberations about rules, we preclude ever achieving the assent of all reasonable persons. So there will be no legitimate grounds for coercion, and thus we seem to face a bad choice: anarchy or illegitimate coercion. Rawls's well-known solution was to seek an overlapping consensus, without reference to comprehensive conceptions, to which citizens could assent.

Rawls allowed that people will continue to hold their comprehensive conceptions privately, as a matter of personal conviction, but before we enter the domain of public reason (deliberations about rules), we (liberals, like all others) must check our comprehensive conceptions at the door. Now, I think it is a fair guess (I have no data, so it's only a guess) that a typical Rawlsian became a Rawlsian because she was convinced by the argument of *A Theory of Justice*, and so believes that she knows the truth (or in any event an important part of the truth) about justice. But if she also accepts the argument of *Political Liberalism*, she is forbidden to offer justifications based on the truth of justice-as-fairness within the domain of public reason. She must surely regard that as a high price, especially if she is an academic political philosopher whose writing and teaching about justice fall within the domain of public reason. But the Rawlsian believer in the truth of justice-as-fairness recognizes that she is not specially disadvantaged; all other holders of comprehensive conceptions face the same constraint in the public domain.

So far so good. But checking our comprehensive conceptions at the door, Rawls claimed, entails leaving *the conception of truth itself* outside the domain of public reason. As Cohen points out, Rawls was concerned that the *singularity* of truth made it divisive and perhaps intolerant; that truth implies *sufficiency*, which encourages sectarianism; and that truth introduces an inappropriate concern with *depth*. In short, Rawls worried that the conception of truth, once it was in the door, would lead to justifications of coercion being grounded in irreconcilable truth-claims, precluding reasonable agreement. With truth left at the door, the standard of reasonableness itself would do the necessary work of determining which justifications would be qualified

(Estlund's term) and which would not. Rawls supposed that the reasonableness standard could yield a good (if imperfect, from the standard of true justice) outcome: People privately holding diverse and mutually exclusive comprehensive conceptions might find common ground by offering one another reasonable justifications, allowing for an overlapping consensus that would be more than merely a modus vivendi between hostile camps; it would allow us to live according to rules that are, we agree, in the neighborhood of what each of us privately regards as truly just.

The problem these two essays address is the inherent difficulty of doing without truth. Cohen argues that when truth is left outside the door, it becomes hard to understand how belief, assertion, judgment, reason, and objectivity—all of which are allowed, indeed *required* by public reason—will be able to operate inside the public domain. Estlund agrees with Cohen's fundamental point here, as do I.

Estlund argues, however, that we might do an end run around the problem by introducing "ersatz truth" on the model of the law court practice of stipulation, whereby one party offers to "treat as factual" a circumstance ("the defendant was at home on the night in question") that may in fact not be true. Stipulated ersatz facts could, Estlund suggests, do the work of truth-claims in "truth-based activities" like belief, assertion, and so on. The problem with this position is that the domain of public reason is relevantly unlike a legal trial. A trial is "two-party adversarial"; arguments are strategies for winning a zero-sum game. The domain of public reason is "n-party deliberative"; arguments are sincerely advanced as justifications for establishing something that we all regard as profoundly important.

Stipulation gives all parties a veto: if, when I say "Let's stipulate that x is F," any other party says "Let's not," we get nowhere. In court I stipulate that x is F because, although it might appear that x being F hurts my case, I believe it does not. My opponent does not veto my stipulation (by saying "Do not assume x is F!") because he cannot see how vetoing will help him win. The stipulation does not (each of us believes) give our opponent a strategic advantage, and it helps us get on with things, in this case a legal decision we each hope to win.

In an n-party deliberation, in which multiple justifications are being sincerely advanced, it is implausible to suppose that all parties will abstain from vetoing my stipulated ersatz fact unless all parties believe it to be true. The key difference with the trial is that in the domain of public reason there are many parties involved, and we are not acting strategically. It is easy to see why stipulation is a handy way to get on with things in a legal trial or, mutatis mutandis, in an academic seminar where the stakes are low and we all agree about most substantive matters. In an n-party deliberation in the domain of public reason, with multiple veto points, where the stakes are high and we disagree on matters of substance, it is hard to see how "Let us stipulate that x is F" will help us get on with things if we do not agree that x *is* F. So Cohen's valid concern is not addressed by Estlund's end run of stipulation. We need "truth" of some sort in the domain of reason, for Cohen's reasons, and "ersatz truth" cannot take its place.[3]

There is a second problem with Rawls's call for checking truth at the door. Rawls's "reasonableness" criterion for justification ultimately depends on a claim about moral truth. As Estlund points out in his argument against Charles Larmore, "reasonable" ought to mean something more than coherent, consistent, and sincere; if it does not, the coherent, consistent, and sincere Nazi (slave owner, torturer, et al.) must be judged reasonable, and so we lose our hope of an overlapping consensus beyond modus vivendi. We exclude the Nazi as unreasonable because he refuses to accept the ground rule by which the domain of public reason was constituted: no coercion without assent. But setting that as a ground rule implies a prior agreement that "no coercion without assent" is morally true. So we are back to the truth-claim problem that political liberalism was meant to solve, albeit with a claim that is much thinner than the truth of justice-as-fairness. Rawls's political conception cannot be political all the way down while remaining liberal; it is grounded in a liberal conception of legitimacy. Nonliberals whose conception of legitimacy is not based on assent, but whose arguments are excluded by the assent ground rule, will not be assuaged because we say that the exclusion was due to *their* unreasonableness, not *our* attachment to a comprehensive conception. "True" ultimately grounds "reasonable" (and "qualified," etc.). Once we admit that, we can turn to the question of designing permits that will allow some conception of truth into the domain of public reason. Estlund argues that the way forward is to abandon the political conception of justice and work on constructing what we will explicitly acknowledge as a truth-based liberal procedural foundation.

It appears, then, that whether we follow Cohen's or Estlund's line of thinking, Rawls was wrong: public reason cannot do without a conception of truth. Having agreed on different grounds that Rawls was wrong to require that all truth-claims be checked at the door of the domain of public reason, these essays offer two options. The options are quite different, although each is explicitly Rawlsian in inspiration and aspiration. Cohen suggests that we can build out from the political conception of justice (the idea that lies at the heart of Rawls's revised political liberalism) by developing a political conception of the truth. Estlund goes the other way, recommending that we abandon the political conception of justice and get on with the business of building a morally true theory of justice by providing justice with truth-based procedural ground rules.

Cohen proposes to thin down the conception of truth in such a way that it can do all the necessary work in regard to the truth-based activities of belief, assertion, and so on, but that does not smuggle into the domain of public reason a comprehensive conception of justice (or of anything else). In effect, truth permits will be issued to those who can show that the truths they propose to bring through the door are nonmetaphysical—neither metaphysical nor antimetaphysical. Cohen answers Rawls's concerns about singularity, sufficiency, and depth by showing first that Rawls's term "reasonable" has "divisive singularity" features that are relevantly similar to truth. Next he shows that truth can be relevant without being sufficient, and finally he shows that assertions may be asserted to be relevantly true without a commitment to depth. Cohen's key argument seems to me right: It is possible, and so ought to be permitted within public reason's domain, to speak of "x as true," while leaving the heavy artillery of "the whole truth" outside the door.

Estlund does not accept this line of argument because he regards the sort of thin conception of truth that Cohen argues for to be a nonstarter. He argues for rejecting Rawls's political conception of justice on the following analogy: "An awkward implication [of a political conception of justice] is that political justice might not be true justice. If it's not true justice, it's not justice. If a painting isn't a true Van Gogh, it's not a Van Gogh." For Estlund, then, justice is true justice as a Van Gogh painting is a true Van Gogh painting.

By rephrasing Estlund's statement using Cohen's terms, the difficulty for Estlund's argument with this analogy becomes apparent: "If it's not *the whole truth about* justice, then it's not *in any sense* justice. If a painting isn't a true Van Gogh, *in that it is not an original work painted wholly by Van Gogh*, it's not *in any sense* a Van Gogh." That all-or-nothing way of thinking about a painting makes sense in some contexts. Suppose an expert is asked to judge a painting suspected of being a forgery and concludes, "It's a Van Gogh." In this case the distinction is between a painting that is what it purports to be and a deceptive fraud—the sort of lying Pinter was concerned with in his acceptance speech. But what do we say about a painting started by Van Gogh and later completed or touched up by someone else (say, a restorer)? Or a project-ed image of a painting by Van Gogh? In these cases, saying "It's a Van Gogh" would not be to speak the whole truth, but would be relevantly true in at least some contexts, for example, if a curator were seeking to distinguish between paintings with Van Gogh's own brush strokes and those without, or if an art history student were asked to distinguish between images of paintings by Van Gogh and Cézanne. The point is that there are many circumstances in which it is neither strange nor deceptive to say "x is true" without in any way imply-ing "x is the whole truth."

　　Cohen's nonmetaphysical "true but not the whole truth" approach offers what seems to me an attractive way of permitting truth back into public rea-son without giving up on the idea of the political conception of justice. The realm of justice, as it is addressed by analytic philosophy, is an important part of the larger territory of democracy and truth. In order to fill out the story we will, of course, need to go a lot further. As Pinter points out, we need citizens who care passionately about the difference between truth and lies. We need artists and humanistic interpreters of art who draw clear lines between the circumscribed role of truth in the realm of artistic creation and the essen-tial role of truth in the realm of politics. We need to design institutions that will resist the tendency of the powerful to lie and the tendency of citizens to accept those lies uncritically. We need citizens who know the difference be-tween "social facts" that are brought into being by felicitously performed acts of speech, and "brute facts" about the world that are unaffected by performa-tive speech.[4] We also need citizens who recognize how difficult it is to parse the complex conglomerates of social and brute facts that confront democratic decision makers. Finally, we need institutions and a political culture that will bring into the public realm the things lying outside comprehensive concep-tions that are known to be true by different people. If it is to address the problems of modernity, democracy must find the right permitting process for allowing truth into the domain of public reason, and it must also take account of the many and diverse things that the demos knows.

Chapter 18

Just Gimme Some Truth: A Pragmatist Proposal

Robert Westbrook

MUCH AS I admire these essays by the philosophers Joshua Cohen and David Estlund, I approach the task of commenting upon them with trepidation. Though perhaps less philosophically challenged than other historians, intellectual historians pride ourselves on bracketing questions of the truth of the ideas of those we study—let alone the truth of any particular conception of what it means to say an idea is true—in favor of putting both the truths and the falsehoods alike that human beings may have told in the past into a context that helps us to understand how they came, rightly or wrongly, to say such things. Most of us blithely leave to others any corrosive doubts about the epistemological underpinnings of the truth of the explanations and interpretations that we ourselves offer.

So rather than engage in unaccustomed amateur philosophizing in the brief space allotted me here, I would like to attempt something else that intellectual historians quite often do well, what one of our number, Daniel Rodgers, has labeled "corralling." By this he means the practice in which intellectual historians, acting as "shepherds," assemble a group of thinkers who may not in their own time have engaged one another at all and construct an engagement that they might well have had.[1]

The horses I would like to put in the corral with Cohen and Estlund are some contemporary neopragmatist philosophers led by Cheryl Misak and

Robert Talisse, whose thoughts on truth and politics seem to me to intersect nicely with theirs. One of the distinct advantages of corralling intellectuals who are still alive is that, in doing so, one might provoke an actual conversation of their own making.[2]

Like many American political theorists these days, both Cohen and Estlund argue within a framework established by John Rawls in *Political Liberalism* (1993), though each seeks to amend that framework in significant and distinctive ways.[3] They share a dissatisfaction with Rawls's attempt to divorce political liberalism from questions of truth and a determination to reunite the two, though in decidedly different fashions. Cohen proposes to package the public reason of Rawls's political liberalism with an underwhelming, non-metaphysical "political conception of truth" that permits truth-claims of a sort that do not threaten the divisive, politically destabilizing consequences that led Rawls to banish all truth-claims from public reasoning. Estlund is less fearful than Rawls and Cohen of a public square filled with contentious ("real" and not merely "political") truth-claims grounded in competing and incompatible "comprehensive doctrines," as long as these truth-claims take a backseat for justificatory political purposes to outcomes generated by the procedures of "a truth-oriented political process" regarded by all reasonable citizens as epistemically powerful (if not infallible). Both of these arguments seem to me to echo those made by the neopragmatists Misak and Talisse.[4]

As Cohen says, Rawls banished all conceptions of truth from the public reasoning of political liberalism on the grounds that they introduced an unduly divisive concept in a polity marked by "doctrinal pluralism." Cohen thinks Rawls went too far: "Truth is so closely connected with intuitive notions of thinking, asserting, believing, judging, and reasoning that it is difficult to understand what leaving it behind amounts to." Public reason cannot do without some conception of truth, and not all conceptions of truth would have to have the unhappy consequences Rawls feared. Hence Cohen aims to "present a view of truth that suffices for public reasoning and could reasonably be endorsed by the adherents of conflicting doctrines, which may themselves employ richer conceptions of truth." He calls his putatively inoffensive, "less committal" conception a "political conception" because it is tailored to "the purposes of political reflection and argument in a pluralistic democracy, characterized by doctrinal disagreements."

A similar "less committal" conception of truth is precisely what some neopragmatists have on offer. (Misak terms it a "low-profile" conception.) They share Cohen's criticism of Rawls's flight from truth. They share his rejection not only of Rawls's "no concept" of truth in public reason, but also of the "no truth bearers," "no substantive judgments of truth," and "no big deal about truth" alternatives. They share Cohen's argument that disquotationalism is *too* minimalist a conception of truth. The "best kind of pragmatism," Misak says, will argue that "there is a conception of truth to be had which captures what is important about truth, is non-metaphysical, and goes beyond the triviality expressed by the disquotational schema."[5]

Misak and Talisse are neo-Peircean neopragmatists. For them, as for Peirce, a true belief is one that meets the test of (communitarian) inquiry, which is the human way of subjecting belief to the challenge of reasons, argument, and evidence. A belief that fully meets this challenge is true: "A true belief is such that, no matter how much further we were to investigate and debate, that belief would not be overturned by recalcitrant experience and argument."[6] But since no inquiry can be exhaustive, we can never know for certain that any of our beliefs are true, however indubitable they may seem at present. Truth is thus a "regulative ideal," an ideal that is unrealizable and yet serves a valuable function, in this case keeping the road of inquiry open. Truth is the aim of inquiry, but the best that can be secured at any moment in its course is well-justified belief, which is not necessarily true. It is *rational* nonetheless to adopt well-justified beliefs, even if these beliefs later prove to be false.

As far as I can see, the principal objection that Cohen might raise to identifying his "political conception of truth" with that of the neopragmatists is he sees theirs as a particular, controversial conception of truth that would not be accepted by those with other conceptions of truth and hence unavailable for public reason under conditions of doctrinal pluralism.[7] But neopragmatists do not claim dogmatically that theirs is the only possible conception of truth. (To do so would be to eschew the fallibilism that is at the heart of pragmatism.) They claim only and more modestly that truth is, *at least*, what they claim it to be. Talisse has anticipated objections such as Cohen's. The epistemic commitments of his neopragmatism, he says, "do not constitute a comprehensive epistemology in their own right, but rather state a set of principles that are consistent with any well-developed epistemology. That is, internalists, externalists, foundationalists, coherentists, and so on all agree that beliefs aim at truth, that when we believe, we take ourselves to be responding to reasons, argument, and evidence, and that reasons, argument, and evidence are *at the very least* reliable indicators of truth." Peircean commitments "attempt to capture the norms we countenance in virtue of the very fact that we are believers. Hence, if they succeed in capturing those norms, the Peircean commitments are not *optional*"—even those who would contest them must presuppose them since they are essential to contestation.[8]

Here Talisse is, in effect, offering a self-conscious version of the argument Estlund attributes to Cohen: "We use, as it were, a fragment of the concept of truth, the fragment that all reasonable views accept." Pragmatists do, of course, suspect that this fragment is all there is to truth, but they see no need to press the claim since it is not one that they can convincingly justify, and inquiry can proceed quite nicely without it. Misak and Talisse are *neo*-Peirceans because they strip pragmatism of notions of a progressive, empirical convergence to truth at the "end of inquiry" with which Peirce burdened his conception of truth and which, as Cohen says, does make a pragmatist conception of truth unduly controversial for purposes of a pluralist politics. As Misak says, "The pragmatist should not connect truth to inquiry with an indicative conditional, but rather with a subjunctive conditional. It is not that a true belief is one which *will* fit the evidence and which *will* measure up to the standards of inquiry as we now know them. Rather a true belief is one which *would* fit with the evidence and which *would* measure up to the standards of inquiry *were* inquiry to be pursued so far that no recalcitrant experience and no revisions in the standards of inquiry would be called for." Insisting on the subjunctive allows pragmatists to avoid "the doomed task of saying just what is meant by the hypothetical end of inquiry, cognitively ideal conditions, or perfect evidence, whatever these might be. Any attempt at articulating such notions will have to face the objection that it is a mere glorification of what we presently take to be good."[9] But the subjunctive formulation also absolves pragmatists of the charge that they confuse truth and current warranted belief.

If Cohen were to marry his political liberalism to this neopragmatist conception of truth, he would not have to call his conception "political truth," a phrase redolent with unsavory connotations and a bloody history from which I would think he would want to distance himself. Misak and Talisse have made available to him a conception of truth that he could simply call "truth" since it manifests the consensual truths about truth that, as a political liberal, he is looking for.

"Epistemic liberal democracy" is a good term for the political consequences that Misak and Talisse derive from their neopragmatism. Hence I think that they would find much to agree upon with Estlund, as well as Cohen. The four basic Peircean epistemological commitments are to the contentions that to hold a belief is to hold it to be true; that to hold a belief to be true is to hold that it would forever meet the challenges of reason, argument, and evidence; that to hold that a belief would meet such challenges is to commit oneself to justifying that belief; and that to acknowledge that the project of justifying a belief is a social project that entails participating in a community of inquiry. As Talisse says, an argument for liberal democracy "follows intuitively from these principles." That is, neopragmatist inquiry is the sort of "truth-oriented political process" that liberal democracy calls for:

> If being a believer commits one to the project of justification, and if the project of justification commits one to the social enterprise of examining, exchanging, testing, and challenging reasons, then one can satisfy one's commitments *qua* believer only within a political context in which it is possible to be an inquirer. Inquiry requires that characteristically democratic norms obtain; in order to inquire, there must be norms of equality, free speech, a freedom of information, open debate, protected dissent, access to decision-making institutions, and so on. Moreover, since the project of justification involves testing one's beliefs against the broadest possible pool of reasons, experiences, and considerations, inquiry requires norms of the sort often associated with "radical democracy" views, such as participation, inclusion, and recognition.[10]

One significant advantage that neopragmatism's proceduralism has over those derived from Rawls is that it begins with such a minimalist set of requirements for participation in public reasoning—shared agreement on what it means simply to hold a belief—that it need not resort to the sort of preemptive dismissal (or repression) of "unreasonable" or "unqualified" participants about which so many critics of Rawlsian political liberalism have complained.[11] Unlike Rawls and so many Rawlsians, neopragmatists do not have to protect liberal politics by smuggling liberal convictions into their supposedly unprejudiced criteria of political "reasonableness." They can even allow the Nazis who haunt these debates to enter into public life, confident that they will immediately find themselves ensnared in a host of performative contradictions.[12]

Rawlsians, Rawls himself said, aim to be "realistically utopian."[13] My suggestion here is that by embedding a neopragmatist conception of truth in public reason, Rawlsians would lend more realism to their utopia, make it more plausible. Indeed, as I have argued elsewhere, one might argue that pragmatism or something very much like it is well on its way to becoming the default mode of argument in pluralist, liberal democracies such as that of the United States.[14]

Of course, whatever conception of truth we embed in our politics, it can provide no guarantee that political discourse will be without lies, even the sort of American whoppers that Harold Pinter lists in his Nobel lecture. All that neopragmatism and other forms of "epistemic liberal democracy" promise is a greater likelihood than would obtain in other truth regimes that such lies will eventually wither under the scrutiny of the sort of free inquiry in which Pinter engages.

Brief though these remarks are, I hope I have said enough to help foster a conversation between neopragmatist philosophers and neo-Rawlsian political theorists. No doubt, they will have much to argue about, though I think they have enough common ground to generate a fruitful engagement for all concerned. If so, I will happily leave it in their expert hands, though someday I might perhaps venture to try to explain why they were having it when they were.

Notes

Introduction

1. This view is sometimes expressed in terms of the importance of liberty. But many of the policies against which this argument is pressed—for example, so-called targeted tax breaks and subsidies for institutions such as public broadcasting and for the arts—involve not restrictions on liberty in the classic sense, but supplements to the market. And while one kind of objection to these policies concerns the particular choices they represent (and that are made in the course of implementing them), there is a another, and deeper objection that denies that there are, in principle, human goods worthy of being publicly promoted independent of market outcomes. As one conservative commentator has put this, writing in opposition to the very notion of "merit goods" (goods whose importance is independent of how they are valued in the market), such a concept "is essentially noneconomic and paternalistic," for it "implies that individual consumers would spend their money mistakenly if left to their own devices." David Sawers, *Should Taxpayers Support the Arts?* (London: Institute of Economic Affairs, 1993), 25. This argument was offered in the context of discussing funding for the arts, but it is a more general claim that appears in opposition to many other policies.

2. Richard Rorty, *Take Care of Freedom and Truth Will Take Care of Itself*, ed. Eduardo Mendieta (Stanford: Stanford University Press, 2006), 57–58.

3. Friedrich Nietzsche, "How the 'True World' Finally Became a Fable," *Twilight of the Idols*, in *The Anti-Christ, Ecce Homo, Twilight of the Idols and Other Writings,* ed. Aaron Ridley and Judith Norman (Cambridge: Cambridge University Press, 2005), 171.

4. Bernard Williams, *Truth and Truthfulness* (Princeton: Princeton University 2002), 2. The explicit critique of truth in the humanities may be less pronounced now that it was several years ago. But Williams is right that

> this does not mean that the real problems have gone away. Indeed, the real problems have been there, as Nietzsche understood, before the label of

"post-modernism" made them a matter of public debate, and they remain there now. Moreover, there is a danger that the decline of the more dramatic confrontations may do no more than register an inert cynicism, the kind of calm that in personal relations can follow a series of hysterical rows. If the passion for truthfulness is merely controlled and stilled without being satisfied, it will kill the activities it is supposed to support. This may be one of the reasons why, at the present time, the study of the humanities runs a risk of sliding from professional seriousness, through professionalization, to a finally disenchanted careerism. (3)

5. As he put it in *Twilight of the Idols*, "The true world—we have abolished. What world has remained? The apparent one perhaps? But no! With the true world we have also abolished the apparent one." Nietzsche, *Twilight of the Idols*, x.

6. Nietzsche, *The Anti-Christ*, in *The Anti-Christ, Ecce Homo, Twilight of the Idols and Other Writings*, §8.

7. Friedrich Nietzsche, *Writings from the Late Notebooks*, ed. Rüdiger Bittner (Cambridge: Cambridge University Press, 2003), 43, 21, emphasis in original.

8. This is not denied by Nietzsche's perspectivalism. Nietzsche did often speak of the truth in *personal* terms—"my truth," as he sometimes put it—and the polemical character of that expression is of course meant to contrast with the standard view of truth as having an impersonal character, to suggest that ideas about the world are incapable of being tested except from a perspective. But Nietzsche, famously dismissive of common opinion and of the press, hardly intended by this anything like an equality of perspective. Relatedly, while Nietzsche was indeed concerned to reclaim the world of "appearance" against a certain metaphysical tradition that, as he read it, began with Platonic forms and continued through the Kantian "thing in itself," this was not for him inconsistent with the idea that many of our most basic conceptions of ourselves and the world—notions of cause and effect, to take just one example—could be mistaken. While there is no good reason to think that, for Nietzsche or for us, the evaluation of opinions should be understood wholly as a matter of discerning truth, there is equally no reason to think that the idea of truth has no role to play.

9. Cited in Simon Blackburn, *Truth: A Guide* (Oxford: Oxford University Press, 2005), 5. Clifford's essay was the occasion for William James's celebrated response, "The Will to Believe." Blackburn rightly observes that James's defense of our right, as James puts it, to "decide an option between propositions, whenever it is a genuine option that cannot be decided on intellectual grounds" assumes that we can see on the face of things which issues are and are not capable of being decided on intellectual grounds, that the odds are even of the correct answer to a given such question being the one we decide upon, and that the social costs of our decision are negligible—all, as Blackburn observes, quite contestable, indeed improbable claims (7–12).

10. Blackburn, *Truth*, 10.

From Nobel Lecture

© The Nobel Foundation 2005. Reproduced by permission. We are grateful to Joshua Cohen, whose reference to this lecture at the beginning of his essay led to our including this excerpt.—Eds.

1. Concerning Practices of Truth

    1. Ron Suskind "Without a Doubt," *New York Times Magazine*, October 17, 2004:

In the summer of 2002, after I had written an article in Esquire that the White House didn't like about Bush's former communications director, Karen Hughes, I had a meeting with a senior adviser to Bush. He expressed the White House's displeasure, and then he told me something that at the time I didn't fully comprehend—but which I now believe gets to the very heart of the Bush presidency.

    The aide said that guys like me were "in what we call the reality-based community," which he defined as people who "believe that solutions emerge from your judicious study of discernible reality." I nodded and murmured something about enlightenment principles and empiricism. He cut me off. "That's not the way the world really works anymore," he continued. "We're an empire now, and when we act, we create our own reality. And while you're studying that reality—judiciously, as you will—we'll act again, creating other new realities, which you can study too, and that's how things will sort out. We're history's actors . . . and you, all of you, will be left to just study what we do."

    2. Harry Frankfurt, *Bullshit* (Princeton: Princeton University Press, 2005).

    3. Plato, *Meno*, 99B.

    4. Friedrich Nietzsche, *Beyond Good and Evil*, trans. Walter Kaufmann (Random House, 1966), §1.

    5. Ibid., §§10, 6. "Gradually it has become clear to me what every great philosophy so far has been; namely, the personal confession of its author and a kind of involuntary and unconscious memoir" (§6).

    6. Ibid., §6. I have altered Kaufmann's translation of *Erkenntniss* and *Verkenntniss* as, respectively, "understanding" and "misunderstanding."

    7. Romans, 7:11 (King James version).

    8. John Milton, *Paradise Lost* (1667), 3rd ed., ed. Gordon Teskey (New York: Norton, 2005), IV: 808–9; V: 70, 454–55.

    9. Romans 2:20.

    10. Edmund Burke, *Reflections on the Revolution in France*, in *The Works of the Right Honorable Edmund Burke,* revised ed., 12 vols. (Boston: Little, Brown, 1865–67), 3:357, 356, 356–59, 274–76, 357–59.

11. For Nietzsche, however, this did not imply that the question of truth should be abandoned, but rather that it needed to be raised anew. On this, see the introduction to this volume.

12. Hannah Arendt, "Philosophy and Politics," *Social Research* (Fall 2004): 433–34.

13. Ibid., 433.

14. In calling on Arendt as I have, I do not suggest that what I say here about the implications of the general idea that opinions are perspectives on a world is the same as what she says—her own concern in "Philosophy and Politics" is different—or even that she would agree with it, and there are grounds, including importantly her essay "Truth and Politics," in *Between Past and Future* (New York: Penguin, 1977), (which I shall discuss shortly) for thinking that she might not. I shall discuss that essay later.

15. Burke, *Reflections*, 222.

16. Aristotle, *Nicomachean Ethics*, VII: 1150b19.

17. Burke, *Reflections*, 332–3. Edmund Burke, "Speech to the Electors of Bristol," November 3, 1774, in *Works*, 2:95; Edmund Burke, "Letter to M. Dupont," in *Correspondence of the Right Honourable Edmund Burke*, ed. Charles William and Richard Bourke, 4 vols. (London: Gilbert & Rivington, 1844), 3:107. Thus, for example, in defending his own past parliamentary measures, he insisted that "I conceived nothing arbitrarily, nor proposed anything to be done by the will and pleasure of others or my own,—but by reason, and by reason only. I have ever abhorred since the first dawn of my understanding to this its obscure twilight, all the operations of opinion, fancy, inclination, and will, in the affairs of government, where only a sovereign reason, paramount to all forms of legislation and administration, should dictate" (Edmund Burke, "A Letter to a Noble Lord," in *Works*, 5:189). Burke did not always use these terms in this way; he sometimes used "opinion" to refer to reasoned opinion, referred to God's law as that in which "will and reason are the same," (*Reflections*, 356), spoke of the importance of passion and sentiment to social cohesion, "which the heart owns and the understanding ratifies" (*Reflections*, 333), and so on.

18. Burke, "Bristol," 95–96.

19. Ibid., 96.

20. Edmund Burke, "Letter to Sir Hercules Langrishe," in *Works*, 4:258.

21. Burke, "Bristol," 96.

22. Ibid., 97.

23. Hannah Pitkin, *The Concept of Representation* (Berkeley: University of California Press, 1967), 186; Burke, *Reflections*, 313; Edmund Burke, "Appeal from the New to the Old Whigs," in *Works*, 4:176.

24. Burke, *Reflections*, 313.

25. Edmund Burke, "Speech on Conciliation with the Colonies," in *Works*, 2:155; Edmund Burke, "Letters to the Sheriffs of Bristol on the Affairs of America," April 3, 1777, in *Works*, 2:216.

26. Michael Oakeshott, "Political Discourse," in *Rationalism in Politics* (Indianapolis: Liberty Press, 1991), 82.

27. Arendt, "Truth and Politics," 262. "Philosophy and Politics," in which Arendt discusses the Socratic project, was written, it seems (it was published posthumously), well after she wrote "Truth and Politics," the essay on which I focus here. But there is little reason to doubt that Arendt's conception of the Socratic project as discerning the truth in opinion was a view that she had long held, including at the time she wrote the earlier essay. But that is in any case just a question of the consistency of Arendt's thought; my concern here with the ideas of "Truth and Politics" is not with that question, but with a certain line of thought of which I take the ideas of that essay to be representative.

28. Arendt, "Truth and Politics," 234, 263–64.

29. Ibid., 231, 235, 255, 259.

30. Friedrich Hayek, *Law, Legislation, and Liberty,* 3 vols. (Chicago: University of Chicago Press, 1973), 1:2.

31. *Brown v. Board of Education* 347 U.S. 483 (1954).

32. Arendt, "Truth and Politics," 262.

33. *Meno,* 97–98.

34. Arendt, "Truth and Politics," 241. These propositions seem closer to what Arendt refers to as interpretation of facts, such as that which takes place within the "historical sciences and humanities," and which Arendt also relegates to outside of the political realm. She writes:

> But do facts, independent of opinion and interpretation, exist at all? Have not generations of historians and philosophers of history demonstrated the impossibility of ascertaining facts without interpretation, since they must be picked out of a chaos of sheer happenings (and the principles of choice are surely not factual data) and then be fitted into a story that can be told in a certain perspective, which has nothing to do with the original occurrence? No doubt these and a great many more perplexities inherent in the historical sciences are real, but they are no argument against the existence of factual matter, nor can they serve as a justification for blurring the dividing lines between fact, opinion, and interpretation. . . . Even if we admit that every generation has the right to write its own history, we admit not more than it has the right to rearrange the facts in accordance with its own perspective; we don't admit the right to touch the factual matter itself [such as that in August 1914, Germany invaded Belgium and not the other way around]. . . . We are concerned here with brutally elementary data of this kind, whose indestructibility has been taken for granted even by the most extreme and most sophisticated believers in historicism. (238–39)

If truth is identified with facts, and facts with brutally elementary data, the interpretation of facts cannot itself be an enterprise concerning matters of truth. But if it is not, what sort of question is, for example, the question of *why* Germany invaded Belgium in August

1914? On the other hand, if interpretation of facts can itself be about truth, the proper distinction is not between truth and opinion, but only (brutally elementary) facts and opinion; and the question of the political role for nonpartisan institutions that are concerned with questions of truth beyond elementary facts cannot be so easily disposed of.

35. Ibid., 257.

36. Burke, "Appeal," 175.

Burke himself did not say much about the role of unofficial institutions such as the press in realizing this aim of politics. Although Carlyle once claimed that "Burke said that there were Three Estates in Parliament; but, in the Reporters' Gallery yonder, there sat a *Fourth Estate* more important far than they all" ("The Hero as Man of Letters," lecture 5, in *On Heroes and Hero Worship and the Heroic in History* [London: Chapman and Hall, 1841], 194), we have, according to the *Oxford English Dictionary*, no "confirmation of Carlyle's statement" (entry for "Estate," 7b). Whether or not Burke actually ever said such a thing, it is not improbable, in light of Burke's view of the purpose of political institutions, that he would have regarded a responsible press as performing an important political function.

37. This was not a point lost on Burke himself. Although he opposed extension of the franchise in England, he was well aware of the tendency of governing bodies to act in the particular interests of those best represented and was among their harshest critics when in his view they did so.

38. "Evolutionary theory," as I shall use that term here, refers to the theory that all forms of life beyond the most basic are the product of evolution and of its basic mechanisms as those have been understood by the evolutionary sciences: natural selection, variation (including "random" mutation), and reproduction. (I put "random" in scare quotes because although the idea of random mutation is taken by many intelligent design advocates and by some evolutionary theorists as implying no ultimate purpose, strictly speaking it need only refer to a material process and not imply the absence of a more purposive final cause.)

There are many differences among critics of the opponents of evolutionary theory, including in the object of their criticism, and this is so even among members of that latest wave of opposition on which I shall focus here, the intelligent design movement. For example, some advocates of intelligent design, such as Michael Behe, accept much of the scientific consensus on the fact of evolution above the level of individual cells, including the idea of common ancestry, whereas others, such as Phillip Johnson, deny a great deal more of it. Opponents of evolutionary theory also differ with respect to the care with which they distinguish Darwin's hypotheses about the mechanism of evolution from contemporary evolutionary theories. Because of all of this, neither "evolution" nor Darwinism is satisfactory as an umbrella term, and "evolutionary theory" is only marginally better. "Evolutionism" would perhaps be the best candidate, for it easily suggests the thesis that unites virtually all evolutionary scientists and separates them from the opponents: that all complex life forms are the product of evolutionary processes. However, "evolutionism" is now a loaded term, having been adopted by Johnson to describe what he claims, but which many evolutionary scientists deny, is the underlying "philosophi-cal materialism" of evolutionary science. I discuss the issue of philosophical materialism later in this essay.

39. For a concise statement of this position, see Francis Beckwith, "Government Sponsored Theology," *American Spectator*, April 7, 2004. The references in this para-graph to Supreme Court decisions are from Beckwith, citing *Lynch v. Donnelly*, and *Epperson v. Arkansas*.

40. Amicus Brief of Christian Legal Society and National Association of Evangeli-cals in *Edwards v. Aguillard*, 1986 WL [Westlaw] 727650, p. 10.

41. The intelligent design movement, which arose after the courts held that the teaching of "creation science" is unconstitutional because it is an inherently religious doctrine, distinguished itself from creationism in not (ostensibly) offering an explana-tion for the specific character of the intelligence which it claims designed complex life forms. According to the Discovery Institute, the leading center of the intelligent design movement, intelligent design does not share with creationism a grounding in "a reli-gious text" (www.intelligentdesign.org/whatisid.php, accessed December 9, 2009). The movement for teaching intelligent design in the public schools has largely been pressed, however, by religious groups, and a leaked planning document for the Discovery Insti-tute itself ("The Wedge") describes its aim as undermining the acceptance of evolution-ary theory in order to restore acceptance of the "proposition that human beings are created in the image of God." Available at www.antievolution.org/features/wedge.pdf, accessed December 9, 2009.

42. Brief for Appellants, in *Edwards v. Aguillard*, 1986 WL [Westlaw] 727653, p. 22. The phrase now covered by ellipses was "evolution is not established fact and." I have removed this in order to cover the views of intelligent design advocates who accept some aspects of evolution.

43. Richard Rorty, *Take Care of Freedom and Truth Will Take Care of Itself*, ed. Edu-ardo Mendieta (Stanford: Stanford University Press, 2006), 57–58.

44. On that debate, see, for example, Richard Rorty, *Philosophy and the Mirror of Nature* (Princeton: Princeton University Press, 1980), particularly Chapter 7; Bernard Williams, *Ethics and the Limits of Philosophy* (Cambridge, Mass.: Harvard University Press, 1985), Chapter 8; Hillary Putnam, *Renewing Philosophy* (Cambridge, Mass.: Har-vard University Press, 1992), Chapter 5; Bernard Williams, "Philosophy as a Humanistic Discipline," *Threepenny Review*, Spring 2001; Hillary Putnam, "Reply to Bernard Wil-liams' 'Philosophy as a Humanistic Discipline,'" *Philosophy* 76, no. 4 (2001).

45. Richard Rorty, "Universalism and Truth," in *Rorty and His Critics*, ed. Robert Brandom (Malden, Mass.: Blackwell, 2000), 2.

46. For example, ibid.

47. They will also involve, for example, such questions as how to weigh the (vari-ous kinds of) costs of getting more accurate information and the risks of being wrong in each direction.

48. The ambiguity concerning what kind of theory intelligent design is has been

both reflected and exploited by some political officials. For example, when Senate Majority Leader Bill Frist expressed his support for teaching intelligent design alongside evolution by arguing that "a pluralist society should have access to a broad range of fact, of science, including faith. . . . In a pluralist society that is the fairest way to go about education and training people for the future," he was running together two very different kinds of truth-practices, for if anything characterizes "science," as it is normally understood, it is its distinction from the kind of religious faith to which Frist was referring. Frist's argument would have been very different had he said that in a pluralist society, the perspective of science ought not to be taught as the only perspective on truth, or not to be treated as displacing religious faith. And he might have offered forthrightly the opposite claim that in general faith ought to be a standard for assessing truth claims in the natural sciences. But he did not do either, and the reason that he did not was evidently that he was at the time contemplating a run for the Republican presidential nomination and was intent on appealing to a fundamentalist audience on a matter of central importance to it, without sacrificing his scientific credibility. Then-President Bush seemed to be pursuing a similar strategy of ambiguity when he responded to the question of whether intelligent design should be taught in the public schools by arguing that "both sides ought to be properly taught . . . so people can understand what the debate is about . . . people ought to be exposed to different ideas" and then refusing to answer whether in saying this he meant to "accept the validity of intelligent design as an alternative to evolution" in the science curriculum. (The strategy was apparently successful. The next day, the President's science adviser insisted that the President had only meant that intelligent design should be discussed as part of the "social context" in science classes, while at the same time a number of fundamentalist religious leaders heralded the statement as defending the teaching of intelligent design as an alternative scientific account.) These rhetorical strategies, stemming from a desire of politicians to express allegiance with a position that they are unwilling to defend, not only reflect the ambiguity in the foundation of intelligent design, but are reflections of just that kind of politics of "will" that it is the point of the Burkean tradition to resist. It is part of the job of political institutions to interrogate these claims, and this requires focusing on second-order questions of truth. ("Bill Frist Backs 'Intelligent Design,'" Associated Press, August 19, 2005; Elisabeth Bumiller, "Bush Remarks Roil Debate over Teaching of Evolution," *New York Times*, August 3, 2005).

49. Phillip Johnson, "Darwinism and Theism," address delivered at "Darwinism: Scientific Inference or Philosophical Preference," sponsored by the Foundation for Thought and Ethics, Dallas, March 26–28, 1992, quoted in Eugenie C. Scott, "Darwin Prosecuted: Review of Johnson's *Darwin on Trial*," *Creation/Evolution Journal* 13, no. 2 (1996).

50. "The Wedge Document: 'So What?,'" www.discovery.org/scripts/viewDB/files-DB-download.php?id=349, accessed December 15, 2008. The introduction to the document reads:

The proposition that human beings are created in the image of God is one of the bedrock principles on which Western civilization was built. Its influence can be detected in most, if not all, of the West's greatest achievements, including representative democracy, human rights, free enterprise, and progress in the arts and sciences.

Yet a little over a century ago, this cardinal idea came under wholesale attack by intellectuals drawing on the discoveries of modern science. Debunking the traditional conceptions of both God and man, thinkers such as Charles Darwin, Karl Marx, and Sigmund Freud portrayed humans not as moral and spiritual beings, but as animals or machines who inhabited a universe ruled by purely impersonal forces and whose behavior and very thoughts were dictated by the unbending forces of biology, chemistry, and environment. This materialistic conception of reality eventually infected virtually every area of our culture, from politics and economics to literature and art.

The cultural consequences of this triumph of materialism were devastating. Materialists denied the existence of objective moral standards, claiming that environment dictates our behavior and beliefs. Such moral relativism was uncritically adopted by much of the social sciences, and it still undergirds much of modern economics, political science, psychology and sociology.

Materialists also undermined personal responsibility by asserting that human thoughts and behaviors are dictated by our biology and environment. The results can be seen in modern approaches to criminal justice, product liability, and welfare. In the materialist scheme of things, everyone is a victim and no one can be held accountable for his or her actions.

Finally, materialism spawned a virulent strain of utopianism. Thinking they could engineer the perfect society through the application of scientific knowledge, materialist reformers advocated coercive government programs that falsely promised to create heaven on earth.

This was followed by the specific statement of purpose quoted in the text.

51. Ibid., 2.

52. Ibid.

53. Some intelligent design advocates have suggested that despite the denials the evolutionary sciences are committed to a philosophical materialism. But since both sides publicly agree that philosophical materialism should not be taught as part of the science curriculum, this is merely a matter of policing.

54. For example, in *Kitzmiller v. Dover Area School District*, 400 F. Supp. 2d. 707, 735 (2005), the U.S. district court held that intelligent design was in essence a religious doctrine with no basis in empirical science and that the intelligent design movement "aspires to change the ground rules of science to make room for religion" based on "cultural and religious goals, as opposed to scientific ones" (720).

Earlier cases that had held that "creation science" was not science include *Epperson v. Arkansas*, 393 U.S. 97 [Arkansas law prohibiting teaching of evolution was adopted "for the sole reason that it is deemed to conflict with . . . a particular interpretation of the Book of Genesis by a particular religious group" (103)], and quoted approvingly in *Edwards v. Aguillard*, 482 U.S. 578, 593; *McLean v. Arkansas Board of Education*, 529 F. Supp. 1255 (1982) [Arkansas's requirement to give "balanced treatment" to creation science grew out of a "resurgence of concern among Fundamentalists about the loss of traditional values and a fear of growing secularism in society"; "[t]here is no evidence that" the sponsors and principal advocates for the Act "were motivated by anything other than their religious convictions"; and that "'creation science' as defined" by the Act "is simply not science" (1259, 1263, 1267)].

55. The phrase "gaps in the record" is sometimes used by intelligent design advocates to refer specifically to the fossil record. I use the term "gaps" here more broadly to refer to the record provided by existing empirical data overall.

56. For example, in response to the argument, which has been pressed most prominently and at the biochemical level by Michael Behe, that some structures could not have come about as a result of evolutionary processes because they are "irreducibly complex" such that the removal of any single part of the structure would make the structure entirely nonfunctional, evolutionary scientists have offered paths by which such structures *could* have developed (acknowledging that there is not yet sufficient evidence as to how they did) and have pointed to the evolutionary pathways by which some larger structures (e.g., the ear), which had once been cited as evidence for irreducible complexity, did in fact come about as a result of evolutionary changes that adapted more primitive structures (in the case of the development of the ear, the lower jaw) for new purposes. On this debate, see, Michael Behe, *Darwin's Black Box* (New York: Touchstone, 1996) and *The Edge of Evolution* (New York: Free Press, 2008); Kenneth R. Miller, "Review of Michael Behe's *Darwin's Black Box*, *Creation Evolution Journal* 16 (1996); Jerry Coyne, "The Great Mutator," review of *The Edge of Evolution*, *New Republic*, June 18, 2007; Niall Shanks and Karl H. Joplin, "Redundant Complexity: A Critical Analysis of Intelligent Design in Biochemistry," *Philosophy of Science* 66 (June 1999).

57. Richard Lewontin, "Billions and Billions of Demons," review of Carl Sagan, "The Demon-Haunted World: Science as a Candle in the Dark," *New York Review of Books*, January 9, 1997.

58. Although the theory of intelligent design disputes that *evolution* is a sufficient material explanation for complex life forms, when intelligent design advocates seek to point to a significant dissent within the scientific community they generally refer to dissents from "Darwinism," which they identify with the idea that "natural selection acting on random mutations is the driving force behind the complexity of life." See, for example, www.dissentfromdarwin.org/faq.php. But that there are scientific debates about the explanatory power of *natural selection* is not in dispute. Indeed, according to Lewontin, "The entire body of technical advance in experimental and theoretical evolutionary genetics of the last fifty years has moved in the direction of emphasizing non-selective forces in evolution" ("Billions and Billions of Demons," 30).

59. Thus if political bodies had good grounds for accepting the accusations that have sometimes been made by intelligent design advocates, that on the question of evolution the organized scientific community has been disingenuous or sloppy or myopic or irrationally stubborn, they would, *pro tanto*, have better reason for demanding that anticonsensus views be taught. But for the reasons discussed in the text these grounds would have to be second-order grounds that did not depend on evaluating directly the scientific evidence.

60. Lewontin, "Billions and Billions of Demons," quoted by Phillip Johnson on *Firing Line*, December 19, 1997 (topic: "Resolved: Evolution Should Acknowledge Creation"), available at www.youtube.com/watch?v=Wrs3FDiyot4 at 00:50–01:16, accessed January 15, 2011.

61. Judge Jones, summarizing testimony of defense (intelligent design) witnesses Scott Minnich and Steven William Fuller in *Kitzmiller*, 400 F. Supp. 2d., 720.

62. It is perfectly plausible, for example, to hold with the District Court in the *Kitzmiller v. Dover* case that we need "[take] no position" on the question of "whether ID arguments may be true" (ibid., 735).

63. I do not mean to suggest that *only* an independent press has a role to play in public life. It is a separate question, which I do not address here, what role partisan publications, for example, might play in contributing to political discourse, and of the relation between that role and the idea of truthful inquiry.

64. I know of no studies that have tried to substantiate that this represents a change in the behavior of the press. The development itself is, I think, apparent, but nothing in the broader argument of this section turns on the extent to which these tendencies have increased in recent years.

65. Bernard Williams, *Truth and Truthfulness* (Princeton: Princeton University Press, 2002), Chapter 6.

66. Even with respect to fixed news budgets, the question of truth comes into play, for the judgment of how to allocate resources, while it includes a judgment about the public importance of an issue, also includes a judgment about what counts as an acceptable level of knowledge for reporting on it. However, in a world in which news outlets are almost entirely owned and operated as subsidiaries of conglomerated corporations, the question of accuracy comes into play again at the level of deciding how much of the company's resources to devote to investigative journalism. Slashing investigative budgets, particularly for news outlets that are not already a revenue drain, is *ceteris paribus* a reduction in the commitment to truth.

67. It is not just a question of what the press reports, but also how it reports on it. What is treated as "hard news" and what as secondary—analysis, editorial, punditry, and so on? What becomes part of the news "narrative" and what appears only as a occasional sidebar? And so on.

68. To take just one example, the overwhelming tendency of the press during the first years after the invasion of Iraq was to treat the Bush administration's claims about its long-term agenda in Iraq as hard news, even though there was substantial evidence

from the beginning that its claims were disingenuous, and even as the evidence for that mounted. This is not merely a matter of reporting on the elementary "fact" of what was said versus "the truth" of what was said, for there has always been an abundance of sources inside and outside of government that could have shed light on the administration's long-term agenda (or on the multiple agendas or conflicting agendas, etc.) and whose statements as such could be reported as facts no less than the statements of administration spokespersons.

69. During the 2004 election, the strategists for the incumbent (Bush) believed that his success depended on focusing almost exclusively on "the war on terror," and the strategists for the challenger (Kerry) worried that raising other issues would hurt his credibility on national security. The press by and large took the position that it was not its business to raise other issues in any sustained way. (National Public Radio's *All Things Considered,* which claims to offer a more in-depth form of reporting, reflected the common, and convenient, conception of "neutrality" when it treated as its centerpiece of reporting on the election the presentation of a series of roughly thirty-second excerpts from the two major candidates' stump speeches.) Thus the decision of the Bush administration to focus immediately after the election on the issue of privatization of Social Security surprised many—the issue of Social Security was mentioned only occasionally during the campaign and the proposal for privatization was alluded to in only the vaguest terms—despite the fact that the administration's plans were well known within political circles.

Several years earlier it had also been well known that the administration had planned to raise the issue of privatization of Social Security after the adoption of the so-called Bush tax cuts of 2001, once the federal budget surplus was no longer available (a plan that was deferred because of the events of 9/11). As with the election of 2004, however, the press did not, by and large, think it part of its role to raise the implications of the tax cuts for the Social Security issue and thus left it to public officials to shape the political agenda on the basis of strategic partisan considerations.

70. To take just one example: What responsibility does the press have—particularly in light of the common practice of candidates' charging their opponents with having "voted against" a particular program—to educate the public on the legislative practice of packaging programs, and the typical strategy of majority legislative parties of coupling popular programs with those the minority party opposes? One can find examples of "news analyses" in which such explanations are given, but these are fairly isolated and generally considered secondary to "hard news" reporting; as such they generally do not become part of the common news narrative.

71. These questions are not only about how the privately owned press as it is currently structured should think about itself, but also have implications for public policy concerning media ownership and the funding and structuring of public stations.

72. It was just that sacrifice that characterized, for example, so much of the politics of the George W. Bush administration. Although, no doubt as a consequence of the common tendency to reduce the political significance of truth to questions of sincerity,

we were subjected during that administration to endless musings by political pundits (and others) about whether the president and vice president actually believed what they said, the deception that characterized that administration did not consist merely in saying what was known to be untrue, but perhaps more importantly in the concerted corruption of the ordinary practices for making truth-judgments. From an institutional perspective, what was so disturbing about the politics of the Bush administration—and disturbing in part because of the role of that administration in helping to normalize this kind of politics—was not just its systematic deception, but how many of its policies *depended* on undermining various kinds of institutional truth-norms and truth-practices: suppressing information to Congress; adopting environmental and other regulatory policies that flew in the face of analyses by the government's own experts; censorship of leading scientists employed at governmental agencies; positing the existence of scientific debates where there was largely consensus; stacking government advisory panels with industry representatives or scientists whose views were at odds with the mainstream views of the scientific community; leaking classified information designed to harm those who challenged the administration's misrepresentations; using the presidential power to review criminal convictions and sentences in order to protect those who engaged in violations, and so forth.

In some of these cases these institutional corruptions involved illegal activity. In many they did not. And of the latter, many consisted of actions against which there can be no simple prohibition. It is easy enough, in principle, to establish rules prohibiting U.S. attorneys from engaging in prosecution or investigations for partisan purposes, or political officials from threatening to fire subordinates for giving truthful information to Congress. It is more difficult to try to establish practices to prevent officials from ignoring the analyses of governmental advisory boards without also hampering their ability to overturn those recommendations for good reasons. But the problem of how to bridle political discretion without diminishing the vitality of political life or unduly cabining political imagination is among the classic and enduring challenges of politics; for any political community that shares the aspiration of a politics that can mediate (in Burke's words) "wanton caprice" and "naked will" or (in Arendt's words) "profit, partisanship, and the lust for domination," the question of how best to do so remains a central task. This kind of question is necessarily—again, not exclusively—concerned with truth, not in the simplistic sense of trying to resolve political disputes by attaining some objectively verifiable certain knowledge of the world in itself, or unanimity, or some other such nonsense, but in what I have called the secondary sense of being concerned with modes of inquiry that are truth-directed, that is, that aim at giving—and in which the disagreements are disagreements about—the best account we can offer of how things are.

For examples of the practices referred to above, see, Robert Pear, "Inquiry Confirms Medicare Chief Threatened Actuary," *New York Times*, July 7, 2004 (suppression of information to Congress); "Bush Aide Edited Climate Reports," *New York Times*, June 8 2005 (ignoring scientific advisory councils); James Glanz, "Scientists Say Administration Distorts Facts," *New York Times*, February 19, 2004 (same); Ron Suskind,

"Without a Doubt," *New York Times Magazine*, October 17, 2004 (quoting former EPA administrator Christine Todd Whitman, who disclosed that she was "accused of disloyalty" for asking, during meetings of political officials to determine environmental policy, "whether there were any facts to support our case"); Juliet Eilperin, "Climate Findings Were Distorted, Probe Finds: Appointees in NASA Press Office Blamed," *Washington Post*, June 3, 2008 (includes statement of James E. Hansen, director of NASA's Goddard Institute for Space Studies, that his warnings on global warming were "censored by NASA press officers," with "several other agency climate scientists report[ing] similar experiences"); Gardiner Harris, "Morning-after-Pill Ruling Defies Norm," *New York Times*, May 8, 2004 (citing interviews with "several former F.D.A. officials [who] said that they could not remember another instance in which" the director of the FDA "had overruled both an advisory committee and staff recommendations"); Jim Morris and Alejandra Fernández Morera, "Network of 900 Advisory Panels Wields Unseen Power: Concerns Raised about Secrecy, Industry Influence and Political Interference," *Center for Public Integrity*, http://projects.publicintegrity.org/shadow/report.aspx?aid=821, accessed December 26, 2008 (stacking government advisory panels with industry representatives).

The charges that administration officials leaked classified information concerning CIA agent Valerie Plame Wilson in retaliation for her husband Joseph Wilson's public revelation that there was no credible evidence to support the Bush administration's claim that Saddam Hussein had attempted to purchase "yellow cake" uranium from Niger was not legally proved, but is strongly suggested by the steps taken by former Vice President Chief of Staff Lewis Libby to cover up the circumstances surrounding the leak. Libby was convicted for his actions in the cover-up, but his sentence was commuted by President Bush. Vice President Cheney, who seems to have been involved in the campaign to discredit Joseph Wilson, apparently assumed that Bush would ultimately pardon Libby after the 2008 election, although Bush resisted Cheney's lobbying to do so.

73. Indeed "Truth and Politics" was Arendt's response to the controversy sparked by the publication of *Eichmann in Jerusalem*.

2. Truth and Politics

Reprinted by permission of *Theory and Event* and the Johns Hopkins University Press. Thanks to Sarah Johnson for her careful editing.

1. The critique of cognitive relativism and that of moral relativism were conceptually distinct and in important ways at odds with each other. As Peter Novick observes, "For critics of moral relativism . . . it was the 'neuter' qualities of objectivity and detachment which had morally disarmed the West for the battle against totalitarianism. For critics of cognitive relativism, objectivity and detachment were the distinctive values of the Western life and thought which distinguished the democracies from the totalitarian regimes." Peter Novick, *That Noble Dream: The "Objectivity*

Question" and the American Historical Profession (Cambridge: Cambridge University Press, 1988), 288.

2. Quoted in ibid., 285.

3. Hannah Arendt, "Truth and Politics," in *Between Past and Future: Eight Exercises in Political Thought* (New York: Penguin, 1993), 227–64, quotation on 232. Hereafter cited as "TP."

4. Jürgen Habermas, "Hannah Arendt's Communications Concept of Power," in *Hannah Arendt: Critical Essays*, ed. Lewis Hinchman and Sandra Hinchman (Albany: State University of New York Press, 1994), 225.

5. Linda M. G. Zerilli, "'We Feel Our Freedom': Imagination and Judgment in the Thought of Hannah Arendt," *Political Theory* 33, no. 2 (2005): 158–88.

6. Hans-Georg Gadamer, *Truth and Method*, trans. Joel Weinsheimer and Donald G. Marshall (New York: Continuum, 1994), quotation on 41. Hereafter cited as *TM*.

7. Mark Danner, "Reply" to "The Secret Way to War: An Exchange," *New York Review of Books*, July 14, 2005. Hereafter cited as "Reply." I discuss Danner's argument below.

8. Hannah Arendt, "Philosophy and Politics," *Social Research* 57, no. 1 (1990): 73–103, quotation on 74. Hereafter cited as "PP."

9. Hannah Arendt, *The Human Condition* (Chicago: University of Chicago Press, 1989), 223, 225. Hereafter cited as *HC*.

10. This would be something like the quest for that which is generalizable in an otherwise "impenetrable pluralism of ultimate value orientations" that governs the work of validity thinkers such as Habermas. On this point see Zerilli, "'We Feel Our Freedom.'" Although there is a plausible interpretation of the dialogic character of Socratic dialectic that would accord with the communicative model proposed by Habermas, this is not the interpretation Arendt offers.

11. Leo Strauss, *What Is Political Philosophy? And Other Studies* (Chicago: University of Chicago Press, 1988), quotation on 11.

12. Ibid.

13. Leo Strauss, *Natural Right and History* (Chicago: University of Chicago Press, 1953), 124. In his reading of Strauss contra Arendt on the teaching of Socrates, Dana Villa criticizes Strauss's insistence on the need for yardsticks or absolute standards and argues that Strauss's "definition of political philosophy assimilates the Socratic position to Plato's, and it is motivated by the demand that there be *some* way of rationally adjudicating the fundamental questions and controversies of political life." Dana Villa, "The Philosopher versus the Citizen: Arendt, Strauss, and Socrates," in *Politics, Philosophy, Terror: Essays on the Thought of Hannah Arendt* (Princeton: Princeton University Press, 1999), 155–79, quotation on 168. However that may be, Strauss's challenge is not so easily dismissed. It raises in a particularly acute form the question of the relation between opinion and truth as the fundamental problem of judgment that arises once we deny the existence and/or desirability of yardsticks or absolute standards.

14. Hannah Arendt, "Thinking and Moral Considerations," in *Responsibility and Judgment*, ed. Jerome Kohn (New York: Schocken, 2003), 159–89, quotation on 170. Hereafter cited as "TCM."

15. Ernesto Grassi, *Vom Vorrang des Logos: Das Problem der Antike in der Auseinandersetzung zwischen italienischer und deutscher Philosophie* (Munich: Verlag C. H. Beck, 1939), 38. Hereafter cited as *VL*. All translations are my own.

16. That the world presents itself or appears (*sich zeigen*) is central to Heidegger's phenomenology of being-in-the-world. Heidegger contests the notion that human beings are subjects standing over and against a world of objects, which they then try to "know." "Self and world belong together in the single entity *Dasein*. Self and world are not two beings, like subject and object . . . [instead] self and world are the basic determination of *Dasein* in the unity of the structure of being-in-the-world." Martin Heidegger, *The Basic Problems of Phenomenology*, trans Albert Hofstadter (Bloomington: Indiana University Press, 1982), 297. Rather, as Charles Guignon explains, "entities in general—the tools in a workshop, the unknown chemical in the chemist's beaker, even the precise kinds of sensation and emotion we can have—these can show up *as* what they *are* (i.e., in their *being* such and such) only against the background of the interpretive practices of a particular historical culture." Charles Guignon, "Introduction," in *The Cambridge Companion to Heidegger* (Cambridge: Cambridge University Press, 1993), 1–41, quotation on 13.

17. The ancient conception of truth as *alètheia*, writes Heidegger, means to "take beings that are being talked about . . . out of their concealment: to let them be seen as something unconcealed (*alēthes*); to *discover* them." This unconcealment happens through speech or *logos*. Not *logos* understood in the modern sense as "reason, judgment, concept, definition, ground, relation," but as that which "lets something be seen (*phainesthai*)." Martin Heidegger, *Being and Time*, trans. Joan Stambaugh (Albany: State University of New York Press, 1996), 29, 28.

18. According to Grassi, Heidegger overcomes the objectivist conception of truth, calling our attention instead to the act or process through which things show up for us. But Heidegger leaves unanswered the question of the various forms of appearance (*sich-zeigen*) and *légein*.

19. In *Kunst und Mythos*, for example, Grassi differentiates between a "hermeneutical *légein*," an "empirical *légein*," and a "*téchne-légein*." For the purposes of this paper, however, I will concentrate on the philosophical, aesthetic, and political forms of *légein* discussed below. Ernesto Grassi, *Kunst und Mythos* (Hamburg: Rowohlt, 1957). In Grassi's later work the notion of *légein* is developed as that of *metaphérein*. See especially *Macht des Bildes: Ohnemacht der rationalen Sprache* (Cologne: DuMont Schauberg, 1970).

20. Villa, "Philosopher versus Citizen," 165.

21. Hans-Georg Gadamer, "The Problem of Historical Consciousness," in *Interpretive Social Science: A Second Look*, ed. Paul Rabinow and William M. Sullivan (Berkeley: University of California Press, 1987), 135. Hereafter cited in the text as "PHC."

22. Gadamer writes, "Those views of the world are not relative in the sense that one could oppose them to the 'world in itself,' as if the right view from some possible position outside the human, linguistic world could discover it in its being-in-itself. No one doubts that the world can exist without man and perhaps will do so. This is part of the meaning in which every human, linguistically constituted view of the world lives. In every worldview the existence of the world-in-itself is intended. It is the whole to which linguistically schematized experience refers. The multiplicity of these worldviews does not involve any relativization of the 'world.' Rather, what the world is is not different from the views in which it presents itself" (*TM* 447). The kind of knowledge of the world that Gadamer has in mind, then, does not presuppose that there is some conception of the world that captures the way the world (already) is, in and of itself, independent of our particular conceptions of it. The very idea of knowing the whole truth in some absolute way is premised on the possibility of attaining the presuppositionless standpoint. By contrast with the Archimedean ideal that has governed the idea of philosophical truth as well as the application of scientific method in the *Geisteswissenschaften*, Gadamer holds that no opinion can be declared absolutely true—or for that matter false—since every opinion expresses a view of the world that is both conditioned and limited by one's linguistic or historical perspective. For a good discussion of these issues see Brice Wachterhauser, "Gadamer's Realism: The 'Belongingness' of Word and Reality," in *Hermeneutics and Truth*, ed. Brice Wachterhauser (Evanston, Ill.: Northwestern University Press, 1994), 148–71.

23. We are, as Heidegger famously describes it, always in "a hermeneutical circle." To see this circle as a limitation, to see it as "vicious," or "even to feel that it is an inevitable imperfection [of human knowing]," writes Heidegger, "is to misunderstand understanding from the ground up. . . . What is decisive is not to get out of the circle, but to get in it in the right way" (*Being and Time*, 143). In other words, comments Gadamer, we need to recognize that "the circle possesses an ontologically positive significance" (*TM* 266), which, far from excluding the possibility of genuine knowledge, is the very condition of all understanding and critical thinking.

24. According to Habermas, Gadamer has no adequate answer to this all-important question of validity: "Gadamer's prejudice for the rights of prejudice certified by tradition denies the power of reflection. The latter proves itself, however, in being able to reject the claim of tradition." Jürgen Habermas, "A Review of Gadamer's *Truth and Method*," in *Understanding and Social Inquiry*, ed. Fred R. Dallmayr and Thomas McCarthy (Notre Dame, Ind.: Notre Dame University Press, 1977), 358. Although Habermas grants the *Vorurteilstruktur* of understanding, he rejects (what in his view is) Gadamer's rehabilitation of prejudices and authority, for this undermines critical reflection. Even if we were to grant Gadamer his claim about the historicity of understanding, says Habermas, we would still be left with the epistemological question of how to establish a universal normative basis to distinguish rational and irrational aspects of tradition, legitimate from illegitimate prejudices. Needless to say Gadamer does not accept the charge and maintains that Habermas overestimates the power of

reason. Be that as it may, my point here is not to elaborate, let alone adjudicate, the debate between Habermas and Gadamer but rather to ask whether the question about the legitimacy of prejudices can even be decided apart from the register in which prejudices guide our quest for truth.

25. Hannah Arendt, *Was Ist Politik?*, ed. Ursula Ludz (Munich: Piper Verlag, 1993), 17. Hereafter cited as *WIP.* All translations are my own.

26. Prejudices can count on the agreement of others without any rational argumentation or recourse to evidence, argues Arendt, because they are based neither on proof nor experience (*weil sie erfahrungslos sind; WIP* 18).

27. What can it mean to unearth the truth of the judgment that is buried in prejudice? In "Thinking and Moral Considerations," another essay that deals with the Socratic search for truth, Arendt talks about this process as that of "unfreez[ing]" a concept or a "frozen thought" (*TMC* 173, 172). This concept can be as everyday as the word "house" or as abstract as the words "happiness," "justice," and "courage." If we think of this concept as the rule under which particular cases are subsumed in a rule-governed judgment, we can perhaps begin to see what is at stake in the Socratic effort to recover "the particular cases as they [originally] *appear* to us (we *see* the happy man, *perceive* the courageous deed or the just decision)" (*TMC* 171). This appearance is not the substance that the concept ("what Plato . . . called ideas perceivable only by the eyes of the mind" [*TMC* 171]) indicates but a process, a becoming that we grasp in the course of our activity (seeing, perceiving, etc.). What we want to recover in the judgment, then, is the particular. More precisely we want to recover that which is no object (as captured by a concept, e.g., courage) but is instead what originally shows up for us, what appears (*sich zeigen*) through the originary act of *légein* in the course of our daily activity.

28. Hannah Arendt, *Lectures on Kant's Political Philosophy*, ed. Ronald Beiner (Chicago: University of Chicago Press, 1982), 39.

29. Quoted in Novick, *That Noble Dream*, 290.

30. See also Hannah Arendt, "Lying in Politics," in *Crises of the Republic* (New York: Harcourt Brace, 1972), 1–48, quotation on 6. Hereafter cited as "LP."

31. Factual truths are clearly relevant to politics, in Arendt's view, for without them we would not be able to form opinions. The mutual entanglement of opinion and truth makes it "relatively easy to discredit factual truths as just another opinion. Factual evidence . . . is established through the testimony of eyewitnesses— notoriously unreliable—and by records, documents, and monuments, all of which can be suspected as forgeries. In the event of a dispute, only other witnesses but no third and higher instance can be invoked; that is, in the same way as the settlement of opinion disputes—a wholly unsatisfactory procedure, since there is nothing to prevent a majority of witnesses from being false witnesses" (*TP* 243). Arendt sees all of these dangers; however, the putative antidote to them (e.g., setting up a higher instance that would not be subject to error or lies by which to judge) is not only impossible (it would be, after all, yet another opinion) but dangerous. It would be an escape into the solidity of order that transforms action into rule and

divides those who know but do not act from those who act (i.e., execute orders) but do not know.

32. Mark Danner, "The Secret Way to War," *New York Review of Books*. June 9, 2005. Hereafter cited as "SWW."

33. The memo, which describes a secret meeting on July 23, 2002, between Tony Blair and top British defense and intelligence figures to discuss the possible war with Iraq, was published by the London *Sunday Times* on May 1, 2005. This led to a huge uproar in Britain and nearly cost Blair the election. In the United States, by contrast, the memo was ignored (see note 33), save for a few exceptions, including a signed letter dated May 5, 2005, from some U.S. senators to George W. Bush asking for an explanation of the memo. For a copy of the memo, go to www.downingstreetmemo.com. According to Bob Woodward, the war was planned as early as November 21, 2001, when President Bush ordered Secretary of Defense Donald Rumsfeld to examine "what it would take to protect America by removing Saddam Hussein if we have to." Military planning between Rumsfeld and General Tommy Franks began during the late spring of 2002. See Danner, "SWW," and especially Bob Woodward, *Plan of Attack* (New York: Simon and Shuster, 2004), Chapters 2–4.

As Jack Straw, former British foreign secretary, observed, there was little legal basis for going to war with Iraq (the desire for regime change was not legal grounds). Danner explains, "In order to secure such a legal base, the British officials agree, the allies must contrive to win the approval of the United Nations Security Council, and the Foreign Secretary puts forward a way to do that: 'We should work up a plan for an ultimatum to Saddam to allow back in the UN weapons inspectors'" ("SWW" 5). Danner remarks, "Thus, the idea of UN inspectors was introduced not as a means to avoid war, as President Bush repeatedly assured Americans, but as a means to make war possible" (7). The Bush administration, especially hard-liners like Vice President Dick Cheney, were opposed to the United Nations route from the start, but the British refused to join the U.S.-led attack on Iraq without the "fig leaf" of UN approval. Pressured by the British, Bush gambled that Saddam Hussein would not let the inspectors in, but even when he did and they found nothing, the politically constructed reality of WMD that had already been sold to the American public proved impervious to empirical evidence to the contrary. For example, Cheney, speaking on August 26 (three weeks before Bush came before the UN Security Council to secure the resolution to demand inspections), declared that the United States already had all the information it needed and publicly denounced the UN route: "Simply stated, there is no doubt that Saddam Hussein now has weapons of mass destruction [and] there is no doubt that he is amassing them to use against our friends, against our allies, and against us." The UN route, said Cheney, would produce the dangerous illusion or "false comfort that Saddam was somehow 'back in the box'" (quoted in Danner, "SWW").

34. Danner, "Reply." "In the United States," writes Danner, "the Downing Street memo has attracted little attention. As I write, no American newspaper has published

it and few writers have bothered to comment on it" ("SWW" 14). In a *New York Times* editorial, Paul Krugman likewise observes, "There has been notably little U.S. coverage of the Downing Street memo." Paul Krugman, "Staying What Course?," *New York Times,* May 16, 2005.

35. Mary Dietz, "Working in Half-Truth: Habermas, Machiavelli, and the Milieu Proper to Politics," in *Turning Operations: Feminism, Arendt, and Politics* (New York: Routledge, 2002), 141–69, quotation on 143.

36. Stanley Cavell, "Knowing and Acknowledging," in *Must We Mean What We Say?* (Cambridge: Cambridge University Press, 1969), 238–66.

3. Truth and Disagreement

1. Hannah Arendt, "Truth and Politics," in *Between Past and Future* (New York: Penguin Books, 1978), 241.

2. Ibid., 233. "The story of the conflict between truth and politics is an old and complicated one. . . . Throughout history, the truth-seekers and truthtellers and been aware of the risks of their business; as long as they did not interfere with the course of the world, they were covered with ridicule, but he who forced his fellow-citizens to take him seriously by trying to set them free from falsehood and illusion was in danger of his life: 'If they could lay hands on [such a] man . . . they would kill him,' Plato says in the last sentence of the cave allegory" (229).

3. Hannah Arendt, "Philosophy and Politics," *Social Research* 57, no. 1 (1990): 81.

4. Ibid., 81, 84–85.

5. Ibid., 85, 80. What relates one man's *doxa* to another's is "the fact that the same world opens up to everyone and that despite all differences between men and their positions in the world" (80).

6. Ibid., 90.

7. Arendt, "Truth and Politics," 238.

8. "For institutions that are identified as 'political,' the notion that their responsibility toward truth is *limited* to respecting brutally elementary truths, certainly held (or this along with certain 'rational' truths), opens up an enormous space in which 'things as they are' plays little or no role" (Elkins, emphasis in original).

9. E. W. Caspari and R. E. Marshak, "The Rise and Fall of Lysenko," *Science* 149 (1965); S. M. Gershenson, "The Grim Heritage of Lysenkoism: Four Personal Accounts. IV. Difficult Years in Soviet Genetics," *Quarterly Review of Biology* 65 (1990); Howard Simons, "Russian Genetics and Chickens," *Science Newsletter* 73 (1958). For a discussion of a similar effort to politicize scientific knowledge in the state of South Dakota, see Robert Post, "Informed Consent to Abortion: A First Amendment Analysis of Compelled Physician Speech," *Illinois Law Review* 939 (2007). This is not to deny, however, that professional knowledge practices may at times require political regulation.

10. Robert Cover calls this the "jurispathic" quality of law. Robert M. Cover, "The

Supreme Court, 1982 Term. Foreword: Nomos and Narrative," *Harvard Law Review* 97 (1983).

11. See Robert Post, *Constitutional Domains: Democracy, Community, Management* (Cambridge: Harvard University Press 1995).

12. Robert Post, "The Constitutional Concept of Public Discourse: Outrageous Opinion, Democratic Deliberation, and *Hustler Magazine v. Falwell*," *Harvard Law Review* 103 (1990).

13. Robert Post, "Democracy and Equality," *Annals of the American Academy of Political and Social Science* 24 (2006).

14. Robert Post, "Reconciling Theory and Doctrine in First Amendment Jurisprudence," *California Law Review* 88 (2000); Robert Post, "Between Management and Governance: The History and Theory of the Public Forum," *UCLA Law Review* 34 (1987).

15. *Gertz v. Robert Welch, Inc.*, 418 U.S. 323, 339 (1974).

16. Ibid., 340; *New York Times Co. v. Sullivan*, 376 U.S. 254, 279–80 (1964); *Gertz*, 347.

17. Robert Post, "The Constitutional Status of Commercial Speech," *UCLA Law Review* 48 (2000).

18. "The kind of truth that is relevant for politics . . . requires publicity" (Zerilli).

19. Elsewhere I have argued that the distinction between law and politics turns on the normative role of disagreement. Robert Post, "Theorizing Disagreement: Reconceiving the Relationship between Law and Politics," *California Law Review* 98 (2010).

20. Mark Osiel, *Mass Atrocity, Collective Memory and the Law* (Piscataway, N.J.: Transaction Books, 1997).

4. "Speaking Power to Truth"

1. To my thinking there was thus something more discomfiting than reassuring in Al Gore's call for a "return to reason" as the rejoinder to G. W. Bush's wanton way with facts and rationality, a return that also happened to neatly line up with a progressive political, economic, and environmental agenda. The dangers of truth's despotism are not limited to its Platonic or overtly theocratic forms. See Al Gore, *The Assault on Reason* (New York: Penguin, 2007).

2. Hannah Arendt, "Truth and Politics," in *Between Past and Future: Eight Exercises in Political Thought* (New York: Viking Press, 1961), 228, 231, 237.

3. Actually the speculative explanation Arendt offers is quite odd. After saying that "it may be in the nature of the political realm to deny or pervert truth of every kind," she adds, "as though men were unable to come to terms with [truth's] unyielding, blatant, unpersuasive stubbornness" ("Truth and Politics," 237). How strange to blame power's subjects for power's perversions of truth!

4. Michel Foucault, *History of Sexuality*, vol. 1, trans. R. Hurley (New York: Random House, 1978), 86.

5. Of course there are theorists such as Marx for whom power is obscured and mysterious only up to the moment in which justice finally appears on earth: "The life process of society . . . does not strip off its mystical veil until it is treated as production by freely associated men, and is consciously regulated by them in accordance with a settled plan." *Capital*, vol. 1, in *The Marx-Engels Reader*, ed. R. Tucker (New York: Norton, 1978), 327. In this line of thought power becomes transparent when it is radically shared, at which point it loses its reason to hide, invert reality, or comport with mystification, fetishism, or ideology. But this dimension of Marx's thought, which also features the reabsorption of politics into the social sphere, is surely its least compelling and is what Foucault so quickly sets aside in his own appreciation of power's permanence and pervasiveness and of its necessary subterfuge.

6. Arendt, "Truth and Politics," 259. But for Arendt, always pathologically anxious about contaminations and boundary breaches, truth is destroyed by consorting with persuasion, violence, and other sordid elements of the political. Truth in her view issues from the "*solitude* of the philosopher, the *isolation* of the scientist and the artist, the *impartiality* of the historian and the judge, and the *independence* of the fact-finder, the witness, and the reporter" (260–61, emphasis added).

5. Cynicism, Skepticism and the Politics of Truth

Reprinted by permission of *Theory and Event* and the Johns Hopkins University Press.

1. Though I will speak mostly of *truth* in what follows, I do not think it is helpful to make a fetish of the word. As J. L. Austin reminds us, "There are numerous other adjectives which are in the same class as 'true' and 'false,' which are concerned, that is, with the relations between the words (as uttered with reference to a historic situation) and the world. . . . We say, for example, that a certain statement is exaggerated or vague or bald, a description somewhat rough or misleading or not very good, an account rather general or too concise." "Truth," in *Philosophical Papers*, ed. J. O. Urmson and G. J. Warnock (New York: Oxford University Press, 1961), 97, 98. Austin, as usual, gives amusing and helpful examples: "Is it true or false that Belfast is north of London? That the galaxy is the shape of a fried egg? That Beethoven was a drunkard? That Wellington won the battle of Waterloo? There are various *degrees and dimensions* of success in making statements." I doubt there are general rules to determine, in the absence of context and good judgment, when the latter forms of what Austin terms *ineptitude* will be politically significant or reprehensible.

2. Regarding the first, I have in mind President James K. Polk's claim (famously challenged by Abraham Lincoln in an 1848 speech in the House) in his May 11, 1846, speech to the Congress that the Mexican War was begun, "notwithstanding all of our efforts to avoid it . . . by the act of Mexico herself," specifically its unprovoked decision to "shed American blood on American soil" in the April 25 attack on American forces on the left bank of the Rio Grande River. As John Schroeder makes plain, Polk here ignores

the extremely provocative actions of the United States toward Mexico and assumes that the Rio Grande marked the border between Texas and Mexico, though he knew full well that few shared this assumption and "the boundary was purposely left undetermined in the joint resolution which annexed Texas to the United States in 1845." *Mr. Polk's War: American Opposition and Dissent, 1846–1848* (Madison: University of Wisconsin Press, 1973), 10–12. Regarding the second, I have in mind Robert McNamara's August 6, 1964, assertion (in President Johnson's service) that the attack on the U.S. destroyer *Maddox* in the Tonkin Gulf was wholly unprovoked and that the *Maddox* was not involved in covert South Vietnamese raids against North Vietnam: "Our navy played absolutely no part in, and was not associated with, was not aware of, any South Vietnamese actions, if there were any. . . . I say this flatly. This is a fact." Cited in Stanley Karnow, *Vietnam: A History* (New York: Penguin, 1983), 375. As Karnow observes, McNamara knew very well this was false, and he quickly backed off from these categorical claims. Regarding the third, I have in mind now infamous claims like the following, the first from Vice President Dick Cheney and the second from President George W. Bush. "Simply stated, there is no doubt that Saddam Hussein now has weapons of mass destruction. There is no doubt he is amassing them to use against our friends, against our allies, and against us." Address to the Veterans of Foreign Wars 103rd National Convention, 2002. "The British Government has learned that Saddam Hussein recently sought significant quantities of uranium from Africa." State of the Union Address, January 28, 2003.

3. On the last two, see Saskia Sassen, "Beyond Flawless Elections: Toward a Privatized Presidency," *Theory and Event* 8, no. 2 (2005): "Whether Congress is involved or not makes a significant difference. Legislatures slow down the political process: they are the site for public deliberation, often moving into public brawls, allowing the average citizen to catch up. . . . When Executive decisions amount to a kind of 'law-making,' we can begin to speak of a serious democratic deficit at the heart of the liberal state." Sassen makes the nice observation, "The position of the Executive is that since September 11 a growing number of citizens must be open to scrutiny, and a growing number of the government's operations must be kept secret. This inverts a foundational aspect of liberal democracy: individual privacy must be protected and the government must be open to public scrutiny."

4. So-called white lies are an obvious exception to this rule, though even here there is considerable variation, and it is hardly unusual for a "beneficiary" of such a lie to feel humiliated by it.

5. Orwell perfectly captures the dazed credulity of 1984 Oceania and contemporary America: "'I thought we'd always been at war with Eurasia,' she said vaguely. It frightened him a little. The invention of airplanes dated from long before her birth, but the switch-over in the war had happened only four years ago, well after she was grown up." George Orwell, *1984* (New York: Harcourt Brace Jovanovich, 1961), 127. The outstanding analysis of this "indifference to how things really are" is of course Harry Frankfurt's "On Bullshit," in *The Importance of What We Care About* (Cambridge: Cambridge University Press, 1988), 125. Frankfurt makes connections between the prevalence of bullshit

and that of skepticism about truth and an interest in sincerity similar to those I make here. He also makes the fine observation that these three do not fit as easily together as many seem to assume: "It is absurd to imagine that we ourselves are determinate, and hence susceptible both to correct and to incorrect descriptions, while supposing that the ascription of determinacy to anything else has been exposed as a mistake" (133). That said, Frankfurt's analysis of bullshit is relevant here only for an understanding of contemporary (political) culture, not of actual political lies such as those listed in note 2 above. None of these meet Frankfurt's criteria, as they work only insofar as they claim to be true in their details.

6. The terms are Bernard Williams's: "Truthfulness implies a respect for the truth. This relates to both of . . . the two basic virtues of truth, . . . Accuracy and Sincerity: you do the best you can to acquire true beliefs, and what you say reveals what you believe." *Truth and Truthfulness: An Essay in Genealogy* (Princeton, N.J.: Princeton University Press, 2002), 11–12. Compare Bernard Williams, "Truth, Politics, and Self-Deception," in *In the Beginning Was the Deed: Realism and Moralism in Political Argument* (Princeton, N.J.: Princeton University Press 2005), 157: "A truthful person both says (with numerous familiar qualifications) what he or she believes, and takes some trouble that his or her beliefs should be true. Because of its connection with accuracy, [truthfulness] is a quality that essentially involves mentioning *the truth*."

7. I follow here the outstanding discussion in Alan Keenan, "The Twilight of the Political? A Contribution to the Democratic Critique of Cynicism," *Theory and Event* 2, no. 1 (1998).

8. See Zygmunt Bauman's helpful discussion (which Keenan also follows) in *Freedom* (Minneapolis: University of Minnesota Press, 1988), 81ff. Suspicion of the idea of the common good has been carefully cultivated by conservative intellectuals. Consider Hayek: "The 'social goal,' or 'common purpose,' for which society is to be organized is usually vaguely described as the 'common good,' the 'general welfare,' or the 'general interest.' It does not need much reflection to see that these terms have no sufficiently definite meaning to determine a particular course of action." Friedrich Hayek, *The Road to Serfdom* (Chicago: University of Chicago Press, 1994), 64. What principle or value ever has done this?

9. This can even take the form of a "democratic theory," as in the influential work of Joseph Schumpeter, whose conception of democracy as nothing more than an institutional arrangement allowing competition for leadership between elites has found wide acceptance. Schumpeter blithely declares that in such competition "effective information is almost always adulterated or selective," where "selective information" is "an attempt to lie by speaking the truth." *Capitalism, Socialism, and Democracy* (New York: Harper, 1942), 264.

10. Machiavelli was, of course, not *simply* cynical, and the *Discourses* advance a form of political idealism that is compatible with his often bleak appraisal of human nature and of the requirements of a successful political actor. On the role of skepticism

in Hobbes's thought, see Richard Tuck, "Hobbes," in *Great Modern Thinkers* (New York: Oxford University Press, 1992).

11. Obviously I am using the word "cynicism" in its current everyday sense, and I do not propose that the classical Cynics were uninterested in philosophy.

12. Hannah Arendt, "Lying in Politics," in *Crises of the Republic* (New York: Harcourt Brace Jovanovich, 1969), 4; Hannah Arendt, "Truth and Politics," in *Between Past and Future* (New York: Penguin, 1977), 227, 251.

13. Hannah Arendt, *The Human Condition* (Chicago: University of Chicago Press, 1958), 7; Cicero, *On Duties*, trans. M. T. Griffin and E. M. Atkins (Cambridge: Cambridge University Press, 1991), 6–10, 26, 37, 51. This omission is particularly striking, given the fact that Arendt cites *De Officiis* repeatedly in *The Human Condition* (at 91 and 110). For an excellent discussion of the manner in which Machiavelli overturns Cicero's elevation of *fides* to the "pivotal" "princely" virtue, see Quentin Skinner, "Machiavelli," in *Great Political Thinkers* (Oxford: Oxford University Press, 1992). 44ff. For another Roman testimony to the importance of truth, see the repeated references to the necessity of the same in Marcus Aurelius' *Meditations*. Arendt is famously dismissive of the Stoics, but there is no denying that Marcus understood the Stoic virtues to be essential to his conduct as emperor. For the Stoics, appropriate action is determined by the various roles or "professions" (*epangeliai*) that our lives mark out for us. As a good man, Marcus was required to use the powers of his office to act for the greater good of the whole of which he was a part—ultimately the universe, but proximately the Roman Empire. His virtues were therefore *political* virtues, and among these virtues "truthfulness" played an important part. See, e.g., Marcus Aurelius, *Meditations*, trans. Martin Hammond (New York: Penguin, 2006), 21. If this does not count as a political virtue for Arendt, it is presumably because she defines a political virtue as being categorically distinct from the kind of virtue that could be exercised by a private individual. But this would reduce what appears to be a telling observation into a self-fulfilling prophecy.

14. See Stuart Hampshire's excellent account of this essentially Machiavellian position in "Public and Private Morality," in *Public and Private Morality*, ed. S. Hampshire (Cambridge: Cambridge University Press, 1978). It is important to note that none of these considerations excuses in any way Polk's or McNamara's or Cheney's lies.

15. Arendt, "Truth and Politics," 257; Arendt, "Lying in Politics," 7. Arendt goes on, in "Lying in Politics," to anticipate the "boy in the bubble" effect of the Bush presidency, where the efforts of the president's handlers to protect him from criticism ended up weakening his grip on reality: "The only person likely to be an ideal victim of complete manipulation is the President of the United States. Because of the immensity of his job, he must surround himself with advisers, the 'National Security Managers,' as they have been called by Richard J. Barnet, who 'exercise their power chiefly by filtering the information that reaches the President and by interpreting the outside world for him.' The President, one is tempted to argue, allegedly the most powerful man of the most powerful country, is the only person in this country whose range of choices can be predetermined" (9).

16. Arendt, "Truth and Politics," 263–64.

17. Ibid., 259–60. "Outstanding among the existential modes of truthtelling are the solitude of the philosopher, the isolation of the scientist and the artist, the impartiality of the historian and the judge, and the independence of the fact-finder, the witness, and the reporter."

18. Hannah Arendt, "Philosophy and Politics," *Social Research* 57 (Spring 1990): 80.

19. Ibid., 81. I am grateful to Jeremy Elkins for reminding me of this passage.

20. Arendt, "Truth and Politics," 239, emphasis Arendt's. Bonnie Honig accurately captures Arendt's concern with the "mode of asserting validity" when she argues that Arendt privileges—in Austin's terms—performative over constative utterances. "In politics, the appeal to the absolute is illicit *because of* its constative character," and not vice versa; "in [Arendt's] view, constatives are violent, despotic, and disempowering." "Declarations of Independence: Arendt and Derrida on the Problem of Founding a Republic," *American Political Science Review* 85, no. 1 (1991): 99, 106; Bonnie Honig, *Political Theory and the Displacement of Politics* (Ithaca, N.Y.: Cornell University Press, 1993), 99, 107, emphasis mine. Honig distances herself somewhat from this extreme position when she argues that Derrida appreciates better than Arendt the "undecidability" between the constative and the performative. This position nonetheless retains the notion that the constative is coercive in a way that the performative is not.

21. The language of courtship is of course Kant's, from the third Critique. See Hannah Arendt, *Lectures on Kant's Political Philosophy*, ed. R. Beiner (Chicago: University of Chicago Press, 1982), 72. It is puzzling to see truth and truthfulness contrasted in this way. (Compare Williams's remarks in note 6 above.) Arendt may not want to identify truthfulness with sincerity, as it might appear, but to distinguish between my experience of the world, which I can in the end not fully control, and my expression of that experience in the dialogue within which we "establish a kind of common world" ("Philosophy and Politics," 84). Compare in this regard Arendt's reference to "the compelling force of factual truth" on the firsthand observers to whom the world "opens up" in Hannah Arendt, *The Life of the Mind*, vol. 1: *Thinking* (New York: Harcourt Brace Jovanovich, 1978), 59.

22. Arendt, "Truth and Politics," 240. In the best book written on the Vietnam War, Michael Herr writes, "You couldn't find two people who agreed about when it began, how could you say when it began going off? Mission intellectuals like 1954 as the reference date, if you saw as far back as War II [*sic*] and the Japanese occupation you were practically a historical visionary. 'Realists' said that it began for us in 1961, and the common run of Mission flack insisted on 1965, post–Tonkin Resolution, as though all the killing that had gone before wasn't really war." *Dispatches* (New York: Avon, 1978), 50–51.

23. Even Dostoyevsky's Underground Man rails against reason in the service of being able to *will* what appears stupid and pointless, not to assert or believe what is false.

24. Consider in this regard Michael Oakeshott's claim, "In a conversation the participants are not engaged in an enquiry or a debate; there is no 'truth' to be discovered,

no proposition to be proved, no conclusion sought." "The Voice of Poetry in the Conversation of Mankind," in *Rationalism in Politics and Other Essays*, expanded edition (Indianapolis: Liberty Fund, 1991), 498. It is true that a good conversation is not a proof or a debate. But does that mean it seeks no conclusion or that there is no truth to be discovered? Good conversations regularly reveal truths about the participants and the topic(s), even if they don't aim at them systematically. That's why we say we learn from them, and part of why we enjoy them. I am grateful to conversations with Dick Flathman for this example.

25. This point is well made by Michael Lynch in *True to Life: Why Truth Matters* (Cambridge, Mass.: MIT Press, 2004), 3. Lynch does a good job of demonstrating how apparent opposites like the relentlessly skeptical Stanley Fish and the smugly doctrinaire William Bennett actually agree upon the false premise that we can speak of truth only if we can be confident of being absolutely certain of the truth of a given claim.

26. Hegel gets this quite right when, in contrasting truth with anything that might be the object of a command, he writes, "Truth is something free which we neither master nor are mastered by." Georg Wilhelm Friedrich Hegel, "The Spirit of Christianity and Its Fate," in *Early Theological Writings*, trans. T. M. Knox (Philadelphia: University of Pennsylvania Press, 1975), 196.

27. Williams, *Truth and Truthfulness*, 211–12. In the earlier and more polished "Truth, Politics, and Self-Deception," Williams gives a more detailed treatment of this general claim, distinguishing an antityranny argument, an argument from democracy, and two versions of a liberal argument, all of which give different reasons for the importance of truth in politics and which therefore support different actual policies. According to the first, governments are disposed to commit illegitimate actions, which they will hope to conceal because of "their peculiar powers and opportunities." According to the second, government is a trust, and it is a violation of that trust for the governing to deceive the governed. According to the minimal version of the third, liberal argument, government should promote freedom, and denial of information is an important limitation of freedom in itself. According to the stronger version of the liberal argument—which Williams notes corresponds to a "positive" notion of freedom—"self-development consists of the exercise and development of one's powers in the light of the truth," and government deceit therefore stymies self-development (157–58). Williams does not argue for one of these against the others. For a good critique of Williams' failure to give the anti-tyranny argument its due in *Truth and Truthfulness*, see Lynch, *True to Life*, 176–77.

28. Ernesto Laclau, "Discourse," in *A Companion to Contemporary Political Philosophy*, ed. R. Goodin and P. Pettit (Oxford: Blackwell, 1993), 431–37.

29. Ernesto Laclau and Chantal Mouffe, *Hegemony and Socialist Strategy* (London: Verso, 1985), 122. I criticize the account of ontology underlying this understanding of the objective in Andrew Norris, "Against Antagonism: On Ernesto Laclau's Political Thought," *Constellations* 9, no. 4 (2002).

30. Jacques Derrida, "Force of Law: The 'Mystical Foundation of Authority,'" in

Deconstruction and the Possibility of Justice, ed. David Carlson, Drucilla Cornell, and Michael Rosenfeld (New York: Routledge, 1992).

31. Chantal Mouffe, *The Democratic Paradox* (London: Verso, 2000), 1.

32. Ibid., 11.

33. Ibid., 11–12. Compare Chantal Mouffe, *On the Political* (London: Routledge, 2005), 121.

34. Mouffe, *The Democratic Paradox*, 96, emphasis mine.

35. Mouffe provides a similarly lengthy discussion of Wittgenstein in Chantal Mouffe, "Wittgenstein and the Ethos of Democracy," in *The Legacy of Wittgenstein: Pragmatism or Deconstruction,* ed. Chantal Mouffe and Ludwig Nagl (Frankfurt am Main: Peter Lang, 2001), but there her focus is on political theorists she sees as being broadly "Wittgensteinian," and not the details of Wittgenstein's own arguments.

36. Ludwig Wittgenstein, *On Certainty,* trans. D. Paul and G. E. M. Anscombe (New York: Harper, 1972), 611, 612, cited in Mouffe, *The Democratic Paradox*, 70.

37. Mouffe, *The Democratic Paradox*, 70.

38. Compare the previous chapter of *The Democratic Paradox,* "Carl Schmitt and the Paradox of Liberal Democracy."

39. Mouffe cites the same lines again in *The Democratic Paradox*, 97–98.

40. Mouffe distances herself from Schmitt when she distinguishes between "two forms of antagonism, antagonism proper—which takes place between enemies, that is, persons who have no common symbolic space—and what I call 'agonism,' which is a different mode of manifestation of antagonism because it involves a relation not between enemies but between 'adversaries,' adversaries being defined in a paradoxical way as 'friendly enemies'" (ibid., 13). The "friendliness" here is a matter of shared commitment to democratic liberty and equality, if not a shared understanding of what this means. This shared commitment allows for the emergence of politics as opposed to the political, where "politics" is "the ensemble of practices, discourses and institutions which seek to establish a certain order" and "the political" is "the dimension of antagonism that is inherent in human relations." But Mouffe's entire argument is premised upon the idea that politics can "defuse" the political for only so long, and that agonism is truly political—that is, antagonistic: in the absence of both an agreement upon the meaning of the terms "liberty" and "equality" and a common practice that would reflect such agreement, the "order" of politics is open to truly political disruption. Here as in Schmitt, the exception that breaks the "order" is privileged over the order of the norm (viz., the hegemonic interpretation of what the terms mean); it and not the norm is "political" (101). Compare Mouffe, *On the Political,* 21: "The agonistic struggle . . . is a struggle between opposing hegemonic projects which can never be reconciled rationally. The antagonistic dimension is always present." For Schmitt, see especially Carl Schmitt, "Definition of Sovereignty," in *Political Theology,* trans. George Schwab (London: MIT Press, 1988) and William Scheuerman's argument in *Carl Schmitt: The End of Law* (New York: Rowman & Littlefield, 1999), 46 that Schmitt's emphasis on crisis situations "distorts much of what everyday politics seems to be about."

41. A similar insensitivity to the differences between these cases is found in Allan Janik's "Notes on the Natural History of Politics," which argues that a political understanding of Wittgenstein's later work will highlight the polemical. Coincidently, Janik cites these same lines (OC 608 and 609) at the start of his piece. On his account, which draws heavily upon William Connolly's classic *The Terms of Political Discourse*, Wittgenstein's discussions of family resemblance and rule following highlight how concept use *as such* is political because it is always potentially a subject of dispute: since any given rule can and will be followed in different ways in different contexts, different senses of any given word are bound to develop that bear only a family resemblance to one another, lacking any common feature. This leaves us with the difficulty of sorting out the relative merits of the various understandings of the resulting "essentially contested concepts." Among these concepts might be ones that we already recognize as political (e.g., "fair" or "just") and others that we had not hitherto recognized as political (e.g., "art" or "Christianity"). In each case, however, "our very descriptions of the world are charged with evaluations that are fundamentally political in nature." Janik, "Notes on the Natural History of Politics," in *The Grammar of Politics: Wittgenstein and Political Philosophy*, ed. C. Heyes (Ithaca, N.Y.: Cornell University Press, 2003), 105. While there is something true and important here, one might well nonetheless protest that there is a *conceptual* difference between "conceptual conflict" and "political conflict" (hence our use of the phrases to describe quite different phenomena), and that Janik is obscuring that as much as he is revealing a neglected feature of our political and conceptual life. The confusion is not one into which Connolly falls, as Janik himself indicates: "Connolly . . . has written, 'When groups range themselves around essentially contested concepts, politics is the mode in which the clash is normally expressed.' What is obscured in this sentence is the fact that for a concept to be essentially contested, groups must have already in some sense ranged themselves around it, since a concept has no existence outside of human actions" (108). Compare William Connolly, *The Terms of Political Discourse*, 3rd ed. (Princeton, N.J.: Princeton University Press, 1993), 203.

42. I specify "*this* sort of challenge" because I am convinced by Thomas Nagel that there is a regularly ignored but real, categorical distinction between such "creation science" (his scare quotes) and scientific theories that incorporate appeal to intelligent design. The former argues, on the authority of the Bible, that the Earth and all the creatures on it were created by God about six thousand years ago—claims that do not amount to a scientific hypothesis because they are not offered as explanations of the empirical evidence available to us, and are not open (in the eyes of those advancing them) to empirical confirmation or refutation. In contrast, Intelligent Design makes a hypothesis (about a supernatural power that intervenes or has intervened in natural history) that is intended to help explain the empirical evidence, a hypothesis that is in principle no less scientific than the alternative hypothesis that a fully naturalistic account of the history of natural organisms like us is possible. Both atheism and theism are religious commitments that cannot be proven by science (at this point, at any rate), but are compatible with it. See Thomas Nagel, "Public Education and Intelligent Design," in *Secular*

Philosophy and the Religious Temperament (Oxford: Oxford University Press, 2010). I note that in an earlier version of this essay I wrote as if this distinction were not real.

43. Wittgenstein, *On Certainty*, 336.

44. Ludwig Wittgenstein, *Remarks on Frazer's "Golden Bough"* (Nottinghamshire: Brynmill, 1979), 1e. See Peter Winch's sensitive account in "Understanding a Primitive Society," in *Ethics and Action* (London: Routledge & Kegan Paul, 1972).

45. Wittgenstein, *On Certainty*, 74, 195. Nagel makes a similar distinction between being mistaken and being irrational in "Public Education and Intelligent Design," 54n13.

46. Wittgenstein, *On Certainty*, 94ff.

47. Mouffe, *The Democratic Paradox*, 105, 103. This evidence notwithstanding, this claim of mine might seem to distort Mouffe's position, especially as Laclau sometimes takes the contrary position. But Laclau is deeply ambivalent about this, and ultimately embraces a version of the decisionism he elsewhere rejects, as I argue in Andrew Norris, "Ernesto Laclau and the Logic of 'the Political,'" *Philosophy and Social Criticism* 32, no. 1 (2006). I am grateful to Alan Keenan for pointing out to me the possible confusion here.

48. Ludwig Wittgenstein, *Philosophical Investigations*, trans. G. E. M. Anscombe (New York: Macmillan, 1958), I, 186. Simon Critchley explicitly takes the tack to which I think Mouffe implicitly commits herself when he cites this passage as possible support for his view that "politics . . . is the task of invention in relation to the other's decision in me—nonfoundationally and nonarbitrarily." Critchley asks, "How does one do this exactly?" and answers, "Perhaps in the following way: in a quite banal sense, each new decision is necessarily different. Every time I decide I have to invent a new rule, a new norm, which must be absolutely singular in relation to both the other's infinite demand made on me and the finite context within which this demand arises. I think this is what Derrida means, in 'Force of Law' and elsewhere, by his qualified Kierkegaardian emphasis upon the madness of the decision, namely that each decision is like a leap of faith made in relation to the singularity of a context." Such a position, he concludes, might be "linked" to the quoted passage from the *Investigations*. Simon Critchley, "Five Problems in Levinas's View of Politics and the Sketch of a Solution to Them," *Political Theory* 32, no. 2 (2004): 179–80. To say I am *inventing* a new rule each time I apply the old one would seem to be considerably less banal than Critchley suggests, however, as it implies that it is, strictly speaking, impossible to apply any given rule without setting it aside and creating a new one. The very concept of a *rule* thus dissolves.

49. Wittgenstein, *Philosophical Investigations*, I, 213. Compare I, 219 and Stanley Cavell's recounting: "We learn and teach words in certain contexts, and then we are expected, and expect others, to be able to project them into further contexts. Nothing ensures that this projection will take place (in particular, not the grasping of universals nor the grasping of books of rules), just as nothing insures that we will make, and understand, the same projections. That on the whole we do is a matter of our sharing routes of interest and feeling, senses of humor and of significance and of fulfillment, of what is outrageous, of what is similar to what else, what a rebuke, what forgiveness, of when an utterance is an assertion, when an appeal, when an explanation—all the whirl

of organism Wittgenstein calls 'forms of life.' Human speech and activity, sanity and community, rest on nothing more, but nothing less, than this. It is a vision as simple as it is difficult, and as difficult as it is (and because it is) terrifying." "The Availability of Wittgenstein's Later Philosophy," in *Must We Mean What We Say?* (Cambridge: Cambridge University Press, 1969), 52. On decision, compare 50: "It is a matter of . . . 'forms of life.' That is always the ultimate appeal for Wittgenstein—not rules, not decisions." Read together with Cavell's differences with Kripke and Rorty, whose reading of Wittgenstein resembles and apparently influences Mouffe's own, such passages suggest that Mouffe is wrong to suggest that Cavell shares her "emphasis on the moment of *decision*" in politics. Mouffe, *The Democratic Paradox*, 75–76. For Cavell's criticisms of Kripke, see Stanley Cavell, "The Argument of the Ordinary," in *Conditions Handsome and Unhandsome* (Chicago: University of Chicago Press, 1990).

50. Michael Williams, *Unnatural Doubts: Epistemological Realism and the Basis of Scepticism* (Princeton, N.J.: Princeton University Press, 1996), 30. Williams gives one of the best accounts I know of *On Certainty*, arguing that of all of the positions Wittgenstein tries on in these inconclusive and very exploratory notes, the best is that found in OC 250: "My having two hands is, in normal circumstances, as certain as anything that I could produce in evidence for it." Compare, e.g., Williams, 70. If Williams's work has a weakness, it is in the hastiness of its reading of Cavell, whose own view anticipates Williams's more than Williams acknowledges.

51. Wittgenstein, *On Certainty*, 92.

52. I am passing over subtleties here. "It may happen," Wittgenstein writes, in his "Remarks on Frazer's *Golden Bough*," "as it often does today, that someone will give up a practice [*Gebrauch*] when he has seen that something on which it depended is an error. But this only happens in cases when you can make a man change his way of doing things simply by calling his attention to his error. This is not how it is in connection with the religious practices of a people; and what we have here is *not* an error [*Irrtum*]" (2e). The nineteenth- and twentieth-century theory of ideology of course argues that politics cuts across this distinction, and that sometimes a perverted, oppressive form of political life rests upon more than error, but practices of passive or active acceptance of oppression. But such theories of ideology and their more Foucauldian successors *expand* the notion of living in error and succumbing to lies, rather than dismissing it.

53. Mouffe, *The Democratic Paradox*, 102.

54. Ibid., 96.

55. Wittgenstein, *Philosophical Investigations*, 1:19.

56. Mouffe, *The Democratic Paradox*, 97; compare 96.

57. Ludwig Wittgenstein, *Culture and Value*, ed. G. H. von Wright (Chicago: University of Chicago Press, 1984), 64e/64. Wittgenstein begins, "It strikes me [*Es kommt mir vor*] . . . " Mouffe mistakenly gives the page citation as 85e.

58. John Micklethwait and Adrian Woolridge, *The Right Nation: Conservative Power in America* (New York: Penguin, 2004), 198ff.

59. To take Micklethwait and Woolridge's examples, while it may to some extent be

in my character to react "decisively," we can also ask, Is it true that a decisive reaction to an attack is likely to ward off future attack, or gain the sympathies of third parties? Is it true that unilateralism is the best foreign policy, either in general or in the current political climate?

60. This is denied by Aletta Norval, who explicitly follows Mouffe on this point (though she makes criticisms of Mouffe and Laclau that are not immediately relevant here). Norval argues that a moment of political identification is essential to democracy, and offers South Africa's 1994 elections as a case in point: "Queuing in the hot sun for hours on end in order to vote condensed the moment in which all South Africans could claim their status as equal subjects of a new democracy. 'We are all democrats now!' 'We are all equal now!' 'We are all humans now!'" *Aversive Democracy: Inheritance and Originality in the Democratic Tradition* (Cambridge: Cambridge University Press, 2007), 136. But note that *being able* to claim this is different from actually *claiming* it, and that there is an immense difference between all being democrats (something that, in any robust sense of the term, is certainly not true of everyone living or even voting in South Africa, or anywhere else for that matter), all being equal (in the eyes of the law, presumably), and all being (acknowledged by the state or many of one's fellow citizens to be) equal. If Norval ignores this, it is because of her eagerness to make *identification* central to political activity. But one can be politically active without having a sharply defined political identity of which one is aware, and one can identify oneself as a democrat while contesting some of the criteria that Norval takes to be definitive of the term.

61. Mouffe, *On the Political*, 121.

62. James Wiley, "The Impasse of Radical Democracy," *Philosophy and Social Criticism* 28, no. 4 (2002): 486. This is a crucially important point to bear in mind when considering the role of the press in modern democratic society.

63. Gopal Balakrishnan, *The Enemy: An Intellectual Portrait of Carl Schmitt* (London: Verso, 2000), 263. On the "empty space" of democratic sovereignty, compare Laclau and Mouffe, *Hegemony and Socialist Strategy*, 186, and Claude Lefort, "The Logic of Totalitarianism," in *The Political Forms of Modern Society: Bureaucracy, Democracy, Totalitarianism*, ed. John Thompson (Cambridge, Mass.: MIT Press, 1986), 279–80.

64. Some will respond here that this is as it should be, and that the very idea of governance or rule is incompatible with democracy. See, e.g., Miguel Vatter, *Between Form and Event: Machiavelli's Theory of Political Freedom* (Dordrecht: Kluwer Academic, 2000), 2: "The concept of event, introduced here, stands in opposition to the concept of form and to its cognate concept of a well-founded order." On Vatter's account, which builds upon Reiner Schürmann's account of an-arche in *Heidegger on Being and Acting: From Principles to Anarchy* and, more generally, Arendt's distinction between freedom and sovereignty, classical political thought revolves around the question of who should rule, a question that assumes the necessity and propriety of domination. It is Machiavelli's achievement to challenge this assumption and "pose the question of the situation or event of no-rule, from which all forms of government and every legal order are to emerge and into which they may be revoked if political life is to remain free" (4).

Readers of Vatter's impressive work will note, however, that he himself makes the rather large assumption that any imposition of order is a form of domination. It would seem to follow from this that democracy is incompatible with education.

65. See Bernard Williams's discussion of "the ubiquitous danger of wishful thinking" in "Truth, Politics, and Self-Deception."

66. Paul Feyerabend goes, if anything, even further than Mouffe, arguing for a relativism in which the initiatives of citizens take priority over epistemology, and in which those initiatives are expressed in "concrete decisions" that can be justified, if at all, by reference to the "tradition" of the citizen in question. Feyerabend in no way privileges science over practices judged by, say, the measures of Protestant fundamentalism. What counts as a tradition for him is hard to say, however, as he speaks of "the tradition of white men." Paul Feyerabend, *Erkenntnis für freie Menschen*, altered edition (Frankfurt: Suhrkamp, 1980), 37–38, 36, 13, 16. For an excellent if brief critique of Rorty's better known views on objectivity, see John McDowell, "Towards Rehabilitating Objectivity," in *Rorty and His Critics,* ed. R. Brandom (Oxford: Blackwell, 2000). For an excellent if over-long critique of Rorty's political writings, particularly his attempt to appropriate Orwell's *1984* (in *Contingency, Irony, and Solidarity*), see James Conant's essay in the same volume.

67. Connolly has recently argued that the tendency of the postmodernist left to regard any claim "of objectivity [as] a myth to be exploded" has "not help[ed]," and that "perhaps we need to articulate a new model of objectivity." William Connolly, "The Media and Think Tank Politics," *Theory and Event*, 8, no. 4 (2005).

68. I am grateful to Anne Norton for proposing this example to me, though she did not agree with my interpretation of its significance for the present discussion.

69. When I first presented this essay at the 2005 annual convention of the American Political Science Association, Rom Coles in his remarks as discussant objected that it is "arrogant" to tell one's political opponents what one believes is true or false or to suggest how one might determine truth or falsity, and that what is needed is greater self-examination and self-criticism. This seems to me profoundly misguided. Not only is it not arrogant to speak of truth and falsity, but self-examination and self-criticism cannot get off the ground without a distinction between the two.

70. For their help on earlier drafts of this essay I am grateful to Richard Boyd, Jeremy Elkins, Dick Flathman, Andreas Kalyvas, Alan Keenan, Tracy Strong, Yashas Vaidya, John Wallach, Eric Wilson, and the audience at the panel on "The State of Democracy: Theoretical Perspectives on the 2004 Presidential Election" at the 2005 annual convention of the APSA in Washington, D.C.

6. Democracy as a Space of Reasons

1. The phrase "the space of reasons" comes from Wilfrid Sellars, "Empiricism and the Philosophy of Mind," in *Midwest Studies in the Philosophy of Science,*

vol. 1, ed. H. Feigl (Minneapolis: University of Minnesota Press 1956), 76: "In characterizing an episode or state as that of knowing, we are not giving an empirical description of that episode or state; we are placing it in the logical space of reasons, of justifying and being able to justify what one says." Obviously I adopt it for my own purposes, purposes which I fancy are not completely distinct from Sellars's own.

2. Richard Popkin, *The History of Skepticism from Savonarala to Bayle* (Oxford: Oxford University Press, 2003); Terence Penelhum, *A Study in Skepticism and Fideism* (Dordrecht: D. Reidal, 1983).

3. Michel de Montaigne, *Apology for Raymond Sebond*, trans. R. Ariew and M. Grene (Indianapolis: Hackett, 2003), 50.

4. Ibid., 102.

5. From remark G on the article on Uriel Acosta, see introduction to Pierre Bayle, *Historical and Critical Dictionary: Selections*, ed. R Popkin and C Brush (Indianapolis: Hackett, 1993), xxi.

6. Montaigne, *Apology for Raymond Sebond*, 164.

7. The connection between autonomy, respect, and reason just illustrated is precisely why so many of us worry about the health of a democracy that allows its leaders to mislead them, as this country did in the case of the invasion of Iraq. Indeed no better example is needed of a lack of respect shown to citizens than the Bush administration's willingness to manipulate the evidence—to disregard reason—in its march to war. Consequently no better example is needed for demonstrating the crucial role that the rational pursuit of the truth plays in democratic politics.

8. John Rawls, *Political Liberalism* (New York: Columbia University Press, 1993), 216ff.

9. For the standard communitarian version of the critique, see Michael Sandel, *Liberalism and the Limits of Justice* (Cambridge: Cambridge University Press, 1982).

10. J. Rawls, "The Idea of an Overlapping Consensus," *Oxford Journal of Legal Studies* 7 (1987): 1–25.

11. Jean Hampton, "Should Political Philosophy Be Done without Metaphysics?," *Ethics* 99 (1989): 791–814.

12. The externalist locus classicus is Alvin Goldman's "What Is Justified Belief?," in *Justification and Knowledge*, ed. G. S. Pappas (Dordrecht: D. Reidel, 1976), 1–23. For an externalist response to the skeptical challenge of the criterion, see E. Sosa, "Reflective Knowledge in the Best Circles," *Journal of Philosophy* 94, no. 8 (1997): 410–30.

13. That doesn't mean that no such argument would be sound. After all, if the standards *are* truth-conducive, then an argument that employs them to show as such may well be correct, even if unconvincing. This is essentially the externalists' point.

14. Richard Rorty, "Universality and Truth," in *Rorty and His Critics*, ed. R. Brandom (Cambridge, England: Blackwell, 2000), 7.

15. Ibid., 2.

16. See Ludwig Wittgenstein, *Tractatus Logico-Philosophicus*, trans. D. Pears and B

McGuinness (London: Routledge & Kegan Paul, 1922); Bertrand Russell, "On the Nature of Truth and Falsehood," in *Philosophical Essays* (London: George Allen and Unwin, 1966).

17. Detailed presentations of this view can be found in Michael Lynch, "Truth and Multiple Realizability," *Australasian Journal of Philosophy* 82 (2004): 384–408; Michael Lynch, *Truth as One and Many* (Oxford: Oxford University Press, 2009).

18. Rorty, "Universality and Truth," in *Rorty and His Critics*, ed. R. Brandom (Cambridge, England: Blackwell, 2000), 4.

19. Richard Rorty, "Ethics without Principles," in *Philosophy and Social Hope* (New York: Penguin Books, 1999), 85.

20. Rorty, "Universality and Truth," 20.

21. My thanks to Paul Bloomfield, Steven Wall, Donald Baxter, and Eberhard Herrmann for helpful discussions and comments.

7. Truth and Democracy

1. For a good summary, see Greg Miller, "Flaws Cited in Powell's U.N. Speech on Iraq," *Los Angeles Times*, July 15, 2004, A1.

2. Bernard Williams, "Truth, Politics, and Self-Deception," in *In the Beginning Was the Deed,* ed. Geoffrey Hawthorn (Princeton, N.J.: Princeton University Press, 2005), 161.

3. For a discussion, see William A. Galston, "Community, Democracy, Philosophy: The Political Thought of Michael Walzer," *Political Theory* 17, no. 1 (1989).

4. This and the preceding three paragraphs are adapted from William A. Galston, *Liberal Pluralism* (Cambridge: Cambridge University Press, 2002), 82–83.

5. Rabban Shimon ben Gamaliel, *Mishnah Pirkei Avot*, 1:18.

6. David Park, *The Truth Commissioner* (London: Bloomsbury, 2008).

10. Response to Norris, Lynch, and Galston

1. There are, of course, examples from across the political spectrum. See, for instance, Eric Alterman, *When Presidents Lie: A History of Official Deception and Its Consequences* (New York, 2004), which begins with an account of the lies Franklin Delano Roosevelt told to get the United States into World War II.

2. For a recent consideration of their interaction, see Bernard Williams, *Truth and Truthfulness* (Princeton, N.J., 2002).

3. Hayden White, *Metahistory: The Historical Imagination in Nineteenth-Century Europe* (Baltimore, 1973). This book has generated enormous discussion. Not all critics are persuaded by his disdain for historical truth-claims.

4. As J. Hillis Miller observes, "Contrary to common sense, a lie is a performative,

not a constative, form of language. Or rather, it mixes inextricably constative and performative language. A lie is a form of bearing witness. It always explicitly or implicitly contains a speech act: 'I swear to you I am telling the truth.' This speech-act aspect of a lie is not a matter of truth or falsehood. It is a way of doing something with words. Its functioning depends on faith or lack of faith in the one who hears it, not on referential veracity. If a lie is believed it is as 'felicitous' as a truth in making something happen." "The Anacoluthonic Lie," in *Reading Narrative* (Norman, Okla., 1998), 154.

5. Ruth Grant, *Hypocrisy and Integrity: Machiavelli, Rousseau and the Integrity of Politics* (Chicago, 1997); David Runciman, *Political Hypocrisy: The Mask of Power, from Hobbes to Orwell and Beyond* (Princeton, N.J., 2008). For an earlier historical account, see Jenny Davidson, *Hypocrisy and the Politics of Politeness: Manners and Morals from Locke to Austin* (Cambridge, England, 2004).

6. Adolf Hitler, *Mein Kampf*, trans. Ralph Mannheim (Boston, 1943), 232.

7. Alain Badiou, Metapolitics, trans. Jason Baker (London, 2005), 11–24.

11. Democracy and the Love of Truth

1. T. Hobbes, *The Elements of Law, Natural and Politic*, (London: Frank Cass, 1969), 2.2; M. Walzer, *Spheres of Justice* (New York: Basic Books, 1983), 304.

2. Plato, *Republic*, 476.

3. B. Williams, *Truth and Truthfulness*, (Princeton, N.J.: Princeton University Press, 2002), 15.

4. This is especially true of the most influential of truth's critics, Friedrich Nietzsche. See Williams, *Truth and Truthfulness*, 1–2, 12–17; B. Yack, *The Fetishism of Modernities* (Notre Dame, Ind.: Notre Dame University Press, 1997), 112.

5. This new vision of deliberative democracy is the focus of my critical arguments in the second section of the paper. On the "great community," see J. Dewey, *The Public and Its Problems* (New York: Swallow Press, 1954). For a sympathetic analysis and critique of Dewey's understanding of democracy, see M. Smiley, "Pragmatic Inquiry and Social Conflict: A Critical Reconstruction of Dewey's Model of Democracy," *Praxis International* 9 (1990): 365–80. On dialectic as engagement, see, in particular, P. Euben, "Reading Democracy: 'Socratic Dialogues' and the Education of Democratic Citizens," in *Demokratia*, ed. J. Ober and C. Hedrick (Princeton, N.J.: Princeton University Press, 1996), 327–60. For a powerful critique, see G. Shiffman, "Deliberation versus Decision: Platonism in Contemporary Democratic Theory," in *Talking Democracy*, ed. B. Fontana, C. Niedermeyer, and G. Remer (University Park: Penn State University Press, 2004), 87–114.

6. The distinction between "strong" and "weak" versions of deliberative democracy is taken from G. Shiffman, "Deliberation versus Decision," 87–88. The strong version looks to deliberation as an alternative source of democratic legitimacy, the weak, merely as a way of improving democratic citizenship.

7. S. Benhabib, "Toward a Deliberative Model of Democratic Legitimacy," in *Democracy and Difference*, ed. S. Benhabib (Princeton, N.J.: Princeton University Press, 1996), 68.

8. Walzer, *Spheres of Justice*, 304.

9. Aristotle, *Rhetoric* 1355b.

10. B. Manin, *The Principles of Representative Government* (Cambridge: Cambridge University Press, 1997), 136.

11. As Aristotle notes (*Rhetoric* 1356b), rhetorical argument is "persuasive to someone," namely the listener(s) whose judgment determines whether it has been successful.

12. As Bryan Garsten suggests, this pair of opposing vices looms very large in most critiques of rhetorical speech. See B. Garsten, *Saving Persuasion* (Cambridge, Mass.: Harvard University Press, 2006), 3–7.

13. Manin, *The Principles of Representative Government*.

14. Garsten, *Saving Persuasion*, 3.

15. This is the heart of what Gary Shiffman ("Deliberation versus Decision," 87–88) calls the "strong version" of deliberative democracy.

16. Benhabib, "Toward a Model of Democratic Legitimacy," 68.

17. J. Cohen, "Deliberation and Democratic Legitimacy," in *Deliberative Democracy*, ed. J. Bohman and W. Rehg (Cambridge, Mass.: MIT Press, 1997), 72.

18. J. Habermas, *Between Facts and Norms* (Cambridge, Mass.: MIT Press, 1997), 448.

19. J. Elster, introduction to *Deliberative Democracy*, ed. J. Elster (Cambridge: Cambridge University Press, 1998), 5.

20. Cohen, "Deliberation and Democratic Legitimacy," 67.

21. M. Saward, "Rawls and Deliberative Democracy," in *Democracy as Public Deliberation*, ed. M. Passerin d'Entrèves (Manchester: Manchester University Press, 2002), 112.

22. Cohen, "Deliberation and Political Legitimacy," 79; J. Cohen, "Procedure and Substance in Deliberative Democracy, in Benhabib, *Democracy and Difference*, 99.

23. Elster, introduction, 5; J. Cohen, "Democracy and Liberty," in Elster, *Deliberative Democracy*, 185–86.

24. Cohen, "Deliberation and Political Legitimacy," 75.

25. Habermas, *Between Facts and Norms*, 448.

26. Cohen, "Procedure and Substance in Deliberative Democracy," 99.

27. Benhabib, "Toward a Model of Democratic Legitimacy," 69.

28. Ibid.

29. Michal Walzer raises a similar question about unconstrained and undirected discussion in "A Critique of Philosophic Conversation," *Philosophical Forum* 21 (1989–90): 195.

30. Socratic examination of opinion is therefore taken in an antidemocratic spirit, despite its challenge to all conventional standards of authority. See Shiffman, "Deliberation versus Decision," 95–97.

31. T. M. Scanlon, "Contractualism and Utilitarianism," in *Utilitarianism and Beyond*, ed. A. Sen and B. Williams (Cambridge: Cambridge University Press, 1982). As I suggested in an earlier essay, when you transfer this expectation that people should accept standards that they cannot "reasonably reject" from a moral to a political context, it begins to sound like you are interested in extending to people an "offer that they cannot refuse." See B. Yack, "Rhetoric and Public Reasoning: An Aristotelian Understanding of Political Deliberation," *Political Theory* 34 (2006): 429.

32. See, for example, E. Markovits, *The Politics of Sincerity* (University Park: Penn State University Press, 2008), 26. She suggests that "expansive mutual accountability is a central component of democratic politics."

33. R. Rorty, "Is It Desirable to Love Truth?," in *Truth, Politics and Postmodernism: Spinoza Lectures* (Assen: Van Gorcum, 1997), 25.

34. Williams, *Truth and Truthfulness*, 15.

35. On Rorty's unstated attachment to the virtue of accuracy, see M. Sleat, "On Relativist Truth and Liberal Politics," *Inquiry* 50 (2007): 288–305.

36. See Williams, *Truth and Truthfulness*, 11–12, Chapter 5.

37. Ibid., 11–12, Chapter 6.

38. Markovits, *The Politics of Sincerity*, 18–31.

39. Walzer, "Philosophy and Democracy," 397.

12. J. S. Mill on Truth, Liberty, and Democracy

Reprinted by permission of Oxford University Press.

1. This essay draws on two previously published essays and other materials developed for a book on Mill's ethical and political philosophy (forthcoming from Oxford University Press). See F. Rosen, "J. S. Mill on Socrates, Pericles, and the Fragility of Truth," *Journal of Legal History* 25 (2004): 181–94; F. Rosen, "The Philosophy of Error and Liberty of Thought: J. S. Mill on Logical Fallacies," *Informal Logic* 26 (2006): 121–47.

2. J. S. Mill, *System of Logic* (1843) in *Collected Works of John Stuart Mill*, 33 vols., ed. J. M. Robson (Toronto: University of Toronto Press, 1963–91), vols. 7–8 (hereafter cited as *CW* in the text). See O. Haac, ed., *The Correspondence of John Stuart Mill and Auguste Comte* (New Brunswick, N.H.: Transaction, 1995).

3. B. Williams, *Truth and Truthfulness: An Essay in Genealogy* (Princeton, N.J.: Princeton University Press, 2002), 211–12.

4. There are echoes of Mill's approach in this passage from G. Frege, "The Thought: A Logical Inquiry" (1956), trans. A. M. and Marcelle Quinton, in *Truth*, ed. S. Blackburn and Keith Simmons, Oxford Readings in Philosophy (Oxford: Oxford University Press, 1999), 85: "The word 'true' indicates the aim of logic as does 'beautiful' that of aesthetics or 'good' that of ethics. All sciences have truth as their goal; but logic is also concerned with it in quite a different way from this. It has much the same relation to truth as physics has to weight or heat. To discover truths is the task of all

sciences; it falls to logic to discern the laws of truth." There have been a number of excellent studies of various aspects of Mill's logic. See, for example, R. Jackson, *An Examination of the Deductive Logic of John Stuart Mill* (London: Oxford University Press, 1941); O. Kubitz, "Development of John Stuart Mill's *System of Logic," Illinois Studies in the Social Sciences* 18, nos. 1–2 (1932); A. Ryan, *The Philosophy of John Stuart Mill,* 2nd ed. (Basingstoke: Macmillan, 1987); G. Scarre, *Logic and Reality in the Philosophy of John Stuart Mill* (Dordrecht: Kluwer Academic, 1989); J. Skorupski, *John Stuart Mill* (London: Routledge, 1989).

5. Texts like H. Aldrich, *Artis Logicae Compendium* (Oxford: Oxford University Press, 1691) and R. Sanderson, *Logicae Artis Compendium,* 2nd ed. (Oxford: A. Lichfield, 1618) were still in use in this period.

6. See J. Locke, *An Essay concerning Human Understanding,* ed. P. Nidditch (Oxford: Oxford University Press, 1975), 671.

7. See ibid., 495.

8. See R. Whately, *Elements of Logic,* 2nd ed., ed. Ray E. McKerrow (Delmar, N.Y.: Scholars' Facsimiles and Reprints, 1975).

9. See *Encyclopaedia Metropolitana, or, Universal Dictionary of Knowledge, On an Original Plan,* 29 vols., ed. E. Smedley, Hugh J. Rose, and Henry J. Rose (London: B. Fellowes, 1845), 1:1–43, 193–240, 241–303.

10. "We shall be more than satisfied if he should derive one hundredth part of the instruction from our criticism, which we have received from his work" (*CW* 11:4).

11. See Rosen, "The Philosophy of Error and Liberty of Thought," 121–47; H. Hansen, "Mill on Inference and Fallacies," in *Historical Foundations of Informal Logic.* ed. D. Walton and A. Brinton (Aldershot: Ashgate, 1997).

12. G. Vlastos, *Socratic Studies* (Cambridge: Cambridge University Press, 1994), 13, 18–20 is one of a few recent scholars who have appreciated the significance of the Socratic elenchus and the work of George Grote, Mill's close friend, in reasserting this perspective.

13. Mill wrote translations and brief comments on nine Platonic dialogues in the 1830s, some of which were published in the *Monthly Repository* in 1834–35. See *CW* 11:37–238.

14. See K. O'Rourke, *John Stuart Mill and Freedom of Expression: The Genesis of a Theory* (London: Routledge, 2001).

15. See N. Urbinati, *Mill on Democracy: From the Athenian Polis to Representative Government* (Chicago: University of Chicago Press, 2002), 14ff; J. Riley, "Mill's Neo-Athenian Model of Liberal Democracy," in *J. S. Mill's Political Thought: A Bicentennial Reassessment,* ed. N. Urbinati and A. Zakaras (Cambridge: Cambridge University Press, 2007), 221–49.

16. See K. Demetriou, *George Grote on Plato and Athenian Democracy: A Study in Classical Reception* (Frankfurt: Peter Lang, 1999), 118ff, 125, 230–43.

17. See ibid., 119–23; M. Cranston, "Introduction," to Rousseau, *The Social Contract* (Harmondsworth, England: Penguin, 1968), 17.

18. G. Grote, *A History of Greece,* 12 vols., Everyman ed. (London: Dent, 1940), 6:181.

19. Not all classical scholars share this view of liberty in Thucydides. See, for example, S. Hornblower, *A Commentary on Thucydides,* vol. 1 (Oxford: Oxford University Press, 1991), 297–99, 301.

20. See Demetriou, *George Grote,* 229ff.

21. Grote, *A History of Greece,* 8:312–59; Demetriou, *George Grote,* 231ff; K. Demetriou, "Grote on Socrates: An Unpublished Essay of the 1820s in Its Context," *Dialogos* 3 (1996): 36–50.

22. Grote, *A History of Greece,* 9:87.

23. See F. Rosen, *Jeremy Bentham and Representative Democracy: A Study of the Constitutional Code* (Oxford: Clarendon Press, 1983), 183–99.

24. See F. Rosen, *Bentham, Byron and Greece: Constitutionalism, Nationalism, and Early Liberal Political Thought* (Oxford: Clarendon Press, 1992), 25ff.

25. See J. Bentham, *Rationale of Judicial Evidence, Specially Applied to English Practice,* 5 vols., ed. J. S. Mill (London: Hunt and Clarke, 1827); J. Bentham, *The Works of Jeremy Bentham,* 11 vols., ed. J. Bowring (Edinburgh: W. Tait, 1838–43), 8:193–293.

26. See G. Varouxakis, "National Character in John Stuart Mill's Thought," *History of European Ideas* 24 (1998): 375–91; G. Varouxakis, *Mill on Nationality* (London: Routledge, 2002); F. Rosen, "La science politique de John Stuart Mill," in "John Stuart Mill," special issue of *Revue d'etudes Benthamiennes* 4 (2008): 121–31, online.

27. See J. Riley, *Mill on Liberty* (London: Routledge, 1998), 144; Urbinati, *Mill on Democracy,* 55ff; Riley, "Mill's Neo-Athenian Model of Liberal Democracy," 221ff. As for the originality of Mill's term, see the *Oxford English Dictionary* and A. Bain, *John Stuart Mill: A Criticism with Personal Recollections* (London: Longmans, Green, 1882), 73. For a good account of Mill's use of the term with Auguste Comte, see M. Pickering, *Auguste Comte: An Intellectual Biography,* vol. 1 (Cambridge: Cambridge University Press, 1993), 527–28, 671.

28. Haac, *The Correspondence,* 52.

29. Comte was much taken with the term "pedantocracy" and used it to attack those opposed to positivism, to him personally in the Ecole Polytechnique, and elsewhere. See ibid., 56, 62–64, 71, 77, 243–44; Pickering, *Auguste Comte,* 527–28, 531, 671–72.

30. See B. Knights, *The Idea of the Clerisy in the Nineteenth Century* (Cambridge: Cambridge University Press, 1978), 169.

31. S. Collini, introduction to J. S. Mill, *On Liberty, with The Subjection of Women and Chapters on Socialism* (Cambridge: Cambridge University Press, 1989), xvi–xvii.

32. See Riley, "Mill's Neo-Athenian Model of Liberal Democracy," 221ff.

33. See F. Rosen, "The Method of Reform: J. S. Mill's Encounter with Bentham and Coleridge," in *J. S. Mill's Political Thought: A Bicentennial Reassessment,* ed. N. Urbinati and A. Zakaras (Cambridge: Cambridge University Press, 2007), 124–44.

34. A. Ryan, "Mill in a Liberal Landscape," in *The Cambridge Companion to Mill,*

ed. J. Skorupski (Cambridge: Cambridge University Press, 1998), 497. In *Why Read Mill Today?* (London: Routledge, 2006), 6, J. Skorupski answers his question by seeing Mill in terms of liberalism, and, particularly, he emphasizes the foundation of liberty of thought within his liberalism.

35.   See, for example, E. Eisenach, introduction to *Mill and the Moral Character of Liberalism*. ed. E. Eisenach (University Park: Pennsylvania State University Press, 1998), 3–7 and references to "liberal" and "liberalism" in the index to N. Urbinati and A. Zakaras, eds., *J. S. Mill's Political Thought: A Bicentennial Reassessment* (Cambridge: Cambridge University Press, 2007), 384.

36. For a different and contrasting view, see N. Capaldi, *John Stuart Mill: A Biography* (Cambridge: Cambridge University Press, 2004), 346ff.

37. See Rosen, "The Philosophy of Error and Liberty of Thought," 142–43.

13. Can This Marriage Be Saved?

1. Rogers M. Smith, "Still Blowing in the Wind: The American Quest for a Democratic, Scientific Political Science," *Daedalus*, Winter 1997, 253–87. Compare Robert D. Putnam, "APSA Presidential Address: The Public Role of Political Science," *Perspectives on Politics* 1 (2003): 250–51. The tensions confronting American political science are actually tripartite, among the three distinguishable goals of furthering scientific truth, furthering democracy, and furthering America, but here I focus on the tensions between truth and democracy.

14. Democratic Politics and the Lovers of Truth

1. Seyla Benhabib, "Toward a Deliberative Model of Democratic Legitimacy," in *Democracy and Difference*, ed. Seyla Benhabib (Princeton, N.J.: Princeton University Press, 1996), 68.

2. Adam Przeworski, "Minimalist Conception of Democracy: A Defense," in *Democracy's Value*, ed. Ian Shapiro and Casiano Hacker-Cordón (Cambridge: Cambridge University Press, 1999), 47.

3. On political realism or "pure politics," see Giovanni Sartori, *The Theory of Democracy. Part One: The Contemporary Debate Revisited* (Chatman, N.J.: Chatman House, 1987), Chapter 3.

4. Vilfredo Pareto, *The Mind and Society*, 4 vols., trans. Andrew Bongiorno and Arthur Livingston (New York: Harcourt, 1935), 4: § 2244.

5. As Sartori explained in *The Theory of Democracy Revisited*, 117–18, "information is not knowledge," and while knowledge presumes information, "it does not go by definition that he who is informed is knowledgeable." This means two things: first, that the exposition of people's opinions to information does not translate into their betterment

or even transformation; second, that no matter how many times we vote we don't learn how to vote (or vote more "competently" or "rationally").

6. Philip Pettit, "Depoliticizing Democracy," *Ratio Juris* 17 (March 2004): 54–55.

7. I discussed this topic extensively in *Representative Democracy: Principles and Genealogy* (Chicago: University of Chicago Press, 2006).

8. Antonio Gramsci, *Quaderni del carcere*, ed. Valentino Gerratana (Turin: Einaudi, 1973), 1625. See also John Dewey, "The Ethics of Democracy," in *The Early Works, 1882–1898*, vol. 1: *1882–1888*, ed. J. A. Boydston (Carbondale: Southern Illinois University Press, 1969), 232–33.

9. Gramsci, *Quaderni del carcere*, 1625.

10. Jane Mansbridge calls this "dynamic" view of representation "anticipatory" because citizens are not seen as static agents of accountability and passive spectators of representatives' behavior; they and their representatives are actually participants in the "continuing communication and potentially changing" of opinions through the entire electoral mandate. "Rethinking Representation," *American Political Science Review* 97 (2003): 518.

11. Compare Pierre Rosanvallon, *La contre-démocratie: La politique à l'âge de la défiance* (Paris: Seuil, 2006), 9–32.

12. Bernard Yack, "Rhetoric and Public Reasoning: An Aristotelian Understanding of Political Deliberation," *Political Theory* 34 (2006): 417–38.

13. Compare Alan Ryan, *John Dewey and the High Tide of American Liberalism* (New York: Norton, 1995).

14. George Grote, *A History of Greece*, 12 vols. (London: J. M. Dent, 1906), 9:22–28, 45–50. Bacon himself endorsed Cicero's interpretation of Socrates as a thinker who did not mix "things human and divine" and thus created not a "fantastic philosophy" but a "useful" philosophy grounded in human creation and potential. Francis Bacon, *The New Organon*, in *The New Organon and Related Writings*, ed. Fulton H. Anderson (Indianapolis: Bobbs-Merrill, 1960), 62.

15. John Stuart Mill, *A System of Logic* in *The Collected Works of John Stuart Mill*, 33 vols., ed. John M. Robson (Toronto: University of Toronto Press, 1963–91), 7:19–20, 27–42.

16. Friedrich D. E. Schleiermacher, "On the Worth of Socrates as a Philosopher," trans. Connop Thirtwall (1833), in *A Life of Socrates*, ed. Gustave Friedrich Wiggers (London: Taylor and Walton, 1840), cxxix–clv. In a letter to Thomas Carlyle, Mill confessed the extraordinary impression Schleiermacher's essay had made on him: "I also am conscious that I write with a greater appearance of sureness and strong belief than I did for a year or two, in that period of recovering after the petrifaction of a narrow philosophy, in which one feels quite sure of scarcely anything respecting truth, except that she is many-sided" (Mill to Carlyle, July 12, 1833, in Collected Works, 12:181). I have analyzed Schleiermacher's interpretation of Socrates and its impact on Mill in *Mill on Democracy: From the Athenian Polis to Representative Government* (Chicago: University of Chicago Press, 2002), Chapter 4.

17. This point has also been made by Gregory Vlastos, "The Socratic Elenchus," in

Oxford Studies in Ancient Philosophy, vol. 1, ed. Julia Annas (Oxford: Clarendon Press, 1983), 46. On the negative function of dialectics in Grote's interpretation, see also John Glucker, "The Two Platos of Victorian Britain," in *Polyhistory: Studies in the History and Historiography of Ancient Philosophy* ed., Keimpe A. Algra, Peter W. van der Horst, and David T. Rumia (Leiden: E. J. Brill, 1996), 385–406.

18. I am borrowing this very effective description from Stephen G. Salkever, "'Loops and Bound': How Liberal Theory Obscures the Goods of Liberal Practices," in *Liberalism and the Good*, ed. R. Bruce Douglass, Gerald M. Mara, and Henry S. Richardson (New York: Routledge, 1990), 194, even if he does not think Mill's philosophy would fit it.

19. Stuart Hampshire, *Innocence and Experience* (Cambridge, Mass.: Harvard University Press, 1989), 57.

20. There are different ways of dealing with these obstacles; some constitutions make the government directly responsible for enacting a welfare system; others propose a more indirect form of intervention that aims to contain inequality rather than promote equality.

21. Keith J. Bybee, *Mistaken Identity: The Supreme Court and the Politics of Minority* (Princeton, N.J.: Princeton University Press, 2002), 12.

15. Truth and Public Reason

Reprinted by Permission. Wiley Periodicals, Inc., from *Philosophy and Public Affairs* 37, no. 1 (Winter 2009).

1. I presented earlier versions of this essay at the Catholic University of Leuven; LUISS Guido Carli; the Harvard Graduate Conference in Political Theory; philosophy departments at Columbia University, Union College, Northwestern University, and Cornell University; the September Group; and the Stanford Law School Legal Theory Colloquium; and as the 2008 Mala Kamm Lecture at New York University. I am grateful to audiences on all these occasions, to the editors of *Philosophy and Public Affairs*, and to Bradley Armour-Garb, Alex Byrne, David Estlund, Erik Freeman, Samuel Freeman, Barbara Fried, David Hills, Erin Kelly, Cristina Lafont, Jon Mandle, Sebastiano Maffetone, Richard Miller, Ingrid Salvatore, Thomas Scanlon, Seana Shiffrin, and especially Paul Horwich for comments and suggestions. I also benefited greatly from generous and illuminating comments by Richard Rorty at the Stanford colloquium. I sketch his concerns below in n53.

2. To be sure, Pinter was thinking about the truth and falsity of assertions about matters of nonnormative fact, for example, about the absence of weapons of mass destruction from Iraq in 2002. Nevertheless, because he states his point in more sweeping terms, just as he had earlier stated a perfectly general claim about truth, I think it is appropriate to interpret him as making a more general claim about the place of truth in the discourse of citizens.

3. I say "conception" or "understanding" rather than "theory" because I am not supposing that a conception needs to have the internal structure that we associate with a theory. See below, final two paragraphs of "Including Truth."

4. In the way that the political conception of objectivity, associated with political liberalism, is a genuine conception of objectivity, though different from and in a way less committal than rational intuitionist and Kantian conceptions of objectivity. See John Rawls, *Political Liberalism* (New York: Columbia University Press, 1996), 110–16.

5. See Gottlob Frege, "The Thought: A Logical Inquiry," *Mind* 65 (1956): 293.

6. There are many versions of the deflationary approach, and not all treat propositions (as opposed to sentences) as truth bearers. I have made that assumption here, but nothing in my discussion turns on it. For discussion of some of the variety, see Scott Soames, *Understanding Truth* (Oxford: Oxford University Press, 1999), Chapter 8; Bradley Armour-Garb, "Deflationism: A Brief Introduction," unpublished manuscript. On propositions as truth bearers, see Soames, *Understanding Truth*, Chapter 1; Paul Horwich, *Truth*, 2nd ed. (Oxford: Oxford University Press, 1998), 16–17.

7. On public reason, see "Political Liberalism," lecture 6; John Rawls, "The Idea of Public Reason Revisited," in *Collected Papers*, ed. Samuel Freeman (Cambridge, Mass.: Harvard University Press, 1999), 573–615.

8. For discussion of the charge, and the ways that it puzzlingly deploys a passion for truthfulness against the concept of truth, see Bernard Williams, *Truth and Truthfulness* (Princeton, N.J.: Princeton University Press, 2002).

9. See "Declaration on Religious Freedom," *The Teachings of the Second Vatican Council: Complete Texts of the Constitutions, Decrees, and Declarations* (Westminster, Md.: Newman Press, 1966), 366–67; John Courtney Murray, "The Problem of Religious Freedom," in *Religious Liberty: Catholic Struggles with Pluralism* (Louisville, Ky.: Westminster, 1993).

10. John Rawls, *Justice as Fairness: A Restatement*, ed. Erin Kelly (Cambridge, Mass.: Harvard University Press, 2001), 37.

11. In emphasizing Rawls's concern specifically with truth, I disagree with Joseph Raz's claim that Rawls is equally concerned with a variety of terms of normative appraisal, including "reasonable." See Raz, "Facing Diversity: The Case of Epistemic Abstinence," *Philosophy and Public Affairs* 19 (1990): 15 (and especially n34). Raz's essay was written before Rawls had developed a number of the main ideas of political liberalism, so the (mis)interpretation is understandable. More broadly, I agree with Raz in thinking that Rawls was mistaken in putting aside the concept of truth. But there are several important points of difference between his view and mine: (1) Raz does not have the idea of a political conception of truth, and thus does not see that doctrinal disagreement imposes any conditions on the understanding of truth that falls within public reason (or perhaps see any need for an account of public reason at all). (2) I think that Rawls, in emphasizing the importance of the political and practical, was never concerned simply with what Raz calls "consensus-based social stability." Because Raz misconstrues Rawls's concern with the political and practical, he misinterprets the reasons for abstaining

from judgments about truth. (3) Raz appears to endorse what I will later call the sufficiency and full display arguments, an endorsement that may be associated with skepticism about the idea of public reason.

12. John Rawls, "Justice as Fairness: Political Not Metaphysical," in *Collected Papers*, ed. Samuel Freeman (Cambridge, Mass.: Harvard University Press, 1999), 394.

13. The passages that follow are from John Rawls, *Political Liberalism*, xxii, 116, 94. In "The Idea of Public Reason Revisited," Rawls does not address the issue of truth at all, though he does not suggest (except perhaps by the sheer omission) any change of mind.

14. Rawls, *Political Liberalism*, 127.

15. John Rawls, "Reply to Habermas," in *Political Liberalism*, 394–95.

16. Political officials and candidates for office have a "duty of civility" to explain their positions on fundamental issues by reference to the political conception that they take to be most reasonable. See John Rawls, "The Idea of Public Reason Revisited," in *Collected Papers*, 576. The point is not that it is advisable or obligatory to assert that one's view is the most reasonable. Instead there is a duty to argue by reference to the view that one judges to be most reasonable. Judgments about the reasonableness of one's views thus belong to the terrain of political reflection and argument. Rawls states that he takes justice as fairness, with its two principles, to be the most reasonable conception. See *Political Liberalism*, xlvi.

17. Samuel Freeman proposed in correspondence that Rawls wishes only to avoid claims about the truth of principles of justice, not about the truth of consequences drawn from those principles. We cannot, then, affirm, within public reason, that the principle of equal basic liberties is true, or that it is true that justice requires equal basic liberties. If that principle is, however, part of the most reasonable conception of justice, then there is no objection to saying about a law infringing freedom of worship that it is true that it is unjust. The acceptable claim of truth is made from "within" the conception of justice, whereas the unacceptable claim is made about the conception itself. The same distinction, however, does not apply to the notion of being reasonable (or most reasonable). I do not see a case for interpreting Rawls this way, and do not, in any case, see the basis for the proposed restriction on the concept of truth. First, if we cannot say that the principles are true, can we nevertheless affirm the principles, or are we limited to asserting that the principles describe the most reasonable conception? If we affirm the principles, assert them, and believe them, what is the force of withholding the judgment that they are true? Second, suppose it is permissible to judge, from "within" a conception of justice, that it is true that certain policies are unjust. Let's say that is because we confine claims about truth to what we can argue for from common ground (not that I wish to accept that thesis). But then why is it not permissible to judge, from "within public reason"—which provides a terrain of argument that different conceptions of justice share—that certain principles of justice are true because they can be argued for from common ground? Third, the case for confining truth to judgments made "within" a conception of justice seems to turn on a sharp distinction, reminiscent of Carnap, between internal questions, which arise within a linguistic framework, and external questions, about whether to adopt a framework. But Carnap's distinction did not permit judgments

about which framework or language (say, a thing-language or a sense-datum language) is "most reasonable." Our attitude to a framework, on Carnap's account, is a matter of acceptance, not belief or assertion; it is, he says, "not of a cognitive nature." So it is nonsense to describe a framework as true, but that is because the framework is not a matter of belief at all. See Rudolf Carnap, "Empiricism, Semantics, and Ontology," in *Meaning and Necessity*, 2nd ed. (Chicago: University of Chicago Press, 1956), 205–21. The idea that cognitive appraisal is entirely internal is foreign to public reason.

18.   Rawls, *Political Liberalism*, 129. I will come back later to this passage, which ties together two arguably very different ideas, one about holding a political conception as true, the other about holding it as the one suitable basis for public reason in virtue of its being true.

19.   Ibid., 92. See also 111 ("in the familiar way") and 114 ("this idea of truth").

20.   On rational intuitionism, and the idea of an independent order of moral values, see ibid., 91–92; John Rawls, *Lectures on the History of Moral Philosophy*, ed. Barbara Herman (Cambridge, Mass.: Harvard University Press, 2000), 69–83, esp. 70–72.

21.   When Rawls states that political liberalism "does without the concept of truth," he identifies this as one of four elements in the contrast between rational intuitionism and political constructivism. See *Political Liberalism*, 91–94. But logically speaking, the alternative to endorsing a "traditional conception" of truth is to not endorse a traditional conception. There are two ways to do that: do without the concept of truth altogether, or endorse a nontraditional (that is, noncorrespondence) interpretation of truth.

22.   On the political conception of the person, see ibid., 18–20, 29–35, 48–54, 86–88.

23.   On the relevant kind of fatality, see Williams, *Truth and Truthfulness*, 67–68. On truth as a standard of correctness, see Nishi Shah, "How Truth Governs Belief," *Philosophical Review* 112 (2003): 447–82; Nishi Shah and David Vellerman, "Doxastic Deliberation," *Philosophical Review* 114 (2005): 497–534.

24.   See Donald Davidson, *Truth and Predication* (Cambridge, Mass.: Harvard University Press, 2005), Chapter 3.

25.   Gottlob Frege, *Basic Laws of Arithmetic*, sec. 5, in *Translations from the Philosophical Writings of Gottlob Frege*, ed. Peter Geach and Max Black (Oxford: Blackwell, 1970), 156; Gottlob Frege, *Posthumous Writings*, ed. H. Hermes, F. Kambartel, and F. Kaulbach, trans. P. Long and R. White (Chicago: University of Chicago Press, 1979), 129. Neither this remark of Frege's about assertion, nor the previous remark about judgment depends on his redundancy theory of truth, much less on his view that true sentences denote the same object.

26.   On the good of accuracy and sincerity, see Williams, *Truth and Truthfulness*, Chapter 3.

27.   For an illuminating discussion of Heidegger on truth, see Cristina Lafont, *Heidegger, Language, and World-Disclosure* (Cambridge: Cambridge University Press, 2000), Chapter 3.

28.   Allan Gibbard initially defended an expressivist account of normative discourse, and argued that such discourse is not fact-stating or truth-apt. See *Wise Choice,*

Apt Feelings (Cambridge, Mass.: Harvard University Press, 1990), 8, 10. For criticisms, see Paul Horwich, "Gibbard's Theory of Norms," *Philosophy and Public Affairs* 22 (1993): 67–78. More recently, Gibbard proposes an expressivist explanation of normative discourse, but recognizes that the expressivist strategy—which starts by asking what states of mind normative claims express—can help itself to notions of truth and fact. See *Thinking How to Live* (Cambridge, Mass.: Harvard University Press, 2003), esp. Chapter 9.

29. Anticipating what will come later: if public reason includes the concept of truth, does this impose a barrier for noncognitivists, who traditionally thought that truth is not in play in normative discourse? The answer lies in the content of the political conception of truth. Noncognitivists have no reason to object to that use, given the relatively minimal commitments that come with it. See Gibbard, *Thinking How to Live*, Chapter 9; Simon Blackburn, *Truth* (Oxford: Oxford University Press, 2005).

30. Rawls, *Political Liberalism*, 110–11. For a forceful statement of the point, see John Rawls, *Lectures on the History of Political Philosophy*, ed. Samuel Freeman (Cambridge, Mass.: Harvard University Press, 2007), 7.

31. *Veritatis Splendor*, paragraphs 34, 99, 4. This is an encyclical by Pope John Paul II on moral theology. See www.vatican.va/holy_father/john_paul_ii/encyclicals/documents/hf_jp-ii_enc_06081993_veritatis-splendor_en.html.

32. David Estlund, "The Insularity of the Reasonable: Why Political Liberalism Must Admit the Truth," *Ethics* 108 (1998): 253. Habermas also misinterprets the claim that the concept is unavailable. He attributes to Rawls the view that "a theory of justice cannot be true or false," and mentions a "weak interpretation" of this thesis on which it asserts that "normative statements do not describe an independent order of moral facts." Jürgen Habermas, "Reconciliation through the Public Use of Reason: Remarks on John Rawls's Political Liberalism," *Journal of Philosophy* 92, no. 3 (1995): 123. A political conception of justice cannot make either of these claims, on Rawls's account. Lacking the concept of truth, it cannot make any claims about the truth or falsity of conceptions of justice, including the claim that they cannot be true or false. Moreover endorsing the moral constructivist thesis that normative statements do not describe an independent order of moral fact (the so-called weak interpretation) would put it directly in conflict with rational intuitionism. See Rawls, *Political Liberalism*, 113. What political constructivism does say is that "once, if ever, reflective equilibrium is attained, the principles of political justice (content) *may be represented* as the outcome of a certain procedure of construction (structure)" (*Political Liberalism*, 89–90). The italicized phrase is essential. It would defeat the purpose of political constructivism to say that the principles of justice are the product of a procedure of construction, and therefore "do not describe an independent order of moral facts." The rational intuitionist may well agree with the political constructivist's claim about how the principles "may be represented," while rejecting the moral constructivist's claim about what those principles are.

33. In saying that it is very different, I am not criticizing the view. My aim in this section is simply to clarify the No Concept account.

34. Thomas Hobbes, *Leviathan* (Indianapolis, Ind.: Hackett, 1994), 180.

35. See John Austin, *The Province of Jurisprudence Determined* (Amherst, N.Y.:

Prometheus Books, 2000). According to Austin, the moral rectitude of laws depends on conformity with natural law, understood as God's law for humankind.

36. See Horwich, *Truth*.

37. See Michael Dummett, "Truth," in *Truth and Other Enigmas* (Cambridge, Mass.: Harvard University Press, 1978), 2–3. On the importance of giving an account of the point of the concept of truth, see Davidson, *Truth and Predication*; Williams, *Truth and Truthfulness*; Crispin Wright, *Truth and Objectivity* (Cambridge, Mass.: Harvard University Press, 1992). Dummett focuses on Frege's redundancy theory. "It is part of the concept of truth," Dummett says, "that we aim at making true statements," but Frege's account of truth "leaves this quite out of account." For criticisms, see Tyler Burge, "Frege on Truth," in *Truth, Thought, Reason* (Oxford: Oxford University Press, 2005), 130, and more generally 88–93 (esp. n3).

38. See Crispin Wright, "Truth: A Traditional Debate Reviewed," in *Truth*, ed. Simon Blackburn and Keith Simmons (Oxford: Oxford University Press, 1999), 203–38; Wright, *Truth and Objectivity*, Chapter 2.

39. A distinction of some kind between truth and warrant seems important to understanding the practice of deductive argument. Deductive argument is both compelling and useful. It is compelling because it is truth-preserving. But it is useful because we are often not antecedently warranted in endorsing the conclusion of a deductive argument, or warranted in endorsing the conclusion independently of its issuing from that argument. See Michael Dummett, *The Logical Basis of Metaphysics* (Cambridge, Mass.: Harvard University Press, 1991), Chapter 7.

40. Horwich, *Truth*; Paul Horwich, "Norms of Truth and Meaning," in *Reflections on Meaning* (Oxford: Oxford University Press, 2005), 104–33; Paul Horwich, "The Value of Truth," *Noûs* 40 (2006): 347–60, esp. sec. 10, on how to explain the desirability of truth without supposing that the concept is "constitutionally normative."

41. Rawls, *Political Liberalism*, 129.

42. Hannah Arendt, "Truth and Politics," in *Between Past and Future* (New York: Penguin, 1977), 241. For an instructive discussion of the complexities of Arendt's views, see Linda Zerilli, "Truth and Politics," *Theory and Event* 9 (2006): n.p.

43. Rawls says that citizens fulfill their duty of civility when they explain their positions to other citizens by reference to "the political conception of justice they regard as the most reasonable" ("Idea of Public Reason Revisited," 576). To be sure, as Philip Kitcher reminded me, several views may be tied for the most reasonable. The relevance of this is uncertain, because you are still left with the judgment that some are less reasonable. Public reason is animated by concerns about tolerance, not by an unwillingness to make judgments.

44. Rawls, *Political Liberalism*, 42, 243; Rawls, "Idea of Public Reason Revisited," 766; emphases added. A number of other passages in *Political Liberalism* also focus their concern on appeals to the "whole truth." See 216, 218–19, 225, 242–43.

45. Raz, "Facing Diversity," 9.

46. For a sketch of the familiar point, see Horwich, *Truth*, 2–5. Horwich begins his

discussion by saying that "the truth predicate exists solely for the sake of a certain logical need." The political conception does not include any such story about the sole reason, but can incorporate the rest of what is said.

47. Habermas suggests that Rawls endorses the full display argument. See "Reconciliation through the Public Use of Reason," 124–25.

48. John Rawls, *A Theory of Justice*, revised ed. (Cambridge, Mass.: Harvard University Press, 1999), 509.

49. Here I follow Rawls's discussion of "declaration," in "Idea of Public Reason Revisited," 594.

50. Harry Frankfurt, *On Bullshit* (Princeton, N.J.: Princeton University Press, 2005), 33–34.

51. John Stuart Mill, *On Liberty*, Chapter 2, paragraph 10.

52. Williams, *Truth and Truthfulness*, 7.

53. See in particular Richard Rorty, "Is Truth a Goal of Inquiry? Donald Davidson versus Crispin Wright," in *Truth and Progress: Philosophical Papers*, vol. 3 (Cambridge: Cambridge University Press, 1998), esp. 41–42. In his comments on my paper at a Stanford Law School colloquium in October 2006, Rorty disagreed that truth is a norm distinct from warrant, for reasons that struck me as assuming some form of pragmatism, and resisted my attribution to him of the cultural proposal. But once we accept that truth and warrant are distinct norms, and distinguish the word "true" from the concept of truth, then we must conclude that Rorty is endorsing something along the lines of the cultural proposal. Or so it still seems to me.

54. Rorty notes the wavering in ibid., 21–22.

55. See Hilary Putnam, "Does the Disquotational Theory Solve All Problems?" in *Words and Life* (Cambridge, Mass.: Harvard University Press, 1994), 264–78.

56. Rorty, "Is Truth a Goal," 29, 41.

57. Michel Foucault, "The Ethics of Concern for Self as a Practice of Freedom," in *Ethics: Subjectivity and Truth*, ed. Paul Rabinow (New York: New Press, 1997), 295.

16. The Truth in Political Liberalism

1. Hannah Arendt, "Truth and Politics," in *Philosophy, Politics and Society*, 3rd ser., ed. Peter Laslett and W. G. Runciman (Oxford: Blackwell, 1967), 122. Her example stems from a remark by Georges Clemenceau in 1919 on how historians would tell the story of World War I: "One thing is for certain: they will not say that Belgium invaded Germany."

2. I discuss this point in detail in David Estlund, *Democratic Authority* (Princeton, N.J.: Princeton University Press, 2008), Chapter 5.

3. John Rawls, *Political Liberalism* (New York: Columbia University Press, 1993).

4. Ibid., 146.

5. Ibid., ix–xx, 94, 116, 126.

6. Ibid., ix–xx.

7. If it is true, then it apparently applies to itself. I trace the implications of this fact, arguing

that it is not the paradox it might appear to be, in David Estlund, "The Insularity of the Reasonable: Why Political Liberalism Must Admit the Truth," *Ethics* 108 (January 1998): 252–75.

8. Below I will consider an alternative form of political liberalism in which political argumentation appeals to truths as such. As I will explain, though, that variant still accepts the sentence here in the text: justification may appeal only to doctrines acceptable to all reasonable points of view, and that is the basis of their justificatory force.

9. Charles Larmore, "The Moral Basis of Political Liberalism," *Journal of Philosophy* 96, no. 12 (1999): 599–625. Subsequent citations are cited parenthetically in the text.

10. See ibid., 600.

11. See Cohen's essay in this volume.

12. John Rawls, *The Law of Peoples* (Cambridge, Mass.: Harvard University Press, 1999), 14.

13. Rawls, *Political Liberalism*, 129.

14. Ibid., 153. The Rawlsian language of overlap (as in "overlapping consensus") can seem to count against me. That can tempt the reading that the reasonable views of the truth about justice share this one part in common. So there is overlap on a view about the truth about justice, even if not the whole truth. But I see no way around the point that there is, according to Rawls, reasonable disagreement about the truth about justice, and even about the most reasonable political conception. So the overlap is best seen, I think, as an overlap on the liberal principle of legitimacy as true, and on the mutual acceptability of any of a family of liberal conceptions of justice, whether they are true or not, for political purposes.

15. I speak mainly of justice in order to easily engage the Rawlsian view and its opponents. But I do not mean to take a view here on whether justice is the master value in politics, nor to imply that I mean my points to apply only to that single value.

16. For example, see Joseph Raz, "Facing Diversity: The Case of Epistemic Abstinence," *Philosophy and Public Affairs* 19, no. 1 (1990): 3–46.

17. John Rawls, "The Idea of Public Reason Revisited," in *The Law of Peoples*, 14418. I discuss this structure of justification at great length in Estlund, *Democratic Authority*. Here I limit myself to a sketch. The structure is just like my epistemic proceduralism, but in the book I assumed that voters must address a shared political conception of justice. That is the assumption whose possible abandonment I am exploring.

19. That is the name I use in my discussion of a similar structure of democratic theory, in Estlund, *Democratic Authority*.

20. For what it is worth, we might spread several approaches to liberalism across a continuum according to how robustly they make use of truth in political justification. Moving from the least robust to the most:

Skepticism: denying that there are truths on these matters.

Rawls: doing without truth altogether.

Larmore: truth of the underlying principle of legitimacy, no truth elsewhere.

Cohen: a political conception of truth in discourse about justice.

Epistemic political liberalism: real truth throughout, but including the truth of the principle of legitimacy, which puts the justificatory weight on reasonableness rather than truth.

Comprehensive liberalism: no boundaries to public reason at all.

17. Truth at the Door of Public Reason

1. Josiah Ober, *Political Dissent in Democratic Athens: Intellectual Critics of Popular Rule* (Princeton, N.J.: Princeton University Press, 1998); Ryan K. Balot, *Greek Political Thought* (Oxford: Blackwell, 2006).

2. Elizabeth Anderson, "The Epistemology of Democracy," *Episteme: Journal of Social Epistemology* 3 (2006):8–22; Josiah Ober, *Democracy and Knowledge: Learning and Innovation in Classical Athens* (Princeton, N.J.: Princeton University Press, 2008).

3. The end run is not Estlund's preferred solution to the problem of carrying on essential truth-based activities without the concept of truth; it is offered as a possible solution for those who prefer, as he does not, to retain the political conception of justice. His preferred position is laid out in admirable clarity and detail in David Estlund, *Democratic Authority: A Philosophical Framework* (Princeton N.J.: Princeton University Press, 2008.

4. Social facts and brute facts: John R. Searle, *The Construction of Social Reality* (New York: Free Press, 1995).

18. Just Gimme Some Truth

1. Daniel T. Rodgers, "Of Shepherds and Interlopers," *Intellectual History Newsletter* 9 (1987): 47–53. Rodgers's essay addresses the work of one of the finest "shepherds" in our guild, James T. Kloppenberg. See Kloppenberg, *Uncertain Victory: Social Democracy and Progressivism in European and American Social Thought, 1870–1920* (New York: Oxford University Press, 1986), a book quite germane to the issues raised here.

2. An engagement that, as Rodgers says, future intellectual historians will not have to construct but which they can overhear as "interlopers" rather than shepherds. As will become apparent, the neopragmatists have already tried to initiate this conversation, and what I am really trying to do here is persuade the Rawlsian political liberals to accept the invitation.

3. Regrettably for future intellectual historians, John Rawls's own part of the conversation I am proposing will definitely have to be constructed, not overheard. The absence of much significant engagement with Rawls by historians of recent American

intellectual life is regrettable, but perhaps explicable. For intellectual historians, both corralling and interloping are designed to set the stage for a contextual explanation of why these conversations occurred when they did or, at least, of why they can be readily constructed. Rawls looms large in the intellectual history of the United States in the past half century; one cannot imagine any survey of this period in which he would not be among the most significant figures. Yet his work is so forbiddingly abstract, so bereft of contextual clues beyond those internal to the history of philosophy and political theory, that he presents a daunting challenge to any intellectual historian who would place *Political Liberalism* in its own time (call it perhaps the age of liberal eclipse, *Roe v. Wade*, and the "culture wars")—and thus far none has. I cannot advance this important project here, but I hope someday to contribute to it. For a pioneering engagement with Rawls's *Theory of Justice* by a talented intellectual historian, see S. M. Amadae, *Rationalizing Capitalist Democracy: The Cold War Origins of Rational Choice Liberalism* (Chicago: University of Chicago Press, 2003), 251–73.

4. The most important texts here are Cheryl Misak, *Truth, Politics, Morality: Pragmatism and Deliberation* (London: Routledge, 2000); Robert Talisse, *Democracy after Liberalism: Pragmatism and Deliberative Politics* (New York: Routledge, 2005); Robert Talisse, *A Pragmatist Philosophy of Democracy* (New York: Routledge, 2007). For brief summaries of their arguments, upon which I draw here, see Robert Westbrook, *Democratic Hope: Pragmatism and the Politics of Truth* (Ithaca, N.Y.: Cornell University Press, 2005), 44–51, 194–200; Robert Westbrook, "Liberal Democracy" in *A Companion to Pragmatism,* ed. John Shook and Joseph Margolis (Malden, Mass.: Blackwell, 2006), 290–300; Robert Westbrook, "The Pragmatist Family Romance," in *The Oxford Handbook of American Philosophy,* ed. Cheryl Misak (Oxford: Oxford University Press, 2008), 185–96.

5. Misak, *Truth, Politics, Morality,* 18–29, 57–63. Misak locates her theory of truth between disquotationalism (insufficiently robust) and Habermas's transcendental argument (too robust).

6. Ibid., 49.

7. Cohen rightly distances his argument from the "cultural program" for the eclipse of truth of the most prominent neopragmatist, Richard Rorty. Like Cohen, I am puzzled by Rorty's apparent oral disavowal of the "cultural program" since it was the lodestar of his "epistemological politics" (see Westbrook, *Democratic Hope,* 139–74). But Rorty's version of pragmatism is highly controversial *among* pragmatists, and his view of truth is arguably the aspect of his thought that has most led other neopragmatists to distance themselves from his views. For Misak's and Talisse's dissents from Rorty, see Misak, *Truth, Politics, Morality,* 12–18; Talisse, *Democracy after Liberalism,* 68–76. Shortly before his death, I suggested to Rorty that his arguments were sufficiently ambiguous to hold open the possibility of closing the gap between him and Misak, but I failed to convince him. See Westbrook, *Democratic Hope,* 45–45n68; Richard Rorty, "Dewey and Posner on Pragmatism and Moral Progress," *University of Chicago Law Review* 74 (2007): 915–27. More recently I have argued that, if Rorty's hope for a wholly "pragmatized"

culture was extravagant, he might more reasonably have hoped for a democratic politics in the United States in which pragmatism provided the default, modus vivendi conception of truth upon which citizens relied in the face of doctrinal pluralism. See Robert Westbrook, "Pragmatism and War," in *Pragmatism, Nation, and Race: Community in the Age of Empire,* ed. Chad Kautzer and Eduardo Mendieta (Bloomington: Indiana University Press, 2009), 242–53.

8. Robert Talisse, "Two Democratic Hopes," *Contemporary Pragmatism* 4 (2007): 24.

9. Misak, *Truth, Politics, Morality,* 68, 49–50.

10. Talisse, "Two Democratic Hopes," 22. These arguments dovetail with those of two prominent pragmatists among contemporary political theorists, Jack Knight and James Johnson. See Knight and Johnson, "Political Consequences of Pragmatism," *Political Theory* 24 (1996): 68–96; Knight and Johnson, "The Priority of Democracy: A Pragmatist Approach to Political Economic Institutions and the Burden of Justification," *American Political Science Review* 101 (2007): 47–62.

11. For the objections of Misak and Talisse to the limits of Rawlsian pluralism, see Misak, *Truth, Politics, Morality,* 18–29; Talisse, *Democracy after Liberalism,* 55–63; Talisse, *Pragmatist Philosophy of Democracy,* 76–98.

12. Misak nicely uses onetime Nazi Carl Schmitt as the exemplification of the sort of participant that her neopragmatism can accommodate and deflect.

13. John Rawls, *The Law of Peoples* (Cambridge, Mass.: Harvard University Press, 1999), 124.

14. Westbrook, "Pragmatism and War," 250–51.

Index

Contributors

Jane Bennett is professor of political science at Johns Hopkins University.

Wendy Brown is Class of 1936 Professor of Political Science at the University of California, Berkeley.

Joshua Cohen is Martha Sutton Weeks Professor of Ethics in Society and professor of law, political science, and philosophy at Stanford University; coeditor of Boston Review; and on the faculty of Apple University.

Jeremy Elkins is associate professor of political science and affiliated professor of philosophy at Bryn Mawr College.

David Estlund is Lombardo Family Professor of Philosophy at Brown University.

William A. Galston holds the Ezra K. Zilkha Chair in Governance Studies at the Brookings Institution.

David Couzens Hoy is Emeritus Professor of Philosophy at the University of California, Santa Cruz.

Martin Jay is Sidney Hellman Ehrman Professor of History at the University of California, Berkeley.

Michael P. Lynch is professor of philosophy at the University of Connecticut.

Andrew Norris is associate professor of political science and affiliated professor of philosophy at the University of California, Santa Barbara.

Josiah Ober holds the Constantine Mitsotakis Chair in the School of Humanities and Sciences at Stanford University.

Robert Post is dean and Sol & Lillian Goldman Professor of Law at Yale Law School.

Frederick Rosen is Professor Emeritus of the History of Political Thought and Senior Research Fellow in the Bentham Project at University College London.

Rogers M. Smith is Christopher H. Browne Distinguished Professor of Political Science at the University of Pennsylvania.

Nadia Urbinati is Kyriakos Tsakopoulos Professor of Political Theory and Hellenic Studies at Columbia University.

Robert Westbrook is Joseph F. Cunningham Professor of History at the University of Rochester.

Bernard Yack is Lerman Neubauer Professor of Democracy and Public Policy at Brandeis University.

Linda M. G. Zerilli is Charles E. Merriam Distinguished Professor of Political Science at the University of Chicago.